HUBBUB

Emily Cockayne

Hubbub

FILTH, NOISE
& *Stench* in
ENGLAND
1600–1770

YALE UNIVERSITY PRESS
NEW HAVEN AND LONDON

Published with assistance from the Annie Burr Lewis Fund.

For information about this and other Yale University Press publications, please contact:

US Office: sales.press@yale.edu   yalebooks.com
Europe Office: sales@yaleup.co.uk   www.yaleup.co.uk

Set in Caslon by MATS Typesetters, Southend-on-Sea, Essex
Printed in the United States of America by Sheridan Books, Ann Arbor, Michigan.

Library of Congress Cataloging-in-Publication Data

Cockayne, Emily, 1973–
  Hubbub: filth, noise and stench in England, 1600–1770 / Emily Cockayne.
    p. cm.
  Includes bibliographical references and index.
  ISBN 978-0-300-11214-6 (alk. paper)
    1. Public health—Great Britain—History—17th century. 2. Public health—Great Britain—History—18th century. 3. Sanitation—Great Britain—History—17th century. 4. Sanitation—Great Britain—History—18th century. 5. Pollution—Great Britain—History—17th century. 6. Pollution—Great Britain—History—18th century. 7. Great Britain—Social life and customs—History—17th century. 8. Great Britain—Social life and customs—History—18th century. I. Title.
  RA485.C62 2007
  363.7094109032—dc22

                                            2006027626

A catalogue record for this book is available from the British Library.

10 9 8 7 6 5 4 3

To erstwhile neighbours
in Cambridge, Oxford, Charlbury, Newark and Norwich

Contents

Maps and Illustrations

Maps

Illustrations

Acknowledgements

Uncomfortable dwellings have been my muses during the writing of this book. They have helped me empathise with the cast of curmudgeonly and complaining characters who populate the pages. At university in Cambridge I shared one college room with ants, and another with bedbugs. Since then I have lived with my husband, Ben, in many dwellings, several provided by grasping landlords. We shared a tiny, shabby and earwig-infested caravan, until it blew over one stormy night. Our first proper home turned out to be a former brothel that still attracted gentlemen callers. We then lived together in surprising happiness in an excessively damp flat equipped with ancient electrical wiring. We moved to another dank property – one in the very centre of Cambridge. This flat led me to sympathise with Samuel Pepys. In Cambridge in May 1668 he 'lay well ill by reason of some drunken scholars making a noise all night'. Nothing had changed by 1998. Our next move took us to a Cotswolds cottage overrun with mice. Although these environments caused irritation and discomfort at the time, they have all served to sharpen my understanding of physical experiences.

Maxims teach us much about the importance of getting along with our neighbours. One proverb starts warmly – 'love your neighbour', but continues with a warning, 'yet pull not downe your hedge'. Bad neighbours were nuisances *par excellence* in the seventeenth and eighteenth centuries and in this book we share the suffering of people whose neighbours filled their cellars with horses, allowed their pigs to rootle through walls, sited their dunghills and privies inappropriately, or created inconsiderate noise. I have endured a few 'ill' neighbours, causing me to sympathise with the eighteenth-century author who wrote, 'No man can live longer in Peace than his Neighbour pleases. For an ill Neighbour, with his Scolding, Noise, Complaints, Law-Suits, and Indictments, may be very troublesome.' However, for the most part we have been extremely lucky with our neighbours, notably Tony Mitton and Elizabeth McKellar, Clare and Jason Gibbons, Joan Cook, and Fred and Jennifer Bartlett. We were fortunate to live for a while near Mary Laven and Jason

Scott-Warren, and I still owe much to both of them. Without their help and continuing friendship I would have fallen in the mire before I had started writing.

The genesis of the book came when I was an undergraduate, discussing 'otherness' with the late, and much missed, Bob Scribner. I went on to do a Ph.D. on sounds and noise in early modern England, largely under the guidance of Keith Wrightson, who taught me more about history than I had the grace to realise at the time. As I worked on my thesis I became increasingly interested in the ways that bodies and minds experience the environment. My doctoral examiners, Paul Slack and Peter Burke, encouraged me to think more broadly about my research and led me to encompass not just noise but also other nuisances to the senses. My agent, Clare Alexander, pulled my ragged ideas together and steered me on the right course, and for her help I am very grateful. Adam Freudenheim, formerly of Yale University Press, noticed the potential of my proposed study, and Heather McCallum has patiently seen my project through since Adam left Yale to become the Classics Publisher at Penguin – I owe much to both of them.

My researches have been assisted by archivists, librarians and academics across the country, and I would like to take this opportunity to thank the staff at the London Metropolitan Archive, the British Library, the Bodleian, Cambridge University Library, the Guildhall Library, the Corporation of London Record Office, as well as Jane Foster at Chetham's Library, and Lucy Powell at the Bath Record Office. Ann Saunders of the London Topographical Society helped me to sort out some images at a late stage, and so did Roger Houghton and Tracey Hill. I am grateful to them. Craig Horner has been of great help in locating texts about Manchester, and the two anonymous Yale readers pointed out various mistakes and missed opportunities.

I would also like to thank Ros Vinnicombe, Anna Stevens and my mother, Yvonne Cockayne, for taking great care of Maud 'while Mummy was doing her working'. My father, David Cockayne, has proved to be a reliable sounding board for my ideas and has created beautiful photographs and maps. Our home life has suffered much disruption to accommodate my writing, and I am grateful to my long-suffering husband, Ben. His understanding and good humour have allowed us to live quietly together while I have been distracted. Our family expanded just as I was completing the book, and now includes Ned, named after the eighteenth-century Grub Street hack Ned Ward, whose witty words are scattered liberally in the text that follows. I hope that he will approve when he is older.

CHAPTER 1

'The City in a Hubbub'

This book is about how people were made to feel uncomfortable by other people – their noises, appearance, behaviour, proximity and odours. It considers physical and emotional reactions to unpleasant things such as poor-quality food, smoke, dirt, dust, stench and putrefaction. I emphasise the unseemly aspects of life in order to redress the balance in favour of the pleasures of the period.[1] The experiences presented here are unashamedly skewed towards the negative. By concentrating on the situations and sights that caused discomfort and displeasure I am deliberately not presenting a rounded view of urban life – I am simply highlighting the worst parts of it. My focus on stomach-churning aspects of everyday life draws on the succulent biases in much of the source material; people are most vocal when they are moaning about things that have disgusted or annoyed them. Complaints filtered into diary entries, letters, civic records and criminal accounts. This is not, however, a litany of misery. Spurred by discomfort, human ingenuity brought innovations in many fields, including urban planning, management of industrial waste, food preservation and clothing design.[2]

It is hard to define nuisances and disgusting things. In a US Supreme Court judgment of 1964 Justice Potter Stewart stated in relation to obscenity that 'I know it when I see it'.[3] To extend this to nuisance, one might say, 'I know it when I sense it'. Contemporaries were well aware of the difficulty in applying standards to subjective matters of taste. In the mid-eighteenth century Henry Home, Lord Kames (an author and a judge), remarked, 'There is nothing more easy, viewing a particular object, than to pronounce that it is beautiful or ugly, grand or little: but were we to attempt general rules for ranging objects under different classes, according to these qualities, we should find ourselves greatly at a loss.'[4]

'Disgust' according to William Ian Miller, the author of *The Anatomy of Disgust* (1997), 'paints the world in a particular way, a distinctly misanthropic and melancholic way'.[5] Inevitably, the people who left the most fulsome comments about such things were the curmudgeons and the grouches. Some people were more liable to be upset or disgusted than others. Without caution, a reliance on personal and literary documents made by (potentially) hyper-sensitive individuals might lead to an exaggeration of the prevalence of nuisances and susceptibilities to annoyance and disturbance. This presents us with a problem. Whose views do we prioritise, those of the ordinary citizens or those of the fastidious ones? We are in danger of presenting a vision of the past based on a few sweeping and bilious comments that amplify occasional unpleasant experiences and package them in hyperbole. At the least, citing those sensitive souls who did document their reactions to nuisances will indicate which things and situations *could* have been considered as a nuisance to other members of seventeenth- and eighteenth-century society.

A modern geographer, J. Douglas Porteous, has proposed that the views of 'inperts' are as useful and valid as those of 'experts' when approaching the world of perception. The subjective views of inperts help us to understand how ordinary people evaluated their sensory experiences in a way that the objective measurements of experts cannot.[6] Our cast of inperts include the following diarists, authors and poets.

Samuel Pepys (1633–1703)   Samuel Pepys, an administrator who imple-mented a successful reorganisation of the Navy Office, is more famous for his frank diary, which he kept between 1660 and 1669. The son of a tailor, Pepys was born in Salisbury Court, off Fleet Street, in London. He was a diligent scholar at Magdalene College, Cambridge, in the 1650s, although he did get into trouble once in 1653 for being drunk in hall. Shortly after leaving Cambridge, Pepys married the fourteen-year-old Elizabeth de St Michel, a spirited woman with a Parisian background. In 1658 the couple settled in Axe Yard, near to the present Downing Street. During the following year Pepys started his thirty-year career with the navy and moved to be near his office in Seething Lane in 1660. Their house survived the Great Fire, an event that Pepys documented in his diary, but was destroyed in a subsequent fire in 1673.[7] Pepys was the sort of man not to make too much of a fuss about being accidentally spat on by a lady in the theatre – providing the lady was pretty.[8] Indeed, he was often led by his libido and found it difficult to keep his hands from wandering all over a variety of female acquaintances and servants. This caused much marital strife between himself and Elizabeth, drawing to crisis point in 1668 when Pepys was caught *in flagrante* with Elizabeth's own maid, Deb. Pepys ended his diary in May 1669, when he thought (incorrectly) that he was going blind, and so he does not describe his reaction to Elizabeth's death, aged twenty-nine, the following November.[9]

Anthony à Wood (1632–1695)   The independent scholar, diarist, biographer of Oxford alumni, and antiquarian who titled himself as Anthony à Wood was born in an old Oxford house opposite Merton College.[10] Although a bit of an outsider, Wood was a keen observer of Oxford society and provides a gossipy account of university life. His note-like descriptions give a good flavour of Oxford from the Restoration to the end of the seventeenth century, considering people, places, buildings, and the development of land use. Wood was not an easy man to like; he was 'notoriously peevish' and quarrelsome.[11] Growing more grumpy and craggy with old age, Wood became increasingly alienated from kith and kin and experienced poor health. The outspoken antiquarian Thomas Hearne, then a scholar at St Edmund Hall, described Wood as looking eighty when he was only sixty-four.[12]

Margaret Cavendish, Duchess of Newcastle (1623?–1673)   The author Margaret Cavendish (née Lucas) was an eccentric figure in Restoration England.[13] In her youth she had been taught some basics of reading and writing by an 'ancient decayed gentlewoman'; later Cavendish was an autodidact, and spent much time studying an eclectic range of books. She travelled to Oxford at the start of the civil wars in 1642 (where the King and court were located), and became one of Queen Henrietta Maria's maids of honour. In exile with the Queen in Paris Margaret met William Cavendish, the Marquess of Newcastle upon Tyne, and they married in 1645. Her first book, *Poems and Fancies* (1653), was described by one contemporary female wit as being 'ten times more Extravagant than her [i.e. Margaret's] dresse'.[14] Although Samuel Pepys admired her as a 'very comely woman', he also drew attention to her 'extravagancies', including a velvet cap, wild hair and 'many black patches because of pimples about her mouth'.[15] Cavendish never really fitted into polite society. In *Worlds Olio* (1655), a broadly philosophical work, she explored a wide-ranging number of topics, but a tendency to veer off at bizarre tangents clouded her message.

Robert Hooke (1635–1703)   Robert Hooke was a polymath with expertise in (among other areas) acoustics, the senses, urban planning and architecture.[16] Hooke had studied at Oxford, where he met other natural philosophers, including the influential Robert Boyle, before becoming the curator of experiments at the Royal Society in London in 1662. Three years later Hooke published *Micrographia* (1665), the seminal text in the field of microscopy. This work did not impress Margaret Cavendish, and she criticised it in her *Observations upon Experimental Philosophy* (1666). Along with Christopher Wren, John Evelyn and other Restoration urban designers, Hooke attempted to replan London following the fire of 1666, becoming one of the city surveyors charged with the oversight of the rebuilding. Hooke managed the project to build a monument to the fire, and hoped to use the space within it for experiments, but vibrations from the encircling traffic frustrated his plans.[17] In some ways Hooke's own body became one of his case studies, and he documented his various maladies and illnesses in his diary (kept between 1672 and 1680).[18] His openness makes him seem like a creepy hypochondriacal nerd. It is easy to visualise him peering into his handkerchief to analyse his 'digested', 'much yellow' or 'fleshy' snot.[19] Hooke was, by the account of his protégé Richard Waller, a physically unattractive man. In adolescence Hooke's body 'grew awry' and eventually became 'very crooked'. He was of short stature, but had long limbs. He 'was always very pale and lean, and latterly nothing but Skin and Bone, with a meagre Aspect'.[20]

Thomas Tryon (1634–1703)   The vegetarian author Thomas Tryon was an almost exact contemporary of both Samuel Pepys and Robert Hooke. Tryon was about a year younger than Pepys and a year older than Hooke. Both Hooke and Tryon lived out their adult lives in London after growing up elsewhere, and both started their careers apprenticed to a trade. However, whereas Hooke swiftly abandoned his apprenticeship to a painter (he was too sickly to continue amidst the noxious substances), Tryon stuck with his apprenticeship to a hatter at Bridewell Dock near Fleet Street.[21] Whereas Hooke remained single, Tryon married, and he lived in the leafy suburbs of Hackney, studying 'Physick' (in its Galenic forms) in his spare time. He began a new career as a writer of popular didactic manuals when he was forty-eight, turning out nineteen volumes in eighteen years. Like the Duchess of Newcastle, Tryon found it hard to stay focused in his writing, and his asides sometimes confuse his arguments. Tryon's key interest was maintaining the purity of the body and he verged on obsessive compulsion at times. He advocated water consumption, a vegetable-based diet, fresh air, and an avoidance of the privy (for fear of diseases).

Edward ('Ned') Ward (1667–1731)   Ned Ward was a hugely prolific and extremely sharp-witted satirist. He is largely unknown now, but was very popular in his time. In humorous fictitious trips around London and dialogues between couples, he exposed low-to-middling lives in verse and prose. By 1702 Ward lived near Gray's Inn (a slightly unpleasant area at that time), and in 1712 opened an alehouse near Clerkenwell Green. He ran a tavern in Moorfields between 1717 and 1730 and then returned to the Gray's Inn area to manage the British Coffee House in Fullwood's Rent.[22] His key work was *The London Spy* (1698–1700), a collection of tavern-to-tavern rambles in which his characters weave through the highways and back alleys of the city and provide an exaggerated, but almost anthropological, view of human excesses in the big city.

Edmund Harrold (1679–1721)   Edmund Harrold was a Manchester-based wig-maker who kept a diary between 1712 and 1715.[23] His barber's business was probably located along the city's long Market Street Lane. Harrold was twice widowed and thrice married and he provides intimate details about his relationships. His diary is richly endowed with reflections about his everyday life, including regular and boastful notes about his sexual relations with his second wife, keeping a detailed tally chart, with comments such as 'did wife 2 tymes couch & bed in an hour an[d] ½ time'.[24] He was born when Manchester had only one parish church but several taverns, and the increasingly industrialised urban milieu forms a faint backdrop to his rambles that took him to many of Manchester's watering holes, especially the Fiddlers and the Gold Goose. A fairly unsuccessful trader, Harrold was unable to make a living from wigs and minor barber-surgery (or, rather, to resist drinking his profits) and supplemented his income with bookselling (diversification was common among provincial barbers).

Dudley Ryder (1691–1756)   The son of a dissenting draper, Dudley Ryder was born in Hackney in 1691. Ryder was a gauche, introverted student at Middle Temple when he kept a diary between 1715 and 1716. He was later to become a judge, and prosecuted the leaders of the second Jacobite Rebellion in 1745. He was appointed Lord Chief Justice nine years later.[25] As a youth, Ryder was painfully shy, especially around women. After spending months plucking up the courage to experience female flesh with a whore, this hapless student ended one night with his virginity intact – but minus a hanky, plucked from his pocket by his chosen paramour.[26]

Bernard Mandeville (c. 1670–1733)   Bernard Mandeville, a physician and political and economic analyst from Rotterdam, came to London for an education and stayed, practising medicine without a licence. His views, published in *Grumbling Hive* (1705) and *Fable of the Bees* (1714), were controversial. Mandeville was keen to expose the symbiotic relationship between rising luxury and falling social and moral standards in a way that suggested he endorsed filth and immorality. He criticised the hypocrisy of people who embraced luxury but also complained about the inevitable degradation that accompanied it, and regarded dirt and squalor as necessary evils in a prosperous community.[27] The English were not fond of having their faults laid out by an interloper from Rotterdam, and Mandeville's ideas attracted much criticism.

James Woodforde (1740–1803)   The Church of England clergyman James Woodforde is much more famous now (as 'Parson Woodforde') than he was in his day, due to his diary-keeping, which spanned forty-three years.[28] Woodforde was a fairly unremarkable man; indeed, in a biographical piece the editor of his diary wrote, 'By any standard James Woodforde was a dull man ... that is his value as a diarist, his personality does not obtrude.'[29] Woodforde was an Oxford scholar when he kept a diary between 1759 and 1763 and recalled his (occasionally drunken) everyday existence. Woodforde became a curate in Somerset, but he returned to Oxford in the 1770s and gives a valuable description of the city during the major developments carried out there at that time.

John Wood, the elder (bap. 1704–1754)   In the 1740s the architect John Wood wrote a key text on the development and history of his native city of Bath, *An Essay towards a Description of Bath* (first published in 1742, revised 1749). Although fascinating, this text is not a fully reliable account of pre-Woodian Bath and served to cast his own projects in a more favourable light. The son of a builder, Wood was born shortly after Bath was popularised by Queen Anne's visit in 1702. He established himself as a joiner in London in the 1720s, returning to Bath to work on the Duke of Chandos's project to build quality lodgings. Wood was partly responsible for the 'rapid development' of Bath, helping to transform it from a compact spa city to a grand and much admired resort. Among his Bath buildings are the quarry magnate Ralph Allen's town house (1727), Queen Square (1728–34), the General Hospital (1738–42) and The Parades (1739–48). Wood suffered from asthma in his middle age and died in 1754, just before major developments were undertaken in Bath, some of which had been suggested by Wood in his *Essay*. His son, who was also called John, continued his work.

Mary Chandler (1687–1745)   Mary Chandler is the other female protagonist in this cast of characters. The daughter of a dissenting minister, she set up a millinery business opposite the Pump Room in Bath in her late teens. Chandler was well placed to observe the hubbub and hurry of the city. Her Bath grew from a basic city retreat to the pre-eminent polite resort. Chandler opened her shop in 1705, just as Beau Nash rolled into town and became the Master of Ceremonies. A period of rapid economic and commercial expansion began. By 1739 Chandler also owned a lodging house, just off the fashionable Orange Grove.[30] Like Thomas Tryon, Chandler was an autodidact, turning her attention to poetry. She published *A Description of Bath* in 1733, recently described as 'a substantial piece of civic propaganda by a propertied local resident'.[31] Alexander Pope, with whom she shared a spinal condition, supported her writing.[32] Abandoning hopes of marriage in her youth, Chandler considered herself to be spoiled goods due to 'the disadvantages of her shape'.[33]

Tobias Smollett (1721–1771) (in the guise of **Matt Bramble**)   Matt Bramble is barbed and prickly, a gouty country gent who appears in Tobias Smollett's final novel, the picaresque and epistolatory *The Expedition of Humphry Clinker*

(1771). Bramble's nephew describes him as being 'as tender as a man without skin; who cannot bear the slightest touch without flinching. What tickles another would give him torment.'[34] He is hypersensitive to sensory stimuli, and says of himself that his 'sense of hearing is painfully acute'. The lodgings, filth, air, water, food and noise of London and Bath all 'mortify' his senses.[35] For Bramble each city corner teemed with 'fresh objects of detestation and disgust.'[36] He was a typically splenetic traveller, of a type that would have been familiar to an eighteenth-century audience.[37] Bramble's propagator was a Scottish-born surgeon who lived much of his life in exclusive parts of London, and also spent some time in Bath.[38] The author Laurence Sterne, a contemporary of Smollett's, thought there was more than a little Bramble in his creator, and portrayed him as the truculent misanthrope 'Smelfungus' in *A Sentimental Journey* (1768). A recent biographer of Tobias Smollett presented Matt Bramble as Smollett's 'alter ego'.[39]

It would be easy to assume that the experiences of these exceptional people are typical. Their lives should be placed in context in order to recognise that cultural mores influenced perceptions of whether certain conditions were tolerable. Therefore a mosaic of experiences is laid down in this book; the voices of a vast number of contemporaries are heard. Our main cast take a more central role because they wrote more copiously about their reactions. It is inevitable that the views of male and richer citizens are highlighted, as they left most records. The geographic contexts for these experiences are the expanding urban centres. The sensory worlds of towns and cities form a focus in order to judge how citizens were unsettled by the environmental consequences of urban development. Reactions to the urban environment from the very young, women and the poor will unfortunately and inevitably have less prominence. However, many voices can also be discerned here – even if some are faint. Anonymous neighbours appear in cameo roles as fleeting reference is made to their views.

Hubbub often ventures into the provinces. Places were associated with particular smells, sounds or atmospheres. Writers were apt to dismiss entire cities in a single sentence, focusing on infrastructure, topography, the built environment, a notable trade or commercial features. At the close of the sixteenth century William Camden had described Birmingham as swarming with 'Inhabitants, and resounding with hammers and anvils, for most of them are Smiths'.[40] Little had changed a century and a half later, when a German tourist marvelled at the 'thickly populated' town, where 'almost every one is busy hammering, pounding, rubbing and chiselling'.[41] John Evelyn thought Leicester was an 'old & ragged Citty . . . large, & pleasantly seated, but despicably built; the chimnies flues are like many smiths forges'. Lincoln faired little better under his quill – it was described as 'an

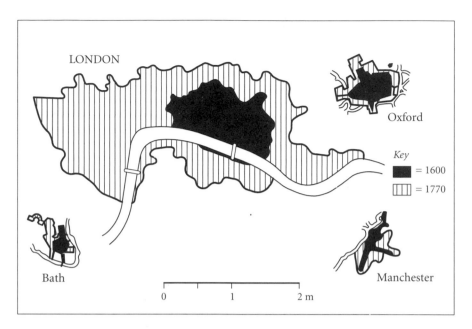

Map 1 The development of Manchester, Oxford, Bath and London 1600–1770. The diagram shows the relative sizes of the four cities.

Map 2 Map of the City of London, City of Westminster, Lambeth, Southwark and the River Thames, *c.*1680 by John Oliver (d.1701).

old confused town, very long, uneven & confragose, steepe & ragged'.[42] Commentators did not condemn all towns and cities. Margaret Cavendish was smitten by Nottingham on a visit in 1660, describing it as 'one of the most pleasant and beautiful towns in England'. She lingered in its long streets and fine marketplace, complimenting the solid brick houses and good food to be found there.[43] Stories are drawn from towns and cities across the nation, with particularly detailed portraits of the university city of Oxford, the spa resort of Bath, and the northern manufacturing town of Manchester. These centres have been chosen because there are sufficient sources to conduct in-depth studies, and they allow for comparisons between different urban areas.

London The capital city of London was one of the largest cities in the world in the seventeenth and eighteenth centuries. The navigable River Thames presented trading opportunities, and much warehousing lined its banks. By 1600 the ancient city walls had already been breached in places by suburban developments into which migrants swarmed, bringing the population to almost 200,000. By the early seventeenth century, London was a wealthy, bustling and expanding city, but infrastructural development could not keep pace and parts of the city became increasingly crowded, dirty and noisy. London suffered an extended *annus horribilis* in the mid-1660s, with a catastrophic outbreak of the plague in the summer of 1665, and the disastrous Great Fire of September 1666. The city rebounded quickly; by 1670 there were more than 370,000 inhabitants, and this was to rise to approximately 600,000 by the close of the seventeenth century – representing a threefold population increase in one century. The population growth for the following century was less dramatic but impressive nonetheless. By the mid-eighteenth century, London was home to nearly three-quarters of a million souls.[44] The growing metropolis consumed outlying settlements; the once remote villagers of Kensington could see the western fringes of London by the turn of the eighteenth century, and Thames-side expansion swallowed eastern villages.

The heart of the political and legal societies lay in the western part of London. Manufacturing and industries were prominent to the east. The City was the focus of the financial and commercial businesses, and was also home to many metalworkers. In Lothbury ears were assaulted by 'scratting' as the founders rasped and filed metals; according to John Stow this made a 'loathesome noyse to the by-passers that have not been used to the like, and therefore by them disdainfully called Lothburie'.[45] Many of the leather, cloth and victualling traders found a home beyond the city walls.[46] Bermondsey was the location of leather industries such as tanneries. A strong smell of pitch lingered in the air around the shipbuilding trades in Wapping.[47]

Local government in London was extraordinarily complex. The Court of Aldermen and the Court of Common Council governed the City's Corporation, making decisions about taxation and citywide central government. Nuisances were presented to the wardmote inquests held in each ward; through these wardmotes the citizens enjoyed a high degree of participation in the government of their own locality. In the suburbs local government was exercised at a parish level through the vestries. Above the vestries in authority came the Justices of the Peace who, on both a formal and an informal level, supervised parish affairs. In Westminster, after 1585, the citizens were governed by a group of twelve burgesses, who acted in a similar capacity to the City aldermen and governed the social and moral life of their citizens. The burgesses suffered increasing infringements on their authority from vestries and commissioners, and by the early eighteenth century their focus was largely confined to the control of street conditions and the upkeep of ceremony. There was a short-lived Annoyance Jury in the mid-eighteenth century, to which nuisances, obstructions and encroachments could be presented.[48] Relations between the various bodies were not always harmonious, and their responsibilities could be unclear. As the period progressed, new layers of authority came with civic bodies and private companies – for example, the turnpike trusts which controlled some of the highways, and the commissioners for the sewers. In addition, trades and crafts were controlled and protected by companies

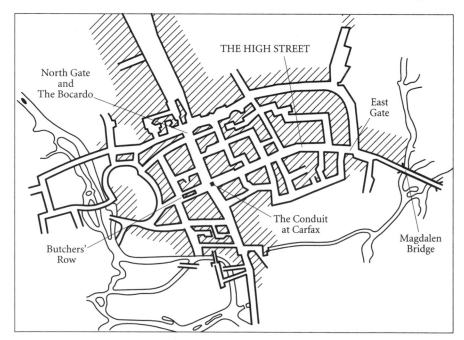

Map 3 Map of Oxford, based on the David Loggan map of 1675.

and guilds. Overlapping jurisdictions caused administrative confusion and disarray.[49]

Oxford   The River Cherwell met the Thames in Oxford, and as a result the city was partially surrounded by floodplains. Sixty miles to the west of the capital, Oxford was a muddy little market town with narrow streets. At the close of the seventeenth century Celia Fiennes judged Oxford to be a 'pleasant and compact' city, with clean, broad and well-paved streets.[50] Fiennes was easily pleased; complaints recorded in the Council Minutes tell a different story, revealing parts of the city that were shabby, dirty and congested. A main highway running east to west bisected the city. This long road was divided into different named sections: walking from Castle Street in the west, the pedestrian would pass the Old Butcher Row, the Carfax conduit (after 1617), before heading out in the direction of London down the High Street in the east. In 1600 London was fifty times bigger than Oxford, but Oxford's population rose swiftly to support a rapid increase in the number of scholars at the university, and by 1650 there were approximately 10,000 citizens.

In addition to being a university city, Oxford was a diocesan see, an important regional market centre and the location of trades (especially the manufacture of gloves, other leather goods and cutlery).[51] The population expansion was brief, and by the turn of the eighteenth century it had started to level, rising to only 11,000 by 1770.[52] Despite this, traders could enjoy a comfortable life in the city; in 1721 one author remarked that 'Oxford daily increases in *fine cloathes* and *fine buildings*; never were *brick-layers, carpenters, tailors*, and *perriwig-makers* better encouraged there'.[53]

Oxford was a corporation city; councillors were elected by and from the freemen. There was a high degree of participation – in the 1630s approximately an eighth of the freemen were active on the Council.[54] Four 'viewers for annoyances' surveyed grounds for building plots and watercourses and checked on the condition of existing properties for the Council.[55] The Oxford Council had long tussled with the university authorities over the rights to control various aspects of the city environment, including market supervision, street maintenance, alehouses, building developments, and noctivagation (seeking people on the streets during curfew hours).[56] The university used its court leet (a manorial institution with jurisdiction over petty offences) to dampen civic pride, and it took every opportunity to complain about encroachments on the city waste (undeveloped land) and other issues.[57]

Bath   Cradled in the Avon valley, the walled city of Bath sat on hot springs that had long attracted sick visitors in search of a cure for their ailments. Describing the city in 1673, Henry Chapman felt that the location was good, but the city centre developments were poor. He thought the streets were

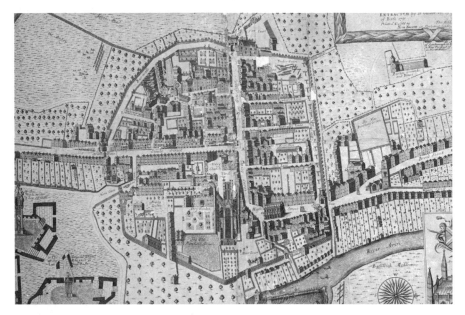

Map 4 Map of Bath by Gilmore, 1694.

mostly 'of the Narrowest size' and were the 'greatest Eyesore to its Beauty, and Cumber to its accommodation'. He guessed the wall, built of 'a Time-defying-stone' to be 'not a full *English* Mile'.[58] When John Evelyn visited Bath in 1654 he had also been unimpressed, finding 'the streets narrow, uneven & unpleasant'.[59] Even by the turn of the eighteenth century almost the entire city sat within the 40 acres encompassed by the walls.[60]

In 1650 Bath was even smaller than Oxford, with just over 1,000 citizens and three churches, including the impressive central Abbey (St Peter and Paul). However, by 1700 this figure had more than doubled, necessitating a burst of building to accommodate newcomers.[61] A more dramatic expansion occurred after 1700 as society folk flocked in greater numbers to Bath when it was popularised by Princess Anne, who first visited in 1692, and then returned as Queen in 1702. Shortly afterwards the first pump room was opened, and in 1707 the turnpike trust improved the roads in and out of the city. The population fluctuated, boosted by visitors in the season. Ned Ward remarked that for five months each year ''tis as Populous as *London*, the other seven as Desolate as a *Wilderness*'.[62]

Avon navigation improved the links between Bristol and Bath in 1727, helping to facilitate a building boom that spread housing beyond the medieval walls. Many new streets were cut, including Avon Street to the west of the city wall. Kingsmead Square was created in 1730. As the city grew the street

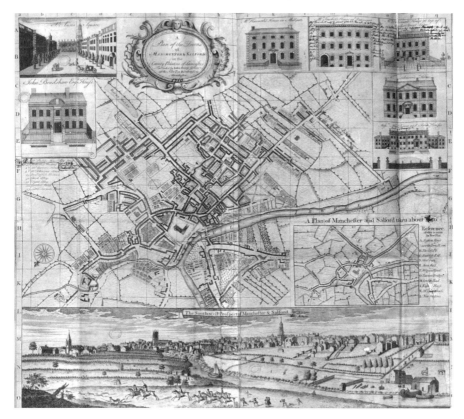

Map 5 The Casson and Berry map of Manchester, 1741.

environment was also improved, with road widenings, the installation of good-quality paving and lighting schemes. The streets would have been unrecognisable to Chapman and Evelyn. By 1750 the population had risen to between 6,000 and 8,000, and it was rising still faster as developments stretched the footprint of the city to the north-east and west of the centre. Fine rows of buildings marched up the hills.[63] *The Bath and Bristol Guide* of 1753 trumpeted the town's recent developments: the 'new Houses are strong, large, and commodious', built from stone hewn from Ralph Allen's quarries.[64] Some very grand and exclusive residencies, including The Circus and the Royal Crescent, were built for wealthy socialites keen to sample the leisure and commercial opportunities of the town in their spare time or retirement.

Like Oxford, Bath was a corporation town, with a mayor, aldermen and councillors.[65] By 1750 there were two city surveyors who helped to collect the rates and supervise properties.[66]

1   St Ann's Square, Manchester (1745).

Manchester   In 1600 the town of Manchester perched on a stony hill, near the confluence of the rivers Irwell (a major tributary of the Mersey) and Irk. Manchester was not walled and in 1600 had fewer than a dozen main streets, which spread out from the only parish church. Open fields, orchards and gardens rolled between the fine residencies lining Deansgate and the River Irwell.[67]

The town had 2,000 inhabitants, at the turn of the seventeenth century – making it bigger than Bath, but with only half the population of Oxford. By 1650, despite a disastrous plague in 1645, this figure rose to over 3,000, and steeper rises were to come in the following century (especially the latter half). By 1717 there were 8,000 townsfolk by 1758 there were 17,100 and by 1773 there were 29,000, making the population of Manchester bigger than Oxford and Bath combined (although it was still dwarfed by London).[68] The town's population roughly doubled between the mid-seventeenth century and the early eighteenth century, and again between the early to the mid-eighteenth century. Buildings started to proliferate during the early eighteenth century, expanding the town about three-quarters of a mile to the east, and the same distance to the south.[69] A student touring the country in 1725 found Manchester to be 'very populous and large, has a great many new and handsome brick buildings, particularly St Anne's [sic] Square'.[70] The pink sandstone church of St Ann's was built in 1712.[71]

Despite the growth in size and population, Manchester was still not a city, but merely a township. Visiting Manchester in 1713, William Stukeley described it as the 'largest, most rich, populous, and busy village in England'.[72] Daniel Defoe mirrored these sentiments: 'You have here', he writes, 'an open village, which is greater and more populous than . . . most cities in England.' Defoe added, with some bemusement, 'it is neither a walled town, city, nor corporation; it sends no members to Parliament, and the highest Magistrate there is the Constable.'[73] Among the peculiarities of local government in Manchester between 1600 and 1770 was the baronial-style local government, led by the Mosely family.[74] A borough reeve was the chair of the court leet, and he was supported by two constables (acting as executive officers).[75] Beneath them were a number of lower-ranking officials, including market lookers for fish and flesh, aletasters, scavengers, officers to care for the conduit, and dog muzzlers. These officers, elected each Michaelmas, managed markets, collected taxes and governed the streets.[76] While the population of the town saw a fourteenfold increase between 1600 and 1770, the number of officers rose from about 100 to 140 in the same period.[77] The manorial court leet, latterly described as a 'half-fossilised relic', found it difficult to keep the inhabitants in check, and was supplemented by the mid-eighteenth century by several bodies established by local acts of parliament. These brought improvement commissioners to the town to oversee street cleaning and to try to combat nuisances.[78]

Migration had fuelled the population expansion: workers were attracted by the opportunities of unregulated trade. John Aikin, a physician and author, described Manchester as 'destitute (probably to its advantage) of a Corporation'.[79] Without a restrictive corporation the town was not held back by laws that controlled apprenticeship, settlement and wages; therefore skilled non-natives could establish business there. Industry was aided by enhanced road conditions combined with the navigation of the River Irwell in the 1720s and the construction of the Bridgewater Canal in 1761, facilitating the transport of cheap coal to the factories. The fabric industries prospered most.

'Each Sense hath a Gate'[80]

The five senses act as the mediators between the outside world and the mind. The senses help people navigate around their environment, and gain a sense of others. However, urban life impacted on the senses of different citizens in diverse ways. As some early modern commentators noted, each person has a varying range of sensory skills and powers. In his *Essay on Taste*, Alexander Gerard, a Scottish minister and professor, considered the 'external senses'. He decided that 'in one man [each sense is] more acute than an another . . . One eye is more piercing, one ear more quick, one palate, one smell, or one touch, more delicate than another.'[81] Sensing is not only highly individualistic, it is also historically constituted. It changes over time and it changes during lifetimes and is dependent on context. Some people's senses became dulled in old age, but ageing could turn people waspish. An elderly contributor to the letters section of the *Manchester Mercury* in 1759 admitted to having 'all that Peevishness about me almost inseparable from old Age'.[82] This tetchiness might have caused elderly people to experience more upset and discomfort through their senses than they had when they were younger.

Discussions of the hierarchy of the senses – judgements about which sense holds the pre-eminent place in human cognition – get some modern (and got some early modern) theorists very excited.[83] However, these arguments often assume that the senses are employed on a rational and conscious basis. This is not the case.[84] The tortuous and usually dull debates often fail to consider linguistic barriers to the description of non-visual and non-aural sensory experiences.[85] In the early modern period an added dimension to these circular arguments came in the form of religious angst, the association of the 'lower' senses of touch and taste with beasts contrasted to the association of the 'noble' senses of sight and hearing with godly men.[86] When considering the sensory perceptions of people long dead it is more important to think of the interactions between the senses, and their practical applications, rather than spending time pondering some imposed and abstracted notion of a sensory hierarchy. The senses worked together; people saw and heard at the same time, they tasted and smelt and touched simultaneously – reactions intertwined.

In the following chapters I have tried to locate the perceiver centrally. Individuals reacted to experiences as beings-in-the-environment, not as detached observers. They formed subjective judgements from their own experiences and sensations. There was no separation between the perceiver and his or her milieu; people absorbed the world with their (functioning) senses, and they inhabited that environment at the same time. They could smell, but their own bodies could also be smelt by others, and by themselves.

In the early modern period the sensory organs were commonly considered to be active.[87] If they thought at all about them, people regarded ears, eyes, noses, tongues and fingers themselves as the barriers and controllers of sensory input and the initial location of sensory interpretation. Although there was increasing recognition among the natural philosophers that the senses merely channelled sensations to the brain, old views prevailed. Some sensory experiences were thought to cause emotional damage; the senses stood guard against injurious things. Thomas Tryon, with his keen eye for the hazards of daily life, turned his attention to the harmful effects of gazing. Puppet shows, dances and games were all 'evil' events with the power to 'wonderfully pollute' vulnerable minds. Even gawping jealously at the fashionable members of the congregation dressed in rich silks brought corrupting danger through the eyes.[88] The damage could be physical as well as moral, especially in the unborn. Whereas now the stress is on dangers through careless ingestion, gravid women were considered to be just as much at risk from damaging sights, smells and sounds. According to Tryon, pregnant women should keep calm and avoid 'Unclean Places, as also all terrifying and melancholly Sights, remembring that all things have an innate Power to impress their signatures on the tender Fruits'.[89]

As avenues to the inner body the senses were regarded as important protectors of both body and soul. When the sensory guardians were lax the body could be exposed to foul words that corrupted morals, or to poisonous food that sickened the body. For Thomas Tryon, properly functioning senses would create barriers against bad things and admit the good. This way the body would not become 'defiled nor adulterated by Intemperance, Uncleanness and Disorders, neither in Meats, Drinks Employments nor Communications'. Tryon asserted that 'each Sense hath a Gate, which it can open or shut as it pleases'. Therefore, you can hold your nose at bad smells, or breathe through the mouth, which, bypassing the sense of smell located in the nose, means that the ill smell cannot be communicated to the 'Central Parts of the Body'. The palate gave orders to the lips to shut the gates to the mouth, to 'withstand any thing that intrudes or is offensive'. The mouth had an additional faculty – of expulsion, ejecting distasteful things that passed over the palate, thus saving the stomach from an unfortunate encounter.[90]

The most sinister sounds that the ears could guard against were 'Evil Words' and 'lewd Discourses'. John Evelyn strove to keep his ears 'incontaminate' from newfangled religious movements.[91] Tryon thought words were so potent that 'Thousands of ignorant People have been utterly Ruined' by absorbing them. Children were most vulnerable, and must be taught to 'shut the Gate of their Ears against all evil sounds and Voices, which will, if admitted, unlock the inmost Cabinets of Nature'. Tryon explains that 'gross stinking Foggs, Scents and Vapours' are hurtful to the mind and body.[92] If the senses detected malign influences, well-honed ones did this best. Tryon's 'Gates' were partly physical and partly intellectual. Experience formed the strongest barrier. By developing their sense of smell a person could 'obtain the Gift of distinguishing Things and Qualities, whether they be good or evil, clean or unclean'.[93]

Sensations were thought to provoke physical responses in the sensory organs and the wider body: 'Doth not your nose swell [or eek, i.e. itch] at that?' asked one proverb.[94] A collator of proverbs noted: 'excrements of the body . . . being offensive to our senses, and usually begetting a loathing in our stomachs'.[95] The frontispiece of an anonymous work entitled *Hell upon Earth: or the Town in an Uproar* (1729) carried the story of a 'coffee-man's wife' who reacted dramatically to a report of a privy being burgled; she 'refunded her Breakfast upon reading the Relation'.[96] The power to recreate an image in the imagination is shown to prompt a visceral response. Even in the mid-eighteenth century the idea that the senses were corruptible (and corrupting) was still current. Painting the scene of drunken debauchery at the Kersal Moor Races, a 'disgusted of Manchester' feared that 'To display that *Scene* of *Iniquity* in its proper colours, would sully the imagination and taint the minds of men afresh . . . if the representation of it only, is so odious, that no pure Eye can see, nor modest Ear can hear, without *Horror* and *Astonishment*; what must it be to have it acted over again, to be display'd in *new*, and more *lively* Colours.' Blasphemy and filthy obscene discourse was to be heard at the turf and was 'so shocking to the Ears of every modest person, as to make them tingle'.[97]

'Better a mischief than an inconvenience'[98]

Sensory perceptions of towns – and the people who inhabited them – shaped cultural and practical responses. The citizens were protected from the worst excesses of urban life by some legal constraints. 'Nuisance' can be used to describe a wide range of experiences, from niggles to extreme discomfort. James Boswell was woken by early dawn light flooding through unfamiliar windows, only half obscured by blinds: 'Such things as these (trifling as they are) disturb human life.'[99] Many seventeenth- and eighteenth-century documents use the words 'annoyance', 'nuisance' (or, more frequently 'nusance') and 'noisome' synonymously. The Manchester leet jurors used the word 'noysome', which came to be reserved for annoying smells, for all nuisances, not just olfactory ones – it was short for 'annoysome'.[100] Some things had the potential to be a nuisance in a variety of ways, but were unhelpfully listed by contemporaries as 'nuisances'. It is not always possible to tell on what grounds the nuisance annoyed the complainer. Take, for example, uneven pavements. A trip hazard, these could jar ankles and injure horses. They made manoeuvres difficult for carriages and trundle carts. They collected water in stagnant puddles and gathered dirt and dust. By adding to visual clutter they looked unsightly. However, unless a passage is particularly descriptive (and many official documents are not) we cannot be sure why such a pavement annoyed the complainant. Another example would be pigs. There was a perpetual battle to contain the numerous swine that roamed city streets because they annoyed citizens in various ways. Their sties and dung were sources of offensive smells and their odours were even thought to tarnish metal and discolour linen. Pigs formed obstacles in busy city streets and savaged sacks of cereals in the market.[101] Their rooting could even damage structures. Swine caused illness, both through the consumption of infected pork and via their ordure. An early zoologist declared the hog to be 'certainly the most impure and filthy of all quadrupeds'.[102] A contemporary defended urban pig confiscations on the grounds that 'Swine are beasts that may cause diseases to bee in a City, and therefore it is against the Common-wealth.'[103] Both in life and at the point of death, they made shrill and unpleasant noises. The eponymous heroine in Henry Fielding's *The Intriguing Chambermaid* (1734) included squeaking pigs in a short list of the 'wild' noises of the universe.[104] The noise of slaughter was distressingly high-pitched and travelled long distances.[105] In most sources, however, we are just informed that pigs were nuisances.

The law on nuisance was not fixed, but the main principle remained 'doing to others' as we want them to 'do unto ourselves'.[106] Legislation demands common standards of tolerance, but individual reactions differ. Generally, in legal terms, a nuisance was 'an actionable annoyance which interferes with the ability of another to use or enjoy his land'.[107] As the legal writer William Blackstone put it, a 'Nusance, *nocumentum*, or annoyance, signifies any thing that worketh hurt, inconvenience, or damage'.[108] There were two basic types of legal nuisance: public (or common) nuisances and private nuisances.

A public nuisance had the potential to annoy all those who passed by it. This was 'an offence against the publick' caused by doing, or neglecting to do, something 'which the common good requires'.[109] Common nuisances included a surprising range of activities considered to be immoral, as well as those that the modern reader might expect. They included keeping disorderly alehouses, gaming houses or bawdy houses; being a common scold or barrator; setting up stages for mountebanks or rope dancers; littering bridges, highways and rivers with dirt or obstructions; building unlawful cottages; eavesdropping (i.e. listening at the doors or windows of others – rather than allowing water to fall from roofs); throwing fireworks; using a speaking trumpet (a primitive loudspeaker invented by Samuel Morland, Samuel Pepys's Cambridge tutor); and running brewhouses or 'melting-houses for Candles' in inappropriate locations.[110] Playhouses could also be regarded as a common nuisance if they tempted the idle and drew disorderly crowds. A common nuisance would need to be suppressed; a structure could be pulled down or taken away. For the more obviously immoral infringements the wrongdoer could be punished with fines and imprisonments or by corporal means; for example a scold could be ducked and a brothel-keeper whipped. [111]

An action (private litigation) would not be taken against a public or common nuisance.[112] This avoided an unwieldy number of cases issuing from one nuisance. Rather than a multiplicity of suits for damages, a single case in the monarch's name was made on behalf of all subjects. The judgment would be more likely to lead to an abatement of the nuisance rather than the recovery of damages, and would therefore benefit the commonweal.[113] The only exceptions were made for those people who suffered extraordinary damage from a common nuisance. For example, if a ditch was dug across a public highway, the digger would be prosecuted for committing a common nuisance, but if a person or their animal suffered an injury by falling into the ditch, they could take an action for damages against the ditch maker.[114]

Indictments as misdemeanours were the oldest defence against common or public nuisances – but indictments did not play a significant role against nuisances in most urban centres because they were costly to obtain (some legal cases were funded by trade companies[115]), and civic authorities established more simple procedures through presentments, bylaws, orders and fines.[116] The authorities focused on annoying dunghills, wandering swine, fire hazards, unkempt pavements, improper market trading, defective drainage, obstructions on the streets and other similar offences. In each city the problems were the same, but the frameworks for countering them differed. The approaches taken by the Oxford Council were not the same as those taken by the manorial officers in Manchester.[117] In an effort to reduce some nuisances civic authorities could forbid the rental of city properties to particular trades. In 1671 a smithy by Liverpool's town hall was proving to be 'noisome to all and several shops and other tradesmen, and the market side'. The authorities decreed that the owner of the smithy must cease leasing the property to a smith, 'but shall convert the same to some other use'.[118] A new weapon became available to the authorities in the mid-eighteenth century – the naming and shaming of miscreants. From 1766 'the New's paper' *Harrop's Manchester Mercury* was to include lists of those fined by the court leet.[119]

A private nuisance hurt or annoyed the land or tenements of an individual (or individuals).[120] Private nuisances included the stopping (i.e. blocking up) of other people's windows, rainwater falling from the eaves on to another person's property, and setting a brick kiln or a hogsty near a neighbouring house.[121] These annoyances could not be remedied by public prosecution as common nuisances because they did not affect the public at large. They could be made the subject of a private action in the hope of recovering damages.[122] The aggrieved party could also abate such a nuisance himself or herself (as long as this did not cause a riot).[123] If a nuisance continued after a plaintiff had successfully sued for damages they could be awarded exemplary damages for each new nuisance ('every fresh Running [down a diverted watercourse] is a fresh Nusance'[124]). Theoretically this could continue for as long as 'the defendant has the hardiness to continue it'. Thus, a nuisance could remain unabated for any person who was unfortunate enough to have a 'very obstinate as well as an ill-natured neighbour; who had rather continue to pay damages, than remove his nusance'. As a last resort, in such circumstances, the sheriff could remove the nuisance on the sufferer's behalf.[125] With the exception of blocked windows, few plaintiffs sought abatement; more sought damages, especially by 1770.[126]

It is hard to say how prevalent different types of nuisance were in the past. For some nuisances there may not have been clearly defined channels for complaint; others might have been dealt with on an ad hoc, informal basis (with or without mediation from local elites and professionals).[127] Aggrieved parties needed to convince the courts that the activities that annoyed them were on a sufficiently widespread or gross scale to warrant abatement, or that they were sufficiently damaging to be a private nuisance to an individual. Decreasing numbers of cases might indicate that a particular nuisance had become less common, or it might suggest that civic or legal officers were more ready to overlook certain offences. Apparent increases in particular nuisances might simply be evidence of crackdowns on some forms of annoyance rather than evidence of increasing nuisance activity.

Location was the key to some nuisances – it was only the proximity of other properties that led to the potential to cause damage or annoyance. 'Nuisance is the common law of competing land use,' noted a legal historian in 1974, and as such had a zoning function.[128] All citizens drank beer, used candles and wore shoes, but few wanted to live near a brewer, a chandler or a tanner. 'For though a Smith is a necessary Trade, and so a Lime-burner, and Hog-Merchant; yet they must be used not to be injurious to the Neighbours.'[129] These dirty, smelly or noisy manufactures needed to be undertaken in remote locations, and only became nuisances when their situation was considered to be too close to other citizens.[130] When considering common nuisances there was a need to weigh up numbers of people involved and the negative effects on trade of closing down an annoying business.[131] Sometimes the types of nuisance – common or private – differed little, apart from the scale of the problem, the numbers affected and whether an authority could be persuaded to take an interest in suppressing it.[132] Some private nuisances became common nuisances when they occurred in an urban setting, for example leaving noisome dunghills on city streets so they increased the risk of disease or obstructed traffic.[133] Dunghills on rural fields and byways would pose little or no nuisance to others.

So what upset the senses of the seventeenth- and eighteenth-century citizens? What made eyes water, ears ache, noses wrinkle, fingers withdraw and mouths close? How did the matter drawn in by the sensory organs affect people, and how did they react when sights, smells, tastes, textures and sounds activated their sensory alarms? What were the sensory nuisances of the time? How did the citizens deal with them? These are the questions behind this book.

CHAPTER 2

Ugly

There is nothing so subjective as beauty. What some people regard as lovely others see as abnormal and irregular. Margaret Cavendish, Duchess of Newcastle, noted that there was no such thing as uniform beauty; each individual had particular preferences for skin colourings, countenances, statures and eye colour; just as 'all Tunes please not all Ears, no more do all Beauties please all Eyes'.[1] Smooth unblemished skin free from spots and sores (collectively known as 'tetters'), freckles and scars was considered desirable by most people, but would have been enjoyed by only a few.[2] Before contracting smallpox in her twenties, Lady Mary Wortley Montagu was a renowned beauty. Stripped of her eyelashes and disfigured by a severe infection, she later campaigned for inoculation.[3] Samuel Johnson's pockmarks added to scars he already had following an operation on his lymph nodes in infancy.[4] A fellow of

2 This detail from Marcellus Laroon's oyster seller illustrates a harelip and smallpox scars: 'Twelve Pence a Peck of Oysters', from *The Cryes of the City of London Drawne after the Life* (London, c.1688).

New College, Oxford, was described in 1655 as being 'squint-ey'd and purblind, and much deformed with the smal pox'.[5] While being disfiguring, the tell-tale marks left by smallpox (visible, along with a harelip, on Marcellus Laroon's oyster seller in figure 2) would have made servants more employable, as they denoted immunity. Blemishes were useful for identification – witness statements mention suspects being 'much Pock-broken', or 'pock-freckled . . . with a large mouth'.[6]

Witnesses also noticed missing teeth.[7] Malnutrition and poor dental hygiene made teeth and gums weak, discoloured and decayed. A taste for sugarplums, coffee and tobacco resulted in missing, rotten and stained teeth, perished gums and putrid breath. As every schoolchild used to know, Queen Elizabeth sported black teeth. Emetics were popular cure-alls, and these would have hastened tooth decay through the acidic erosion of the enamel. Archaeological surveys suggest that the majority of early modern adults suffered tooth decay.[8]

'The blind man's wife needs no painting'[9]

The face is the most exposed part of the body, and facial irregularities are difficult to conceal. In 1766 the German intellectual Gotthold Ephraim Lessing published *On the Boundaries of Painting and Poetry*. In this he argued that 'a scar in the face, a hare-lip, a flattened nose with prominent nostrils, an entire absence of eyebrows, are uglinesses which are not offensive either to smell, taste, or touch. At the same time it is certain that these things produce a sensation that certainly comes much nearer to disgust than what we feel at the sight of other deformities of body.'[10] Throughout the seventeenth and eighteenth centuries consumers tried to correct their facial deformities. An advert in the *Athenian Mercury* directed people to a shop supplying 'Secrets to remove all Deformities of the Face or Skin, as Freckles, Sun-burn, Pimples, Redness, Morphew &c.' and washes to leave an 'Artifical tho' undiscoverable Whiteness'.[11] One advert plugged 'True, Original, Chymical Washballs' made without 'the least grain of mercury or anything pernicious' for those hoping for soft and smooth skin. The balls could remove 'all deformities, tetters, ring-worms, morphew, sunburn, scurf, pimples, pits or redness of the small-pox, keeping it [the skin] of a lasting and extreme whiteness'.[12]

Refined Georgians preferred a pale complexion; the sun was avoided and numerous recipes claimed to remove freckles.[13] Away in London for long periods, the poet and stenographer John Byrom wrote home urging his wife to keep herself and the children out of the sun, fretting, 'Prithee let the children have some sort of things that will keep the sun off 'em; why should one let their faces be spoiled when a little custom might prevent it?'[14] It was, however, possible to be too pale. A contemporary expert on occupational diseases singled out wan mathematicians as men needing to get out more. These proto-nerds are described as 'nearly all dull, listless, lethargic, and never quite at home in the ordinary affairs of men'.[15] According to his biographer, John Aubrey, the mathematician and theologian Isaac Barrow was 'a strong man but pale as the candle he studied by'.[16]

Tans and freckles were associated with country folk and outdoor labourers such as hawkers and construction workers.[17] The Earl of Westmorland immortalised the milkmaid as a 'wholesome' beauty in his poem of 1648. This 'bony Lass' had 'skin like silk' browned by the elements, and complemented with perfect teeth and hair.[18] In defence of his fellow rural dwellers, Matt Bramble cast the fashionably pale citizens in an unfavourable light, with their 'languid, sallow looks', against the appearance of 'those ruddy swains that lead a country life'.[19] Fashions are contradictory and fickle, and sometimes the bucolic look became à la mode. In the eighteenth century there was a brief fashion for milkmaid garb among refined English ladies – anticipating Marie Antoinette's later fetish.[20]

Small facial blemishes such as spots and scars could be covered with black patches. In 1662, as the Restoration fashion for patches and beauty spots was starting to bloom, a 'Well-wisher to modest Matrons and Virgins' penned 'an invective against Black-spotted Faces'. This work, entitled *A Wonder of Wonders: or, a metamorphosis of Fair Faces voluntarily transformed into foul Visages*, implores readers to reject the new fashion. It complains that applications of 'ugly black spots and loathsome patches' implied criticism of God's handiwork: 'Whereas you suppose that by applying such spots and patches to your faces ye beautifie and adorn them, ye indeed make them visibly deformed and abominable in the eyes of all beholders, especially of the more judicious people.' The 'well-wisher' also suggested that patch-wearers would be suspected of prostitution.[21] Ranting about the *Loathsomnesse of Long haire* (1654), Thomas Hall, master of King's Norton grammar school, called beauty spots 'Beastly spots', and listed seven arguments against them.[22]

'The Rubbish and Ruins of our vile Bodies'[23]

In *Fanny Hill* John Cleland outlined the features required in a beautiful young 'Woman of Pleasure'. Her stature would be moderately tall, thin-waisted and slight; her bosom pert, with the promise of further growth to round firmness. Fanny had long, glossy, naturally curly auburn hair, and neat, white teeth and delicate features. Her only minor flaw was a 'rather too ruddy' complexion.[24] Petite features were prized in women. Corpulence, especially when coupled with floridness, was associated with country alewives.[25] Dudley Ryder, smitten with a young lady in 1716, was dismayed when his aunt Billio described her face as 'too large for a beauty'. His father was even less generous, opining that she was 'a very clumsy women, her face broad and flat, her hands thick and big and her voice very rough and masculine'.[26] Ryder was also quick to dismiss women who lacked physical appeal. Admitting that the minister's sister was 'very pretty', he criticised the short stature and flat chest that diminished her good looks.[27]

For women, large breasts have swung in and out of vogue throughout the centuries, and were selected among features of an ugly woman by Edward Phillips (John Milton's nephew), alongside a lank belly, hemp-like red hair, a hammer head, a beetle brow, plump cheeks festooned with carbuncles and warts, a bottle nose, and a 'scattering [of] teeth enamel'd . . . with blew, and black, and yellow'.[28] An Italian physician declared that fat bodies were nauseating, and that most people 'shudder at the sight of women who are too fat or have abnormally large breasts'.[29] One book of cosmetics contained recipes for ointments to 'keep the Breasts small . . . hinder their growth' and 'harden soft and loose Breasts'.[30] There were some moderate voices, however. Margaret Cavendish painted an image of the ideal wife in *The Worlds Olio* (1655), and listed her physical attributes as being 'healthfull of Body, plump of Flesh, not deformed, nor exactly handsom; gracefull in Carriage' – resembling Cavendish herself.[31]

The ideal male physique depended on status and occupation. Labourers were expected to have big, strong bodies – 'rusty Hides' and 'Herculean Limbs and Rawbone Sides'.[32] Working men were ideally rugged and strong. They displayed their bodies warts and all. This ideal contrasted with the foppishness increasingly popular among young rich men who did not work. Corpulence in older men was often regarded as a sign of well-fed success. Gouty gentlemen recumbent in their armchairs feature in Hogarth's illustrations. The eminent physician George Cheyne was still consulted for dietary advice by society gentlefolk despite his 32-stone enormity.[33] Men *were* risible if their size hindered their activities. Charles I mocked a fat man who could not keep pace with him when descending the stairs, 'puffing and blowing very much which made the King laugh heartily'.[34] Hurrying along London streets and trying to avoid slipping on the greasy pavements, one of Ned Ward's fictitious 'Merry Travellers' was a large man. He 'blow'd and snorted like a Porpus'. As the journey continued he 'puff'd and blow'd, and waddl'd' along the streets.[35]

In Hogarth's *The Stage Coach, or A Country Inn Yard at Election Time*, ugly passengers queue to board a stagecoach (figure 3). Jenny Uglow has described this as an image of 'comic rotundity'.[36] The focus of the scene is the wedged posterior of the large woman eclipsing the coach door. A portly queuing traveller looks concerned that space is filling up. To the far left a robust refreshment vendor fills her booth, and calls time. The stout innkeeper

3   Engraving, William Hogarth, *The Stage Coach, or A Country Inn Yard at Election Time* (1747).

discusses a bill with a well-fed election agent who is also hoping to board the coach. In the background of the scene a thin, mean-spirited old woman wags a bony finger at a crying baby. Standing by the huge coach wheel, a dwarf hunchback postilion stands in oversized boots.

Ugliness was no bar to male success. Robert Hooke enjoyed success in many fields despite having a reputation for being very ugly. A fellow natural philosopher and Hooke's protégé, Richard Waller described his mentor as 'very crooked' and as having 'a thin weak habit of Body, which increas'd as he grew older'. He had a stunted stature and was pallid and gaunt. In old age he was described as 'nothing bit [sic] skin and Bone', with a thin nose, 'meanly wide' mouth, a thin upper lip, a sharp chin and a large forehead. Hooke shunned wigs until his dotage, preferring to wear his own long dark brown hair, which hung 'neglected over his Face uncut and lank'.[37] If the frontispiece to Thomas Tryon's *The Knowledge of a Man's Self* (1703) is accurate, Tryon had a massive angular head and a bulbous nose (figure 4, opposite). A posthumous edition of his *Memoirs* (1705) described Tryon as being 'of middle Stature, a little stooping or incurvated, Slender, but well compacted . . . his Eyes Small, a little sinking into his Head'.[38] Bath's Master of Ceremonies, Beau Nash, credited with boosting the fortunes of the spa city, was not known for his good looks (see figure 5). Visiting Bath in 1725, one diarist described Nash as 'a batter'd old Beau turned

4 Frontispiece image of the author, from Thomas Tryon, *The Knowledge of a Man's Self* (London, 1703), from a copy in the British Library.

of fifty years and not at all handsome'.[39] Dudley Ryder, while acknowledging that Nash was a good conversationalist and impresario, also noted his 'very ugly' face. By his own account Dudley Ryder himself was no oil painting: his 'littleness and want of beauty' combined with an 'ill complexion'.[40] Unlike Ryder, Nash was much beloved and esteemed by the ladies.

'Ugglesome monsters and fearful mishapen creatures'[41]

People who were clearly disfigured or deformed were viewed with pity, suspicion or distrust. Pondering the notion of 'Monsters', the redoubtable Duchess of Newcastle bred in her fertile imagination a man with two heads, eyes in the chest, arms and legs in the wrong place, and limbs sprouting from the head. She declared that monsters are those in both the animal and human kingdoms with 'more parts than they should have, or fewer, or when their parts do not fit into their proper place'. The Duchess considered deformities a 'Vice in Nature', but others declared 'ugglesome monsters and fearful mishapen creatures' to be divine warnings.[42] Many of the reported oddities of birth came from the Low Countries. These included 'the Hog-faced Gentlewoman' born in Wirkham in 1618 and 'a female creature borne in Holland, compleat in every part save only a head like a swine' (see figure 6).[43]

5   Portrait of Richard 'Beau' Nash (1674–1761) towards the end of his life by William Hoare of Bath (1707–92).

Freakish physical specimens attracted gawping audiences; Jonathan Swift captured the peepshow thrill of mutant humans in *Gulliver's Travels* (1726) with his depictions of very small and very large people. In 1616 Humfry Bromely was given permission to show to the people of Norwich a 'strange Child with two heades'.[44] Top of the bill were humans straddling the hominid/animal divide – the horse-men, the pig-women, the fish-scaled-boy and the hedgehog-boy. People who were extremely tall or unusually short, or overly hirsute were also good for business.[45] John Evelyn visited a famed Lincoln tavern, popular due to its keeper being a woman over six feet tall.[46] Samuel Pepys and Anthony Wood both joined the crowds to see 'Battles', a man seven and a half feet tall from Cheshire.[47] Wood also viewed an adolescent girl who was 'not much above eighteen inches long', paraded to the paying Oxford public in 1679.[48]

It was commonly believed that a pregnant woman exposed to grisly sights or sounds might induce congenital abnormalities in the child she carried.[49] When a woman with '16 fine children' gave birth to 'a monster, with nose and eyes like a lyon, no palate to the mouth, hair on the shoulders, claws like a lion instead of fingers, no breast-bone, something surprising out of the navel as big as an egg, and one foot longer than the other', some speculated that the cause was the roar of the old lion at the Tower of London, which had 'much terrify'd'

6   Image from L.P., a ballad, *A Monstrous Shape. Or, A Shapelesse Monster* (1639). Note the marginalia.

her when pregnant.[50] It was thought that cosseting was needed during pregnancy to avoid such unhappy outcomes.[51] Anthony Wood deemed 1665 a 'cursed' year filled with strange happenings, including peculiar weather and numerous monstrous births. One 'monster', born in Oxford, was reported to have 'one hand, one leg, one eye in the forehead, noe nose, and its 2 eares in the nape of the necke'.[52]

These were not politically correct times. Tourists gawped at the Bedlam lunatics, and deformed children were paraded in fairs and as street spectacles. Some were afflicted from birth, others during life. Most people born with large birthmarks, hermaphrodite extras, club feet and other blemishes and deformities endured them for life. Specially adapted clothes could disguise some features – those born with one leg shorter than the other could wear a built up shoe.[53] Very few sought corrective surgery. Those wishing to pay could secure the services of Nicholas Bowden, who in the early seventeenth century claimed he could cure – 'with the helpe of almightie God' – conditions such as 'wrie necks, wrie legges, and crooked bodies, by a rare meanes newly practised'. Without testimonials, or before and after images, the prospective patient would have to trust Bowden's boast that 'All hare or cleft lippes, I cure in short time.'[54] Such procedures would have been risky and might have exacerbated the condition through scarring.

'If all the World were ugly, Deformity would be no monster'[55]

Long-term skeletal stress induced by poor ergonomics at work would malform the spine, and tailors and shoemakers could be identified by their rounded shoulders and crooked backs as their work necessitated stooping for long periods.[56] Porters were chaffed by their heavy loads and suffered from growths and distortions.[57] Bakers could be recognised by their wry 'mishapen legs', caused by 'unfit burdens'.[58] Other workers suffered the consequences of prolonged exposure to toxic substances. Some potters had cadaverous faces, and sallow, pale skin due to lead poisoning and damp working conditions. A metalworker was characterised by 'a beetle head, and a leaden heele' – lumbering and slow.[59] From the myriad noxious substances painters used in their work, their limbs could wither, their teeth blacken and their complexions become pallid. The irony that these damaged folk would exaggerate the health and beauty of those whose portraits they painted was not lost on the Italian physician Bernardino Ramazzini. Similarly the apothecaries who mixed the potions and pills to beautify and mollify their customers' skin could themselves be palsied and rendered blear-eyed and toothless by toxic concoctions containing lead and mercury. Ramazzini described the plight of one chemist: the 'mere sight of him was enough to ruin the reputation of the medicaments, the cosmetics especially, that he used to sell'.[60]

Old faces scarred by disease and accidents showed the ravages of time. People with particularly stressful or labourous occupations aged quickly. In 1705 two authors described old soldiers as being 'known by their Roughness, Ugliness, and Scars' and having 'Slashes and Scars'.[61] Tobias Smollett's former soldier, the dishevelled Lismahago, who features in *Humphry Clinker*, is a good example of how a sound physique could be wrecked through abuse and damage. He is tall but he stoops. His narrow shoulders further undermine his masculinity, and create an imbalance with his long and thick legs. His face, elongated, tanned and 'shrivelled', has projecting cheekbones, small eyes, a large hook nose, a pointed chin and 'a mouth from ear to ear very ill-furnished with Teeth, and a high narrow forehead well furrowed with wrinkles'.[62]

Hogarth depicts a collection of infirm, maimed, dying and disabled men wheeled out for corrupt polling purposes (figure 7). A maimed soldier with missing limbs swears with his hook on the Bible. An imbecile is pinned to a chair and prompted by a manacled man to his rear. The pipe-smoking nurse, one of the two who flank a dying man with bandages on his head, has a skeletal appearance, and is missing a large chunk of his nose due to third-stage venereal disease. By contrast, the nurse to his right has a warty, oversized nose. Henry, Lord Kames, discussing 'risible objects' in the mid-eighteenth century, asserted that a 'nose remarkably long or short, is risible, but to want the nose altogether, far from provoking laughter, raises horror in the spectator'.[63] 'The

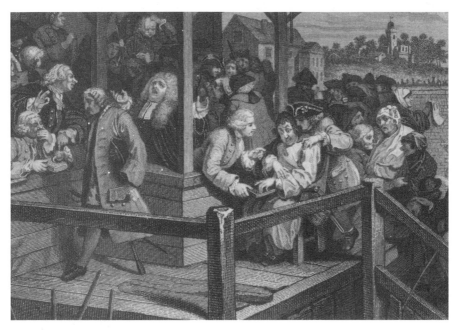

7   A collection of maimed and infirm men are gathered to vote in William Hogarth's engraving, *The Election* (1758), Plate III, 'The Polling'.

syphilitic nose marked the body as corrupt and dangerous', notes a modern cultural historian, who explains how the collapsed cartilage of the nose combined with infections to sink the nose into the face, casting the noseless as 'polluted and polluting'.[64] The maid pouring tea in plate VI of William Hogarth's *Harlot's Progress* has a nibbled nose and a beauty spot, suggesting she was in an advanced stage of syphilis (see figure 25 on p. 71).[65] Lost noses might be congenital rather than the result of disease, but the taint of syphilis was unavoidable. In Laurence Sterne's *Tristram Shandy* (1760–7) the eponymous protagonist was born without a nose (possibly due to forceps mismanagement) and suffered the stigma of noselessness.[66] Faces were judged for symptoms of disease. Noses were not the only facial casualties of syphilis: teeth would also decay as the disease progressed, especially if treatment was sought in the form of mercury pills – contributing to the 'equation of loose teeth with loose morals'.[67]

Accidents and trauma could also mangle bodies. Eliza Haywood advised servant maids to give due and proper attention to any children in their care. She asked them to think about how guilty they would feel if a child became 'lame, crook-back'd' through neglect. Haywood speculates that 'of the many unhappy Objects we see of this Kind, Ninety nine in a Hundred owe their

Misfortune to the Disingenuity of those who attended them in their Infancy.'[68] Alexander Pope suffered a congenital spinal deformity that was exacerbated when he was trampled by a wild cow in his youth. Joshua Reynolds described Pope as 'four feet, six inches high, very humpbacked, and deformed'.[69]

Nonetheless, the 'normal' body was not recognised as 'perfect', and minor physical anomalies were accepted, especially in the male physique. Even those with fairly extreme physical deformities were deemed able to work for their living. Mr Powell, 'a crooke legged man', had gone to school with Samuel Pepys, and later preached a good sermon.[70] In 1761 Count Kielmansegge watched a 'humpbacked' jockey at the Newmarket races 'who seemed to make up for this deformity in skilfulness'.[71] Oxford colleges occasionally employed men with physical deformities. A 'dwaff' called Edward Price was among the staff of Merton College in the 1660s.[72] The likeness of Thomas Hodges, the son of the New College porter, was captured by a portrait painter in 1768, displaying his wooden leg and withered hand (figure 8). The reactions of some people towards the physically challenged were childish. The footboy of the coach that took William Schellinks to Gravesend in 1661 was a dwarf dubbed 'frog'.[73] During his visit in 1652 Lodewijk Huygens joined the laughter at a 'little hunchback' called Mr Kirch.[74]

Women with deformities experienced more negative reactions and could be considered unmarriageable. Some features were thought to pass through the generations. Imparting fatherly advice to his son in 1671, Caleb Trenchfield tried to steer him away from physically blemished women, as their union could bestow 'an hereditary deformity or disease' on further generations. Using the example of a crook-shouldered woman raising a family of crook-backed children, he worried for his future grandchildren, and the honour of the family name. Such a woman should not be taken as a 'breeder', as this would 'leave your name running in the winding-Chanel of a crooked deformity'. Counselling his son to take the most handsome woman available, he reminded him that 'comely' mothers produce 'comely' daughters, and these were more easily dispatched with smaller dowries, to greater marital effect.[75] It was such attitudes that made the poet Mary Chandler dismiss the possibility of marriage and establish herself in business instead. Describing herself as 'crooked', Chandler versified that she was 'a true maid, deformed and old: That she never was handsome ne'er needed be told'. Consequently she was shocked at the age of fifty-four ('when hoary Age' had 'shed Its Winter's snow, and whiten'd' her hair) to be proposed to by a wealthy fan. Chandler spurned his offer, marvelling in a poem: 'Fourscore miles, to buy a crooked wife / Old too! I thought the oddest thing in Life.'[76] She continued to adorn the beautiful ladies of Bath with pretty frills and ribbons in her milliner's shop until retiring in 1745 because of ill health.[77]

8   Portrait of Thomas Hodges (1768). Note his withered hand and wooden leg. He holds a huge silver tankard, which further diminishes his tiny frame.

'Old enough and ugly enough'

Margaret Cavendish claimed to value riches over beauty because wealth lasts longer. In 'the Winter season of Life' therefore, beauty 'seldom or never appears'.[78] To Francis Bacon, beauty was 'as Summer Fruits, which are easie to corrupt, and cannot last'.[79] Nothing could hold back the inevitable sag of age. In the late sixteenth century William Harrison asserted that 'our women through bearing of children doo after fortie begin to wrinkle apace'. He patriotically added that French women weathered worse. In Ned Ward's depiction of a fighting couple the wife is described by her husband as 'More ugly than the Witch of *Endor*', and as approaching her 'despicable Forti'th Year'. Rebuffing her claim to be attractive to other men, the husband announces:

> Faith, my dear Dowdy, thou'rt mistaken,
> Thy skin's too much like rusty Bacon,
> Too rancid and too old to be
> Fancy'd by any Fool but me.[80]

Women past childbearing age were often thought to be unsuitable candidates for marriage. Lady Sarah Cowper rubbished the betrothal of 'a lady, old, decrepit with the palsy and other infirmities'.[81] Samuel Pepys was disappointed when his uncle Fenners married a 'pitiful, old, ugly, ill bred woman in a hatt, a midwife'.[82] Thomas Tryon thought that women over the age of forty-nine were unfit to be brides, but men should feel free to marry until they were sixty.[83] Widows were considered to have more sexual experience than was good for a younger man, and betrothals between older women and younger men were also suspected of being driven by a desire for business advancement as a widow often inherited her husband's established trade. The old woman's purse might have been her most beguiling attribute – 'Old Women's Gold is not ugly.'[84] Another of Ned Ward's *Nuptial Dialogues* is held between a 'young Libertine, and an old canting rich Widow, he had marry'd for her Money'. As they argue, the husband spits invective at his wife:

> old Granny, hold thy jarring Tongue;
> Tho' you are old and toothless, I am young.

The husband claims his wife was motivated by greed: she has purchased a stud to satisfy her 'sweet tooth', her lust for youth. Little wonder, sneers the husband, that he should take a young lover, so he can bear life with a 'wither'd Relict, toothless and decay'd'. The wife – an 'old Hag', a 'grizly Jade' – is cast as

> Fitter for Witchcraft, than a Nuptial-Bed,
> Can ne'er be pleasant to an airy Spouse,
> Too young for barren Joys, and wrinkl'd Brows.

The husband is offended by his wife's 'toothless Mouth', which 'affords such Fumes,/ That smell of Death, and stink of rotten Gums'. He is repelled by her groaning body, which he describes as a 'wither'd skinful of such mouldy Bones'. Her aches and pains put him off sex.[85] 'Unequal marriages' are explored in a manual for bachelors, teaching *The Art of Governing a Wife* (1747). The author scoffs at the absurdity of 'an old decay'd worn-out Widow cast by a Veil, and fairly set up for a Beauty and Fortune, when her shrivel'd Skin looks like so much Parchment, and serves only for a coarser Sort of Bag to carry her tatter'd Limbs and decay'd Joints . . . with an ugly Hag's Face, looking like the true Picture of Envy'.[86]

Sexuality and fertility helped to define a woman's social status and to establish her power. Bodily decay was a problem because much of her worth depended on her ability to provide sexual gratification and to reproduce. Once these qualities had faded, what use was a woman's body? Older ladies were

9   Detail from engraving, William Hogarth, *A Rake's Progress* (1735), Plate I, 'The Young Heir Takes Possession'.

expected to sit out the society balls in Bath on the second bench, along with the children, 'as being past, or not come to perfection'.[87]

Elderly women were particularly vulnerable to calumny in print. This poor press was at least in part due to the fact that most 'wits' and writers were male. There were few positive characterisations of old women. The bawd, the hag, the beldam and the crone were female tropes distinguished by unappealing features and unfeminine behaviour. Bawds were generally depicted as large women, but hags and crones were often frail, with hunched backs. Women were at greater risk than men of the bone-weakening disease osteoporosis, and the 'widow's hump' was a common skeletal response to the ageing process (as in the old woman assembling firewood in the grate in Hogarth's *The Rake's Progress*, figure 9 above). Arthritis and other degenerative illnesses caused limb contortion and general twisting in configurations.[88] These women had gaunt faces and hollow cheeks unsupported by long-lost teeth. Hooked noses and crooked chins added to the overall image. Wrinkles and hunchbacks did not make a hag; ugly, harridan-like behaviour was important. Spite and vengefulness could even throw the suspicion of witchcraft their way.

Old codgers were less abused, but they could still be vilified for their physical degeneration. As they aged, men were characterised as toothless, lame and subject to baldness and diminishing strength and sensory perception.[89]

Although at less risk of damage caused by osteoporosis than women, men would still have suffered from creaking bones as they aged. Anthony Wood complained of weak joints and poor hearing in his old age.[90] Many men changed their jobs during their later years, taking other forms of employment that were not necessarily less arduous, but would have been less skilled, such as portering or hawking.[91] In Ned Ward's *Dialogue* the 'young noisy wife' of 'an old, prodigal, new-sworn Constable' dwelt on his physical features. She described his 'Roman Nose', and 'wrinkl'd Pair of Lanthorn Jaws, / Anatomiz'd by Age, to Skin and Bone'. She goes on to criticise the 'wither'd Hide' of this 'gouty Leader of a scabby Crew / Of louzy tatter'd Scrubs'.[92]

10   Marcellus Laroon (III), *Town Crier Tolling a Bell and Reading from a Paper.*

Some old men took little interest in their appearance and lived shabbily. The wrinkled attorney in *The Rake's Progress* sports a warty face, a bent nose and a dishevelled wig. The clothes of Marcellus Laroon's town-crier, above, are crumpled and hang awkwardly on his body. Two buttons are fastened, two are not. Old men were often depicted with disgusting habits and poor personal hygiene. Wye Saltonstall's 'Old Man' in his *Picturae Loquentes* is 'a candle burnt to the snuffe'. Telling tedious tales in an indulgent and ponderous fashion, his 'soule has long dwelt in a ruinous tenement'. These metaphors point to the decay of his body, mind and manners.[93] 'Old men', began the character in Thomas Overbury's *Overburie His Wife*, 'are to bee knowne blindfolded: for their talke is as terrible as their resemblance.' It was a blessing that the aged lost their various senses, else they might have offended themselves. Thus as 'they can hardly smel at all' they would not notice their own 'putrified breath'. Counting it an 'ornament of speech' to end each sentence 'with a cough', they 'spend their time in wyping their driveled beards'.[94]

Sexual relationships and marriage between elderly men and nubile women attracted almost as much criticism from the satirists and novelists as relations of old women and young men. Nicholas Breton's servant 'Mauillia' finds no pleasure in kissing an old man, an erstwhile traveller in the Low Countries, 'where he hath bene subjected with some unwholsome ayre'. The 'stubble of his olde shaven beard new come up, so pricks mee, and tickles my lipps, that I am ready to scratch them after every kisse: but yet his nose is so great, that hee hath much adoo to kisse kindly: Besides, he hath a stinking breath, and a hollow eye.' Additionally, this old 'foole' has a poor complexion and rotten teeth, has only one ear and is deaf, has gout, is half blind, 'hath almost no hayre on his head', is 'crup shouldred', and spits and coughs continually.[95] When Fanny Hill – John Cleland's 'woman of pleasure' – is paraded in front of her first client she gasps that the sight of him would be dangerous to pregnant women. A short man in his sixties, he had 'a yellow cadaverous hue, great goggling eyes, that stared as if he was strangled; an out-mouth from two more properly tushes than teeth, livid lips, and breath like a jakes'. Fanny is struck by his ghastly grin.[96] Ned Ward depicted a marriage between an ancient gentleman 'whose head Age had Powder'd like a Beau's' and a beautiful young woman, attracted by his 'filthy Lucre'. The wife became frustrated when her seventy-year-old partner could not consummate the nuptials, and the marriage swiftly broke down amid jealously, acrimony and conflict.[97] Another marriage – between a 'Pert Lady' and an 'Old fumbling Libertine' – was equally doomed. 'Go, you old fumbling Letcher', says the wife to the husband, 'blush for shame / To be so lewd, when gouty, old, and lame.'[98] One author lamented the foolishness of an 'Old Doting Fellow of Sixty, to fall a Dying, Sighing, and Languishing, for a sprightly Girl of Sixteen'. Such a sight was comical, as he sported spruce accoutrements, the '*allamode* combing of the Wigg, the careless placing of the Hat', on his 'Monkey's Face and a Death's Head'. This was beastly. This was 'Ape-like'.[99]

'Ugly Women, finely dress'd, are the uglier for it'[100]

Elderly folk who refused to age gracefully were lampooned in print, prose and poetry. Fashions designed for younger figures sat awkwardly on older frames.

A long beard and a balding pate were no longer seen as marks of sagacity, so the hair loss and whitening that often accompanied the march of time could be masked with wigs and borders. Wigs were the one form of head covering for those with only wispy tufts left which did not need to be removed in the presence of superiors or in church.[101] However, head furnishings for the elderly offended some contemporaries. One critic noted the disjuncture of a 'youthful bush of hair' with wrinkled faces and trembling joints ('they have December in their bones').[102]

The creators and traders of cosmetics and potions to enhance or cover the skin played on fears of ageing. With no advertising standards to uphold, claims could be wild. Ned Ward parodied pedlars of cosmetics and toiletries, detailing an uncommon beauty wash that made nonagenarian women appear in the first flush of youth, and 'so repair old wither'd Maids, / And set off founder'd wrinkl'd Jades, / That Bawds of sixty shall go down / With Country Squires at half a Crown.'[103] In a characterisation of 'an old decay'd worn-out Widow' her face is plied with 'Paint and Patch' to fill the furrows, and her figure is disguised by artful tailoring. The author did not approve of such 'disguises' – 'for all such unnatural Things carry with them a Deformity so gross, as can never be concealed'.[104]

Dudley Ryder was neither the first nor the last man to be embarrassed by his mother's lack of sartorial propriety. After she wore a 'scandalous gown' in August 1716, Dudley cringed to his diary: 'my mother is very much to blame in wearing clothes that make her friends blush for her and ashamed of being seen in her company.'[105] While visiting Bath in 1766 the Revd John Penrose wrote to his daughter Peg. One of the things that captured his attention was the clothing worn by the old ladies in the town. Noting that 'your Mamma is the only old woman in Town', he tells Peg that 'Ladies without Teeth, without Eyes, with a foot and half in the grave, ape youth, and dress themselves forth with the fantastic Pride of eighteen or twenty.'[106] The Grub-Street Journal of 2 September 1731 spins the tale of an 'elderly Lady, whose bulky, squat figure, / By hoop and white damask was render'd much bigger'.[107] Men could also fail to dress appropriately for their age. When Huygens visited the philosopher Thomas Hobbes in 1652 he found the sickly sexagenarian dressed 'in the French manner' in trousers with points, white buttoned boots with 'fashionable' tops and a long dressing gown.[108]

'Mutton dressed as lamb' hardly begins to describe the couple in Marcellus Laroon's An Ancient Couple shown opposite. This gaudy couple are so affected by the ravages of time that they are animal-like in their fine and frilly clothes. Their sticks appear ornamental, yet we suppose them vital equipment for balance, especially for the woman as she totters in high heels. This couple are stepping out together as though still in the prime of their youth, and the viewer is invited to join in Laroon's gentle scorn. Erasmus Jones warned against the

11   Marcellus   Laroon   (III),   *An Ancient Couple* (*c.*1730).

inappropriate adornment of old bodies, such as a 'glittering Buckle upon the gouty Foot' or a 'white stocking tightly garter'd upon the lame Leg'. He commented on the ridiculousness of 'grey Hairs decorated with Ribbons' or attire that revealed 'a wither'd naked Neck'. 'Gaudy Grandmothers and gay Grandfathers', Jones asserted, 'are equally contemptible in the Eyes of all People.'[109]

'He is handsome that handsome doth'[110]

Ugliness could be a symptom of behaviour as much as appearance. Acting outside one's station, or in an extreme way, could be deemed ugly, or beastly. The effete fop and the thuggish tradesman were both character types displaying such excesses. Overly masculine or effeminate behaviour in men was unattractive. Both types of men are represented in Hogarth's *The Cockpit* (figure 12). Cockfights were raucous events. Foreign visitors were bewildered by the sounds; one mentioned a 'continuous hubbub', another exclaimed that 'no one who has not seen such a sight can conceive the uproar by which it is accompanied.' The spectators 'gentle and simple . . . sit with no distinction of place'. Among the unappealing bunch gathered to watch Hogarth's cockfight are men of all ages and classes, and some of the wealthier spectators show obvious discomfort about mixing with the hoi polloi. A well-dressed gent peers disdainfully at his arm as he is barged by the post-boy, who is grabbing the

12   Engraving, William Hogarth, *The Cockpit* (1759).

central character, Lord Albermarle (a blind man). All the senses are involved here, from the smell of tobacco to the jostling contact. There is a toothless man who grins inanely; a curmudgeonly gouty deaf old man with an ear trumpet; a porcine man snorting out his snuff; a thief with a sullen face and sunken cheeks; a gambler with eyes bulging in knuckle-cracking anticipation; and a chubby aristocrat with piggy eyes. The scuffling and shoving brutes push one man into the arena, knocking his wig off. A Quaker is visible among the gathered throng, praying at the back. A curious addition to such a noisy crowd, his inclusion might signal his hypocrisy. It is hard to separate the appearance from the behaviour – both contribute to the ugly scene. Men could be accused of effeminacy or mincing foppishness, a charge risked by one man on the far left who represents continental chic and looks disdainfully down on the English rabble. Another, a roman-nosed rake, front right, has been targeted by a hook-wielding thief, and will imminently lose his purse. The fop was 'no great Friend to the Tobacconist, for Fear of his Lungs', tells the author of *Hell upon Earth* (1729), 'yet he holds a Pipe in his Mouth to make his Diamond Ring the more conspicuous'. Fops were mere gaudy baubles parading like showy peacocks. Describing the head of a fop as 'a dark and unfurnished Garret', he notes that fops consulted tailors rather than ancient Greek sages.[111]

Men should look like men. The university authorities struggled to prevent the scholars abandoning their academic garb and embracing fussy fashions. In 1636 a Cambridge college master worried about scholars with 'fair Roses on the Shoe, long frizzled haire upon the head, broad spred Bands upon the Shoulders, and long large Merchants Ruffs about the neck, with fayre feminine cuffs at the wrist'.[112] Anthony Wood thought that the 1660s were a 'strang effeminate age when men strive to imitate women in their apparel, viz. long periwigs, patches in their faces, painting, short wide breeches like petticotes, muffs, and their clothes highly sented, bedecked with ribbons of all colours'.[113] In April 1661 an acquaintance told Samuel Pepys that he had spent a day with both legs 'through one of his Knees of his breeches'. 'Petticoat-breeches' could be so voluminous that such a mistake would have been fairly easy to make.[114]

The ultra-fashionable fops attracted much criticism in this period for their subversion of status and gender.[115] These fashions arrived from the continent, causing John Evelyn to fulminate against the 'Forreign Butterflies' who fluttered about town.[116] Critics grumbled about beaux bedecked with frizzled curls and wanton ringlets, and bemoaned the clouds of powder and pomatum. Effeminate men who minced around 'furnished only with Ribbands and Laces, Flounces and Falbelows' offended a 'Disgusted of Manchester'.[117] The author of *Satan's Harvest Home* (1749) complained about the difficulty in distinguishing a mincing fop from a footman. He felt that the worst excess of foppery was 'the Hair strok'd over before and Cock'd up behind, with a *Comb* sticking in it', condemning such styles as overly feminine.[118]

The caricature of the butcher was diametrically opposed to the fop. In *The Cockpit* a man towers over the central character taking bets. He has one arm over the back of the arena in an aggressive stance. He appears to be a butcher, with a stocky physique, wearing oversleeves, cap and jacket, carrying a knife or steel, and seemingly blood-spattered. Butchers had enjoyed a respectable status in most provincial centres in the medieval period, and it was common to find members of their trade in positions of local governance. Their status declined during the early modern period, perhaps due to heightened sensibilities. City butchers were connected with corrupt meat, spilled blood, and pavements covered with offal. Their trade offended the olfactory and visual senses. Their animals obstructed traffic, polluted streets and poisoned consumers. By the eighteenth century the caricatured butcher was a common sight in images depicting the unruly mob.[119] In *The Beaux Disaster* (*c*.1747) (see figure 33, on p. 90), a bullying butcher hangs a fop by his clothes on a hook, to be barked at by a dog. Ned Ward depicts a group of butchers as a herd of animals ('greasy Killcalves') trotting by. Their steels hang at their rears like tails. Their appearance, smell, demeanour and language are all beastly. Accompanied by their dogs ('sheepbiters'), this brutish gang strike each other with 'bended sticks' and play 'twenty rude unlucky Tricks'.[120] Ward returned to these images in 'The Merry Travellers', when he described a drunken pork and poultry butcher:

> His blund'ring Head looks Sarazantick,
> His Body's of a bulk Gygantick,
> So fat, so weighty, and so large.
> 'Twould frieght a little Western Barge;
> His Belly, in its spacious hollow,
> Contains at least ten Stone of Tallow,
> Besides of Filth such ample store,
> 'Twould dung a Rood of Land, or more;
> His Legs, Like Paviers Rammers, level
> The Stone, wherever they walk or travel . . .[121]

Thomas Tryon considered butchers in a letter bearing the gothic title 'Of Employments arising from the Fountain of Darkness'. He grouped them together with other men whose 'Trades . . . bear the marks and signatures of Violence', such as fishermen and hunters and 'all that buy or sell Dead Bodies of Creatures for Funeral-Shows, Embalmings etc'. These men, Tryon asserted, 'are toucht with the like pernicious Evil'.[122] Tryon was a zealous oddball, and few would have subscribed to his worldview. Mr Campbell, author of a compendium of trades, was more prosaic. He wrote that 'Butchers are necessary; yet it is almost the last Trade I should chuse to bind a Lad to. It requires great Strength, and a Disposition no ways inclinable to the Coward.'[123]

Was the butcher truly violent or beastly, or just a convenient target for satirists? There were certainly cases in which butchers physically attacked others; a butcher beat a man in Gosport with a pitchfork in 1682, and another threatened to attack the house and wife of a Portsmouth painter-stainer in 1687.[124] Three years later the wife of a Stepney butcher accused her husband of beating and manacling her with irons. He also threatened to amputate her legs. The butcher was accused of similar acts six years later.[125] In 1769 a butcher almost beat to death a youth in Bath.[126] Butchers can be identified in images of ugly crowd scenes, but their accoutrements made them irresistible candidates for inclusion. Were the stereotypes and caricatures therefore warranted? There were thugs in all trades – even among the foppish perruquiers. Anthony Wood was horrified that the courtiers who sheltered from the plague in Oxford in 1665, although 'neat and gay in their apparell', were 'very nasty and beastly'. Wood claimed that 'at their departure' the 'Rude, rough . . . vaine, empty, carlesse' courtiers left 'excrements in every corner, in chimneys, studies, colehouse, cellars'.[127]

13 Image opposite the frontispiece, from Thomas Heywood, *Philocothomista, or the Drunkard, Opened, Dissected and Atomized* (London, 1635).

Beastly behaviour took other forms. Drunks were frequently identified with animals. 'Wine', remarked Jonathan Swift, 'doth not inspire politeness.' Drunks stuttered, stammered, staggered, reeled, vomited, pissed and blasphemed their way into the sober moralists' bad books. The frontispiece of Thomas Heywood's *Philocothomista* (above) depicts the boorish behaviour of tavern drinkers who have morphed into animals: the 'Dogge-drunke' fought like spaniels and those drunk like calves would prattle, prance and laugh giddily. The swine-drunk wallowed in puddles, emerging 'durty and daubed'.[128] A pipe-smoking cow sits opposite a quaffing goose, and to the rear a dog attacks a donkey. The seventeenth-century herald Randle Holme explained the need for a chamber pot (front left) by 'the Jolly crew when met togather over a cup of Ale; not for modesty sake, but that they may se[e] their owne beastlynesse, in powering in, and casting out more then sufficeth nature, which if it went not suddenly downwards, would force its way upwards'. However, the pig misses the pot, and vomits on the leg and shoes of a goat struggling to stay on his chair. John Hart, 'a lover of Sobriety', used similar imagery for his *Dreadfull Character of a Drunkard*, coupled with 'brief Exhortations to perswade men from that Swinish and abominable sin'.[129]

14   Image from page 8 of Samuel Ward et al., *A Warning-piece to all Drunkards and Health-Drinkers* (London, 1682).

In *England's Bane, or, The Deadly Danger of Drunkenness Described* (1677) Edward Bury asserted that drink 'turns a Man into a Beast' engaging in 'nasty behaviour, wallowing in their Vomit, and moiling themselves in their Dung, and dirt'. Bury likened drunken behaviour to the behaviour of swine, 'for I know not any other Creature that will drink till he Burst, and doth delight so much in Swill, and wallowing in the mire'. The sight of a drunken man was, Bury tells us, 'enough to overset a mans stomack'.[130] The drunkard often lost control of his senses, his limbs, his bladder, his stomach and his tongue. [131] Drunks could become unsteady, noisy and sweaty. When men see a drunkard, Edward Bury notes, they yell 'yonder goes a Toss-pot, a Swill-bowl, a Drunken

Swine, a Belly-god, do you see how he reels? how he vomits? . . . here the Swine lies, sleeping, snorting, wallowing in his Vomit more fit for the Dunghill than the House.'[132] Drunks fumbled, stumbled and staggered.[133] 'Let the Drunkard alone; and by and by he'll fall of himself,' noted a contemporary proverb.[134] Horse riding could be hazardous under the influence of drink. The Aldermen and Mayor of Oxford were so drunk one night in 1685 that many of them fell off their horses.[135] Alcohol affected moods as well as bodily functions. Dudley Ryder found that wine did not agree with him one night, and found himself in an 'uneasy state of mind', becoming 'dull and heavy'.[136]

A Cambridge University Act of 1607 was designed to repress 'the odious and loathsome synne of Drunkennes' apparently common among the scholars.[137] Because alcohol affects bodily functions, the moralists worried that drinkers would not be able to work effectively. An Act of Parliament of 1728 to lay a duty on 'compund waters' stated that 'the drinking of Spirits . . . is become very common amongst the People of inferior Rank, and the constant and excessive Use thereof tends greatly to the Destruction of their Healths, enervating them, and rendring them unfit for useful Labour and Service, intoxicating them, and debauching their Morals'.[138] Hogarth's image of 'Night' (see figure 62 on p. 226) reveals a blind-drunk barber slicing his customer (whose pinched nose makes him look like a pig). Edmund Harrold, a Manchester wig-maker, never became a successful tradesman – due to his inveterate socialising. During one night Harrold alienated a customer and worried his pregnant wife. The loss of credibility, money and reputation he suffered through his addiction often caused him to be introverted and self-critical. He recorded how he had made himself 'a great fool', or 'a laughing-stock to men'. Harrold took widowhood badly and went on an eight-month bender, drinking heavily in various Manchester taverns.[139]

An early careers advice manual argued that silk weavers worked a profitable trade, as long as 'they refrain from the common vice of Drinking and Sotting away their Time and Senses'.[140] The Manchester moraliser John Clayton weighed in against men who 'mingle strong drink' all day 'till their Liquor has enflamed them'. These drunkards ignore the cries of their starving families while 'wallowing in *Riot* and *Drunkenness*, in *Chambering* and *Wantonness*', as the streets of Manchester fill with their 'idle ragged children'.[141] Edward Bury would have agreed. Several decades earlier he had described drunkards as 'gormandizing wretches' and condemned them for drinking away the money that should have filled their children's plates. 'How many Wives and Children', he wondered, 'lie weeping and wailing, and wringing their hands at home, not having Bread to eat, or Cloathing to put on, when their Prodigal Husbands or Fathers are merry enough amidst their cups.'[142] Campbell, the author of *The London Tradesman* (1747), held distillers responsible for 'debauching the Morals, and debilitating the Strength of the common People . . . if the Evil increases in the next ten years as it has done in the last, Drunkenness must become the Characteristick of the People . . . The Children must be born in Gin, brought up in a Gin-shop, live in Drunkenness.' Campbell desired the closure of many distilleries, and controls on chandlers' shops, where many servants got their first taste of gin.[143]

Bath had relatively few inns – only twenty-two are named on Gilmore's map of 1694 (see p. 8).[144] By contrast the scholars and citizens of Oxford could choose to drink in one of ninety-four unlicensed and three hundred licensed premises in 1634.[145] Anthony à Wood suggested that there were in excess of 370 alehouses in Oxford in 1678, and described them as 'Means to create idleness and debauch scholars'.[146] Christopher Guise, a student at Oxford's Magdalen Hall in the early seventeenth century, downed innumerable 'unwilling glasses . . . without any advantage from those woemen'. Others imbibed to such a degree that they developed 'an unhealthy, evill and deborch't habitt'.[147] Like many students, Parson Woodforde had been fond of a tipple when an Oxford undergraduate in the mid-eighteenth century. In the early hours of 21 May 1761 six of his friends broke both his inner and outer doors 'all to shatters for Funn'. 'N.B.', added Woodforde, by way of justification, 'They were all drunk as Pipers.' Woodforde became temporarily abstemious two years later after falling in a drunken stupor and gashing his head.[148] Anthony Wood singled out St John's College in Oxford as a 'debauched colledg', with much drunkenness – a clique of scholars had even been known to 'come drunk into the chapel and vomit in their hats or caps there'.[149] Oxford don and erstwhile Puritan Thomas Brace reeled down the street after drinking himself into a stupor at the Blue Boar in 1664. The moralisers had much to say when those who were meant to set the moral standards fell victim to the pot. Wood described the preaching of a Corpus Christi fellow as 'ridiculous', affected by drink 'like a monkey rather than a Xtian'.[150] In 1691 a fellow of All Souls College (the son of a Westminster brewer) died at the Mitre Inn in the city 'after immoderate drinking'. Within the week another Oxford death was partly attributed to the effects of drink when Dr Edward Farrar, Master of University College, breathed his last on his close-stool. Farrar had lived a life of excess and his demise was hastened because in life he had been 'much given to bibbing and smoking and but little to exercise'.[151] A fellow of Magdalen College who spent a life enjoying 'a good deal of coffee, and abundance of small beer' died of alcohol poisoning in 1724.[152]

Gin, a disgusting and potent brew, was the subject of many licensing acts throughout the eighteenth century.[153] The reeling freemason depicted in Hogarth's 'Night' was Thomas de Veil, who introduced stringent legislation in 1736. Bernard Mandeville thought that all forms of alcohol were harmful to the constitution, but he identified gin as the worst. Nothing was more destructive to 'the Health or the Vigilance and Industry of the Poor than the infamous Liquor'. It 'burns up the Entrails, and scorches every Part within', stops them thinking about hardships – 'Brats that cry for Food, hard Winters, Frosts, and horrid empty Home'. It is readily available: 'In the Fag-end and Out-skirts of the Town, and all places of the vilest Resort, it is sold in some part or other of almost every House, frequently in Cellars, and sometimes in the Garret.' The sellers endure 'filfy Actions and viler Language of Nasty Drabs, and the lewdest Rakehells', bear 'the Stench and Squallor, Noise and Impertinence that the utmost indigence, Laziness and Ebriety, can produce in the most shameless and abandon'd Vulgar'.[154] An infant living in St John

15   Engraving, William Hogarth, *Gin Lane* (1751).

Wapping slept top-to-toe with her mother and two men above a gin shop. When she died it was suspected that she had been infected with a venereal disease by one of her bedmates. The case fell apart given an absence of proof, but witness statements paint a horrifying image of debauchery fuelled by liquor.[155]

Gin Lane, Hogarth's contribution to the reform movement, is set in the notorious district of St Giles-in-the-Fields, London, at a time when every fourth building there was a gin shop (see figure 15). This is a wretched scene of depravity, murder, suicide, starvation and disease – the results of gin consumption. At the centre of this horrifying image, a shabby mother with legs ulcerated by syphilis is so paralytic she drops her son to a certain death. Hogarth used the image of a forlorn mother with child in many of his images to represent pitiful poverty (see also *The Enraged Musician*, figure 40 on p. 128). To the left a man fights a dog for a bone. The only flourishing trades are pawn brokerage and undertaking – the barber hangs himself in a ruined building, the carpenter pawns his gear, and the ballad-seller (bottom right) has sold most of his clothes, to reveal a skeletal frame. Above, a mother decants gin into her baby's mouth, and behind, a blindfolded cripple is attacked with his own crutch. Below the hanging coffin a hysterical woman pursues a crazed man with bellows on his head, presumably the mother of the wriggling child he has skewered on his stick. The teetering buildings will soon make more casualties. In *An Enquiry into the Causes of the late Increase of Robbers etc* (1751) Henry Fielding discussed drunkenness induced by gin: 'Many of these wretches there are, who swallow pints of this poison within the twenty-four hours; the dreadful effects of which I have the misfortune every day to see, and to smell too.'[156]

'Hug your ugly selves, and hug your ugly sin'[157]

The lack of inhibition and the need to service an addiction could lead to lewd behaviour or prostitution. Living down to her name in 1611, Mary Beast conducted lewd acts and was punished by the Westminster burgesses by being stripped naked from the waist upwards, fastened to a cart, and whipped through the streets on a cold December day.[158] These sadistic punishments publicly censured licentiousness and made noisy examples of the lewd. Brothel-keepers were whipped at a cart's tail.[159] In 1743 a witness at an Old Bailey trial described prostitutes who plied their trade around St Bride's parish as 'such poor ragged dismal Toads, and drunk'. Another witness continued with the bestial imagery, describing a brothel filled with 'Creatures who had scarce Rags to their Backs . . . the House is like a Hog-sty. They get drunk, and the men and women are like Hogs and Pigs lying altogether.'[160] The author of *The London Jilt* (1683) warned of the dangers of the 'Misses of this Town', who cause 'all manner of diseases'. 'A Whore', he asserts, 'is but a Close-Stool . . . that receives all manner of filth, she's like a Barber's Chair, no sooner one's out, but t'others in.' The writer wonders 'what greater Folly can there be than to venture one's All in such rotten Bottoms . . . only for a Momentary Pleasure, considering that filthy, nasty, and stinking Carcasees, are the best and finest of our Common Whores'.[161] Descriptions often stressed the animalistic physiognomy and odour of the lewd – they looked like toads and acted like filthy swine. Some even dwelt on their smell. One lexicographer gave the definition 'a sluttish Woman who smells rank' to the term 'fustilugs'.[162]

The face distinguished honest from dishonest women.[163] Crudely daubed maquillage suggested whorishness. The arch-puritan Phillip Stubbes moaned about women who busied themselves with such beautification. To this purist, cosmetics were a 'putrifaction', and he likened a painted woman to 'a dunghil covered with white & red'.[164] These views were mirrored by Thomas Hall, who saw make-up as an affront to God's workmanship and the 'badge of a harlot'. Hall thought that women resorting to paints 'deceive themselves, getting deformity instead of beauty', they poison their skin and wrinkle their faces.[165] A fictional prostitute is described at the close of the seventeenth century as a 'damn'd rotten pockify'd Whore' with a 'Tauney face daub'd over thicker with Paint than her skeleton Carcass with Flesh, with a flat *African* Nose, a Wide Mouth, a Pigg's Eye, and a stinking Breath'.[166]

Pausing in Westminster on his fictitious journey around the world in 1691, the journalist John Dunton found a 'Paucity of honest Women', but a 'magnitude of Whores'. The very idea of such polluting females would make a 'modest stomack' turn up 'all the green and yellow ropey stuff, fat eggs, and snotty glib soft substance'.[167] John Stewart of Manchester's Sugar Lane was fined a huge amount in 1759 for running a brothel, and entertaining a notorious prostitute called 'Phanny Heap'.[168] Ever the pragmatist, Bernard Mandeville thought prostitutes made a necessary sacrifice to preserve the majority of womankind. Lusty men unable to attract 'clean Woman, will content themselves with dirty Drabs'.[169]

'Ugly as sin'

The once alluring looks of Ned Ward's 'Insinuating Bawd' had deteriorated, hammered by ageing and the pox. Her once rosy cheeks paled and yellowed, her breasts drooped and her breath turned rancid. Disgusted at her own wretchedness, the bawd holds herself as a warning to the young harlot.[170] The woman in plate I of Hogarth's *The Harlot's Progress* represents the notorious bawd Mother Needham (figure 16). Like a market officer for fish and flesh, she paws young Moll Hackabout with her bare hand like a piece of meat in an image contrasting the innocence of youth with knowing decrepitude. Beauty patches (which Moll sports in later plates) are visible on the bawd's forehead.

16 Detail from engraving, William Hogarth, *The Harlot's Progress* (1732), Plate I, 'The Procuress'.

In Hogarth's images these symbolise the effects of venereal disease.[171] This procuress cuts a relatively fine figure compared to Thomas Overbury's bawd, whose 'teeth are falne out; mary her Nose, and chin, intend very shortly to be friends, and meete about it . . . a *Bawde* is like a Medlar, shee's not ripe, till she be rotton'.[172]

Bile was also directed at scolds or harridans. Not all were old, and there was something particularly tragic about a young or attractive termagant, but the scold and the shrew are preserved in mythology as middle-aged or older. Physical imperfections and a hatchet face, although not essential qualifications, certainly helped. Descriptions of the scold joined the whore and witch as classic female stereotypes. The scold's ugliness had more of an aural than a visual basis. Nicholas Breton compared the voice of an 'unquiet woman' to the 'skrieching of an Owle'.[173] Richard Brathwaite directed his attention to the shrew, remarking that she even made sounds when asleep, when 'she falls into a terrible vaine of snoring and foams at the mouth as if she were possessed . . . she is most out of her element when she is most at quiet'. When awake this woman, with 'ferret eyes and hooke nose', is like 'a bee in a box, for she is ever buzzing'.[174] Brathwaite rhapsodised that the 'wheele of her tongue does with a perpetuall motion: yet she *spits* more than she *speakes*: and never *spits* but in *spite*.'[175] According the *The Spectator*, a shrewish woman would be 'always busy and barking . . . and live in perpetual Clamour'.[176] In *Poor Robin's True*

Character of a Scold (1678) the 'rank scold' was described as 'perpetually hissing, and spitting of venom; a composition of ill-nature and clamour'.[177] Scolding turned the woman into an animal; she is a shrew, a bee, a snake; she has a tongue 'as glibberie as an Eele', and is as spiteful as a wasp.[178] Old before her time, 'shee frets like a gum'd *Grogram*'. Eventually her husband is worried 'out of his senses', and his 'miserable eares are deafed with her incessant clamour'.[179]

A curious little work of 1672 illustrated a misogynistic fantasy (figure 17, below). It described a Dutch invention to help all unhappy husbands: a windmill to reform bad wives. Deemed suitable for such treatment were 'the old, Decreped, Wrinkled, Blear'ey'd, Long-Nosed, Blind, Lame, Scolds, Jealous, Angry, Poor, Drunkards Whores, Sluts' and, indeed, any other problematic spouse. Ground by the mill, these women would emerge refreshed – young, active, pleasant and handsome, 'Without any Deformity'. A frontispiece completes the fantasy, depicting men transporting their womenfolk by all means: carriage, barrow, even piggy-back, in order to have them cured. A happy couple depart with the woman a picture of poise, kindling renewed feelings of love in her husband.[180]

17   *The Merry Dutch Miller: and New Invented Windmill* (London, 1672).

Ducking stools or cuckstools were equipment for punishing scolds and were items of town furniture. Although such devices were not in common use, they were still used as a deterrent in the eighteenth century. Ducking was a rite of humiliation intended to put the woman in her place and to teach her a lesson.

It was a way of meting out punishment on behalf of the entire community, as the whole neighbourhood was thought to suffer with a scold in their midst.[181] Phillipa Winslowe of Holborn was described as 'a turbulent wrangling woman . . . one that by her disorderly living doth disquiet all her neighbours'.[182] Acting contrary to her name, Widow Makepeace, a woman in the Portsoken Ward of London, was a 'Common Schold and a common Disturber of the Neighbourhood'.[183]

Across the country the civic authorities ensured that their cuckstools were functioning. In 1603 the Southampton authorities complained that 'the Cuckinge stoole on the Towne ditches is all broken' and expressed their desire for a new one, to 'punish the manifold number of scoldinge woemen that be in this Towne'. The following year they wondered whether a stool-on-wheels might be invented. This could be 'carried from dore to dore as the scolde shall inhabit'. This mobile stool would, it was explained, be 'a great ease to mr mayor . . . whoe is daylie troubled w[i]th suche brawles'.[184] The Oxford Council erected a cuck stool at the Castle Mills in 1647.[185] The Manchester stool was set up in 1602 'for the punyshement of Lewde Wemen and Scoldes'. It was located in the daub holes, an artificial pond created by digging clay for house building at the upper end of Market Street Lane (figure 18, below). The stool was fragile in 1619, but must have been repaired or replaced, because six scolds were immersed in 1627. A decade later the town added a scold's bridle to their armoury of reform. A new ducking chair was erected in 'the usual place' in 1738.[186] Even as late as 1770 a knot and bridle hung from the door of the

18   Manchester's 'Ducking Stool for Punishing Prostitutes' (c.1775).

stationers, near the Dark Entry in the Market Place 'as a terror to the scolding huxter-women'. [187]

There were no simple definitions of physical beauty or ugliness in the seventeenth and eighteenth centuries. Women felt more pressure to be attractive than men. People who did not look or act in ways appropriate to their station in life were lambasted. Physical imperfections caused by immoral activities or excessive abuse of substances attracted more opprobrium than some other conditions. Physical damage caused by an excess of alcohol or risky sex revealed moral decay. One commentator described how alcohol 'doth so deform, deface, and defile'. The 'red firey measled pimpled' face was swollen like a 'bladder' and the body slipped into a dropsical, gouty and deformed state.[188] Some even blamed a misuse of new luxury items such as tea for removing a woman's bloom.[189] The normal body was not perfect, and everybody suffered some deterioration in their looks as they aged. Elderly couples with fashionable props and underpinnings were chided for silliness, but the nastiest invective was reserved for those with trophy spouses. Couplings of old with young were considered to be vain, silly, beastly and went against accepted norms: 'a merry old Fool, and a gay apish Matron are things so unnatural, that a very ingenious Person has deservedly reckoned them amongst the tamer sort of Monsters.' To 'couple together a young lusty Piece of Flesh with an old frigid Statue' was like uniting summer with winter, or light with dark. [190] A young woman with shrewish habits would be marked as ugly and improper regardless of her looks, while a 'vertuous woman, tho' ugly' was the 'Ornament of the House'.[191] Excessive drinking, overtly sexual behaviour, even being a slave to foreign fashions could all lead to an association with beastliness, subversion and ugliness. Behaviour mattered as much as looks.

CHAPTER 3

Itchy

A lack of sanitary facilities in the seventeenth and eighteenth centuries meant that skin would have been more dirty and sweaty than in modern times. Hair, wigs and clothes became greasy and grungy in the city conditions. Proverbial wisdom dictated that 'he smells best that smells of nothing', but owing to the lack of products for personal hygiene and laundry, 'one is not smelt, where all stink' was a more apt maxim. All experiences are relative and the normal condition of the early modern body, although different from the modern body, would not have exercised the mind of its owner unduly. Discomfort was experienced when the skin of an individual came under attack from disease or parasites. Extreme weather conditions and contact with harsh, greasy or toxic products added to the daily discomfort of many, as did coarse fabrics and ill-fitting footwear.

'An itch is worse than a smart'[1]

'Too much scratching hurts the skin' was one of the more banal proverbs in Edward Phillips's collection of 1658, but it would have struck a chord with contemporary readers.[2] Many conditions would have caused itching, including eczema, impetigo, 'psorophthalmy' (eyebrow dandruff), scabies, chilblains, chapped and rough skin, 'tetters' (spots and sores), 'black morphew' (leprous or scurvy skin) and ringworm. Few citizens enjoyed smooth unblemished skin. Cuts and grazes could lead to ugly and uncomfortable scabbing and unattractive scarring. In this pre-antibiotic era, skin eruptions in the forms of bulging pustules, lesions, acne and gout-induced ulcers could all have become infected, causing chronic wounds.[3] Various diarists recorded their battles with boils. In 1761, as an Oxford undergraduate, the parson-in-waiting James Woodforde suffered from a boil on his bum that made him feverish until it 'discharged itself in the night excessively'. A few months later he was plagued by a 'bad Boyle on my Eye-brow'. This boil reappeared the following year, to be joined by a stye among his lower right eyelashes.[4] Plenty of authors came forward with recipes to treat skin complaints. In an extraordinary leap of tangential thinking, Thomas Tryon managed to introduce a recipe for a poultice to soothe 'all itchy and Leprous Sores' into a discussion about bricks.[5]

Venereal disease was the secret epidemic that blighted the entire period.[6] In addition to weeping sores on the lips, venereal diseases necessitated scratching in embarrassing places. Prostitutes and their clients were most frequently exposed to sexually transmitted diseases, and whores, strumpets, harlots and lechers were often given the sobriquets of 'itchy' or 'pocky'.[7]

> Whores and common Drabs,
> Pepper'd with Pocky Itch, or Scabs,
> Who have for Years been never free
> From the Venereal Leprosy[8]

Despite donning prophylactic 'armour', James Boswell was punished by his aggressive sexuality in 1763 when he felt 'a little heat in the members'. His suspicions were later confirmed by 'damned twinges, that scalding heat, and that deep-tinged loathsome matter'.[9]

Other maladies affected the genitals too. Elizabeth, Samuel Pepys's wife, had a nasty vaginal complaint, now supposed to have been Bartholin's abscess. The pain from boils and a 'hollow sore place below in her privities' incapacitated her on several occasions.[10] Thomas Tryon discussed diseases contracted from the privy in *Wisdom Dictates* (1691). 'Be careful that you do noe sit on Common house of Easement, which oftentimes proves of eveil consequences and infects the Party with Diseases of various kinds.' Tryon recommended his readers to defecate in a vessel and then, on cooling, to decant it into the house of office.[11]

The abundance of dogs and pigs on the city streets provided the perfect breeding ground for a variety of intestinal parasites, many of which wormed their way into humans. Eliza Smith asserted that 'vast numbers' were infested.[12] Many bottoms would have itched with discomfort thanks to the presence of thread and tape worms in the digestive system. According to the numerous contemporary adverts, worms created a myriad of physical discomforts, including 'pinching Pain in the Belly, when hungry, a stinking Breath', vomiting, nightmares, pallidness, fever and teeth gnashing.[13] Ned Ward parodied the sales pitch:

> Pale languid Looks, and fainting Fits,
> False and Voratious Appetites,
> Vomiting, Looseness, Trembling, Griping,
> Laziness, and immod'rate Sleeping,
> Want of Digestion, craving Drowth,

Dull Eyes, dry Lips, and feav'rish Mouth,
Unsav'ry Belches after Drinking,
Foul Stomach, and a Breath that's stinking,
All these are Symptoms, that will tell ye
You've crawling Insects in your Belly,
Nor is it there alone, we know,
That these destructive Vermin grow.
But also in the Tail and Head,
That these intestine Monsters breed.
This makes young Wenches so unsettl'd,
When the Worm bites, their Rumps are nettl'd.[14]

In 1756 a Manchester newspaper carried an advert that offered hope to worm-riddled readers. 'Dr Walldron's Worm destroying Cake' promised to void the bowels of worms, plus, as a bonus, any 'slime and Filth'. A Leeds stuff weaver was reported to void 'upwards of three hundred worms, some of them of Uncommon Thickness' after he took only a few doses.[15]

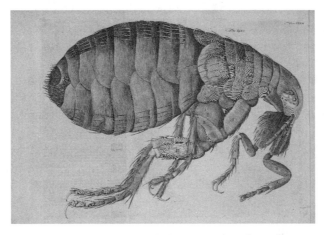

19   A magnified flea from Robert Hooke, *Micrographia* (1665).

Other parasites focused their attentions on the skin. When experimenting with his microscope at the time of the Restoration, Robert Hooke chose to magnify a flea. Fleas would have been a common feature of institutions and inns, as well as domestic settings. One of the inmates in the Bridewell with Moll Hackabout, in plate IV of Hogarth's *Harlot's Progress*, crushes a flea between her fingers (figure 20). Fleas proliferated in sea ports.[16] While lodging at the White Swan in Gravesend, William Schellinks discovered that 'the

20 Detail from engraving, William Hogarth, *The Harlot's Progress* (1732), Plate IV, 'Scene in Bridewell'.

English fleas are very aggressive'. Indeed, they were so aggressive that he forsook his bed for a hard bench.[17] Many fleas would have been brought into contact with humans from their livestock or pets – 'hee that lies with the dogs, riseth with fleas.'[18] The entomologist Thomas Muffet (assumed to be the father of the 'little miss Muffet' tormented by a spider as she tucked into her curds and whey) observed that fleas molest people when they sleep – especially 'young maids' (they were apparently attracted by their moist parts). Muffet remarked that fleas, while troublesome to all, do not stink like 'wall-lice' (bed bugs), and added that it is no 'disgrace . . . to be troubled with them, as it is to be lowsie'.[19] Keen to market his fumigating product and service, John Southall wrote *A Treatise of Buggs* in 1730. Observing that bed bugs bite in all seasons, Southall noted that they were most bothersome in the summer when the skin was most apt to inflame. He also declared that bugs were not choosy – they bit indiscriminately, but only some people reacted badly to the bites. Southall boasted that bugs bit him regularly as he offered his services as a fumigator.[20]

Beds, Thomas Tryon taught, absorb a variety of 'pernicious Excrements' from sweaty and leaky bodies. Passed down through the generations, these

21   The frontispiece to John Southall's
A Treatise of Buggs (London, 1730),
showing the growth of a bug.

beds became fetid and unclean. Tyron believed that bed sharing was the cause
of many diseases, and worried that although evil stinking beds were 'the most
injurious to the Health and Preservation of Mankind', few took the hazard
seriously. Painting a vivid image of lice, fleas, moths and small worms feeding
off the dust, debris and moist substances left in beds, Tyron explains that the
outcome of this feeding frenzy is a stinking bed. Not all beds were equally
affected. The excrements of some bodies were more unclean than others. In
cities and large towns, where the air was sulphurous and humid, bed putrefaction was more prevalent.[21] For those willing to heed his advice, Tryon
conducted a step-by-step routine leading to total bed freshness. Regular
applications of fresh linen were essential to avoid verminous infestations.[22]
Noting the inconsistency of domestic cleaning, Tryon observed that, although
much time was spent cleaning furniture, floors and clothes, beds were rarely
aired. He claimed that if even a tenth of the time and effort exerted in making
clothes and furniture clean was spent instead on bedding, 'there would be no
Matter for the getting of Diseases, nor for the Generation of Bugs'.[23]

The upheavals in the Pepys house on washday reveal the complexity of the
washing process in this period – the routine started in the early hours.[24] Advice
contained in Eliza Haywood's *A Present for a Servant-Maid* (1743) suggests
washing was a laborious and disruptive chore. [25] If maids had been members of
the Royal Society in 1677 they would have ensured a more enthusiastic

welcome was given to Sir John Hoskins's method of 'Rinsing fine linen in a whip cord bag, fastened at one end and strained by a wheel cylinder at the other ... whereby the finest linen is washt wrung and are not hurt'. Patents for prototype washing machines did not trickle in until over a century later, and the majority of these were for industrial rather than domestic purposes.[26]

Eliza Haywood's instructions were targeted at the maids in grander houses and focused on care for delicate fabrics and the removal of stains. For poorer citizens, with limited space or no outdoor land, washing and drying linen would have been a challenge. Water could be difficult to obtain, and fuel to heat water or dry clothes was costly. Their ingrained, worn and moth-eaten clothing would be weak and less able to withstand washing. In his sanctimonious *Friendly Advice to the Poor* (1755) the Revd John Clayton registered a dislike of the poor disporting themselves 'in Rags and Tatters, Filth and Grease'. Clayton suggested that to attract quality acquaintances the poor should dress well, but his friendly advice did not stretch to practical tips about how the low waged, or unwaged, might care for these garments.[27]

Unlike Haywood, Tryon's emphasis was not on stain removal or the aesthetics of the wash, but the removal of bugs and other nasties that might cause disease. In 1691 Tryon advised his readers that if their children are 'afflicted with the Rickets, Blotches, Boils, Scabs, or Leprous Diseases, then ... let all their Linen, Woollen, and Beds be kept very clean and sweet'.[28] Tryon saw the problem in broader terms and suggested that clean linen was only part of the solution. Claiming that 'most or all Beds do perfectly stink', Tryon placed the blame for stinking beds on the materials from which the beds were first constructed. Feathers were dirt-sucking magnets. When they were imported from even older beds feathers retained 'all evil Vapours ... breathed forth by various Diseased People'. Furthermore, feathers contain the excreta of the birds from which they were plucked. Eschewing feather beds, Tyron opted instead for 'Chaff-beds' (straw-stuffed mattresses). The hardness of the chaff will prevent the sagging that occurs in softer featherbeds, where the body sinks and is enveloped, a situation exaggerated by the roll-together of a slumbering couple. By overheating the sleeper, feather beds cause undue sweating, thus exacerbating the problems. Deemed less costly to restuff, such beds, he claimed, 'send forth no stinking fumes or steams ... Certainly nothing is more healthy, next to Temperance in Meat and Drink, than clean hard Beds.'[29]

'Wash your hands often, your feet seldom, and your head never'[30]

According to Lawrence Stone, this was a 'time when personal and public hygiene was largely disregarded. Men and women rarely, if ever, washed their bodies, and they lived in the constant sight and smell of human faeces and human urine.'[31] Keith Thomas has since exposed this view as misleading and ahistorical, as it does not pay due regard to the different concepts of hygiene that held sway in the period. Thomas acknowledges that full body immersion was rare, a fact partly attributable to the relative shortage of appropriate facilities. However, Thomas argues that body parts were cleaned, even if the whole body was rarely immersed. Cleaning was more often a dry process, with a rub down using a brush of pig's hair to dislodge the lice.[32] 'Rub the Hair with a Napkin is to dry it from its swettiness and filth in the head' was included among the descriptions of the barber's work in Randle Holme's *The Academy of Armory* (1688).[33]

Washing routines were so unexceptional they are usually ignored in contemporary diaries, autobiographies or letters. Consequently it is difficult to be sure how people washed in the period. Diarists do occasionally record changes to their cleansing rituals, but then often refrain from mentioning whether they continue with their new regime. James Boswell once mentioned having his feet washed in 'milk-warm water' in his journal in 1762.[34] John Byrom chivvied his wife by letter to keep his children clean in his absence in 1729. He later observed that there is 'nothing more healthful than keeping the pores of the skin free from any obstruction'.[35] However, Byrom does not instruct his wife on the method. Samuel Pepys rarely mentions washing himself, and for him cleansing did not need to involve water – on 5 September 1662 he records 'rubbed myself clean'.[36] It is unlikely that soap featured much in the cleansing routine. Made from rancid fats and alkaline matter such as ashes, most cakes of soap would have been quite greasy and would have irritated the skin. The finest soaps were crafted from olive oil, and were kinder to the skin, but these were expensive and would not have been used widely.[37]

Some authors did extol the virtues of a wet wash. The physician Thomas Cogan suggested that on rising, 'wash your face and hands with clean cold water, and especially to bath and plunge the eyes therein: For that not onely cleanseth away the filth, but also comforteth, and greatly preserveth the sight.'[38] Tryon considered frequent washing in pure water to be beneficial.[39] Some washers preferred to use warm water for cleansing – Hooke found that washing his feet in hot water helped him to sleep.[40] At the age of thirty-three John Evelyn began 'a Course of yearly washing my head with Warme Water, mingl'd with a decoction of sweete herbs, & immediately with cold spring water'. This 'much refreshed' him.[41]

In line with other physicians Joseph Browne thought that many conditions were improved with cold bathing, which could cure scrofula, rickets, venereal diseases and 'weakness of Erection, and a general disorder of the whole Codpiece Oeconomy'.[42] Dudley Ryder took regular cold baths when he was a student.[43] Tobias Smollett was another aficionado of the cold bath.[44] The implication was that the value of bathing was more to give a shock to the system and bring it back into working order than to slough away dirt and dead skin cells.

Workers in dirty trades such as sweeps, coal-heavers and blacksmiths would have more need to wash away ingrained irritants and particles from their skin. Bernardino Ramazzini catalogued the afflictions induced by particles thrown up in work. He noted the sore eyes of the sawyers, scavengers and bakers. Pounding starch-makers threw up clouds of penetrating acidic dust, and flax-dressers worked in similarly dusty circumstances. [45] Chimney sweeps were besooted from head to toe and known as part of the 'black Fraternity'. 'I would not recommend my Friend to breed his Son to this Trade,' remarked Mr Campbell in 1747, adding, 'I think this Branch is chiefly occupied by unhappy Parish Children.'[46] Sweeps effectively acted as the chimney brush – their clothes were tattered on the way up the chimney and their skin endured grazes, burns and scratches. Soot, a carcinogenic substance, would not have washed readily from skin.[47] Millers were prone to lice, which fed off pockets of flour held in folds of skin.[48] Grocer's itch was a condition caused by handling flour or sugar. One contemporary thought this condition was equal in 'malignancy [to] any leprous complaint . . . and . . . often deprives them of the use of their hands'.[49] Plumbers, painters and glaziers – all handling lead in their craft – often became palsied, and frequently died of lead-induced illness.[50] An apprentice glass-cutter suffered lead poisoning from the 'pernicious particles' produced during polishing.[51]

Salesmen proclaimed the magical qualities of cures to take away the harmful particles of the workplace. An advert in a Manchester newspaper sang the praises of 'Imperial Golden Snuff', which promised to 'bring away all Mercury which lodges in the Head, occasion'd at Working at some Trades that are offensive to the Brain, as Plumbers, Refiners, Gilders, Silversmiths and others'.[52] In order to reduce the exposure to such toxic and unpleasant substances, workers in these trades would have benefited from complete body washes. However, it is unlikely that they were presented with the opportunities for such ablutions and would have been stained, splattered and sooty most of the time. Jonas Hanway reported that some sweep masters washed their apprentices annually.[53] Highlighting the polarity between the workers and those who did no manual tasks, the Earl of Chesterfield looked to the hands for evidence: 'nothing looks more ordinary, vulgar, and illiberal than dirty hands, and ugly, uneven, and ragged nails'. Nails, he added, should not be 'tipped with black as the ordinary people's always are'.[54] 'Blame not the cobbler for his black thumbs', implored the proverb; likewise the tanner's hands were indelibly stained with bark.[55]

A few citizens would bathe in nearby ponds and rivers, immersing their whole body, rather than just washing parts. In Anthony Wood's time, Oxford citizens bathed in the Cherwell, although few could bathe in the drought of

1685 when the waters were low and stagnant.[56] Despite the pollution Londoners used the Thames for bathing. John Evelyn noted that even when they bathed in water 'some Miles distance from the City', they still became coated in a 'thin Web, or pellicule of dust' gathered from the clouds of city smoke by falling rain.[57] There were more immediate dangers attached to outdoor dips. A man drowned while bathing in Manchester in 1744.[58] 'Swimming Girdles' could be purchased to prevent this calamity.[59]

Those really serious about bathing headed for one of the spa towns, such as Bath. Here, the body could be subjected not only to full water immersion, but also a range of pampering services, including manicures and pedicures. On a visit to Bath in 1662, the Dutch artist William Schellinks gawped at the people by the poolside, 'ready with knives, scissors etc to cut people's corns, warts and nails'.[60] Not everyone was convinced about the merits of communal spa bathing. Samuel Pepys pondered the matter in 1668: 'methinks it cannot be clean to go so many bodies together in the same water.'[61] The same concerns were voiced during the eighteenth century.[62] The anonymous versifier of *The Diseases of Bath* (1737) found himself sullied by the waters. The poet plunges the reader into waters polluted by 'Nameless Diseases' and 'foul Infections'. In the morass of bodies the bathers push through particles of brawn cast from greasy cooks and the smut of porters and chairmen:

> Here *Lepra* too, and *Scabies* more unclean,
> Divest their Scurf and invent a purer Skin:
> Whose pealing Scales upon the Surface swim,
> Till what th' Unwholesome shed the Wholesome skim.
> . . .
> Hence mad and poison'd from the Bath I fling
> With all the Scales and Dirt that around me cling:
> Then looking back, I curse that Jakes obscene;
> Whence I come sullied out who enter'd clean.[63]

The most fastidious citizens were concerned about their body odours, and feared the potential for offending others with stale sweat or bad breath. Members of certain trades and professions whose work duties included close contact with the public might have prospered more if their bodies did not offend. Barber-surgeons with rough hands and noisome breaths might have repelled clients.[64] Common courtesy and decency towards others in close quarters bolstered the desire to uphold regimes of personal hygiene. An Independent minister believed that 'a Degree of Cleanliness' (clean hands, face and clothes) was necessary 'to render my Company agreeable and inoffensive to others'.[65] *The Spectator* judged cleanliness to be a 'mark of politeness' to make bodies 'agreeable to others' and 'easy to ourselves'.[66] Echoing this, the philosopher David Hume regarded cleanliness as a virtue; a lack of personal hygiene excites an 'uneasy sensation' in others.[67] William Buchan, a physician, cast the want of cleanliness as an inexcusable fault, and also blamed dirty people for wantonly spreading disease and infection. Making personal hygiene a concern of public health, Buchan concluded that 'few virtues were of more importance to society than real cleanliness. It ought to be carefully cultivated every where; but, in popular cities, it should be almost revered.'[68]

Given the relative limitations of the cleansing routine, many citizens resorted to cosmetics and perfumes to hide the dirt and mask the odour. However, both types of product carried risks and hazards. Caustic and toxic ingredients lurked in many ready-made and home-mixed cosmetics and toiletries. Eliza Smith's cure for pimples included brimstone (sulphur).[69] Johann Jacob Wecker suggested the use of arsenic and 'Dogs-turd' as ingredients for ointments to 'make the nails fall'.[70] The Duchess of Newcastle warned that the mercury in some cosmetics could cause consumption and oedema. Indeed, some preparations were so toxic that they could 'take away both the Life and Youth of a Face, which is the greatest Beauty'.[71] The Countess of Coventry was said to have died from toxic properties in her cosmetics.[72]

There was a healthy market in products to mask the smell of human discharges. Perfumers sold washes, pomatums, soft soap, powders and essences – some also sold snuff and tobacco, both used to mask body smells.[73] Masking and concealing carried risks – they might make the situation worse. Those who thickly spread 'Pomatum and Pultis' would have 'wet and greasy' complexions, and 'all the while they have it on, it presents to their Nose a Chandler's Shop, or a greasy Dripping-pan'. Such women shunned hot places for fear of melting visages.[74] Observing the Queen at a banquet in 1662, William Schellinks made a rather cutting observation in his diary about her make-up running down her sweaty face.[75] Rather than masking body odours, scents could simply combine with them. 'Imagine to yourself a high exalted essence of mingled odours, arising from putrid gums, imposthumated lungs, sour flatulencies, rank armpits, sweating feet, running sores and issues, plasters, assafoetida drops, musk, hartshorn, and sal volatile; besides a thousand frowzy streams, which I could not analyse.'[76] Matt Bramble's account of a high society ball in Bath is a pungent one. In this description the odours of bodies mix with the scents applied to mask them.

The effete fop soaked with ambergris contrasted with the manly grime of workers. Effeminate fumery contrasted with the smell of hard physical labour. Critics who favoured a more natural approach to life disapproved of the use of 'Stench to Stench oppose', especially when applied by men.[77] Men who laboured smelt of taverns, beer, smoke and sweat. In Ned Ward's world the men who comprised the trained bands (the civic militia) and worked in tough trades such as butchery, stone-cutting and sawyering smelt of manly body odour. Some smelt a little too much. Ward described greasy cooks in dirty shirts who were 'Tinctur'd beneath the Arm-pits, yellow, By their own nauseous Tallow'.[78]

'The tongue is ever turning to the aching Tooth'[79]

While the eighteenth-century beaux were criticised for spending too much time on their image and dousing themselves in perfume, they were also accused of overlooking their teeth, even though 'none can be attended with more disagreeable and offensive sensations both to themselves and their friends, than the neglect of the teeth.'[80] Knowledge of their own bad breath made some citizens reluctant to have intimate contact with other people; Dudley Ryder fretted about his stinking breath on several occasions. He was unable to relax in the company of an attractive young widow in 1715 for fear that she would detect his halitosis. Readers of his diary will imagine him inhaling the exhaled air caught by his cupped hands. He resolved to ask his mother but was too embarrassed, and resorted instead to various cures such as orange juice, cream of tartar, and Islington Spa water, and foreswore milk.[81] Others advised against the consumption of radishes, turnips and garlic.[82] An advert that appeared in the *Weekly Journal* ten years later would have attracted Ryder's interest. This promoted a 'pleasant ODORIFEROUS TINCTURE for the breath, teeth and gums, a few drops of which instantly make the most offensive breath smell incomparably fine and charming, and in a very short time perfectly cures, so that a disagreeable breath will never return'.[83]

There was an array of dentifrice powders and cures on the market. Although most would have had little or no effect on cavities or diseased gums, some of these products and recipes would have carried away some dirt and plaque from teeth. Powders were concocted from cuttlefish, cream of tartar and sal amoniack (ammonium chloride). These abrasive substances could be rubbed on as they were, or mixed with rose syrup. Ambergris, musk or other potent scents could be added to mask bad breath.[84] Thomas Cogan enjoined his readers to 'rubbe and cleanse the teeth. For the filthinesse of the teeth is noisome to the Braine, to the breath, and to the stomacke.' He suggested a gargle made from cold water or rose water and vinegar, and hard rubbing with a dry cloth or a sage leaf.[85] In contrast, Thomas Tryon advised against rubbing and picking the teeth, favouring instead a simple mouthwash with pure spring or river water after meals.[86] Too-good-to-be-true adverts carried in the newspapers pushed the virtues of powders to freshen 'noxious' breath, clean teeth, fill cavities 'which the scurvy hath eat away', and prevent further decay.[87] The odoriferous tincture advertised in the *Weekly Journal* apparently made 'the blackest and most foul teeth extremely white, clean and beautiful at one using, infallibly preserves them from decaying, and those a little decayed from growing worse, absolutely cures the scurvy in the gums, when almost eaten quite away, and infallibly fastens loose teeth again . . . it has not an equal in the world.'[88] Such bluster would have appealed to those afraid to visit the barber-surgeon to have teeth drawn or scraped with the dentiscalp.[89]

A lack of adequate tooth cleansing and an inappropriate diet led to bad breath and also caused tooth decay. Thomas Tryon argued that toothache could be caused by 'filthy phlegmy Matter' from the stomach lodging in the mouth, rotting and displacing teeth. The want of regular cleaning, he argued, let this matter putrefy, rotting gums 'as though Worms had eaten them'. This condition, he asserted, was frequently mistaken to be a symptom of scurvy. Tryon also suggested that certain types of foods, especially meats and sweets, fouled the mouth, particularly during sleep. This explained why on waking the teeth were furred 'with a gross slimy matter'.[90] Paul Hentzner, a German lawyer who travelled to England at the end of the sixteenth century, reported that Queen Elizabeth had black teeth from the English habit of making 'too great use of sugar'. He noted that it was common to put great quantities of the stuff into drinks.[91] A character in an early eighteenth-century play bemoaned the poor dental state of London's women: 'with drinking hot Liquors, and eating Sugar-Plumbs at Church, not one in ten has a Tooth left.'[92] Frederick Slare was not convinced of the ill-effects of sugar. Aiming to discredit views that sugar rotted the teeth, he rubbed 'fine sifted Loaf-Sugar' on to his gums and teeth for several weeks, reporting that his teeth were whitened in the process.[93]

After spending a month in 1715 chewing just on one side of his mouth to avoid the pain of a severely decayed tooth, Dudley Ryder finally summoned up the courage to have it drawn. In the process, a little of his jaw was broken off, but he rallied, claiming it didn't hurt. Much.[94] By the mid-eighteenth century wealthier citizens would have the option of trying out a transplant, using teeth from a paid donor.[95] David Povet advertised his skills in the *Old Bailey Proceedings* of 1716. Perhaps Dudley Ryder noticed his adverts. Based in Exeter Exchange in the Strand, Povet boasted he had treated royal teeth. He claimed to be able to make rotten and blackened choppers smooth and white, and set 'Artificial Teeth easie, neat, and firm, that they need not be removed seven Years'. The wearers would even be able to eat with them. This was a unique selling point – other false teeth were removed prior to mastication. The wearer would probably have needed to be quite ginger in his jawfalls.[96]

'A barber learns to shave, by shaving of Fools'[97]

The barber-surgeons provided services to protect and care for the external features of the body. Their concerns were with skin and hair and mouths – with shaving, dentistry, cleansing, plucking, treating skin complaints and, later in the period, wig-making.[98] Male middling sorts and professionals usually displayed a smooth beard-free face. Pepys used a pumice to remove facial hair in 1662.[99] The shabby street hawkers depicted by Marcellus Laroon and Paul Sandby often sport face fur, indicating their lowly status and lack of concern for personal hygiene.[100] One of Ned Ward's dishevelled rakes wears a threadbare coat, a 'Peruke lank' and a fortnight's growth of stubble.[101]

Numbers of specialist barbers and peruke-makers increased in the cities during this period, to meet the new market for head furnishings and to remove unwanted hairs. The numbers of peruke-makers establishing businesses in Oxford rose steadily in the 1670s.[102] Edmund Harrold's diary gives a portrait of the work of a minor provincial wig-maker in the early eighteenth century. In two days in July 1712 he finished one wig, started another (a brown one), curled one wig and shaved one head.[103] A hairdresser from Bath came to serve the ladies of Manchester in 1765 and offered to dress hair so that it kept its form for six weeks.[104] Seventy-seven young men were apprenticed to barbers and perriwig-makers in Bath between 1724 and 1769.[105] The Revd John Penrose was scathing about the way the fine ladies in Bath cared for their hair and how they concealed 'the stick of their filthy Heads' with perfume. Noting that they 'do not comb their Heads for three months together' (for fear of spoiling their coiffures), he wondered if they used mercury to keep the lice at bay.[106] Hair goes greasy and itchy when unwashed so it is not surprising that 'wiry', 'dangling' and 'disheveled' appear among Edward Phillips's epithets for hair.[107] Citizens could apply powder to soak up greasy secretions. However, these products would clog the hairs at the roots and needed to be combed out. The combs of Celia, Jonathan Swift's lady in her dressing room, were choked with 'Sweat, Dandriff, Powder, Lead and Hair'.[108]

Testimony to bad hair days came in the rising craze for wigs. Among men the fashion for wig-wearing really took off in the Restoration period. Initially the most fashionable wigs were the longest and bulkiest, sometimes rising in horns at either side of the head in a showy display of wealth. Wigs could be fashioned from the wearer's own hair, but most were made from the hair of other people.[109] The Manchester wig-maker Edmund Harrold purchased hair from a carrier's daughter in 1712, and two other heads of hair from which he made one wig.[110] Wigs made from fashionably blonde hair could command a price of upwards of forty shillings. Travelling to see hair in June 1712 Edmund Harrold rejected it for being 'too dark'.[111] Manchester was not a corporation town, so there would have been little demand for the horsehair wigs worn by some civic officials. The vast majority of the wigs Harrold made were crafted from human hair – although he did once buy a second-hand long horsehair wig for nine shillings.[112] Harrold wore a wig himself. He sold one of his own cast-offs for nine shillings and six pence.[113] Wigs freshly woven from the hair of country women were the most desirable, as this was thought to be free of city miasma.[114] During the plague, concerns were raised that wigs had been made from the hair of victims of the epidemic.[115]

Initially wig-wearing attracted Puritan disapproval. The author of *Coma Berenices; or, The Hairy Comet* (1674) saw the donning of wigs as criticism of God's handiwork. This author envisioned an 'Epidemical fashion or disease of wearing Artificial hair' sweeping the cities, and heaped blame on the heads of wearers for the shameful practice of sending 'Women-factors' across the country to pay high prices 'for the hairy excrement' of country women and children. The country poor were shorn like sheep to maintain the 'ignoble Traffick and Pride of the City'. The men who bought wigs crafted from women's hair donned 'unmanly disguises' and looked like 'Women in mans Apparel'.[116] The practice of topping male heads with tresses from lasses also made the Quaker Richard Richardson bridle. To Richardson wig-wearing men were deformed and emasculated. He disapproved of girls cropped of hair because they looked like boys.[117] John Wesley disparagingly described a wig as a 'Heap of borrowed hair'.[118] John Mulliner, a Northampton barber who quit his job in the 1670s because he was so disgusted with the fashion for wigs, found comfort among the Quakers and wrote *A Testimony against Periwigs, and Periwig-Making* (1677). This treatise was less hardline than some, and Mulliner thought it was acceptable to wear borders for 'health sake' if a man was bald, but he felt that those with a good head of hair should be content with their lot.[119] Those feeling left behind by the new fashions contrasted their times with the halcyon days a few generations back. In *Truth of our Times* (1638) Henry Peacham included perfumes and perukes in a list of '*fooleries*, unknowne to our manly forefathers'.[120] Even in the mid-eighteenth century authors were harking back to times when 'Our Forefathers were contented with their own Hair, and never dreamed of thatching their Sculls with false Curls'.[121]

Heads were usually shaved or cropped closely to accommodate the wigs.[122] This would have reduced the likelihood of infestation with lice and improved the potential for scalp cleanliness but may have made the head itch with hair regrowth, or be irritated by the coarse underside of the wig. Women did not enter so wholeheartedly into the fashion for false hair, probably because of the need for shaving. Samuel Pepys tried out some wigs in May 1663. He confessed to having 'no stomach' for wig-wearing, but found keeping his hair clean to be a great trial. He was still ambivalent three months later, and only finally succumbed at the end of the year. Five years later he set his wig alight by sitting too close to a candle.[123]

For men wigs gave signals about rank, profession and gravitas.[124] Some professional men took to wig-wearing with enthusiasm and physicians became especially associated with big, full-bottomed wigs.[125] The big wigs worn by professionals distinguished them from other occupational groups and signalled their aloofness, giving indications about their position in the professional hierarchy (it was the physicians, not the surgeons or the apothecaries, who

22 A proud physician: Richard Mead in his smart coat and full-bottomed wig, painted by Allan Ramsay (1740).

wore the biggest wigs in the medical world).[126] Samuel Adams, a fellow of Magdalen College and Doctor of Physic, was described in 1711 as 'an extravagant, haughty, loose man. He went in a long power'd wig, and affected the Beau as much as any young spark in Oxford.'[127] A portrait by Allan Ramsay shows the physician Richard Mead in his full-bottomed wig (figure 22). The importance of this medical sartorial code was made apparent in the 1730s when Arthur Pond produced an etching of a wig-free and closely cropped Dr Mead (figure 23). Mead 'passionately desired Mr Pond to suppress it'.[128]

To James Boswell's chagrin, the physicians started to abandon their fulsome wigs in favour of smaller and lighter bag-wigs in the late 1770s.[129] However, the lawyers retained their characteristically big wigs, and members of the bar are still associated with wig-wearing. In his *Five Orders of Periwigs* (1761) William Hogarth illustrates the 'Lexonic' wigs of the lawyers as flamboyant and curly (see figure 24). By 1752 the erstwhile law student Dudley Ryder was Attorney General. In that year he became the butt of a popular ditty concerning his headgear following his involvement in a celebrity libel case.

23 A more humble depiction of Richard Mead, by Arthur Pond (1739).

> Mr. Attorney's grim wig, though awfully big,
> No more shall frighten the nation.[130]

By the mid-eighteenth century even clergymen had adopted the practice of wig-wearing, partly to distinguish themselves from the laity. In 1765 John Clubbe advised young clergy to don a full wig 'and not one that scarce covers your Ears; the latter looks, at best, as if it had been in a Fray, and come off with no inconsiderable Loss.'[131] Clerical garb was modified to accommodate the wigs. Surplices that split down the centre removed the hassle of dragging the fabric over the bewigged head. Archbishops' mitres were abandoned in favour of tricorn hats or scholars' caps. Hogarth places the 'episcopal' or 'parsonic' wigs at the top – these are distinctive thick, full, bobbed wigs. These wigs were reputedly modelled on Bishop William Warburton's wig. Warburton did not wear the cope of Durham Cathedral as the collar got in the way of his full-bottomed wig. Wigs with ribbons or other decorative features such as bags or tails at the back became popular among the clergy, as these features could be displayed to the congregation during certain parts of the service.

The popularity of heavy wigs had waned among non-professionals by the mid-eighteenth century; they made scalps hot, especially in the summer. Wigs

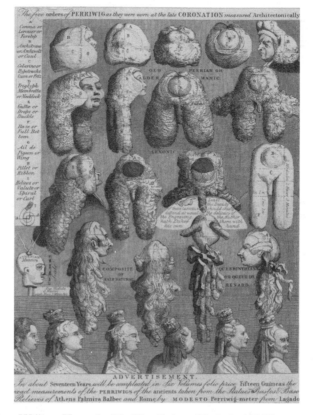

24   Engraving, William Hogarth, *The Five Orders of Periwigs* (1762).

became shorter and less full during the eighteenth century, and a market developed for scratch wigs – shorter wigs allowing fingers to access the scalp.[132] Shorter and lighter bob wigs gained in popularity. These would have relieved pressure on the head. Bags reduced powder spillages around the shoulders by encapsulating the ends of the hairs, and were often secured by black ribbons that tied around the front of the neck – a possible precursor to the black tie.[133] In competition with a massive variety of wigs in the mid-eighteenth century, Lady Mary Wortley Montagu's son still managed to turn heads when he returned from Paris sporting an iron wig spun from fine wire.[134] An advert in the *Ipswich Journal* from May 1750 guided readers towards a peruke-maker who could craft 'a wig of copper wire which will resist all weathers and last for ever'.[135] History does not record whether this wig eventually turned verdigris-green.

By 1765 wig-wearing had become less common among all citizens except some occupational groups, such as coachmen and lawyers. Most ordinary

25 Detail from engraving, William Hogarth, *The Harlot's Progress* (1732), Plate VI, 'The Funeral'. The frisky clergyman wears a coy expression and a bobbed wig.

citizens wore their own hair by this period, often having it styled and powdered to look like a wig. Peruke-makers petitioned the king, seeking help in their failing business, caused by the 'almost universal decline of the trade, occasioned by the present mode of men in all stations wearing their own hair'.[136] The trade picked up again by the close of the century. The ultra-fashionable were still fond of extravagant wigs, which were to grow to extraordinary heights and fashions in the 'Macaroni' period of the 1770s. Hugely ostentatious and ridiculously heavy, the wearer of these wigs would need to take special care when walking under a chandelier or clambering into a sedan chair.

Wigs attracted smoke, grease and dust and needed much care and attention to stop them getting matted, lugged, lank and greasy. Big, full-bottomed wigs would have been especially high-maintenance. Visits to the barber or wig-maker were necessary to maintain their tip-top condition. In the seventeenth century, wigs could be cleaned using fuller's earth. Wigs were kept fresh with powder made from low-grade flour in the eighteenth century, and could be scented with pomatum.[137] Wig-wearing could be a costly business. In London in the 1730s 1lb of powder cost two pounds ten shillings and 1lb of pomatum cost two shillings.[138] As the wig was placed on the head, a mask or a funnel-shaped cone would need to be held in front of the face to avoid powder getting into the eyes and up the nostrils when it was puffed on.[139] Wigs could be recurled, and even enhanced with new tresses. Once they had become lank and greasy, wigs would have smelt vile and sat uncomfortably around the face. As they became disgusting and dirty, wigs became undesirable. Ned Ward's 'Copper-nos'd Cadator' rested a 'shabby Pissburnt Wig worth not a Groat' on his scalp.[140] Consequently, claims portrait historian Marcia Pointon, 'the wig acquired a capacity to symbolize human filth and corruption'.[141]

'It is much like a Blacksmith with a white silk Apron'[142]

In the seventeenth and eighteenth centuries the signals and messages given off by outward appearances were vital to help place citizens within the social hierarchy. The ability to buy wigs, clothes or fabric was limited by location, income, status, gender and occupation. The types of garment worn, and the fabrics from which they were made, strongly affected physical comfort. The market was made-to-measure – clothes were crafted to fit the original owner.

Metropolitan fashions changed quickly in the seventeenth and eighteenth centuries, but fashion spread slowly across the nation. A fictitious Middle Temple lawyer who rode the Western Circuit in 1711 observed that the further from London one travelled, the less opulent clothing became: 'the Petticoat grew scantier and scantier, and about threescore Miles from London was so very unfashionable, that a Woman might walk in it without any manner of Inconvenience.' By the time London fashions reached the provinces they were already dated. Near Salisbury the lawyer spies the wife of a JP 'at least ten Years behind in her Dress' yet still in fine attire, bedecked with wrinkled ribbons and curls. He also spots scallop-top shoes and ruffled shirts, fashions from Charles II's reign, and was informed that there were even 'greater Curiosities' in the Northern Circuit and that fashions were even slower to penetrate into Cumberland than into Cornwall.[143] Shortly after arriving at Oxford new scholars would adopt increasingly fashionable garb.[144] Turning up dressed in linsey-woolsey coats, with 'sun-burnt heads of hair, clouted shoes, yarn stockings, flapping hats . . . and long muslin neckcloths' and accompanied with their 'rusty, old country fathers', the new intake would rapidly transform. Bob wigs, new shoes and the '*Oxford-cut*' were the first signs of change. Next '*drugget cloaths* and *worsted stockings*' were replaced with '*tye-wigs* and *ruffles*', before moving to *silk gowns*, until the scholars were 'metamorphosed into compleat SMARTS, and damn'd the old country *putts*, their fathers, with twenty foppish airs and gesticulations'.[145]

The type of clothing worn varied according to the nature of a person's daily activities. Frilly white clothing was not suitable attire for the butcher, the baker or the candlestick-maker. Lustrous wigs were inappropriate headgear for anyone employed in dirty trades or hard physical labour. Labourers and

26 John Riley, 'A scullion of Christ Church' (late seventeenth century).

craftsmen working with noxious, dirty or dusty materials donned special clothing to shield their hair, clothes and skin from the dangerous particles particular to their work. Masons and carpenters rolled their sleeves and wore aprons so their clothes were not peppered with dust. Some aprons were durable and tough. Coopers' aprons were made from leather. Marcellus Laroon's knife-grinder (see figure 38 on p. 125) wears a tattered apron and splatterdashes guard his lower legs from the wheel debris. Sow gelders wore leather aprons to protect themselves from the mess of castrating pigs and spaying sows. Other aprons were fashioned from washable cloth – such as those worn by bakers and victuallers.[146] Butchers wore oversleeves to protect their shirts from splatter and dustmen wore hats, but no amount of protective clothing would help the chimney sweep. Indeed bulky attire would have increased his chances of becoming lodged in a chimney. The Oxford college scullion occupied the lowliest of positions among college servants and would have spent much of his time undertaking menial and dirty tasks in the kitchens. John Riley painted a scullion of Christ Church, Oxford, in his protective headcovering, and a dark smock and leather straps protect his hands and wrists (figure 26, above).

Part of the point of a gentleman wearing fine attire was to show to all observers that he did not need to make any physical exertions – his employment included nothing dirty or sweat provoking. Cambric ruffles and other frilly wear was ill-suited to chimney sweeping and butchery – and, like wigs, suggested the wearer had an indoor existence. The violinist in Hogarth's *Enraged Musician* (see figure 40 on p. 128) wears ruffles and a bag-wig. Card-players could don muffetees to protect their ruffles from the dirt of the table.[147] These were far removed from the leather aprons and oversleeves of the workers. Silken finery and brocade announced a citizen with staff to do the dirty work. Only ladies served by mob-capped maids could carry off hooped skirts in delicate pastels. Puritanical critics of the idle rich, often fuelled by a strong work ethic, were upset by the laziness implicit in fashionable clothing. 'How self-sufficient and daring a powdered Beau in an embroidered Suit?' asked one commentator, expecting a negative response.[148]

Clothing was not just a matter of practicalities. The semiotics of clothing was vital to reinforce the authority of superiors and to ensure the deference of the poor. If people did not dress according to their station they could not expect to be given due credit and respect. To highlight the importance of wearing the right gear, Erasmus Jones used the example of '*a Lord*, wrapt in a Horseman's Great Coat, and with a hairless Perriwig' who was asked for assistance by a 'Carcass Butcher'. Jones reminded his readers that 'Persons of Figure, when they chuse to amble the Publick streets, should always appear in a Dress suitable to their Dignity' – otherwise they risk losing the right of way, the pavement nearest the buildings, and respect, so might attract insults.[149] Conversely, the wife of a Ludlow smith was subjected to derision for her inappropriately fine clothing. As she walked along the street 'gentle-woman-like', her arrogant pride was reproached with hoots and shouts from a jeering crowd of boys.[150] In 1674 Anthony Wood vented his spleen after noticing the increasing numbers of 'men women and children of the common sort' disporting themselves in 'lace, fals hair, lace whisk, aprons, petticotes, lac'd shoes, fals towers of hair. This in Oxford.'[151] Dudley Ryder's grandmother was 'much offended' by Dudley's attire in 1715. Her indignation stemmed from the belief that a mere tradesman's son (Dudley's father was a draper) should not 'go as fine as her husband the counsellor'.[152]

It was expected that people would be judged by the cut of their jib. A witness in a larceny case of 1761 was asked if the husband of a suspected criminal looked like 'a man of substance and credit, or a poor shabby dirty fellow'.[153] The rich dressed in an opulent manner, and the poor in simple garb. This was not a new idea, and there was nothing distinctly English about it. While fashions changed, the notion that master and servant should be distinguishable from each other remained. Eliza Haywood condemned the habit of servant maids of aping the fashionable ladies, declaring that 'nothing looks so handsome in a Servant as a decent Plainness. Ribbands, Ruffles, Necklaces, Fans, Hoop-Petticoats, and all those superfluities in Dress, give you but a tawdry Air.' Haywood fretted that this 'folly' is 'epidemic' among servant maids who spend their entire wage on 'these imagin'd Ornaments of your Person'.[154] Daniel Defoe bemoaned the difficulty of telling apart a maid from her mistress by their dress, 'nay very often the Maid shall be much the finer of the two.' He argued for regulation and the introduction of liveries for maids. He was concerned that the current trends led to the maids being work-shy, for fear of spoiling their clothes.[155]

Suspicions were aroused when outward signs jarred and notice was taken of clothing worn out of place. A man whose rent was fifteen pounds, but who could not afford to wear ruffles, was suspicious of another man who rented a house worth only five pounds per year but wandered around 'with the ruffles'.[156] When Dudley Ryder spied his brother sporting extravagant garb, including ruffles and white gloves, he worried that he was embezzling or overextending himself.[157] Polarities of dress are evident in witness statements in criminal cases. In 1749 some girls 'in a sad dishabil, ragged and bare-footed' were thought to be stealing small silver items.[158] A 'Notorious Pilferer' claimed that a stolen ship bolt had fallen into his ragged breeches without him noticing. His 'silly excuses excused him not' and he was whipped to teach him a lesson.[159] Young victims of kidnap might be identified by the superiority of their garb to their captors. Ragged Mary Ann Lawless stood out from the crowd as she carried a well-dressed child. 'Very ragged' Mary Billingsby attracted suspicion as she held the hand of a 'neatly Clad' girl. She later stripped the girl of her pretty frock and stays.[160] A servant could be suspected of stealing from her mistress if she transformed from being 'prodigiously ragged, with great holes in her stockings' to become 'dressed out with fine fly caps, and as good things as any lady in the parish'.[161]

Ned Ward's 'generous Termagant' complained to her 'wealthy Niggard' husband that she lacked the fine clothes that a woman of her rank should wear. Her discussion reveals the importance not just of the need for finery for show, but also the desire for comfort. Although she demanded silks, as would befit her 'Birth and Quality' and suit her tender skin, she was compelled by her husband's meanness to wear itchy underwear and to dress 'like Rural Joan, with an old Granum's nasty Grogram on'. She fidgeted in clothing 'as coarse as camels Hair', fit only for an alewife.[162] 'Yarn Stockings' were inferior to 'fine Worsted ones, with silk Clocks'. A 'scanty Linsey-Woolsey Petticoat' was no match for a wide 'good Silk one'.[163] Linsey-woolsey was a fabric woven from wool and flax. It was coarser than wool, and much coarser than silk.[164] 'Hair shagg breeches' and a 'Fustian Petticoat' don't sound very comfortable.[165] Grogram was a coarse fabric made of from various combinations of silk, mohair and wool. Grograms with high mohair content would have been itchy, and the coarsest grograms were stiffened with gum or paste. 'Everlasting' and 'grogram' breeches suggest durability rather than luxury.[166]

On the whole, the coarser folk were destined to wear rougher stuff.[167] Some justified the inequality of fabric by arguing that the bodies of the poor were tougher, so they would tolerate more textured clothes. Phillip Stubbes felt that rough shirts would 'chafe' and 'ulcerat' the 'lyllie white bodyes' of wealthy folk.[168] While some citizens enjoyed a choice of fine fabrics, others made do with whatever garments they could find. When it came to apparel, apprentices were often at the mercy of their master. Some of the appeals to discharge an apprentice from indenture rested on the inability of the master to provide sufficient clothing.[169] Sarah Pickford was granted a discharge from her apprenticeship to a London button-maker in 1706 after complaining she was not provided with sufficient clothing and neither shoes nor stockings.[170] Another apprentice, given ragged clothes and oversized shoes, became so 'very lowsie and nasty in his clothes that the lice might be seen crawling on him'.[171]

'Borrowed Garments never fit well'[172]

Shoes were made by cordwainers to fit the feet of the original purchaser from measurements and lasts. Buying a new pair of shoes was no guarantee of good quality, however. In 1624 some Manchester shoemakers were found to be using horse leather to make shoes, and the leather searchers also discovered shoes that were insufficiently tanned, would not have been durable and may have smelt and rotted. [173] Old shoes were rejuvenated or modified by cobblers, or 'translators'. The subsequent wearers of shoes would have worked their feet into spaces stretched to fit a foreign shape, which might have caused blisters, bunions and corns.

Partial unstitching and 'turning' – the inner parts becoming the new exterior – could prolong the life of coats and other garments.[174] Even the rich eked out the life of their favourite garments by turning, dyeing and scouring. Linings would be renewed, and new pockets, cuffs and ruffles might be added to revive old clothes.[175] As an Oxford student, James Woodforde had a white coat and buff waistcoat turned in 1763. He had them dyed black at the same time, presumably to conceal stains.[176] However, clothes could only be refashioned a limited number of times before they became napless, threadbare and tattered. If enough good fabric remained, this could be reused to make a smaller item of clothing, a garment for a child, or a cloth cap.[177]

Tired garments were passed down to apprentices or servants. Butlers often claimed the old shirts and wigs of their master as employment perks.[178] In his student days, James Woodforde passed on several items to his bedmaker, including his 'old suit of Brown Cloaths being extremely bad'. An old college servant received from him a pair of old leather breeches in 1761, and the son of a bedmaker got an old hat and old black stockings a couple of years later. His oyster merchant was given two cast-off wigs.[179] It is likely that many of

27 Marcellus Laroon (II), 'Old Shooes for Some Broomes', from *The Cryes of the City of London Drawne after the Life* (London, c.1688).

these hand-me-downs were sold on to ragmen, slopsellers and clothes dealers. The clothes from the man who drowned while bathing in Manchester were sold on for nine shillings and sixpence to recoup the costs of recovering and burying his body.[180] Poorer citizens rarely bought new items of clothing, but made do with second-, third- and fourth-hand clothes.[181] The second-hand market was a thriving one. John Matthews travelled around Bath, London, Oxford and Cambridge giving money for cast-off clothes.[182] In London the second-hand clothing sales were focused around the Tower Hill and Barbican areas.[183] Some sellers specialised in old shoes, or even old boots.[184] Marcellus Laroon included an image of a trader who exchanged brooms for cast-off shoes (figure 27, above) in his *Cryes of London* (1688).

A high demand for second-hand clothing meant that garments constituted a considerable proportion of property that was stolen.[185] Thomas Sevan was apprehended at the Hayes turnpike wearing three stolen shirts in 1724. He had left his old ragged shirt behind at the scene of the crime.[186] Elizabeth Pepys's new farandine waistcoat was snatched from her lap as she sat in the traffic in Cheapside.[187] On Easter Monday 1732 John Elliott became the victim of highway robbers who relieved him of his hat, wig, waistcoat and shoes. One of the robbers swapped his own 'ragged Coat' for Elliott's coat at the scene of the crime. The coat and waistcoat were reportedly sold on in Chick Lane.[188] No item of clothing was immune from theft – even odd shoes and bundles of dirty washing were lifted.[189]

However they obtained their garments, subsequent owners might have needed to undertake some alterations to ensure a good fit. The poor donned the exhausted, ill-fitting cast-off garments of the richer citizens with discomfort. Clothes could be taken to a botcher, or a botching tailor, for patching and repair. The wife of Ned Ward's botcher complains of her life surrounded by 'nitty Coats, and stinking Hose'.[190] By the time they reached the poorest members of society, garments would be smutted, food-stained, sweat-ridden, pissburnt and might shine with grease. Richard Brathwaite's 'Ruffian' wears an 'ancient Buff-jerkin; whose lapps you may imagine, by long use, so beliquor'd and belarded, as they have oil enough to fire themselves without any other material'.[191] Clothes in such a state would be hard, unyielding and smelly. Readers of *The Spectator* and *The Tatler* would know how to place a 'Poor Fellow . . . with a rusty Coat' or a 'tatter'd vest' and a 'greasie Gown sully'd with often turning'.[192]

'Neither Coat nor Cloak will hold out against Rain upon Rain'[193]

In the seventeenth and eighteenth centuries comfort was often in the gift of the gods. According to the poet John Bancks, streets were 'unpleasant in all weather'.[194] On dry and hot days coal dust, cart spoil and dried dung swirled up from the streets into the eyes and mouths of the hurrying pedestrians. In London in 1735, John Byrom sought respite from the dust by walking in a park (the paths of which might have been sprinkled with water from a cart).[195] In inclement weather clothes became heavy and sodden – especially the tatty and shabby garments made of thick fabrics such as sacking-like fustian, or coarse woollen clothes worn by the poorer citizens. In his 'Description of a city shower' (1710), Jonathan Swift asked where a 'needy Poet' could find shelter when the dusty rain 'invade; / His only Coat . . . Roughen the Nap, and leave a mingled Stain'.[196]

In addition to being champion of the chimney sweeps, Jonas Hanway has been immortalised as England's umbrella populariser. Umbrellas had been available for decades, but Hanway was the first man to carry one habitually, despite being ridiculed for this.[197] Umbrellas were black so that the sooty rain did not stain them.[198] Umbrellas would have been especially useful on those streets lined with houses not yet equipped with downpipes. Water spluttered out of protruding spouts, giving the pedestrian an impromptu shower. Evelyn thought overhead spouts were 'troublesome and malicious', and created 'a continual wet-day after the Storm is over'.[199] Evelyn would have welcomed the post-fire legislation that insisted that London's new buildings be supplied with downpipes. Increasing numbers of properties across the country were fitted

28   This statue of Jonas Hanway, with umbrella aloft, used to adorn the exterior of 9 Pelham Street, Nottingham.

with downpipes, but even as late as the 1750s one Manchester house had a lead spout projecting eight inches out, which jetted 'the water and filth from an upper room . . . on to the Street called the Hunts back'. This 'nauseous matter' was a particular nuisance in the summer, when it occasioned 'very unwholesome and naucious smells'.[200] If the contents of chamber pots were cast from a window on to a pedestrian's head it was ensured that 'the party to have a lawful recompense if he have hurt thereby'. A guide for JPs included details of how to deal with 'one that shall cast down Chamber-pots on men . . . of purpose to spoil, or do mischief'.[201]

The Revd John Penrose took a sedan chair from the Abbey in Bath to his lodgings 'because of the Rain'.[202] Sedan chairmen wore thick overcoats to ward off some of the rain.[203] In a telling remark, Bernard Mandeville described a porter on a rainy evening dash as returning with his clothes 'as wet as Dung with Rain'.[204] Although they would have made more use of hackney coaches and sedan chairs in foul weather, the well-heeled were not immune to street daubing.[205] Robert Hooke noted rather pathetically in his diary on 17 September 1675 that he 'Fell into the Dirt in Fleet Street'.[206] Erasmus Jones commented on the delight of the rabble when 'a well-dress'd Person is dash'd over Head and Ears with Dirt . . . a sorry Scoundrel with scarce shoes to his Feet shall shake his sides'.[207] Jonas Hanway feared being 'overwhelmed with whole cakes of dirt, at every accidental jolt of the cart'.[208]

Umbrellas would have reduced the amount of water falling on to the body, but the feet still sloshed through muddy puddles. An article in the *Gentleman's Magazine* (1731) described a 'walk through *Rag Fair* in dirty Weather among . . . *Basket Folks*, Drays and Caravans; a jostle in one place, a slip in another, a stop in a third, a Kennel-dash in a fourth'.[209] Street surfaces would become dangerously slippery and miry in inclement or sleety weather. Shoes did not have rubber soles, and would have maintained a poor grip on street surfaces, especially if they were strewn with detritus.[210] The streets could be lethal in frosty conditions, especially in Bristol, where, Daniel Defoe noted, the pavements are 'worn so smooth' by the sledges that transported goods about that 'in wet weather the streets are very slippery . . . 'tis dangerous walking'.[211] It is hard to imagine how milkmaids and water bearers managed to carry their heavy pails without slipping over. While poorer pedestrians skidded in the slimy mud, wealthier walkers plashed in their galoshes. These wooden or leather shoes formed 'a case for a shooe, to keep them clean in foul weather'

29   Marcellus Laroon (II), 'Troop every One one' (hobby horse seller) from *The Cryes of the City of London*.

and were described and illustrated by Randle Holme in 1688.[212] Robert Hooke invested in a pair of 'Goloshoos' in 1675.[213] Other citizens tinked in pattens, iron and wood contraptions to elevate the foot 'by means wherof clean shooes may be preserved though they go in foul streets'.[214]

Even without such cumbersome contraptions, hard, stony pavements were wearing on long walks and jarred the joints. In 1764 William Huddesford moaned that the 'sharp Points' of the pebbles cobbling Oxford's streets made the pedestrian wish for the 'flat Pavements of Bath, or of London' instead. Only the shoemakers were happy.[215] Halfway through a journey, one of Ned Ward's 'Merry Travellers' became wearied by the going. In his 'ruffl'd Socks' he was forced to 'hobble, pick and chuse / His way, as if ha'd Peas in's Shoes'.[216] Poor and puddly pavements punished old and poorly constructed shoes. Four toes peep from the flimsy shoe of Marcellus Laroon's hobby horse seller (figure 29). Wearers became literally 'down at heels', and water squelched around their toes. In 1733 a suspect in a burglary was identified by his dirty shoes, which were 'Rent in the Side' and lacking a sole.[217] The vendors who paced the streets in all weathers in ill-fitting second-hand shoes would have suffered from chafed feet.

30   Marcellus Laroon (II), 'Buy my fat chickens', from *The Cryes of the City of London*.

The proprietor of a second-hand clothes shop in New Rag Fair in Wapping slept in her shop on rainy nights rather than venturing home in the wet.[218] Long garb – such as women and Oxbridge scholars wore – would wipe the pavements; skirts and long gowns became daggle-tailed with clots and spots of mire.[219] It was prudent to pin up petticoats when striding the dirty streets.[220] The clothes of those who spent much time in the pavement mire, such as hawkers and tradesmen, became especially bedraggled and sodden. Indeed, rainy days would have provided a boost to trade, as citizens would have been reluctant to travel to shops and markets, and so would have maximised their exposure to wet pavements. The garments of pedlars faced extreme wear. Their more active lives wore them out quickly, especially when the streets were rain-sodden, or their goods heavy. The male hawkers rarely wore wigs, but often wore shabby and battered hats. The hobby horse seller and the chicken vendor are both ragged and wear tattered breeches and torn jackets. Laroon's female mackerel seller, below, wears multiple layers of patched garments, including a very tatty man's coat.

31   Marcellus Laroon (II), 'Four for Six pence Mackrell', from *The Cryes of the City of London*.

The skin of seventeenth- and eighteenth-century citizens was irritated by disease and infestations and chafed by coarse fabrics and dirty linen. Workers in dirty trades battled to reduce exposure to caustic substances, while at the other end of the social scale fine ladies applied toxic products to their skin in the name of beauty. Opportunities for personal hygiene were limited, especially for the poorest members of society. People with the time, money and space to be fastidious were more likely to notice oversights in the cleansing regime of others. Some of the wealthier citizens blamed the poor for their tatters without really considering the limitations and stresses of cramped conditions and meagre resources. Vagrants had few opportunities to launder, but their piteous condition was still seen as symbolic of a lack of pride by those with washerwomen and maids to clean for them. Others were more compassionate and recognised physical hardships, not just the outward signs of poverty. Warm-hearted Thomas Tryon worried for the 'poor indigent People' who 'fare very hard, having ragged Cloaths, and Shoes without sole, being all Dirty, going about the streets Cold and Hungry'.[221] Ultimately, skin comfort was governed by the rank, station, activities, occupation and wealth of the citizen. The rich man gibed at the poor man – who wore clothes not to adorn but to keep warm and to protect his body from harmful substances and inclement weather.

CHAPTER 4

Mouldy

Diet and taste are cultural constructs. In all social groups the decision to eat or reject a foodstuff is based on both collective and individual preferences.[1] In seventeenth- and eighteenth-century England much vegetable matter (including the humble potato) was routinely overlooked, and although most animal flesh, from slug to human, would nourish, most was taboo. Edible dogs thronged the city streets but did not end up in the pot, although they were sometimes fed to hawks. The English have consistently refused to consume horseflesh, although they have fed it to their dogs.[2] Food consumption was also linked to social status. The poor ate more root and brassica vegetables than the rich. They also consumed more cheese. The physician Thomas Cogan cast cheese as 'no good meat for students', but added that 'labouring men commonly use it without harm'. Cogan was especially disparaging about 'rosted' cheese, favoured by the Welsh. He thought it was best saved for the mousetrap.[3] Readily available common crude foods such as offal, cabbage and salted fish were at the bottom of the food hierarchy. The diet of a poor person also included a greater proportion of legumes and unrefined cereals. Heavy tooth-challenging loaves made of rye, barley or beans were digested slowly, and therefore, ran the argument, filled hungry stomachs.[4]

'Where bad's the best, bad must be the choice'[5]

Marginal foodstuffs were eaten in dearth years when regular supplies dwindled. There were fewer opportunities for hedgerow foraging, mushroom picking and rabbiting in the cities than there were in the countryside. Proverbs hint at the desperation of the hungry:

Hunger makes hard bones sweet beans.[6]

All's good in a famine.[7]

Hunger finds no Fault with the Cookery.[8]

Hungry Dogs will eat dirty puddings.[9]

Although England avoided the famines that blighted other countries, there was still hunger in the bad years. Recording a high rate of corn spoilage in 1693, due to a wet summer season, Anthony Wood noted that scarcity pushed prices out of the pockets of the poor, who were forced to 'eat turnips instead of bread'.[10] During this dearth Thomas Tryon outlined a diet for a person on a budget of twopence per day. The recipes are uniformly bland: flour, water, milk and peas, all boiled to differing consistencies.[11] Broken victuals, the remnants and scrapings from the more affluent plates, were a perk of service for some servants, and the saviour of many paupers. In hard times the poor ate badly. The wife of Ned Ward's botching tailor complains to her husband that his alehouse haunting has forced her to live off 'a Mouldy old Cryst and a Cucumber' while breastfeeding.[12] Personal hardship forced some to root out alternatives: witnesses reported that a young London servant girl was so hungry in 1766 that she ate cabbage leaves and candles.[13] A prisoner who

32   A hungry girl is not too proud to eat fallen pie from the dirty street: detail from engraving, William Hogarth, *The Four Times of the Day* (1738), 'Noon'.

absconded from the Tothill Fields Bridewell in the middle of the century was driven to her actions by hunger, 'being obliged to eat the cabbage stalks off the dunghill'.[14]

In post-famine conditions, more people are able to crave or dislike particular foods. Dislikes and aversions are not constant in communities or individuals, and food was subject to the whims of fashion, causing some products to be avoided for fear of scorn. For most urban dwellers the choice of foodstuffs expanded during the seventeenth and eighteenth centuries. Developments in internal and overseas transport, agriculture and the organisation of commerce increased the range and freshness of food for many consumers. As urban supplies became reliable and abundant in the eighteenth century, there was markedly less demand for seventeenth-century staples like dry rye bread, salty meats and muddy stewpond fish. During a period of cereal shortage in 1756–8, Parliament authorised the sale of Standard Bread. These loaves, identified by their 'S' mark, contained a higher proportion of bran. Although one penny cheaper than the wheaten loaf, this bread did not prove popular.[15] The well-fed minority thought this was picky, but it is understandable when one considers the habituation of tastes: once palates and digestive systems get used to more refined foods, they do not want to revert to the rough.

Differences between rich and poor diets and rural and urban ones increased. However, the 'fine' foods found in the cities were not universally appreciated and some people hankered after simpler rustic fare. One author complained that the natural taste of meat and fish had become 'nauseous to our fashionable stomach', and they needed to be daubed with 'pernicious sauces'. The entire world, opined this compiler of a guide to trades, was being 'ransacked for Spices, Pickles and Sauces, not to relish but to disguise our Food'. He thought something more sinister was afoot, warning that each dish is 'seasoned with slow Poisons, and . . . pregnant with nothing, but the Seeds of Diseases both Chronick and acute'.[16]

Freshness was not always of prime consideration when judging food quality; it was not neatly divisible into rotten and fresh. Indeed, some decay was necessary to improve the shelf-life of certain foods. Apples were fermented into cider, milk soured into cheese, and game tenderised as it decomposed on the hanging hook. However, food that didn't smell, look, taste, feel or even sound right was rejected by all but the hungry. Reactions were based on lifelong experience and relied on all the senses. Individual experiences led to personal preferences within culturally proscribed limits, and foods with unpleasant side-effects such as flatulence, indigestion or bad breath were also avoided. Food poisoning, as suffered by Dudley Ryder in 1715 when a meat pie caused him to be 'extremely sick in the night', would make the consumer wary.[17] John Byrom wrote home from London in 1729 complaining that he was 'out of order, being forced to eat of some lamb that was wretched bad'.[18] These were true gut reactions.

So how are we to judge the quality of eighteenth-century foods? We cannot apply modern shrink-wrapped standards. To twenty-first-century tastebuds, many of the recipes in Hannah Glasse's popular *The Art of Cookery* (1747) seem disgusting, but her contemporaries would have relished most of her dishes. With hindsight and the development of chemical analysis and biological engineering we now know a little more about food quality, and would find fault with many techniques of animal and crop husbandry and food technology and preservation. However, as E. P. Thompson warned us, we must guard against the 'enormous condescension of posterity'.[19]

Individual tastes differ, and this colours our assessment of quality. Contemporary assertions about the propriety of diets according to status started to replace Galenic humoural views, which prescribed different diets to melancholic and sanguine people, adjusted for age (both the very old and very young were thought to benefit from a pappy diet).[20] Such ancient views were still evident in the seventeenth-century works of authors such as Thomas Cogan, and to some extent Thomas Tryon. Cogan thought that cucumbers were unsuitable for 'flegmaticke and delicate persons which do not labour'. He also asserted that 'Burned bread, and hard crusts . . . doe engender adult choller, and melancholy humours', advising his readers to cut their crusts off. Bread with a high ratio of bran to wheat contained too much roughage for some constitutions and 'filleth the belly with excrements, and shortly descendeth from the stomacke'.[21] By the eighteenth century the rich had adapted these ideas, comforting themselves with the notion that the poor thrived on crude and starchy food. Labourers were thought to have iron stomachs able to digest the blackest, driest breads. As a child Robert Hooke had lived off dairy products and fruit, shunning meat as it disagreed with his weak constitution. In adulthood he knocked back emetics in a quest to purge himself, and in 1675 he hoped that 'small beer and spirit of Salamoniack' would 'dissolve that viscous slime that hath soe tormented me in my stomack and gutts'. Ever the empirical scientist, his diet was the object of inquiry and his diary is stuffed with references to consumables that disagreed with him. Cheese gave him nightmares. His sweat became pungent after eating buttered parsnips. Grilled chocolate made him lightheaded and sick. Port made him very sick, as did goose 'not well rosted'.[22] In May 1674 he overate 'water grewell'. (This was no mean feat, as water gruel was a thin salty porridge.)[23] Unsurprisingly, this 'agreed not well'.[24]

The sourest critic of London's food in the 1770s was Tobias Smollett's gouty country gentleman Matt Bramble, who keeps his doctor informed about his diet, complaining bitterly about gastronomic miseries. We will hear much about his views in this chapter. Bramble was set up by Smollett in his last novel, *The Expedition of Humphry Clinker,* as a stodgy curmudgeon wedded to his country estate, to contrast with his giddy companions who frolic in fashionable society. Unfortunately some food historians have taken Bramble's rantings literally. Certainly contemporaries would have recognised Bramble as a clichéd personality type – a grumbler. In order to gain a truer picture of the quality of food supplies, it is necessary to look outside fictional representations.

The whole chain of supply, from growth, harvest, slaughter, market, larder, pan to consumption, played a role in the maintenance of quality. The seasonal nature of supplies meant that the best pear in January was inferior to a normal pear in September. Likewise, mackerel was desirable and expensive in early spring, when prime fish were scarce. By June it was dirt cheap and increasingly prone to spoilage.[25] Spring brought relief from salted larder supplies, pulpy apples and musty grains. Summer heralded plentiful supplies of fresh fruit, but the heat frustrated attempts to store it – delicate fruits rotted quickly and vegetables would sweat and wilt in hucksters' barrows. Poor-quality food was badly husbanded, carelessly stored or transported, deliberately adulterated, unwittingly contaminated and under- or overcooked.

'If fools went not to market, bad wares would not be sold'[26]

Gardens replete with pot herbs and orchard fruits were squeezed out as urban land values rocketed, and infill building replaced vegetation. Industrial smut would have increasingly polluted the produce of the gardens that survived.[27] Each town or city absorbed comestibles from the rural hinterland – 'The chicken is the country's, but the city eats it.'[28] Citizens became divorced from the countryside as their cities expanded, and opportunities to gather hedgerow nuts or mushrooms were curtailed. Draconian game laws, such as the Black Act of 1723, made it dangerous to poach. City dwellers were increasingly reliant on market supplies.

The location of each urban centre constrained the sourcing, storage and sale of produce. Bath's produce came from choice areas: meat from the Welsh mountains, fruit and vegetables from the Cotswolds and the Vale of Evesham, dairy produce from Somerset and fish from Devon and the Severn.[29] These supplies were supplemented from further afield. Eggs that came to London from Scotland or Ireland were often rotten by the time they arrived.[30] Fish travelled upwards of a hundred miles before reaching metropolitan plates. As the cities grew over the period, ever greater supplies needed to come from ever wider areas. Cattle were driven from field to fair to market. London meat came from as far away as North Wales and Yorkshire.[31] The state of the roads was still generally poor, although improving. Grain-burdened carts creaked along rutted tracks, which were alternately dusty and boggy. Pushing for road reforms in 1675, Thomas Mace promised that were his improvements to be adopted, 'there will be very much corn saved from daily spoiling' en route from the fields.[32] Extensions to the navigable limit of rivers and the cutting of canals alleviated some of the pressure on the roads and meant that supplies had a better chance of arriving in fit condition. The River Avon between the port of Bristol and the spa at Bath was made navigable in 1727, and forty years later the Bridgewater Canal served Manchester. City life was not conducive to good food hygiene. London, as the biggest city, was the most effective heat trap, and the pressure of space further limited opportunities for cool storage in the summer months. Nottingham's citizens enjoyed a geological advantage in the form of cellars that were cut out of underlying sandstone and used by tradesmen to keep provisions cool.[33]

Despite transportation improvements, there is evidence of food quality deteriorating, especially of that sold to the poor. The lust for profit made the temptation to trade unwholesome goods irresistible for some unscrupulous middlemen.[34] Purchasing grain in bulk, engrossers stored it until shortages forced up prices and generated greater profits. In addition to inflating prices, stockpiling attracted weevils and damp. This was not a new problem. In the seventeenth century, an 'Ingrosser of Corne' was depicted as unable to abide 'sweet smells' and wishes all 'ayre were generally corrupted', or that his customers lack a sense of smell, then 'his corne might not bee found mustie'.[35] Dishonest dealing was increasingly widespread in the metropolis. Provincial markets, less dependent on middlemen, enjoyed a stronger link between producer and consumer. There was a greater potential for consumers to ask questions about quality and provenance.

All civic authorities sought to control the markets within their jurisdiction. Regulations established permitted days, hours and places of sale. Rules were adopted variously across the country, with ad hoc enforcement, and highly discretionary structures of fines and punishments. High or petty constables could present to civic courts any bakers and brewers found trading 'unwholsome Bread or Beer'.[36] Constables had the power to search out barley malt 'made with Mowburnt or spired Barley' or malt which had been insufficiently processed, or which contained 'half a peck of dust or more' per quarter.[37] Both the London City authorities and relevant livery companies attempted to ensure only wholesome wares were put up for sale.[38] A Market Act of 1674 had preserved the right held by officers of the London Butchers' Company to inspect, and they retained their powers to confiscate and dispose of unwholesome supplies of meat. Market officers were elected in the provinces. Bread-searchers, ale-tasters and others sniffed out stale or contaminated food and condemned it as unfit for human consumption. Lacking chemical tests and carrying equipment no more sophisticated than a knife, officers examined products with their eyes, hands and noses.

In Manchester officers patrolled the markets identifying vendors of bad supplies and presenting them to the manorial court. There was a steady rise in the number of market lookers for fish and flesh, from three in the early to mid-seventeenth century to six by the mid- to late eighteenth century, in line with the expansion of the market. Nearly a dozen officers checked supplies of whitemeats (dairy products, fowl and game) throughout the period. There were two officers policing ale sales. The number of officers checking the bread varied from two to seven, depending on the extent of corn dearth.[39] In Oxford, the civic appointed officials were supplemented by university clerks of the market, whose servants appraised and inspected produce 'in Oxford market, shambles, or other houses or places within the precincts of the University'.[40]

Market lookers did not grub out all the bad supplies. Some were more diligent in their searches than others, and there was a fine line between the stale and the inedible. As the market day progressed, perishables became cheaper, as they were more likely to be fly-blown or decayed. Much food bypassed the markets and shops, carried directly from the producer to be hawked by street vendors. By the time the street vendors were officially permitted to stock up, the good produce had gone. Meat sold illicitly outside permitted trading hours was not subject to any checks, and it was difficult to examine produce during sales conducted after dark. Butchers could be fined for

33   Anthony Walker, *The Beaux Disaster* (*c.*1747).

selling at unlawful hours: 'whereby bad & unwholesome Meat is often Sold by Escaping the Notice of the Officers'.[41] In 1662 the Manchester leet jurors were concerned that 'divers persons' carried meat from door to door, 'whereby they pr[e]vent the sworne officers to viewe the same'. Information gathered at the time suggested that such traders peddled unwholesome flesh.[42] A letter in *The Spectator* called for greater vigilance, claiming that everything sold in the moving market was 'perished or putrified', and recalling wheelbarrows of rotten raisins, almonds, figs and currants.[43] The market stalls, and the streets on which they stood, were frequently described as being filthy and strewn with rotting debris.[44] Butchers' shops, like other sales premises, were commonly open-fronted, and therefore produce was vulnerable to smutting, mud splashes and insect contamination. In the grubbily lyrical words of Ned Ward:

> As thick as Butchers Stalls with Fly-blows,
> When every blue-ars'd Insect rambles
> Abroad, to persecute the Shambles.[45]

The street scene depicted by Anthony Walker in *The Beaux Disaster* (figure 33) includes open-fronted shops common in the mid-eighteenth century. These gave ready access to the goods to customers and insects alike.

'Adulterated bread, and celibacy, diminish our numbers'[46]

Bread has been a priority of lawmakers and enforcers since at least the early thirteenth century.[47] The number of Manchester market lookers for wholesome bread increased from three in 1755 to seven a year later, indicating concerns about bread prices and quality during this dearth year.[48] Of greatest civic concern was the common offence of making underweight bread. Baking rank bread was also punished. In 1603 six Southampton bakers were found with all sorts of bread described as 'verie unwholesome for mans boddie of mustie meale'.[49] Some loaves were deliberately adulterated with stones and other items to bulk them up. Alice Gallaway was booked by the Liverpool market officials in 1642 when she tried to sell a white loaf that contained a stone, to make up the weight.[50] This sort of practice would have been widespread – the baker could claim that the stone had not been removed in milling, and blamed the miller. Stones, grit and other unwelcome contaminants would have posed dangers to the teeth of the unwary.

Ingredients which came together in the cheapest, blackest and coarsest breads included meal, bran, beans, 'Scuftings of other Corn', potatoes and turnips.[51] In the rural backwaters of Leicestershire, folk gnawed on bread made partly of peas.[52] Bread made from bean flour was reputed to be the 'rankest in taste', with a hard and brittle consistency.[53] 'White' bread (akin to our brown bread) was regarded as the most desirable in the towns and cities. During food shortages, civic authorities ordered that the process of making fine white bread should be suspended, as it wasted much of the edible whole grain, and exacerbated shortages.[54] It concerned the authorities that citizens might be unwilling to consume inferior grades. As demand for white loaves rose, so did the temptation to add alum. This astringent mineral salt improved the texture and bleached the loaf. A 1757 pamphlet triggered a consumer panic when the author declared that alum was the least of the bread buyer's problems. The histrionic author of *Poison Detected* claimed to have credible evidence of unwitting cannibalism: 'The charnel houses of the dead', he shockingly declared, 'are raked to add filthiness to the food of the living.' Chickens and a dog were reported to have died immediately after eating bread, and the bakers were held responsible for rising mortality.[55] Joseph Manning, a physician and author of *The Nature of Bread* (1757), compounded the hysteria by claiming to trace the problem back to the mealman: unfavourable storage in damp conditions corrupted the corn, which was then milled to musty flour. The miller, wanting to disguise this, added beanmeal, chalk, animal bones and slaked lime.[56] Unrest spread to Manchester, where rioters broke into shops and warehouses belonging to millers following rumours that beans and whiting had been added to flour.[57]

The inevitable baker-sponsored counter-attack came in the form of *A Modest Apology*, by 'Sampson Syllogism a Baker' and Emanuel Collins's *Lying Detected*, both published in the late 1750s.[58] These works presented the critics as scaremongers, the latter satirically suggesting that adulterants had a long history. Didn't the reader remember that the beanstalk giant, with all his Fe, Fa, Fo Fumming, threatened to grind Jack's bones to make bread?[59] Although disputing the more preposterous claims, neither denied that alum was added.

Signalling the start of scientific chemical analysis and experimentation, chemist Humphrey Jackson revealed that the suggested contaminants, including chalk and bone ash, were unlikely to be added to bread because they were easily detected, impaired the texture and reduced the size of a loaf, and did not even whiten it.[60] The scandal persisted despite Jackson's measured analysis. Millers and bakers were still vilified when Smollett penned Matt Bramble's missive to his doctor, describing London bread as 'a deleterious paste, mixed up with chalk, alum and bone-ashes, insipid to the taste and destructive to the constitution'.[61]

'Crying cabbages and savoys'[62]

Fresh fruit and vegetables were purchased from urban markets or street sellers. Choice was limited by the season, and the quality of the produce would have been variable, depending on the growing conditions, pest epidemics and the length of the journey from soil to stall. A French visitor in 1772 disliked the

34 Marcellus Laroon (II), 'Ripe Assparagus', from *The Cryes of the City of London*.

taste of produce available in London, and identified cabbage, radishes and spinach as vegetables likely to be impregnated with coal smoke pollutants.[63] Barges carrying garden produce to London markets returned with the contents of cesspits to fertilise crops. This could have spread human diseases such as dysentery, especially if not desiccated before use, or not washed from the produce in that rare commodity, clean water.[64] The inferior and wilted remains were bought up from London's Covent Garden Market by the street vendors. Marcellus Laroon's asparagus seller vends produce that has gone to seed and has thick stalks (figure 34, above).

The criers who touted exotic or seasonal foods on the city streets were more respected than those selling mundane ones such as turnips.[65] Appearing for only two months a year, dill and cucumber purveyors enjoyed great popularity, unlike the scorned sellers of cabbages that were available all year and distinctly bucolic.[66] Cabbages were unpopular and cheap. John Evelyn had much to say about brassicas, reminding his contemporaries that Hippocrates had condemned rotten cabbages as unhealthy, and pointing to their flatulent effects. '*Cabbage* ('tis confess'd) is greatly accus'd for lying undigested in the stomach, and provoking Eructations.'[67]

Any Baking Pears.

35 Marcellus Laroon (II), 'Any Baking Pears' from *The Cryes of the City of London*.

In the seventeenth century, fruit had been blamed for a variety of ills from indigestion to the plague. There would be no daily apple for Thomas Cogan, who dismissed apples as 'unwholesome' and liable to 'breed winde in the second digestion'. All except the unruly scrumper with a 'wanton appetite' rejected them.[68] Cogan had advice about figs too: they were blamed for the spread of lice.[69] Anthony Wood's notes reveal that fevers sweeping Oxford in the 1670s were commonly put down to the consumption of fruit.[70] By the eighteenth century many people had started to appreciate the health benefits of fruit, and even Matt Bramble conceded that some of London's fruit wasn't too bad.[71]

Fruit was vulnerable to damage and quick decay. Orange sellers were thought to freshen their wares by polishing them or by boiling and puffing them up, leaching their juice away in the process.[72] Small conical basket punnets, available on deposit from the street vendors, afforded delicate soft summer fruits some protection.[73] Bramble complained about the 'pallid contaminated mash, which they call strawberries; soiled and tossed by greasy paws through twenty baskets crusted with dirt'.[74] Laroon's costermonger holds aloft a basket with legs to keep it away from the street dirt when placed on the ground (figure 35, above).[75]

'No choice among stinking fish'[76]

Just a few hours separated meat that was stale from that only fit for dogs. Low profit margins in the victualling trades tempted people to make false claims about freshness. Butcher John Bentley, robbed of a loin of pork in 1752, readily admitted that it was stale, and concluded that the thief must have taken it in hunger, as it was neither desirable nor resaleable.[77] Clearly, many could identify the stench of decaying flesh. In 1736 a bundle of rags that concealed a suffocated newborn baby was mistaken for a joint of meat by its stinking smell.[78] Didactic literature aided the shopper's hunt for good-quality meat by highlighting tricks of the butchery trade. These included painting stale flesh with fresh blood.[79]

In *The Complete Housewife* Eliza Smith taught that fresh beef, when dented with a finger, will spring back quickly, while the dent would remain in stale, rough and spongy beef. Bull beef had hard and skinny fat, and carried a rank odour even when fresh. Bruised beef turned dusky or blackened.[80] Butchers were apt to wrap veal in wet cloths and Eliza Haywood advised 'you cannot be too careful in examining the Scent . . . what looks beautiful to the Eye may prove musty', adding that London butchers were known to inflate meat with their breath, a practice known as blowing.[81] Others stuffed rags into cavities to bulk out a carcass.[82]

Pork was potentially a more dangerous product than beef; it deteriorated more quickly, and carried a greater number of communicable diseases. Since the early seventeenth century, the ordinances of the London Butchers' Company had set a closed season for the slaughter of swine, both to preserve supplies and to prevent heat decay.[83] Thomas Cogan thought wild swine were superior to domestic hogs, as the latter 'live in a more grosse ayre than those that live wilde'.[84] While rootling in the back alleys and dunghills, pigs picked up contamination from city industries and noisome ditches filled with night soil and street sweepings. Mingling with dogs increased the circulation of disease and intestinal worms. Pork from city pigs needed to be cooked thoroughly to ensure it did not cause illness or worm infestation. Some signs of poor quality were clearly visible. Pork with flabby fat and a hard rind, or with any part that felt 'clammy', should stay on the block. Small kernels in the fat 'like Hail-shot' were warning signs of measly flesh, potentially harmful if consumed.[85] Between 1648 and 1687 there were over thirty cases of fines for selling measled swine, with a peak of offences in the 1670s and 1680s. Measled pork was the meat from a pig infested with a tapeworm or bladderworm.[86]

Salted or smoked bacon was popular, versatile and kept well. However, hanging meats were vulnerable to attack by hopper-fly, and if they got too warm they would rust and spoil.[87] Country supplies were best, and John Evelyn warned against meat hung in London, exposed to the corrosive qualities of smoke pollution. The smoke of London chimneys would 'so *Mummife*, drye up, wast and burn it [hanging meat], that it suddainly crumbles away, consumes and comes to nothing'.[88] Bacon that sagged in inclement weather was ill-cured, and Haywood warned that it 'is either rusty, or will very soon be so'. Haywood also advised carrying a knife to market to test ham, which when inserted should come out cleanly, and not be smeared or smell rank.[89]

Cogan felt that the mutton from rams ought to be left to 'those that would be raummish, and old mutton to butchers that want teeth'.[90] The test of mutton was to peel away the fat, and the easier this was, the fresher the meat. Old mutton would wrinkle when pinched, and strings of sinew held the fat tight.[91] If rot had been a problem in the flock, this would manifest itself in yellowing fat and pale flesh, from which 'a Dew like Sweat' would be emitted when squeezed. Lamb was best examined by sight, and good flesh was full of white fat and the lean was pale pink. To Eliza Haywood, a fine light blue hue to the neck vein denoted a recent slaughter. The buyer was wise to avoid the stale lamb with 'greenish or yellowish' veins, as this meant the meat was 'near tainting, if not tainted already'. A canny punter sniffed under the lamb's kidney and the knuckle, rejecting flesh with 'a faint scent'.[92]

Poultry could be bought live, for fattening in backyards, or ready killed and dressed. Ann Cook, author of *Professed Cookery* (1760), advised that live chickens stuffed into small baskets should be avoided as they bruised easily and became ill with the motion of carriage en route to market (see figure 30 on p. 81).[93] Old dead cocks and hens were told by their sunken eyes and hard, dry feet. When picking a partridge, the careful buyer would 'smell at their Mouths'.[94] Butchers could disguise stale slaughtered birds. Ned Ward warned of one such operator who greased the skin and dredged on a fine powder to make the bird strike 'a fine Colour in a Minute'.[95]

References to butchers selling unmarketable flesh abound in civic and company records.[96] Vendors of corrupt meats could be fined and their produce confiscated. Dogs and pigs devoured some impounded supplies and the rest was disposed of. Any rotten meat found in the York Shambles was 'openly burnt in Thursday-Market' and the butchers were 'severely fined . . . to prevent Sickness and Disease'.[97] In December 1763 meat seized from Richard Whitehead in London's Newgate Market was cast into the Thames.[98]

In Manchester, where court leet records are available for the periods 1600–87 and 1731–70, it is possible to trace cases of bad meat supplied to the city. Fines levied for quality control offences in butchery and fishmongery varied greatly, reflecting the discretionary powers of officers. The market lookers singled out some butchers in particular and their wares were scrutinised carefully. The first cases do not appear until after the period of the civil wars. This suggests that in the early seventeenth century the market officials dealt with corrupt meat sales on an informal basis, or through unrecorded confiscation.

After 1648 the market lookers for flesh and fish were keen to discover carcasses affected by the 'turne'. The turne was a disease affecting sheep and cattle that made the beast 'turne about' while grazing. The unsteady animal would lose its appetite and wither. Husbandry manuals describe the presence of a 'bladder' (known now as hydatids) in the forehead of the infected beasts, suggesting the presence of parasites in the brain.[99] It was thought that the disease could be transmissible to humans if infected meat was consumed, and therefore sales were banned and fines were relatively high for those found to be marketing meat with the turne. The market lookers presented over thirty cases of the turne between 1651 and 1687, but none in the eighteenth century.[100] The Costerdine family of butchers was responsible for seven of these cases.[101] Market lookers also hunted for meat affected by 'chance', a vague term suggesting the presence of cankered flesh. There were fewer cases of chance meat than turne and measled meat, although some cases were reported between 1655 and 1678.[102]

Beef that was not baited (that is, harassed and attacked by dogs) prior to slaughter was considered to be tougher than meat that had been baited. Unbaited beef, while not presenting the hazards to health caused by turne, measled and chance meat, was thought to be of inferior quality, and so was presented by the market lookers. Over forty cases were presented between 1661 and 1687. The lookers displayed especial concern about unbaited beef in the 1670s. In that decade twenty-nine cases were presented to the court leet. In 1662 Thomas Stevenson, one of the market lookers for flesh and fish, was fined for selling unbaited bull meat.[103]

The jurors labelled butchers with previous convictions as 'Old Offenders', and among the worst culprits was Henry Kemp, who in 1741 was found selling bad beef on five separate occasions. These recidivist butchers were often fined at a higher level; thus John Sidebottom of Stockport was fined one pound for his first unwholesome beef offence in 1739, and three pounds for his next.[104] Even so, these fines did not prevent future offending. As a general rule, the smaller or less valuable the product, the lower the fine. Offal attracted the lowest fines and those caught peddling unmarketable calves were fined approximately half the amount of those with bad beef. Some lookers, when presenting cases, would specify particular parts of animals. Stockport butcher Thomas Carteret (aka Cartwright) had a 'Beefs Tongue not Marketable' for sale in 1756. Offering 'part of a cow unmarketable' for sale in 1732 cost Robert Langton fifteen shillings, and in 1740 John Battersbee of Bury, who had already been found trading bad mutton that year, was fined two pounds for a 'whole cow bad'.[105]

Fines were steeper for butchers whose products were especially putrid. Widow Chorlton was fined five shillings for selling mutton described as 'not mans meat' in 1648.[106] Richard Rogers of Chorlton was fined ten shillings in

1664 for plying 'meate [that] Dogs would not eate'.[107] George Leigh of Lymm, whose 'Stinking' beef was sniffed out by the market lookers in 1751, was fined ten shillings more than the standard fine.[108]

As the nearest substantial settlement surrounded with good pasture lands, Stockport was the source of a large quantity of Manchester's corrupt meat. From this town came several notorious butchery families, including the Fallowses, whose offences between 1731 and 1768 exposed them to fines of more than twenty-five pounds. Perhaps hoping to set an example to his wayward kin, the jurors imposed on William Fallows a massive fine of six pounds six shillings in 1766 for plying unmarketable beef.[109] Along with the Cartwrights,[110] other Stockport traders known for bad meat were the Brooks family,[111] the Pass family,[112] and James Green, who was fined almost annually.[113] The Chorlton family, also from Stockport, appeared frequently in the records of the seventeenth and eighteenth centuries – John Chorlton's veal was often vile.[114] The Kenyons of Manchester tried to sell various forms of corrupt cow meat throughout the period.[115]

One might expect the nose to have been the ultimate organ to detect the bad, and sayings testify to the stench of putrid fish ('fresh fish and new guests smell, by that they are three days old'[116]). Fish did not enjoy a long shelf-life ('Daughters, and dead fish, are no keeping wares') and stale fish was not a marketable commodity ('no man cryeth stinking fish').[117] Richard Brathwaite warned that the stench of rotten fish is 'not for queasie stomacks'.[118] For Eliza Haywood the sense of sight seemed to be an effective judge of fish too, with peaky, off-coloured fish finding her displeasure. Haywood warned that some fishmongers coated gills with fresh blood, as red gills indicated a recent netting, so she reminded her readers to check for stiffness, bulging eyes and shrivelled tails – all signs of staleness.[119]

Britain was an island surrounded by fish, but fish were not especially popular in England in this period. Problems transporting sea fish inland may have decreased their popularity and pond fish were notoriously muddy. Dried salt fish, once a larder staple, were also falling out of favour.[120] Thomas Cogan was a fan of fresh fish, however, and praised the quality of sea fish caught in deep waters, 'whereunto runneth no filth nor ordure comming from townes, or cities'. He was less keen on eels and red herrings, which he labelled as being as bad as 'restie bacon'.[121] Some fish were affected by parasites; Samuel Pepys's stomach turned at the sight of a dish of sturgeon on which he saw 'very many little worms creeping'.[122] Cases of rotten and stinking fish and seafood were presented periodically to the Manchester court leet. Much of the poor fish supplied to the town in the seventeenth century was brought in by Henry Shaw, who was fined seven times in the mid- to late seventeenth century, including three shillings and fourpence for his 'stinking salmon' in 1663.[123] Unmarketable fish and shellfish did not figure as much in Manchester markets as putrid meat did, but the town was inland, and had fewer fishmongers than cities like Hull or Liverpool. Nevertheless, shoppers were exposed to unmarketable cockles, cod, herrings, oysters and salmon.[124] William Crompton, a 'Manchester fishman', committed various fish-related offences in the mid-eighteenth century. Thomas Idle came from Yorkshire to sell his rotting fish.[125] Joseph Moss, 'the Warrington Post Carrier', saw an opportunity for a sideline trade in fish while he travelled, but was found in possession of unmarketable cod in 1753 and fined a shilling.[126] Fines for fetid seafood remained low throughout the period. Fines were steeper for fishmongers selling especially putrid fish; Daniel Macanney was fined double the usual amount for his 'Stinking fish' in 1731.[127]

'Bread with eyes, cheese without eyes . . .'[128]

Until the development of the railways most country milk was churned to butter or worked into cheese. In London fresh milk came from the keepers of dairy cows in the city and suburbs, and like mackerel, it was a foodstuff traders were permitted to sell on Sundays, as it would not keep until the next day.[129] Bramble reserved his thickest bile for a description of London's milk:

> the produce of faded cabbage leaves and sour draff, lowered within hot water, frothed with bruised snails, carried through the streets in open pails, exposed to foul rinsings, discharged from doors and windows, spittle, snot, and tobacco-quids from foot passengers, overflowings from mud-carts, spatterings from coach-wheels, dirt and trash chucked into it by roguish boys for the joke's-sake, the spewings of infants . . . and, finally, the vermin that drops from the rags of the nasty drab that vends this precious mixture, under the respectable denomination of milk-maid.[130]

Smollett here exaggerates the accidental impurities in milk by combining all potential contaminants in one pail, and extends the view that cows fed on cabbages and draff produced tainted and insipid milk.[131] With a small and diminishing number of grazing opportunities and little space to store fodder, beasts were left to wallow in their own excrement, tied in dark hovels, where they fed on brewers' waste and rank hay.[132] Their milk was known as 'blue milk', and was only good for cooking.[133] By suggesting it was almost entirely water, Smollett extends a contemporary accusation that milk was diluted.[134] A lack of hygiene at milking time ensured that the bacterial count in milk would have been high by the time it reached the consumer. Carried in open pails, the occasional entry of mud, street dust and stones would have been difficult to avoid.[135] London supplies were not all so terrible, and fresh drinking milk was available in small quantities from cows that were walked along the streets, as mobile bovine vending machines. The Lactarian in London's St James's Park provided some fashionable milk, drunk warm, fresh from the udders of cows able to exercise. Zacharias Conrad von Uffenbach watched the fine English cows grazing there in 1710.[136]

Butter was eaten in great quantities in the eighteenth century. The overfed cooked with it, melting it over vegetables until they swam. It was so indispensable that the price of butter fluctuated according to the availability of vegetables. The underfed spread butter thickly on bread (this was often necessary to facilitate swallowing dark or stale bread). Cheap butter was poor grade, akin to grease and was often imported from Ireland.[137] The butter described by Bramble as a 'tallowy rancid mass' made of candle ends and kitchen grease was the worst type, and a person of his status would not often have encountered it. Preserved and packed for sale in salted layers, butter was beaten into large pottery or wooden vessels and knuckled down to exclude air. Since the mid-seventeenth century, as a result of known abuses such as adulteration with tallow and pig's lard, the producer stamped butter pots so supplies were traceable.[138] Previously, it had been known for pats of butter to be packed around old supplies, a fresh exterior concealing a musty core.[139] Even quality supplies could melt and go rancid in the summer. Elizas Smith and Haywood, and Hannah Glasse, all implored their readers to take great care when choosing butter, and clearly did not regard the stamping policy as a safeguard against adulteration. 'Trust not to that which will be given you to taste', warned Glasse, repeating Smith's caveat that a buyer may be 'deceived by a well tasted and scented piece artfully placed in the lump'.[140] The conscientious buyer would push a knife into the middle to test the whole pat. If 'crumblings' stuck to the knife, the butter would not keep well. Thomas Tryon recommended unhooping a cask of salt butter to taste deep within.[141] The canny shopper would ask for a block near the centre, which had not absorbed the 'ill flavour' of the tub that contained it.[142]

Cheese was not especially prone to adulteration, but hairs and other stray impurities from the dairy could infiltrate at the processing stage. Slovenly dairying was hard to conceal, and casual workings were evident in the product. The physician Thomas Cogan looked to the Bible for inspiration when he warned that 'Cheese should not be white as snowe is, nor ful of eyes as Argos was, nor olde as Mathusalem was, nor full of whey or weeping as Marie Magdalen was, nor rough as Esau was, nor full of spots as Lazarus.'[143] Overly white cheese had been skimmed too thoroughly. Cheese with 'argus eyes' was made from improperly worked curd. It was thought that dairy maids, whose 'scabbed and scurvie hands' had much contact with the curds they worked, squeezed and washed into shape, made poor-quality cheeses: 'such filthiness of hands hinders curdling and makes cheese full of eyes.'[144] Good cheese came with a 'rough moist coat', but not too moist, as this was 'apt to breed

Maggots'.[145] Wormy cheeses were thought to be fit only for the Dutch, who love cheese 'for being worm eaten and mouldy'.[146] Glasse recommended that the buyer judge how far rot and holes penetrated the whole block, warning that worse horrors may lurk within.[147] Cheese was apt to dry out and sweat in heat. Mr Campbell described the trade of the cheesemonger (akin to a modern delicatessen) as a risky business – 'It is liable to a great many Accidents', whereby cheeses shrivel and dry out, hams putrefy and bacon goes rusty, 'notwithstanding all the Care they are able to take'. The high wastage meant that profits from this trade were meagre.[148]

'No larder, but hath its mice'[149]

Salt and brine had traditionally been used to preserve meat, dairy and even vegetable supplies. With improvements in agriculture, importation and transportation, the taste for salted foods declined (as they could lead to mouth ulcers and extreme thirst), and they became regarded as of inferior quality, more fit for the poor and needy. Before 1776, when scientists taught otherwise, it was commonly thought that the key to good preservation was the exclusion of air.[150] Eggs were sunk into wood-ash small end down, where they would remain edible for some months.[151] Jarred foods were buried in yards or stored in cool cellars. Advances in the glass and pottery industries afforded the housewife an increasing variety of vessels. These stackable pots and jars could even be made insect- and rodent-proof with bungs and stoppers. Although preserving and conserving was more widespread in rural areas, such activities were not unknown in the cities.

Potting was a common method of prolonging the shelf-life of vegetables, cuts of meat, small birds and fish. Even lettuce could be potted and topped with mutton fat. Glasse advised her readers to use the finest quality fats available; else 'you will spoil all'.[152] Food was usually cooked and then cooled prior to being bottled or jarred, allowing bacteria to multiply in the process. The probability that the product might putrefy, or go maggoty was factored into many preserve recipes. Compilers suggested ways of dealing with such irritations when they arose, including reboiling, repotting or immediate consumption.[153] Imparting some dubious tips for restoring rotting larder supplies, Hannah Glasse's strategy 'to save Potted Birds, that begin to be bad' (indeed, those which 'smell so bad, that no body [can] . . . bear the Smell for the Rankness of the Butter') involved dunking the birds in boiling water for thirty seconds, and then merely retopping with new butter.[154] Not everyone agreed with Glasse's methods. Ann Cook, a sharp critic of her rival, grumbled that 'such monstrous prodigious Inconsistencies I am asham'd any Cook should recommend'.[155] Glasse had another technique to ensure the longevity of her preserves. In her recipe to make potted beef taste like venison she added large and potentially hazardous quantities of salprunella (melted nitre reacted with charcoal dust). Ann Cook was aghast, and William Ellis, author of *The Country Housewife's Companion* (1750), shunned such practices because nitre (the main constituent of gunpowder) made food 'unpleasantly dry' and gave it an 'unsavoury Twang'.[156] Modern science has shown that nitre is carcinogenic, and can turn humans blue.[157]

'God sends Meat and the Devil sends Cooks'[158]

Once the purchaser managed to source and store supplies, the next hurdle was to cook them before they perished. Each process could lead to a diminution of quality. A skilful cook could disguise salted meats with a powerful sauce; one author suggested that slightly tainted meat be served with root vegetables and onions, to mask the taste.[159] When cooking meat, the most important consideration was to cook it long enough to make it edible and tender, but not so much that it became dry or charred. Hannah Glasse gave basic instructions, suggesting boiling times for types of meat. The pot should be very clean, and the scum skimmed off when it rose. Unskimmed scum would boil back into the meat, turning it an unpalatable black. Glasse also advised that before roasting, the spit should be scoured with sand and water, 'for Oil, Brick-dust and such Things will spoil your Meat'. One can infer that Glasse's contemporaries cooked their greens to a grey sludge. 'Most people', she lectured, 'spoil Garden Things by overboiling them: All Things that are Green should have a little Crispness, for if they are over boil'd they neither have any Sweetness or Beauty.'[160]

To be able to cook, a householder or tenant would need a fireplace, fuel and the ability to wash utensils and pots. Many citizens did not have access to all of these. To cook elaborate meals the householder would need a variety of cooking vessels, a suitable grate, plus the ability to modulate the heat with cranes, jacks and other attachments. Elizabeth Pepys struggled with her new oven in November 1660 – 'not knowing the nature if it, did heat it too hot and so did a little overbake her things'.[161] Ovens were located mostly on lower storeys in buildings, but in spite of the compromised conditions, some very poor folk in loftier rooms managed to set up ovens in a variety of places.[162] It was possible to make a fairly substantial one-pot meal with just an open fire, although an unlidded pot carried the risk of contamination with soot. Those with the space and equipment for basic food preparation could send their pies to a local baker (patted, pricked and initialled).

The thriving second-hand market meant that pots and pans were increasingly available.[163] Damaged cooking pots could pose a danger to health, for if the interior had shed its protective tin lining the metal would leach into food, giving a brassy taint.[164] In one of Ned Ward's *Nuptial Dialogues*, a

London wife orders her maid to keep the saucepan dirty to avoid scouring the tin lining away.[165] Cooking acidic foods in copper pans released toxic verdigris.[166] An anonymous pamphlet entitled *Serious reflections on the dangers attending the use of copper vessels* was published in the mid-eighteenth century, warning that acids and fats could leach copper from pots.[167] Opportunities were further limited by the lack of storage space for ingredients and equipment. Without cool larders for perishables, or dark, dry corners for hanging meats, the poor relied on chandlers and hawkers for daily supplies, and suspended loaves in cloths from the ceiling, away from mice.[168] (See the (empty) cupboard of William Hogarth's *Distressed Poet*, figure 45 on p. 150.)

Not everyone had sufficient time or space for the hassle of cooking or the funds to purchase the necessary fuel supplies.[169] Those renting rooms without cooking provision or space relied on ready-cooked food sold in taverns, ordinaries where you would take pot luck on a fixed price meal, and by itinerant sellers such as pie men. Spitalgate victuallers found good trade among the poor weavers located there, many of whom relied on such outlets for all their meals, from their broth at breakfast to their leeks, meat and ragout for supper.[170] Ned Ward highlighted the disgusting state of some of London's cookshops, where he found 'rotten mutton, Beef that's Turnip fed, [and] Lean meazly Pork on *London* Muck-hills bred'.[171] This low-grade meat is 'basted with a Flux of mingl'd fat, which greasily distils from this and that'. The beef is charred and sweated, and the pork is thrice roasted, recalling and extending the maxim 'Take heed of enemies reconcil'd and of meat twice boil'd'.[172] To Ned Ward pork served in a London cookshop tasted 'nurs'd up in T[ur]d and Mire'.[173] Such eateries were often located in cellars and must have been the source of many an upset stomach.

The more processed an item was, the more opportunities for the trader to disguise tainted or corrupt victuals, and the greater the exposure to poor hygiene in preparation. All kinds of horrors could be concealed in a pie. Pies were originally packaging and contents in one. The pastry outer was not intended for consumption, but to contain the filling during baking until consumption, when the contents were scooped out with a spoon. The pork pie is a throwback to such pies, but it has survived thanks to an edible pastry case that keeps the meat moist and clean in a neat enough package to eat with the fingers.[174] By the eighteenth century, pottery vessels had largely replaced the thick pastry walls. Piecrusts remained on top, often with chimneys through which clarified butter might be added to prolong the pie's shelf life.[175] In her *Art of Cookery* Hannah Glasse included a recipe for a pie with thick and heavy walls, well built for sending as presents.[176] Pies could be eaten hot or cold, and would store for fairly long periods, providing they were not nibbled by vermin. Some vendors tried to keep them too long; 'Truder', a cook, was fined twenty nobles in 1689 for 'selling stinking Pyes, knowing them to be so'.[177]

Unwanted food contaminants came in many forms, but one that attracted the attention of high society was the dirt from the hands of their inferiors, or from crockery or cutlery not sufficiently washed up. 'Better no pies', suggested the maxim, 'then pies made with scabby hands.'[178] The scrupulous Eliza Haywood thought that thorough hand washing was a vital activity for the servant maid to undertake regularly.[179] Jonathan Swift suspected servants of using their hands more than necessary to touch food. His tongue-in-cheek advice reminds cooks not to forget to put a pinch of salt on the side of the porridge plate, remembering first to 'lick your Thumb and Fingers clean, before you offer to touch the Salt'.[180] Pepys found it difficult to maintain his appetite when dining with his Uncle Wight in April 1663, remarking that 'the very sight of my aunts hands and greasy manner of carving did almost turn my stomach'.[181] Haywood shuddered at the thought of dirty or rusting utensils and abhorred the idea of them entering unsuspecting, respectable mouths. It is possible that not only would the condition and cleanliness of the utensils play a role in keeping a mouthful safe, but also the material from which they were constructed. Modern researchers have identified naturally occurring anti-bacterial qualities in silver, and thus those who ate from silver spoons might have enjoyed added benefits.[182]

It seems that views about urban food voiced by the characters in satires by Ned Ward and Tobias Smollett should be taken with a pinch of salt. These were worst-case scenarios, and contained only a grain of truth. It must be remembered that as a tavern keeper Ward would have lost trade to the cookshops, and might benefit from casting their produce in a poor light. That said, most people would have encountered poor-quality food regularly, and these items might have smelt rank, tasted bad, or made them ill. Immune systems on the whole seemed able to cope with the apparent lack of hygiene (compared to modern standards).

As with most aspects of life, to be sure of having a good diet eaters would need to take as much control as possible, or be able to trust their food providers. Urban dwellers, rich and poor alike, were at the mercy of others. At each point along the supply chain, and into the kitchen, the consumer relied on the honesty and integrity of the producer, the wholesaler, the vendor and the cook. Those who would have eaten the highest-quality foods in the cities were rich householders with trustworthy, honest and careful servants. The tactile and sensory tests of freshness – digging with knives, poking with digits, slicing, sniffing, wrinkling, pulling and teasing, holding to the light and being generally choosy – first outlined by Thomas Tryon and repeated by Eliza Smith, Eliza Haywood and Hannah Glasse, were options only for those with time, inclination and cash. Justifying an elaborate checking routine, Haywood lectured that 'if one Cheesemonger refuses to do this, go to another; but if you carry ready money, there is no Danger of his turning you away'.[183] The uncompromising and knowledgeable buyer *au fait* with all the latest scams and alarms could test the goods. A slipshod servant or a tired and busy working housewife might not have had the time or temperament to buy early from the market. The upper middling sorts, to whom the cookery books were directed, would, on the whole, have enjoyed fairly high-quality food by the standards of the day, especially if they had the time and knowledge to choose well, were on good terms with the local traders, and had fully equipped kitchens and room for storage, preparation and cooking. However, even these city dwellers could not have enjoyed the fineries available in well-managed country estates. In his fecund rural retreat of Brambleton Hall, Matt Bramble literally ate his view.[184] Spoilt by a wealth of fresh quality produce, he found the cities wanting.

CHAPTER 5

Noisy

James Gibbs, architect of the church of St Mary-le-Strand, realised that 'being situated in a very public place' the church would be surrounded by the tumultuous traffic of London's eighteenth-century streets. To mitigate this he designed the ground floor without windows 'to keep out the Noises from the Street'.[1] By the mid-eighteenth century, London was not the only city blighted by traffic noise. The Sessions House in Chelmsford was located in the marketplace and as a consequence it was common for the assize judges to be forced to halt proceedings because the words of witnesses and counsel could not be discerned above the noises of carts and carriages.[2] The noise of the

36 John Maurer, 'A Perspective View of St Mary's Church in the Strand near the Royal Palace of Somerset, London' (1753). Note the windows on the ground floor. These are not pierced – they are false windows.

traffic was a common topic of conversation among citizens and visitors, especially the sounds made by coaches and cartwheels. An Act of the Common Council had set down regulations for London's transport in 1586. Fines were fixed for any coach or cart heard to creak or 'pype' for want of oil.[3] As the volume of traffic increased in the cities, the irritating and debilitating effects of traffic noise were widely felt.

The street hawkers of London who advertised their wares and services with sounds also appear frequently in descriptions of daytime noise. In order to be heard above the din of rattling coaches and the clamour of their business rivals, the criers would have needed to keep the volume high.[4] William King, in his *Art of Cookery* (1708), described the cries of London as a 'hideous din'.[5] As shouts were varied to attract attention, words degenerated into sounds, and many consumers would have had difficulty distinguishing one slurred yell from another.[6] Milk, explained Joseph Addison, was sold in shrill sounds and one milk-seller became infamous for her inarticulate scream.[7] According to Addison a lack of clarity often led to confusion: 'I have sometimes seen a Country Boy run out to buy Apples of a Bellows-mender, and Ginger-bread from a Grinder of Knives and Scissars. Nay, so strangely infatuated are some very eminent Artists of this particular Grace in a Cry, that none but their Acquaintance are able to guess at their Profession.'[8]

The pigs that thronged the city streets were not just inconvenient and dirty, but they were noisy too. The proverb 'he that loves noise must buy a pig' is testament to the fact that these animals are particularly raucous.[9] Pigs were not the only noisy animals to inhabit the streets. Hunting, spit-turning and pet dogs scampered on London's streets, playing and fighting with each other, and with numerous strays – 'one barking Dog sets all the Street a barking.'[10] On 15 January 1660 Samuel Pepys was disturbed by the barking of a neighbour's dog and recorded the consequences in his diary: 'I could not sleep for an hour or two, I slept late; and then in the morning took physic, and so stayed within all day.'[11] Even dying dogs taxed the ears. Two men were presented to the wardmote inquest of St Dunstan-in-the-West in 1622 for 'anoyinge of divers Inhabitants in Fleet street and the white Fryers' by killing dogs to feed to hawks. Mention was made of their practice of keeping the dogs prior to their slaughter 'longe alyve, howlinge and crying'.[12]

Noises made at night were more likely to disturb. Curfew rules and conventions meant that the streets should, theoretically, have been devoid of noisy people at night, but they were generally neither observed nor enforced. The night-time economy boomed in the cities. Diners and drinkers could visit taverns, inns or other eateries. In 1619 the landlord of an ordinary (a venue for a set price meal) at the Marigold in Fleet Street disturbed the 'quiet of John Clark and his family being neighbours late in the nightes from tyme to tyme by ill disorder'.[13] One source of persistent nocturnal nuisance was a noisy alehouse, and one proverb warned 'chuse not an house neer an inn (viz. for noise)'.[14] Neighbours of alehouses were disturbed by the noises of the patrons coming and going at night.[15] In *Amusements Serious and Comical* (1700), London hack Tom Brown described his city as 'prodigious, and noisy', a place 'where repose and silence dare scarce shew their heads in the darkest night'.[16] The author of *Low-Life* (*c*.1755) described the London streets of the mid-eighteenth century, detailing how urban sounds changed throughout the day and the night. Between midnight and one o'clock in the morning on a Sunday in June alehouse keepers are portrayed encouraging their patrons ('noisy Fools and Drunkards') to leave the premises for fear of prosecution. According to this account, traders were still active at this hour, as were prostitutes and itinerant musicians. During the following hour the streets gradually quietened, 'as the Whores, Bullies and Thieves have retir'd to their Apartments; noisy drunken Mechanicks are got to their Lodgings, Coachmen, Watermen and Soldiers are mostly asleep'. The noise of the morning swelled after five o'clock, when the dog-skinner, with strays in tow, searched for more, and bells tolled for morning services. Sounds intensified and then plateaued over the following hours, until night-time, when the crowded streets thinned and the sounds of customers leaving alehouses were joined by 'Great hallowing and whooping in the Fields, by such Persons who have spent the Day Abroad, and are now returning Home half drunk'.[17] When a newly erected playhouse in Hampstead became a magnet for undesirables in 1709 the vicar and churchwardens condemned it as a location of 'great scandals, annoyances and disorders'.[18] The inhabitants of St James's Clerkenwell petitioned the Middlesex jurors, hoping to prevent disorders in their neighbourhood caused when several venues (including Sadlers Wells, Lord Cobham's and Sir John Oldcastle's) closed, disgorging hundreds of noisy patrons. The petitioners hoped that existing laws against disorderly behaviour and ale selling would be enforced to prevent these disturbances.[19]

Curfews were not intended specifically to limit noise, but this would have been an inevitable consequence – marking off periods of noise from periods of relative quiet. While limiting the amount of noise, the curfew would have also created a symbolic boundary, with sounds heard during curfew arousing heightened suspicion. The constable or members of the watch were empowered to take anybody acting suspiciously, or 'nightwalking', to a house of correction if they could not provide a reasonable excuse for their whereabouts during curfew hours.[20] In the recognizances for each of the eleven men seized by the guard of Hackney in 1662 it was stated that he 'is a p[er]son suspicious for that he cannot give any good Accompt of his being here, at that unseasonable tyme'.[21] Watchmen were supposed to keep a check on the streets during the curfew, but many failed in their duty. Citizens frequently complained that the watch was comprised of men too old, drunk or weak to pay attention or stay awake. In 1604 it was reported that the watchmen of Southampton were 'verie olde poore weake and unhable p[er]sons' who provided an insufficient watch on the city streets, leading to disorders at night.[22] Ned Ward characterised watchmen as a 'bearded Rout' of 'Old, frowzy, croaking sots' who were 'too infirm and lame to walk without their staves'.[23] Some watchmen were even blamed for causing much of the noise nuisances at night themselves. Matt Bramble complained, 'I start every hour from my sleep, at the horrid noise of the watchmen bawling the hour through every street, and thundering at every door; a set of useless fellows, who serve no other purpose but that of disturbing the repose of the inhabitants.'[24] The wife of Ned Ward's 'old, prodigal, new-sworn Constable' complains that her husband even disturbed her when he was not on duty, with his habit of croaking the hours with farts. 'I always sleep the best', she admits, 'when you're abroad disturbing others rest.'[25]

'You shall ask your neighbours if you shall live in peace'[26]

In his play, *Epicoene or the Silent Woman* (1609), Ben Jonson introduces the character of Morose, a man newly betrothed to the eponymous bride, who during the course of the play finds her to be neither silent nor a woman. Morose, 'a gentleman that loves no noise', is duped into marrying Epicoene, 'a yong Gent. suppos'd [to be a] silent woman'. Preferring life as a quiet bachelor to the state of marriage (which he supposed would be noisy), Morose puts the word around that he is in the market for 'a dumbe woman'. Silent until the wedding ceremony, the 'bride', Epicoene, suddenly becomes loquacious. When the wedding guests wreak auditory havoc in Morose's house his suffering becomes extreme and he demands a divorce. Morose pays Dauphine to help him secure release. He obliges by throwing off Epicoene's disguise and revealing the young man. Morose's obsession with noise is portrayed as anti-social, self-important and tyrannical. Resenting knocks on his door, Morose bids Mute (his servant) to remove the 'ring' from the door and to fasten a thick quilt or feather bed to the outside of it, 'that if they knocke with their Daggers, or with Brick-bats, they can make no noyse'. When the sounding of a postman's horn permeates the padded door, he launches into a tirade. The church bells tolling at the funerals of plague victims drove Morose to distraction. Morose's pathological aversion to noise is manifested in his taking umbrage at the sounds of creaking shoes and hair-trimming. When the parson, whom Morose has paid to perform his wedding ceremony, coughs, Morose demands to be reimbursed. A sonic theme persists until the dramatic crescendo of the post-nuptial celebrations. The 'noise' of the musicians overwhelms Morose, who exclaims, 'Tis worse than the noise of a saw.' Thronged with spitting, coughing, laughing, 'neezing' and farting guests, Morose's once quiet haven becomes a roaring hell. [27]

Morose was crafted to show the inflexible, unreasonable and anti-social aspect of community living. He is a caricature. Yet many of the sounds at which Morose takes umbrage did annoy and irritate the citizens of the seventeenth century. What Jonson's study does not indicate, however, was the importance of good neighbourliness to guarantee aural ease.[28] Francis Bacon advised that on choosing a location for a dwelling one should avoid 'ill Neighbours'.[29] Good neighbours would have ensured that those in their vicinity were not unduly disturbed by sounds made by their animals, their children, their pastimes or produced by their 'living unquietly' together. When Samuel Pepys recorded that he had upset his neighbours by forcing his wife to beat a servant, his shame did not stem from the possibility of his acquiring a reputation for cruelty, but from the noise nuisance generated by the thrashing.[30] A proverb started warmly, 'love your neighbour', but continued with a note of caution, 'yet pull not downe your hedge.'[31] Some thought that wealthy neighbours were the worst, as they proved to be argumentative 'and they will often let loose their *servants* to defy, provoke, insult, and do mischief to those they love not'.[32] Some people preferred not to have trading neighbours, some shunned pauper neighbours.

'The apothecary's morter spoils to Luter's music'[33]

Some neighbours were noisy because of their occupation. The homes of urban craftsmen often doubled as workshops, especially when the trade involved the production of small items, requiring only one workman and his apprentice. Michael Power notes that the soap-makers, gunpowder-makers, tailors and smiths, among other craftsmen of seventeenth-century London, worked predominantly at home.[34] Additionally, dedicated workshops were often interspersed with residential buildings. In 1611, Abraham Shakemaple, a yeoman of Finsbury, was bound over to appear at the next Middlesex sessions of the peace to answer to the charge that he had caused a nuisance by erecting and using a forge. In the meantime he was ordered to 'pull downe his Smythes forge which he hath lately erected in Grubstreet, being a great Annoyance to the neighbours by the filthie smoake and the hameringe &c'.[35]

Particular locales were more menaced by work noise than others. The London pewter industry, for example, was concentrated around the Billingsgate and Bishopsgate wards.[36] John Stow described the practice of the founders of Lothbury, who 'cast candlesticks, chafing dishes, spice mortars, and such like copper or latten works', in his description of London in 1598.[37] In his unimplemented plans for the reconstruction of London following the fire of 1666, John Evelyn segregated shopkeepers from artificers. The shopkeepers would occupy the sweetest quarters and the artificers would occupy 'the more ordinary houses, intermedial and narrower passages . . . that the noise and tintamarre of their instruments may be the less importunate'.[38]

Sir Thomas Blount described 'those several Tradesman whose Noise displeases us so, and who dwell in Mills and Forges'.[39] The noise of mills was so loud that millers could be deafened by their work. 'Millers need no noise,' tells one adage, 'yet cannot grind without it.'[40] Coopers (barrel-makers) and other craftsmen producing hollow goods had a special reputation as noise-makers. In November 1639 the Norwich Court of Mayoralty investigated a case of 'extraordinary noise' from a cooper's shop, and the compiler of *A View of the Penal Laws Concerning Trade and Trafick* (1697) described the cooper as 'a man that makes a great Noise in the World'.[41] In *Epicoene*, pewterers, armourers and braziers are singled out as particularly noisy craftsmen.[42] Although large-scale industrialisation was more a characteristic of the nineteenth century, the sounds of new machinery were appearing across the country in the two preceding centuries. Both Ned Ward and Charles Coffey identified the sounds of paper mills as apt metaphors for incessant noise.[43]

The focus of much early modern concern was the noise of coppersmithery, especially during the eighteenth century. Swift's poem 'On Wood the Ironmonger' (1725) likens the sounds of the coppersmith to thunder.[44] Campbell, in his 'compendious view of all the trades', noted that the journeymen of the coppersmith trade 'ought to live by themselves, for they are very noisy Neighbours'.[45] A complaint recorded in the repertories of the Court of London Aldermen concerned Andrew Niblett, a noisy coppersmith who in September 1722 had 'lately taken a messuage in Birchin Alley'. Neighbours petitioned the court saying they had been led to believe that Niblett only intended to use his premises to warehouse goods for the plantation trade. Yet 'the said Niblett contrary to his agreement and the Intentions of his Landlord has used his sledges and other large Hammers in his Trade to the apparent Interruption and annoyance of the Neighbourhood which is inconceivable and hardly to be Expressed they being almost incapable of Negotiating their Affairs through the intolerable and continial Annoyance of the said Niblett.' The petitioners were unsure to whom they should take their problem and it was noted that they 'presume a Power is vested in this Court to prevent such Nusances, wherefore they pray such reliefe as the Court should think fit'. The aldermen did not seem to know whether they had the jurisdiction to deal with it, and if they did, how they should proceed. It was ordered that the town clerk should search through the records to discover how the court had dealt with any similar complaint in the past, and to report his findings to the next meeting. No reference to any previous similar incident is recorded at this meeting.[46]

Coppersmiths would have been singled out for particular attention because of the nature of their materials, tools and methods and the historical development of their trade. Copper was generally beaten when cold and it offered greater resistance than the other metals that were also beaten cold (gold, silver and tin); therefore it needed to be hammered more vigorously and for protracted periods.[47] Struck with iron hammers the solid copper produced high-pitched notes, and the hollow copper vessels would have amplified the hammer blows.[48] Highlighting the incessant noise of their trade, the Italian physician Bernardino Ramazzini noted that coppersmiths

> are engaged all day in hammering copper to make it ductile so that they may manufacture vessels of various kinds. From this quarter [a district of Venice] there rises such a terrible din that only these workers have homes and shops there; all others flee from that highly disagreeable locality . . . they beat the newly minted copper, first with wooden then with iron hammers till it is as ductile as required. To begin with, the ears are injured by that perpetual din . . . that workers of this class become hard of hearing, and, if they grow old at this work, completely deaf.[49]

Although the craft of the coppersmith was not a new one to England, the numbers of workers in this field did swell during the early modern period, especially after the late sixteenth century.[50] Rapid increases in the home production of copper goods soon reduced imports to 'negligible dimensions' and during the eighteenth century the home demand for copper increased greatly.[51] Craftsmen new to the trade established themselves in areas unfamiliar with the sounds of coppersmithery. Lacking the need for safety in numbers, coppersmiths did not group together in the way that goldsmiths did. Wide dispersal would have exacerbated their unpopularity by increasing the numbers of people irritated by them.

'Beat not your wife after the hour of nine at night'

The prime culprits of city noise in the seventeenth and eighteenth centuries were traffic, traders, animals, craftsmen and drunken revellers. However, there is more to the study of noise than simply identifying likely noise sources.[52] The word 'noise' connoted a variety of imprecise and often contradictory meanings. 'Noise' was used to describe sounds that were musical or unmusical, pleasant or unpleasant, and could also be applied to quarrelling, strife or the spreading of rumours.[53] Randle Holme declared that 'a Sound, is any noise' and used both words interchangeably throughout his tome of 1688.[54] Contemporaries understood the concept of 'noisiness' in a more narrowly defined sense. When he defined 'noisy', Samuel Johnson was more precise than when he defined 'noise', describing the former as 'Sounding Loud' and 'Clamorous; turbulent'.[55] Noisy sounds irritated the hearer because they were irregular, intrusive, disturbing, distracting, inexplicable or shocking.[56] In *Of Building* (1698), Roger North explained that some sounds, such as the 'clapping of a door', annoyed the hearer because, in contrast to musical sounds that have 'equall time pulses', they have 'unequall movements' and 'uncertain periods'. The reason for the disturbing quality of these 'unequall movements' is that 'every stroke is various, and depends not on the past, nor the future on that; and nothing of the measure is understood'.[57] Robert Hooke remarked that 'noise is displeasing because the ear cannot keep up with the constant change of tuning required.'[58] Noise theorists have noted that the pitch of some sounds makes them more likely to be regarded as noise, but that 'in the final analysis it is the social (and in turn political) context which deems them acceptable'.[59] A sound acceptable in one setting could be inappropriate in another and deemed to be noise. Echoing anthropologist Mary Douglas, who judged dirt to be 'matter out of place', Peter Bailey had defined noise as 'sound out of place'.[60] Sounds are out of place when issued in an inappropriate place, or at inappropriate times. People are more sensitive to sounds at certain times of the day, and a sound produced in the day might have been regarded as a noise if it had been made at night. Sounds are especially irritating when they prevent sleep or concentration. On his arrival in Northampton in 1669, Cos[i]mo the Grand Duke of Tuscany was delighted by the parish bells rung in his honour, 'being well tuned, the sound of them was very agreeable'. However, when the ringing continued for a great part of the night he found them to be 'a great interruption to sleep'.[61]

Noises were particularly annoying to the sick. The chimney expert Robert Clavering asserted that 'in high winds nothing can be more irksome and disagreeable to a delicate and sickly person, than the horrible noise the wind makes in whistling round' the chimney pots.[62] Ailing citizens were especially discomforted by the clangour of church bells. The bells that signalled the death of a parishioner were often silenced during plague epidemics, partly to preserve the bells and save the sexton's time, but also to avoid lowering morale. Anthony Wood described Oxford in November 1683 (during a period of sweating sickness): 'some bells were orderd not to toll for persons, because many dying frighted people away and caused trading to decay.'[63] The bells of New College Chapel, Oxford, were silenced while the proctor lay ill in bed with smallpox in 1762, following reports that the noise disturbed him.[64] John Wood noted that the ringing of the Abbey bells to welcome strangers to Bath was considered by some to be the 'greatest Inconvenience' to the invalids.[65] Living near Hammersmith church in the 1720s, Lady Arabella Howard, who was 'of a sickly and weak Constitution', was disturbed by the sound of the five o'clock bell each morning. She and her husband first considered moving to another parish, but it was suggested that she might like to 'purchase her Quiet'. Her husband, Dr Martin, struck a deal with the churchwardens, exchanging a cupola, a clock and a bell for a promise 'to stay the ringing of the five o'clock Bell'. However, when Nutkin, a new and officious churchwarden, resumed the morning ringing after a lapse of two years, Martin brought an action against him, the other churchwardens, the parson, the overseers and several inhabitants of Hammersmith. He secured an injunction from the Court of Chancery. In the hearing it was ruled that the bells should not ring at five during the lifetimes of both Martin and his wife, as such ringing was of 'very ill Consequence to the Plaintiff the Lady Howard'.[66] This is a rare instance of an individual using the law to silence a sound. However, the fact that it was brought before Chancery, a court which heard matters of equity, suggests that the ruling was motivated not by a desire to protect the plaintiff's health, but to ensure that the deal was honoured. The case is interesting nonetheless, because to a woman unable to attend morning service through disability the signal that called people to church was 'undesired' – it was noise.

The legal historian J. H. Baker has detected growing contemporary speculation about the scope of action on nuisance, 'particularly with respect to nuisances affecting the senses. Already by Tudor times the law recognised that nuisances could be occasioned by noise, heat and smell.' However, he notes, not every inconvenience could be the subject of legal redress, and the need to weigh up the rights and freedom of all parties was recognised.[67] This is the nub of the problem. Common noises associated with urban living, such as crying babies, barking dogs and traffic, were not easily preventable, so there would have been little point in taking issue with them. As extraordinary sounds were, by definition, occasional and unpredictable, their prevention was also unfeasible. All the authorities could realistically try to deal with were those continual sources of noise such as rowdy alehouses, quarrelling spouses and inappropriately located workshops. Whether other complaints about noise were heard or recorded would have been influenced by the prospect of remedial action.

Morose dramatises the fact that personal boundaries of tolerability to noise were not uniform; he was an unusually sensitive character. However, to create laws to deal with noise as a nuisance, a consensus on thresholds of tolerability is required. The subjectivity of the sound/noise distinction creates a legal dilemma: who determines what is noise? Specific noise legislation would have been difficult to draft in an age before the decibel meter. Lord Selborne, presiding over a case brought to trial in 1872 involving the noise and vibrations of a steam engine in a mill, stressed that the court should be careful to avoid being unfairly swayed into making too harsh a judgement by a hypersensitive plaintiff. He warned that 'a nervous, or anxious, or prepossessed listener hears sounds which would otherwise have passed unnoticed, and magnifies and exaggerates into some new significance, originating within himself, sounds which at other times would have been passively heard and not regarded.'[68] Although the case post-dates the period under consideration here, Lord

Selborne's caveat is an important one to bear in mind when trying to assess differing susceptibilities to noise, and when considering definitions of acceptable noise. In order for a case to be actionable as a private nuisance, a plaintiff would have needed to argue that damage had occurred to himself or to his property. Whether or not 'damage' would be occasioned by noise was a moot point. In *Jeffrey's Case* (*c.*1560), John Jeffrey had let out a room of his London house to a schoolmaster, but found that the sounds distracted him in his study, which was immediately above the schoolroom. When it was judged to be lawful to keep a school anywhere, he moved his study to another room in his house.[69]

The problems inherent in drafting laws to deal with noise were never coherently addressed in the seventeenth or eighteenth centuries, but people afflicted by noise could theoretically seek redress from a variety of bodies with overlapping and conflicting jurisdictions, depending on the type and location of the noise. In London the wardmote inquests, the London Court of Common Council, and the London Viewers could all be presented with evidence of noise nuisances, as could provincial civic authorities and manorial courts.

The London Viewers of the early modern period absorbed responsibilities previously held by the medieval Nuisance Assize. A viewer (the title hints at a visual bias) would visit a property to resolve a neighbourly dispute, often involving building encroachments and unwelcome chimney smoke. The medieval Nuisance Assize had occasionally dealt with work practices, and back in 1378 had examined the case of a noisy armourer.[70] On the evidence of the surviving certificates, the London Viewers rarely followed up complaints about work practices, even though crafts and trades created smells, noise and waste. Priority was given to residential structural problems such as inconsiderate guttering and building that blocked sunlight.[71] For a complaint to be upheld the complainant would have to prove potential or actual damage to his property. (For the 1378 case the neighbours detailed both the fire risk posed by the forge and the hammer-falls that shook the party walls and damaged alcohol stored in the cellars.) The Oxford Viewers also focused on building construction rather than usage.

Civic authorities crafted specific bylaws to deal with particular nuisances. If expectations of good neighbourliness were not sufficiently persuasive to restrict noise, rule 30 of *The Lawes of the Market* (1595) required Londoners to observe that 'No man shall after the houre of nine at the Night, keepe any rule whereby any such suddaine out-cry be made in the still of the Night, as making any affray, or beating hys Wife, or servant, or singing, or revyling in his house, to the Disturbaunce of his neighbours.'[72] Craftsmen who used hammers in their work were restricted by rule 25 of *The Lawes*, which ordered that 'No hammar man, [such] as a Smith a Pewterer, a Founder, and all Artificers making great sound, shall not worke after the houre of nyne in the night, nor afore the houre of four in the Morninge.'[73]

Some leases included noise-limiting clauses to reduce the likelihood of tenants annoying those nearby. These often stipulated times when certain activities could be carried out. When a second-floor room known as Oxford's Dancing School was leased to a musician in 1610, the agreement prevented dancing between two and five each afternoon.[74] Two decades later the council renewed musician John Bosseley's lease only on condition that he did not 'daunce nor suffer any dancing after tenne of the Clocke in the night nor before fyve of the Clocke in the morning'.[75] The master of a dancing school in Three Coney Walk, Lambeth (later Lambeth Walk), was refused a licence in 1755 on account of the nuisance caused by his dancers.[76] In 1636 one of the Oxford bailiffs was granted permission to open up a door from his backyard to Guildhall Court, providing that the schoolboys taught by his brother did not use the passage. The opening was walled up in 1664 after schoolboys took liberties.[77] Among the conditions for the lease of a plot to the west of Prince Street, Bristol, held by a merchant in the 1720s, was the following: 'No part of the ground to the rear to be used for yards, for timber etc., or for stabling, but to be used solely for warehousing.' Tenants could not use the property as smiths' workshops, tallow chandlers' warehouses, or any other shops for traders likely to 'annoy the neighbouring Inhabitants'.[78]

Although not commonly the subject of specific regulations and laws, noise could be limited coincidentally by other laws, such as the control of alehouses. Alehouse keepers were required by an Act of 1552 to gain a licence from a justice of the peace in order to guarantee the prevention of 'hurts and trobles . . . abuses and disorders'.[79] Keepers who regularly failed to prevent drunken disorder might have found themselves before the justices, with their licence in jeopardy.[80] Adherence to prescribed hours of trading limited nocturnal noise for those in the neighbourhood, yet licensed keepers frequently flouted these laws and regulations, and unlicensed alehouses proliferated. Six alehouse keepers were presented to the Worcester Sessions of the Peace between 1634 and 1638 for disturbing neighbours at night. In 1634 it was claimed that John Browne, selling ale at 'undue times' of the night, kept 'odious and sinful drunkenness in his house at all times so that his neighbours cannot rest in their houses for the odious noise of drunkenness and the voices of drunken men in the night time'.[81] Ecclesiastical courts could be presented with noises made in the church or churchyard during divine service. One woman was presented in Nottingham in 1620 for bringing a 'most unquiet child to the church to the greate offence of the whole congregacion'. It was reported that the vicar could not be heard 'for the offensive noyce'.[82]

Communities afflicted by protracted noise could petition the authorities and claim the noise was a public nuisance. Public nuisances that might have involved the production of noise included illicit alehouses, the use of a speaking trumpet, the keeping of a disorderly house (which drew together noisy crowds), and playhouses (because coaches and people gathered nearby to the inconvenience of the 'Places adjacent').[83] In 1743, James Newbold, a porter from the London parish of St Bride's, was indicted for keeping a disorderly house. Witnesses at his Old Bailey trial listed a catalogue of disorders, including supplying gin and entertaining drunken whores who were unfit for the streets. He beat these 'poor ragged dismal Toads' until they cried out. One witness claimed, 'I have heard Noises all Night long; I have heard too much cursing and swearing, and everything that is obscene; I have it at my Door every Evening, as soon as it is dark; – the House is like a Hogsty.'[84]

Noise was afforded a lower priority than inconsiderate building practices, such as blocking out a neighbour's windows or rerouting guttering to drain into their property, as it was not considered to cause actual damage or a deprivation of rights.[85] Noise was not controlled as rigorously as street dirt. Although wardmote inquest minutes are littered with references to dumping carcasses in ditches, failure to clear dunghills and throwing 'soyles' on the pavement, noise is rarely mentioned. Piles of filth and decaying animals created a more lingering and permanent problem than noise. Noisome offences were considered to pose an immediate danger to public health; noise was not. In contrast to smells, noises rarely featured as causes of private or public nuisance in court records.

When cases involving noise nuisance were presented by petitioning neighbours, the key issue was frequently not noise; it was only one of several causes of complaint. When neighbours complained to the wardmote inquest of St Dunstan-in-the-West in 1622 that two men in the hawking trade created a nuisance in Fleet Street and Whitefriars when they killed dogs for meat it was not the noise of the dogs or the slaughter they stressed (although this was noted), but that the blood from their corpses grew noisome and posed a threat of infection.[86] In 1744 parishioners from St James's, Clerkenwell, called for action to be taken against the keepers of disorderly houses in that parish, namely Old Sadlers Wells, New Wells, Lord Cobham's and Sir John Oldcastle's. The petitioners claimed that each establishment held up to five hundred customers, and pointed out that they sometimes remained open until four o'clock in the morning. When they left patrons 'frequently assembled in bodies, hallowing and knocking on doors, ringing bells and singing obscene songs'. This, it was claimed, led to the disquiet and danger of the petitioners in particular and the public in general. Their petition stressed not the noise but, rather, the lewd and corrupting nature of the clientele, possibly because this would be more persuasive with authorities wishing to tighten moral standards.[87] Canny petitioners would have known which social threats to stress in order to secure redress.

'There is but a thin Deal-Partition betwixt his Room and ours'

Ben Jonson wrote *Epicoene* after a plague epidemic. The incessantly tolling church bells that bid farewell to victims caused Morose much consternation. The lengths to which he goes to avoid their clangour are detailed, 'now by reason of the sicknesse, the perpetuitie of ringing has made him devise a roome with double walles, and treble seelings; the windores close shut, and calk'd: and there he lives by Candle-light.'[88] Morose adapts his property in order to reduce the noises permeating in from outside. In a much less dramatic fashion, citizens across England were carrying out modifications to limit noise intrusion in the seventeenth and eighteenth centuries.

As if Londoners had not suffered enough with the plague, on a windy September day in 1666 a conflagration succeeded the disease. Sweeping through the city, flames destroyed countless homes and businesses. People listened in horror as timbers cracked and exploded, slates spat and splintered, thatch fizzled and hissed, and church bells melted. An alarm was raised – one account recalled 'a great noise of drums' – and as John Evelyn's fellow citizens ran about 'like distracted creatures', crying and lamenting, he heard 'the noise & crackling & thunder of the impetuous flames'.[89] Once the fire was extinguished, a thick blanket of ash muffled the sounds of those rummaging among the ruins.

Although the rebuildings that followed the fire may not have put into reality the grand schemes of designers and thinkers such as John Evelyn, they did intensify the pace of building improvement already apparent in the capital and would have changed the citizens' aural perspectives.[90] Measures to avoid a repetition of the disaster led to the abandonment of timber for the construction of buildings.[91] The Act for the Rebuilding of the City of London (1667) brought about standardisation in metropolitan house building by dictating both materials and wall thickness. That London was rebuilt in brick, tile and glass had implications for the levels of noise disturbance experienced by the citizens. The use of brick increased the ease with which private spaces could be created and also reduced the noise porosity of the walls. The rebuilding jolted the citizens into a new way of perceiving their city spaces. A proclamation of 13 September called not only for a rebuilding in brick, but also for a widening of alleys and secondary lanes.[92] Noise disturbance would have been further reduced as a result of the distancing of neighbours and neighbourhoods. Sound would also have travelled in a different way through the streets, lined with solid new buildings.

The general outline of the changes in building construction, layout and use between 1600 and 1770 reveals that the richer members of society, especially affluent urbanites, would have had increasing access to noise-reducing building innovations – such as glazing, panelling and ceilings – as the period progressed. Some wealthier householders would have hung sound-absorbing tapestries and oak panelling on their walls. Panelled chambers and plaster ceilings were typical characteristics of the houses built for gentlemen in Gloucester during the late seventeenth century. These measures were ostensibly designed to serve other purposes: panelling and tapestries insulated and covered up damp and glazing admitted light, but they did also deaden noises. Not all of these measures would have appeared in the same building, especially in the early part of the period. However, as the eighteenth century progressed, these features would have been available to increasing numbers of households as ideas percolated downwards.[93]

It was long known that the debilitating impact of sounds could be alleviated with thoughtful building design and construction. Homes became more complex and compartmentalised as the period progressed. A heightened desire for privacy, segregation and symmetry in house layout led to a transformation in architectural style. As domestic buildings of almost all ranks of society were 'transformed almost out of recognition', there would have been implications for the movement of noise and therefore exposure to noise.[94] Spaces used for noisy activities were separated from those intended for quiet repose. The period saw the gradual obsolescence of the single-storey house and the rise of more complex structures, with second floors, outbuildings and corridors. The development of the parlour, the use of rooms above the parlour for sleeping, and the insistence on a separate kitchen were characteristic elements of seventeenth-century urban houses.[95]

The ability to escape external noises and to limit the spread of noise through a property depended on ownership of space. The richer the householder, the greater the space that could be afforded and the more solid the materials used. The dwellings inhabited by the poorest city residents would have offered little resistance to noise intrusion, especially in subdivided houses of multiple occupation. Partitions between dwellings could be flimsy; some were merely wainscot partitions.[96] Deposition statements reveal the ease with which people listened through thin dividing walls to the conversations and activities going on in neighbouring properties. Mary Jeffry, a witness in a murder case, lived next to a man accused of murdering his wife in 1725. She asserted that 'there's only a thin Partition betwixt their Stair-Case and mine. I was going to Bed between 11 and 12 o'Clock, when I heard a Disturbance in her Room, and a Noise of two or three People running down Stairs.'[97] In another murder case a witness stated that 'I live next Door to the Prisoner, there is but a thin Deal-Partition betwixt his Room and ours, so that one may hear in one Room what passes in the other, very plainly.'[98] Houses that were two rooms deep offered some insulation against street noises to the back rooms, especially on the upper floors. Many citizens, however, inhabited dwellings that were only one room deep, and for these people the chances of reducing their exposure to exterior noises were reduced.

Architects considered the best use of rooms in order to prevent noises moving through buildings. Roger North compared sprawling houses with those where the storeys are 'lay'd on an heap like a wasps-nest' (a 'pile'), and listed the relative advantages and disadvantages of each type of structure. At the head of his list of five 'inconveniences' of a pile, North places 'all the noises of an house are heard everywhere'.[99] Piles were most commonly built in the cities, where ground space was in short supply, and building plots were narrow, so the way that buildings were used needed to be carefully considered in order to limit noise intrusion. Servants needed to be accommodated within their master's house – to sleep, to work and socialise – preferably without causing undue disruption to the rest of the household. Setting out rules for *The Conduct of Servants in Great Families* (1720) Thomas Seaton instructed servants to resist quarrelling among themselves, 'for otherwise, surely it is not fit to alarm a whole House, and make an Uproar to the Molestation of every Member in it; because every great House wou'd be at this Rate a Scene of Confusion, a Place of Tumult and Noise; to avoid which, a Man wou'd chuse the meanest and most despicable Cottage, where he might be quiet and still, and removed from Clamour'.[100] To deal with servants who lacked this restraint, North made suggestions to reduce the impact of their noise. He argued that servants should not live in attics and garrets, 'for all offensive things fall, rather than rise, and their noise by stirring is trouble-some', so instead they should be situated 'underneath'.[101]

Sir Roger Pratt, Charles II's commissioner for the rebuilding of London after the Fire, suggested that when servants were located in the garrets, they should not be placed directly over the guest rooms, or they might disturb the sleepers below at night and in the morning. Rooms that were above these apartments for 'strangers' might be used for functions such as drying clothes that do not need to be accessed at anti-social times. Pratt also advised that the kitchen, the buttery and all the rooms connected to these should be located in the basement, 'with their backcourts, convenient to them; in that no dirty servants may be seen passing to and fro by those who are above, no noises heard, nor ill scents smelt'. The kitchen should be located near to the 'little parlour', sufficiently far from entertaining rooms to avoid disruption, but near enough for servants to hear 'the least ringing or call'. He recommended an ingenious design for a window like a service hatch, through which the master and mistress could supervise and summon servants without having their senses of smell and hearing assaulted.[102] The compiler of 'Draughts of a House proposed for a Merchant' (1724) detailed how his design would allow the young men who would staff the office to slip quietly to their own chambers at night, through the use of backstairs without 'disturbing or dirtying the best part of the House'.[103] Considering the domestic sphere, Mark Girouard remarked that the use of back stairs meant that the householder 'walking up the stairs no longer met their last night's faeces coming down them'.[104] Quite how many London houses could have incorporated features such as backstairs and serving hatches into their often cramped footprints is a matter for debate, but some of the larger West End developments would have enjoyed them.[105]

'The cry of the poor is unpleasing to the rich'[106]

By the early seventeenth century London was a wealthy, bustling and expanding city. Infrastructure development could not keep pace with the ever growing population, making the capital crowded, shabby and noisy.[107] However, many commentators enjoyed this mêlée and, when describing the sounds of St Paul's Walk in 1627, John Earle revelled in the atmosphere, noting the 'humming or buzze, mixt of walking, tongues and feet . . . a still roare or loud whisper'. On comparing London to Paris in the mid-seventeenth century, John Evelyn noted that what London lacked in houses and palaces it made up for in shops and taverns 'which render it so open by day, and cheerfull in the night', and remarked that 'as *mad* and lowd a *Town*, is no where to be found in the whole world'.[108]

By contrast, impending catastrophes would jolt Londoners into a permanently altered perception of their city. There was a subtle shift in attitudes towards the end of the seventeenth century. Before, visitors had made most of the comments about London's noise, but after that time even Londoners found that noises attracted their attention. They started to grumble about their noisy city; the bustle did not seem to please people as it had pleased Evelyn and Earle. An attractive feature of Mrs Packer's lodgings in Crooked Lane, according to her advertisement in a late seventeenth-century trade paper, was the 'freedom from Noise' one would enjoy there.[109]

From the mid-seventeenth century, London's citizens muttered darkly about the noise of the city in their diaries, turning their attention to the sounds of servants, workmen, the poor, hawkers, drinkers and men who fought each other with cudgels. At the same time, artists and literati portrayed London as distractingly noisy. It is perhaps significant that *Epicoene* enjoyed a period of popularity after the theatres were reopened at the Restoration. Between them, Elizabeth and Samuel Pepys attended at least six performances of it (or extracts from it) during the 1660s.[110] In 1668 John Dryden took a sympathetic line towards Morose, writing, 'We may consider him first to be naturally of a delicate hearing, as many are, to whom all sharp sounds are unpleasant; and secondly, we may attribute much of it to the peevishness of his age, or the wayward authority of an old man in his own house.' Dryden asserted that although risible, Morose was an entirely believable character.[111] Morose, an eccentric figure at the start of the century, had found a home among like minds at the close of the century.

The change of mood apparent in the last half of the seventeenth century was cemented in the eighteenth century.[112] In *Amusements Serious and Comical* (1700), the London hack Tom Brown described his city as 'prodigious, and noisy', a place 'where repose and silence dare scarce shew their heads in the darkest night'.[113] The dissatisfaction with urban noise (and especially London's noise) is also evident in John Gay's *Rural Sports* (first published in 1713):

> I Have long been in the noisie Town immur'd
> Respir'd its Smoak, and all it's Toils endur'd.[114]

This heightened sensitivity might simply be attributable to the swelling population and the knock-on effect of increased trade and traffic. Indeed, the sounds of London's streets multiplied throughout the early modern period. When pedestrians trod the wet and muddy pavements, some chinking with their pattens (iron devices to keep the feet off the ground), others bawling their wares, they could not have failed to hear the sounds of coaches and carts rattling and trundling along the cobbles.

By the mid-eighteenth century, some other cities were also becoming blighted with noises. Tobias Smollett wrote *Humphry Clinker* when Bath was experiencing an unfavourable press. Matt Bramble complains that 'this place, which Nature and Providence seem to have intended as a resource from distemper and disquiet, is become the very center of racket and dissipation. Indeed, of that peace, tranquility and ease, so necessary to those who labour under bad health, weak nerves, and irregular spirits; here we have nothing but noise, tumult and hurry.'[115]

However, an apparent dissatisfaction with urban noise did not manifest itself in a noticeable rise in official complaints about noise, or even in calls to strengthen laws on noise nuisance. Citizens may not have considered it to be economically desirable to reduce some city noises – especially those created during manufacture. The types of noise that attracted most complaint among the literate and vociferous citizens were those sounds made by the poorest citizens – especially the sounds made by popular entertainers and low-profit traders.

Street musicians featured in descriptions of urban din. Instruments most closely associated with cacophony were fiddles and pipes, especially ones that were damaged, ill-tuned or homemade. Common fiddlers were plentiful in towns. Described as 'poor and silly Fellows' who 'get a livelihood . . . playing on their unpleasing and tuneless Musick', their efforts were described as 'scratching', 'scraping', 'grating' and 'twanging'. In his character of 'A Fidler', Samuel Butler exclaimed that he commits 'a rape upon the ear . . . He is an earwig, that creeps into a mans ear and torments him, until he is got out again.' Considering it a greater act of charity to listen to a 'poore Fidler' than to pay him, John Earle remarked that he 'sells nothing dearer than to be gone', thus echoing the proverb 'Give the piper a penny to play and two pence to leave off'. Players of 'tooting' or 'farting' wind instruments were similarly berated.[116] Many harpers, fiddlers and pipers were blind. Unable to perform some skilled labours, they gravitated (or were pushed) towards music to make their living.[117] In Oxford a one-eyed local character called 'blinking Hyatt' sawed at his 'vile Crowd' to make a 'wretched Tune'.[118]

In Marcellus Laroon's *Execrable Concert* (1770) ugly and scruffy musicians play a range of decrepit and discordant devices (figure 37, below). It is implied that the resulting output was more cacophony than music. A fiddler in ragged clothes gives his all to the left, next to a man playing a one-stringed viol. Behind him a character seems to be rubbing or banging a box or a washboard,

37   Marcellus Laroon (III), *The Execrable Concert* (1770).

while another crashes fire irons together. To complete the scene, the 'musician' (far right) pulls the tails of three cats imprisoned in a piano-like contraption similar to one described by Athanasius Kircher in 1650. Cats were positioned according to the pitch of their cries, issued when a spike was driven through their tails. This device was reportedly invented to cheer up a stressed Italian prince.[119] Although Laroon's image is a caricature, written accounts of impromptu street concerts describe a similar level of amateurism. It was traditional for the city musicians to welcome elite visitors to Bath. However, some felt that this was insensitive and shocked those retreating to Bath to soothe their nerves. One poet felt that the fiddlers' 'squeaking catgut' was 'worse than the gout'.[120]

Many studies have shown how the class structure became more complex, and central to this was the burgeoning growth of a professional urban class, into whose 'polite' lifestyles the noise of tinkers, waits, common fiddlers and alehouses did not fit.[121] Participants in football games and other sports and pastimes vocalised their enjoyment, but disapproving witnesses heard only noise and rowdiness.[122] A clash of urban lifestyles and the increasing concern among the professional classes to control the sound environment saw attempts to take music off the streets and to place it indoors.[123] This antagonism had increased steadily during the early modern period, and was connected to distrust of the people who crowded the urban streets. It highlighted a growing gulf between polite and low society. The polite urbanites of the eighteenth century desired separation; they wanted the street cleared of noisy, humdrum performers and hawkers. Concern was expressed about sounds that were alien or irrelevant to professional lifestyles.

Although the ditties of asparagus sellers were welcomed, the noises of sellers of bucolic and cheap vegetables were thought to be unbearable. Criers who touted infrequently because they purveyed seasonal goods, or whose cries were harmonious, enjoyed the greatest popularity with the citizens of London.[124] Comparing it to the 'Song of Nightingales', 'Ralph Crotchett' regretted in *The Spectator* that the cry of the dill and cucumber sellers was only heard for two months. Most criers did not enjoy such approbation. Cabbages were sold all the year round and Jonathan Swift moaned, 'Here is a restless dog crying cabbages and Savoys, plagues me mightily every morning about this time. He is at it now. I wish his largest cabbage was sticking in his throat.'[125] *The Spectator*'s 'Ralph Crotchett' did not appreciate the 'excessive Alarms' of the turnip sellers that he regarded as unnecessary because their wares were in no danger of cooling. He asked that criers 'take care in particular that those may not make the most Noise, who have the least to sell, which is very observable in the Vendors of Card-matches to whom I cannot but apply that old Proverb of Much Cry but little Wool'.[126] Those who cried loudest were perhaps those most desperate to sell – usually the service providers and traders peddling very small items at low profit.[127] The poet Samuel Butler claimed that sellers who 'have but a little wit are commonly like those that cry things in the streets, who if they have but a Groatsworth of Rotten or sticking stuff, every body that comes nigh shalbe sure to heare of it, while those that drive a rich noble Trade, make no Noyse of it'.[128] Generally, it seemed that the poorer you were, the more noise you were perceived to generate, and the deeper your alienation and stigmatisation became.

38   Marcellus Laroon (II), 'Knives or Cisers to Grinde', from *The Cryes of the City of London*.

In February 1685 Richard Hookam was fined one shilling for wandering 'the places and lanes' of Middlesex carrying a wooden cart and a rotary wheel, crying 'Have you any knives to grind?', an action which the Middlesex sessions jurors interpreted as a ploy to disguise his vagrancy and escape punishment for that crime.[129] Knife-grinders feature in both Marcellus Laroon's engraving, above, and William Hogarth's print *The Enraged Musician* (see figure 40 on p. 128). It is implausible that someone would push such a cumbersome wheel for no other purpose than to disguise his vagrancy. Hookham had upset the inhabitants for another reason – perhaps it was his noise.[130] Francis Bacon described knife-sharpening as a 'skreeching noise', which makes 'a shivering or horror in the body' and sets the teeth on edge.[131] Henry Fielding's *Intriguing Chambermaid* (1734) included the sounds of knife-grinding and 'the whetting of saws' in her brief list of 'wild' noises.[132] The knife-sharpener's cry and the piercing shriek of his wheel marked him as one of the county's most reviled vendors.

A tinker, Anthony Sanders, late of St Giles-Without-Cripplegate, was taken to be an 'idle and vagrant person' a month after Hookam. This was despite the account that he was discovered crying in a loud voice, 'Have you

39 Marcellus Laroon (II), 'A Brass Pot or Iron Pott to mend', from *The Cryes of the City of London.*

any worke for a tinker?'[133] Often regarded as beggars, tinkers were the poorest of all hawkers and they were thought to 'make more noise than work'.[134] A letter in *The Spectator* bemoaned the tinker menace, arguing that these men had 'the Privillege of disturbing a whole street for an Hour together, with the Twancking of a brass Kettle or Frying pan'.[135] The polite, with money enough for shiny new buckets and servants to see that knives were sharpened, would not have called on the services of the impolite tinkers and grinders.

Before licensing was introduced in 1697, there were no laws governing vocal criers, and without direct recourse to law, the authorities may have manipulated vagrancy laws to silence them.[136] A vagrant was one who lacked land or master and who worked at no recognised trade, yet Sanders was clearly working as a tinker, and Hookham was, by all accounts, a knife-grinder.[137] The indictments of this pair do not seem to have resulted from beggarly conduct. Hookham and Sanders shared the same offence: their trades were both noisy and in little demand from the elite members of urban society.

Early in the seventeenth century, Nicholas Breton had noticed that 'the cry of the poore is unpleasing to the rich'.[138] Dramatising this division at the turn of the eighteenth century, William Burnaby's Lady Dainty whines about the vulgar plebeians, distinguished by their 'common Discourse . . . some Degrees above the Noise of a Drum'. She proposes a 'Government order' restricting the waking hours of the noisy common folk to 'defend' the ears of the betters 'against offensive sounds' by prohibiting 'all that had the little Breeding to rise before Eleven a Clock'.[139]

'Enter Sir Peaceable Studious with a book in his hand'[140]

The bylaws ensuring that noisy work ended at nine in the evening would have been established to ensure the citizens got enough sleep to work effectively, and perhaps to reduce the risks associated with candle illumination. The church regulations that called on congregations to be quiet were established so the word of the minister could be heard. The need for quiet to sleep and to worship had long driven the fairly meagre noise-reducing regulations in force in the cities. In the seventeenth and eighteenth centuries a new desire became apparent among the richer citizens – to have some peace in which to read and study. This desire was not entirely novel: the scholars and dons had long locked themselves into their quiet, cloistered colleges, and the lawyers had enjoyed the relative peace of their inns. The wish to retain tranquillity had played a part in the lawyers' attempts to scupper building projects near their inns. The Society of Lincoln's Inn unsuccessfully petitioned against house building nearby, arguing that it would disquiet them in their legal studies.[141] The lawyers of St Clement Danes Inn secured a royal writ of nuisance in 1632 against a tenant who enclosed part of a nearby field in the hope of erecting a bowling alley. It was feared that the noise of the patrons would disturb the lawyers in their studies.[142] The eponymous young lawyer of Fielding's *The Temple Beau* explains that he moved from chambers that were 'so noisy, they discompos'd me in my Study'.[143] However, the desire to concentrate was extending more widely into the cities, fuelled no doubt by the rise in literacy and the increasing availability of books. A letter in *The Spectator* suggested that in order to secure enough quiet to be able to study in the eighteenth century a Londoner would have needed to take lodgings 'in a very narrow Street', in order to avoid the noise of coaches and chairmen.[144] Visiting London in 1770, German traveller Georg Lichtenberg was overcome by London's bustle and noise, complaining in a letter that 'I am living here in a house where I have neither time nor peace to collect my thoughts.'[145]

As urban professionals sought quiet spaces in their homes to concentrate on their books, a desire to further segregate living and working areas grew. Wealthy amateur musicians were among those keen to ensure they had the optimum conditions in which to work. In the mid-seventeenth century a tutor suggested that the lute should be played in 'a Wainscote Roome where there is noe furniture if you can let not the Company exceed the number three or fower for the noise of a Mouse is a hinderance to that Musicke'.[146] Upon moving to a house in Manchester's Deansgate in 1661, Reverend Henry Newcome was distracted by noise when preparing a sermon, writing in his diary: 'I was ill put to it amongst the noise & clatter in the house at such a time.'[147] The citizens wanted studies, libraries, music rooms and parlours: rooms sheltered from noise.[148] Whereas studies in the sixteenth and early seventeenth centuries were often located with an exterior wall in order to maximise light, by the eighteenth century these were sometimes tucked inside the property.[149]

For many, and especially the rising middle classes and professionals, the home was becoming a haven, a space in which sounds could be controlled to some degree. Describing a much later period, Jenni Calder argues that, given the noise, dirt, filth and degradation encountered on the streets, a priority of many Victorians was to establish 'an interior environment that enables such things to be forgotten'.[150] There is evidence of the beginnings of this drive from the mid-seventeenth century. That homes were becoming quieter may have led to a heightened sensitivity towards noise; where noise was encountered it would have been less familiar and more noticeable.

The clamour of mid-eighteenth-century London was illustrated by William

40 Engraving, William Hogarth, *The Enraged Musician* (1741).

Hogarth in *The Enraged Musician* (1741).[151] This image rings with urban disorder and disharmony. The violinist (no common fiddler he) cannot work. Distracted by noise he covers his ears. Jenny Uglow, in her biography of Hogarth, described the scene as 'rapid noise'.[152] A parrot caws beside a bill-poster for Gay's *The Beggar's Opera*. Beneath the parrot a female ballad-seller, with crying babe-in-arms, sings *Lady's Fall*, a cheerless ballad.[153] A girl, rattle in hand, watches the young boy as he urinates into a hole. Close by, the piper plays his instrument and a boy demonically beats his drum, while a dog yelps at the sound of the grindstone. The knife-sharpener is not the only street worker depicted, for a dustman ringing his bell and a sow gelder, astride his horse and blowing his horn, also feature. The 'small coals' seller bawls off to the right and a pavior bashes the pavement.[154] Henry Fielding exclaimed that this engraving was 'enough to make a man deaf to look at'.[155] Besides illustrating the noises of the moment, Hogarth also skilfully shows the latent potential for noise. The urinating boy, when he is spent, will make another sound as the object attached by rope to his waist is dragged along the ground. The flag on the church shows that the bells will ring that day. The sign on the wall to the right reads 'John Long, Pewterer', a notoriously noisy metal-hammering trade. Uglow describes this print as 'curiously ambivalent', because whereas Hogarth appears to sympathise with the musician's plight, he is also criticising his arrogance. Why are his sounds more valuable than those around him? The professional musician cannot create harmony in the midst of the disharmonious plebeians.[156] He tries to make order by quietening them, and by covering his ears, but this provides no solace. The poised milkmaid, the central figure, is also depicted with an open mouth, but her beauty and grace form a contrast with the other sound-makers. The milkmaid's implied sweet sounds highlight both the artificiality of the musician's music and the noise of her companions.

The sources of noise in urban England were manifold. They included traffic, animals, revellers, inconsiderate neighbours, artisans and street musicians. The increase in traffic during the period was, in large part, necessitated by an increase in trade and industry. People engaged in certain trades generated noises that affected people living or working nearby. The contexts in which the noises were made, and the sensitivity of the listeners, determined how irritating noises were. Noises that prevented the citizens from sleeping, worshipping or concentrating were the most grating. There seems to have been a rise in the perceived levels of noise nuisance during the period, especially in London. By the end of the century, mutterings about the ambient noise of the capital seemed to get louder; citizens chuntered in their diaries, letters and journals about the jarring, exhausting sounds of their city. This heightened sensitivity might simply be attributable to the swelling population, and the knock-on effect of increased trade and traffic. In London, the psychological effects of the plague and the fire could also have played a role. The process of disillusionment might have been already underway before the crises of the 1660s, and it is difficult to divorce the architectural developments from other social changes of the period. Yet the timing of the shift seems to provide evidence for an acceleration of disquiet caused by the need to acclimatise to a newly formed city.[157] When the city's streets were repopulated after the double disaster of pestilence and fire, the bustle and commotion would have gained emphasis through juxtaposition with a previously (albeit temporarily) quiet state. Indeed, in an expanding London which serviced greater numbers of inhabitants and became more busy, the opportunities for this noise increased: there were more people, more trade and more traffic, and, for a few years, a massive amount of rebuilding. Safely installed in new, solid brick buildings, more Londoners were shielded from noise than ever before. Once people were able to escape noise by retreating indoors they would have become more attuned to it outdoors, and therefore more likely to moan about it.

The built fabric was not the only thing to change during this period. The citizens were dividing into groups: the elites, the professionals, the middling sorts, the industrious poor and the low-life types. The sounds of people with a radically different lifestyle, or with different priorities, could annoy others. The rich were especially quick to complain about the noise of poorer citizens. However, when their noises were associated with industry, specific noise legislation would have been economically unwise. The satirist Bernard Mandeville pointed out that it was not possible to remove the nuisances associated with a booming economy.[158] To corrupt the old saying, 'where there was noise, there was brass'; efforts to secure urban quiet would have been unpopular if they hampered domestic trade. All the authorities could realistically deal with were continual sources of noise such as the rowdy alehouses and the inappropriately located workshops. Denied any hope of ridding the sound environment of most undesirable sounds, wealthy Londoners had two choices: make their houses less permeable to sound, or decamp to the relative quiet of the more salubrious suburbs.

CHAPTER 6

Grotty

Many medieval oak-framed buildings had twisted into terminal dilapidation, leaving early modern urban dwellers a legacy of poorly maintained buildings. Before the Great Fire of 1666, some London houses were little more than ramshackle wooden sheds with earth floors, lacking chimneys and glazing. Post-fire legislation restricted the use of timber in construction. However, even before then the use of brick had been gathering momentum across the country; Alderman Metcalf of Leeds had his Red Hall built of brick in 1628.[1] A description of Bristol in the mid-eighteenth century dwelt on the contrast between the 'broad and handsome' streets lined with new buildings and the narrow irregular streets with houses 'like those of London, before the fire in 1666 . . . built with upper floors projecting beyond the lower; they are crowded close together, and many are five or six stories high'.[2] A visitor to Nottingham in 1725 was surprised to find a city 'constructed almost entirely with brick'.[3] However, some brick-built houses were badly constructed from poor-quality materials, and minimal attention was paid to the ground conditions before construction. Concern about the vulnerability of properties to damage by water and fire was mounting during the period. At the same time, speculative building – an increasingly popular way of making money – drove down the quality of construction, and leasing arrangements did not always ensure that householders cared for their properties. The result of these combined factors was that much of the nation's building stock was insufficiently robust to withstand the depredations of time and climate.

'Fools build houses . . .'[4]

One important factor in ensuring the longevity of a structure is to select quality materials and use them wisely. There is evidence that many of the building supplies were substandard, and that the labourers who used them were insufficiently skilled. Structural collapse was often due to defective materials. Bricks were in such great demand during peaks of construction that several manufacturers spun the clay out with impurities such as scavengers' sweepings.[5] The addition of 'Spanish' (the soil or excrement collected in the cities) or sifted ash from the scavengers' sweepings was generally acceptable, as long as the maker did not give in to the temptation to use too much, or particles that were too large.[6] 'Samel' or 'sandal' bricks were soft and friable. One expert warned that they would 'soon moulder to dirt'.[7] The Frenchman Pierre Jean Grosley, touring London in 1772, described humble houses fabricated from 'the first earth that comes to hand, and only just warmed at the fire'. Grosley peered down his nose at bricks that were bulked out by 'the excrements taken out of necessary houses'.[8]

Such practices were not confined to the capital; poor-quality building materials were common across the country and throughout the period. In 1623 a Southampton brickmaker was fined for failing to temper and fire his bricks sufficiently. These had a slack consistency, causing them to 'multer away and decay to the great damage of all those that doe use them'. The civic authorities hoped the brickhouse would fall into the hands of a more diligent brickmaker.[9] Had he turned his hand to brickmaking, Thomas Tryon, the son of a tiler and plasterer, would not have been so slapdash. In offering advice to aspirant brickmakers he stressed the importance of good preparation. His recipe for strong bricks called for brittle and dusty virgin earth to be wetted gradually, combined with good beatings and temperings, to draw out natural oleaginous qualities which were 'hid and captured in the innermost Centre' of the clay. Tryon warned that some labourers, finding a sloppy consistency easier to work, overwatered the mixture. This meant that the oily binding substances were not released and 'such Mortar becoming dry, is almost as brittle as the Earth of which it was made and is the ruin of many noble Structures'. Tryon believed that poorly constructed bricks were the norm in England; that bricks were commonly 'light, full of cracks and spungy, occasioned by the want of due Working and Management; and the mixing of Ashes and light Sandy Earth, to make them work easy'.[10]

Historians considering the rebuilding of London after the Great Fire have tended to argue that the basic housing stock was much improved as a result of the disaster. Thomas Reddaway largely endorsed this view in his classic *The Rebuilding of London after the Great Fire* (1940): 'the rickety wooden houses and the deep over-crowded basements which had been one of the curses of the old city were abolished from the rebuilt area.'[11] However, more recently some architectural historians have qualified this orthodoxy. In *The Small House in Eighteenth Century London* (2004) Peter Guillery points to the instability of some of the properties that were hastily erected to rehouse Londoners.[12] The eighteenth-century architect Nicholas Hawksmoor would have agreed with Guillery. Like John Evelyn before him, Hawksmoor believed that opportunities presented by the blank canvas left by the fire were not taken up. Instead of glorious new strong buildings, London got shoddy structures surrounded by 'Lakes of Mud and Rills of Stinking mire' that ran down 'winding crooked passages'. Hawksmoor was annoyed that the inadequate government legislation had allowed London to 'run into an ugly inconvenient self-destroying unweildy Monster'. He blamed the 'new fantasticall perishable Trash' on 'unskillful knavish Workmen', labelling them as 'brutall & Stupid'. Furthermore, Hawksmoor asserted, 'the longer they worke the worse they grow, as you may see in all the Additionall Scoundrell streets they are continually cobling up to Sell by wholesale.'[13] John Evelyn had also decried 'Vulgar Workmen, who for want of some more solid Directions, Faithful and easy Rules . . . fill as well whole Cities as Private Dwellings with Rubbish and a thousand Infirmities'.[14] Even John Wood, the celebrated architect of Bath, had problems managing his unruly labourers.[15]

Some contemporaries voiced concerns about the poor quality of much bricklaying. In his *Mechanick Exercises* Joseph Moxon advised that brick be dipped in water immediately prior to use, yet he acknowledged that this practice was often ignored because 'it makes the Workman's Fingers sore'. Moxon also worried about the 'ill custom of some bricklayers to carry up a whole storey of party walls before they work up the fronts that should be bonded with them'.[16] Such shoddy practices would result in cracks and structural weakness. Evidence of this could be concealed if the most meticulous bricklayer of the team then ran up a veneer of good bricks to conceal the rough inner walls. However, problems were stored up for the future when this outer skim was not keyed into the interior brickwork, causing sinking, slippage and bulging over time.[17] In many Georgian buildings well-worked and strong grey stock bricks were used to make fine and showy facades, while friable ashy place bricks were used 'out of sight' and bore the structural load. Such were the hazards of 'economy in speculative building'.[18]

Due to the nature of leasing contracts, terrace houses of the eighteenth century were frequently constructed on a 'stringently economical basis' and were 'technically ill built'.[19] As Peter Guillery puts it, 'in a trade that was rooted in speculation poor building was endemic.' Houses had 'in-built obsolescence'.[20] The contemporary author Richard Neve worried 'that Few houses at the common rate of Building, last longer than the Ground-lease, and that is about 50 or 60 Years'.[21] Isaac Ware also saw the nature of tenures as at the heart of the problem, as this led to houses being constructed that were not expected to see out a century, 'nay some have carried the art of slight building so far, that their houses have fallen before they were tenanted.'[22] This was not a new phenomenon – Thomas Broad, an Oxford apothecary and speculative builder, erected twenty squalid houses in St Thomas's parish in the early seventeenth century – but the scale was becoming alarming.[23] Ware identified a need for control and regulation to avoid 'continual disasters'.[24]

'No good building without a good foundation'[25]

The demand for land in towns and cities was high, and this led to building on substandard plots, former rubbish dumps, along rivers and on flood plains. The need for solid foundations and soil analysis was little understood throughout the period.[26] Isaac Ware's advice in the mid-eighteenth century concerning site preparation amounted to little more than observing the condition of the ground in pluvial conditions: 'it is a very good sign when every shower of rain does not melt it into dirt.'[27] As the cities expanded in this period, many developed on to their dumping grounds and former claypits and gravel pits.[28] Cold Bath Square near London's Mount Pleasant was 'the ironic designation for what had been a rubbish tip', and was by the 1770s approached along Laystall Street ('laystall' being a contemporary term for a dumping site).[29] It is now well known that such reused sites need special treatment but there is no evidence of contemporary concern, and the same was true of waterside areas.[30] The first house on Oxford's Fisher Row was erected in the mid-seventeenth century. It was well built, despite the low-lying and damp riverside situation, which later caused the buildings along the row to degenerate into slums.[31] The low-lying areas of Bath between the abbey and the curve of the River Avon to the west were vulnerable to flooding and the area gradually became colonised by small-scale industry and cheap housing.[32] Without careful site preparation and management, properties built on these substandard plots could have suffered subsidence and eventual collapse.

'When thy neighbour's house doth burn, be careful of thine own'[33]

City houses in the seventeenth and eighteenth centuries were generally narrow but tall, and became taller during the period to maximise the use of precious urban space. Following the Great Fire of London in 1666, the Building Act of 1667 went some way to ensuring vertical separation in an attempt to stop fires migrating, but not all tenancies were neatly contained upwards. Some spread sideways and tenants could occupy rooms laterally through buildings in an ad hoc fashion.[34]

London was not the only city to be devastated by fire in the period. In October 1644, as Royalist Oxford billeted Civil War refugees and militia, the citizens suffered a major catastrophe. Nearly one-sixth of the houses were lost in a blaze rumoured to have started when a stolen pig was roasted. A high demand for victuals kept the fires of bakers stoked longer than normal. Fuel and munitions were stored in makeshift sheds across the city.[35] The conditions suited a flaming disaster. Oxford had long enshrined laws to reduce the opportunities for fire to spread, but these were extraordinary circumstances. The blaze started outside the city walls, in the area now occupied by George Street.

It spread quickly to the south, bursting through the city wall and the North Gate, to destroy properties around Cornmarket Street. A row of butchers' shops was gutted as the fire leapt towards the parish of St Ebbe's. Here it wrought extraordinary damage to the streets filled with the premises and houses of tradesmen and craftsmen, all with supplies of stacked gorse (for fuel) that the fire consumed greedily.[36]

Urban authorities across the country periodically reminded citizens of their obligation to reduce the risk of fire. Central to this was the correct use and installation of chimneys. In Manchester the chimney of a house belonging to William Barlowe was described in 1618 as 'verye daungerous and hurtefull' to his neighbours and posed a fire risk to the whole town. Barlowe was ordered to remove it and raise the height above the building line 'so th[a]t it maye not be noyesome nor hurtfull'.[37] At the same time, neighbours of another Manchester property were fearful of the consequences of fires lit in a room without any chimney.[38] That same year, down in London, neighbours of a tobacco shop in Ram Alley, off Fleet Street, worried that there was no chimney in the shop although fires were lit there.[39] When the furnace and forge of a goldsmith and tanner on Fleet Street were judged to be a fire risk, the aldermen ordered its removal.[40] Forty years after the Fire of London, a chandler melted wax in his shop in the Cornhill area despite 'having no Chimney for that purpose'.[41] In 1740 Elizabeth Beresford, an unlicensed gin dealer in Chancery Lane, caused 'great disquietude to the Neighbourhood' by 'keeping a Charcoal Fire in a Tinn Pott sett upon bricks on a boarded Floor'.[42]

Civic authorities in the seventeenth century prohibited the storage of flammable materials. The manorial authorities in Southampton made regular pronouncements to remind bakers to take care of their fuel supplies and ensure they were stored a safe distance from bakehouses. Lax storage was deemed 'likely to endanger the whole Towne w[i]th fyer'.[43] Outbreaks of fire in Manchester sparked reminders to protect fuel supplies and keep them away from bakehouses.[44] This was to be a constant theme in the manorial deliberations – bakers were regularly and vehemently warned to keep stocks away from flames. As fires revealed a shortage of fire-fighting equipment, buckets, hooks and ropes were purchased.[45] In 1613 the Manchester leet jurors demanded that gorse be stacked at least one hundred yards from houses.[46] Such orders were repeated regularly, and backed up with fines for offenders.

Noting the combustibility of thatched roofs, the Bath Corporation ordered after 1633 that when city-owned properties with thatched roofs needed mending they should be replaced with slates or tiles.[47] At the same time the Oxford Council drafted a clause to be added to all future city leases: houses were to be henceforth 'slatted' and have chimneys built of brick or stone.[48] The lease of a tenement in Oxford's East Gate required the promise to 'slatt' it within four years.[49] After another fire destroyed seventeen houses in the

St Aldate's Parish in 1671, the city and university authorities stepped up their attempts to prevent a recurrence.[50] Threatening uncooperative businesses with boycott, the heads of colleges ordered bakers, brewers, cooks, chandlers and others to remove wood piles and fuel to a 'convenient distance from the City' or provide secure storage. Chandlers were instructed to move their melting houses 'to places where they may not annoy nor endanger their Neighbours'.[51] Orders stated that no outhouses should be thatched.[52]

A fire spread along Bath's Horse Street (now Southgate) in 1726. It was reported that the flames consumed 'the principal part of the old low thatch'd Hovels fronting the street'.[53] Fifty years later the Bath Fire Office identified buildings that were especially hazardous. These included all thatched buildings, and buildings of timber and plaster used as the premises for various dangerous trades and crafts such as china, glass and pottery making, and for the storage of straw, hay, fodder and unthrashed corn. Other properties deemed most likely to catch fire included brick or stone buildings used for the storage of incendiary material or dangerous trades. Apothecaries, tallow-chandlers, chemists, bakers, dyers, stable keepers, innkeepers, maltsters and those ware-housing hemp, flax, tallow, pitch, tar and turpentine were all on this list.[54] In 1742 Dudley Ryder, by then Sir Dudley Ryder, Attorney General, heard the case against 'Taylor' for 'keeping great quantities of gun-powder, to the endangering the Church and houses where he lived'.[55]

By the early eighteenth century some architects were taking the issue more seriously. In 1724 the architect of a house for a Bristol merchant recommended the use of transverse beams that avoided the chimney walls, and the use of wall hangings rather than the more flammable wooden wainscoting. The hangings would have acted as smoke warnings, as they would 'make more smel and sooner give the allarm in case of such accidents'. He also suggested that dressers and shelving should be made of stone 'for there is scarce a Family that do not often find themselves exposd to that hazard by the carelessness of Servants putting their Candles very often under Shelves and against Wanescot Partitions'.[56]

'Hee that repaires not a part, builds all'[57]

Structural decay could be avoided by careful attention to maintenance, but many citizens failed to care for their properties. In congested city centres, with increasing degrees of infill building, some people would have had difficulty gaining access to all the walls of their property in order to maintain them. Many landowners followed the maxim 'let him that receives the Profit repair the Inn'.[58] This proverb was at the heart of the system of beneficial leasing, which was becoming increasingly popular in this period. Beneficial leases obliged the tenant to undertake repairs and these were common among

Oxbridge colleges, landlords of much property in Oxford and Cambridge. Passing responsibility for repairs on to the tenant allowed the landlord to save the money previously spent on maintenance. The system worked well if the tenant wished to sublet the property on a yearly basis rather than dwell in it. To take advantage of a buoyant market, it was in the leaseholder's interests to maintain and improve properties, for which they could charge higher rents.[59] However, tenants without long-term interests in mind might let the property fall into decline. Considering the housing of Oxford, the travel writer Thomas Salmon noted the lack of incentive to modernise: 'lessees patch up their Clay Tenements as long as they can, and sometimes chuse to let their Leases run out, rather than be at the Charges of renewing them and repairing their Houses.'[60] Salmon decried the state of many of the private houses in Oxford, especially along the High Street. Dismissing them as 'meanly built', he thought they diminished the overall glory of the street: 'I do not remember six Houses in this fine Street, built either with Brick or Stone.' Houses to the east of Queen's College 'would disgrace an ordinary Market-Town'.[61] The close proximity of Oxford to a number of stone quarries suggests that Salmon's hunch was correct. The popularity of timber-framed houses in the seventeenth and eighteenth centuries probably reveals the short-term tendencies of the tenants, who selected the more economical and less durable materials for their rebuildings.[62]

"To bring an old house on one's head"[63]

Civic authorities condemned unsound buildings and fined citizens who failed to prop up or underpin tumbledown structures. When city-owned properties became derelict, the tenants could be obliged to make good the repairs as a condition of their lease.[64] At the close of the sixteenth century the Oxford Viewers for annoyances were ordered to inspect all city-owned buildings and force the tenants to 'repaire and bewtyfie'. Properties deemed 'ruynouse' and irreparable were earmarked for demolition.[65] One of Oxford's Carfax houses needed support in 1629 to prevent it falling down.[66] A 'decayed cottage' blighted the western end of Beef Hall Lane in 1651.[67] In 1656 the Oxford chamberlains were granted permission to re-enter property that had fallen into such disrepair that collapse was imminent.[68] The manorial authorities in Southampton frequently dealt with decaying tenements and unsteady walls. By 1613 a bakehouse on William Merriet's property had become 'so Rotten and Rewinous as it is daylie and suddainlye like to fall downe verie dangerouslye'. Worrying for the safety of 'Baggs', Merriet's neighbour, and also hapless passers-by, the jurors demanded he pull it down.[69] In 1677 John Moxon's Manchester house was 'much out of repayre leaninge upon Mr Foxes house to the damage thereof'. Moxon was ordered to set his property straight.[70] The

Oxford Viewers were called to examine a tenement in George Lane damaged by removing soil from beneath it in 1660. The wall on the west side was so undermined that it was reported to be 'like suddenly to fall', and needed to be rebuilt.[71]

A proverb warned that 'old buildings may fall in a moment'. So familiar was the sound of collapsing masonry that in 1688 Randle Holme included 'a crash, a noise proceeding from a breach of a house or wall' in a list of only nine descriptive sentences to illustrate the 'Sense of Hearing'.[72] Portmeadow House in Oxford collapsed in the early seventeenth century.[73] Among the casualties recorded in the Bills of Mortality for 1664 was one hapless soul killed by a falling house in St Mary's Whitechapel.[74] This precariousness was caused by a combination of poor-quality bricks, bad preparation, shoddy workmanship and disincentives to build well in contemporary leasing schemes.[75] The poor state of the housing stock continued through the period. Dr Johnson described London of the 1730s as a place where 'falling Houses thunder on your Head'.[76] The architect Nicholas Hawksmoor grumbled that 'we have noe City, nor Streets, nor Houses, but a Chaos of Dirty Rotten sheds, always Tumbling or takeing fire'.[77] In the 1740s, 'Props to Houses' appeared among a list of common items hindering free passage along the pavement in London.[78] A German visitor wondered if he should go into the street in 1775 during a violent storm, 'lest the house should fall in, which is no rare occurrence in London'.[79]

One author, Joseph Massie, deeming ruinous houses to be 'a Nuisance of a shameful and dangerous kind', singled out two recent London cases for particular criticism. One property was on Fleet Street and the other could be found at Pye Corner – 'both which remained, for many Years, a Terror to Passengers, both on Foot, and in Coaches!'[80] Another property, tucked away in a court off Fleet Street and belonging to 'Prat of Vauxhall', was 'very ruinous' in 1752, with 'part of it continually falling Down whereby the same is a great nusance to all the neighbours'. One nuisance property along Fleet Street was described as a 'House without a front'. It could be found between the Boars Head Alehouse and the passage to the Bolt & Tun Inn.[81] The social reformer Jonas Hanway thought London needed specific regulations to permit the pulling down of 'old houses, after they become uninhabitable'. Without these measures houses became 'the rendezvous of thieves; and at last ... fall of themselves, to the great distress of whole neighbourhoods, and sometimes to bury passengers in their ruins'.[82] In 1768 three 'Old uninhabited Houses' in the Minories were described as having fallen into such a 'ruinous and decayed condition, that the lives of his Majestys subjects passing and repassing that way are thereby greatly Endangered'.[83] Massie wondered if the current laws governing ruinous structures were tight enough, or sufficiently enforced in London. He complained that dilapidated buildings were tolerated for long

41 Old houses on Manchester's Deansgate, *c.*1750. Deansgate was a relatively upmarket part of town, but note the botched repairs to the shutters.

periods by the authorities, and when they were demolished they were frequently not rebuilt, leaving ugly gaps on the street frontage. 'If the present Laws be insufficient, a new one may enable the Chamberlain of London [and the Benches of Justices in the several Suburbs] after proper Notice given to the Proprietors or Litigants, to pull down and rebuild such Houses.'[84]

'Wind and Weather do your utmost'[85]

A contemporary author wrote that 'the first, and chiefe use of an house is to defend men from the extremity of the winde, and weather. And by the receit of comfortable light, and wholesome aire, into the same to preserve mans body in health.'[86] Unfortunately, many houses did not satisfy these requirements.

Due to a phenomenon now known as the 'urban heat island', cities and larger towns would have experienced exaggerated temperature increases. The quicksilver was raised higher by industrial activity, domestic heating, surface heat absorption and retention, and blanketing by smoke particles.[87] Inhabitants suffered in extreme temperatures because the homes of seventeenth- and eighteenth-century England were relatively poorly insulated. In inclement weather properties could become saturated, and penetrating damp would

42   Another illustration of the same Deansgate houses (see figure 41 on the previous page). The ramshackle shutters appear to be missing now.

create unpleasant internal conditions. In the colder months homes might freeze, especially if fireplaces were few.[88] With rising fuel prices in the mid-eighteenth century, some worried about the consequences for the urban poor 'who cannot afford. . . Firing enough to keep them warm in a Place where Fuel is so excessive dear'.[89] Many urban dwellers would have experienced draughts through floorboards, keyholes and gaps in partitions, down chimneys, around warped window frames and under doors. Draughty chambers led to a fashion for bed drapes, bed closets and poster beds. John Wood described the houses of Bath prior to his developments as rustic and spartan, with slight and thin doors, draughty windows and little insulation.[90] Lodging in Bath in 1726, James Brydges, the first Duke of Chandos, complained that the windows of his 'old rotton lodgings' couldn't 'keep out the least puff of wind'.[91]

Fragile buildings suffered much during storms and tempests. Samuel Pepys remarked on the 'extraordinary Winde' that battered London in February 1662, rendering it 'dangerous to go out of doors'. A lady in Covent Garden was among several killed 'by the fall of things in the streets'.[92] Gales swept the capital in 1690, leaving 'very many houses shattered, chimneys blowne downe'.[93] During a storm in 1716, Dudley Ryder lay in bed fretting, his mind cast back to the last great winds when a chimneystack had blown down into his room.[94] Even the well-constructed stone buildings of Oxford colleges were vulnerable in high winds.[95]

The inconsiderate actions of neighbours could exacerbate damage, discomfort and damp. A stone chimney erected in a passage between two Manchester houses in the early seventeenth century decayed the walls of one house, annoying the tenants with water falling from the eaves which 'rotte and washe downe the walls of the house'.[96] In 1604 a wooden gutter on a house owned by Sir John Jeffry, a Southampton citizen, was found to be decayed and 'doth putryfe & rott' the timbers of a neighbouring property.[97] Ancient custom laws prohibited building less than two feet from a land boundary in order to prevent damage or trespass caused by water falling from neighbouring roofs, although there is some evidence to suggest that this was not always rigidly enforced in cities.[98] An awareness of the potential for water run-off to cause penetrating dampness was evident in contemporary lease conditions.[99] Edward Bussell, allowed a plot of land under the Borough Walls of Bath, was not permitted to build higher than the walls, or to let rainwater fall on to nearby roofs.[100]

Watery threats to neighbouring properties also came from ground level. Samuel Pepys awoke on the morning of 29 November 1660 to discover that 'a great deal of foule water' had seeped from his neighbour's house into his parlour 'from under the particion'.[101] Neighbours who allowed their drainage to become diverted or blocked caused problems for others. A Coventry widow was presented for a nuisance because she had allowed her 'sinke' (the pit that collected waste water – sometimes filled with sand, to act like a soakaway) to let her neighbour's house become 'dampnified'.[102] A tailor called Edward Cushin coursed water into 'a Sinke not able to contain the same'. Neighbours complained that the collected water grew 'verye noysome . . . whereof maye ensue a pestilent infectious harme'.[103] In 1611 a foot of water collected in the cellar at the home of Baggs, a Southampton hatter (possibly the same Baggs who lived in fear of the fall of his neighbour's bakehouse, see above p. 137) after a neighbour diverted a watercourse.[104] The blockage of a watercourse between two houses in St Mary's Gate, Manchester, in 1622 caused filthy water to flow into a barber's shop – where minor surgery was performed.[105] In the same year, the inhabitants of a court next to the sign of the Three Broad Arrows on Fleet Street in London created a 'Sinke passinge out of the Court' that flooded the cellar of a shoemaker.[106] In 1680 servants were found to be sweeping dirt into the grate at Hanging Ditch in Manchester, risking blocking the passage of water and flooding nearby cellars. Their masters were fined.[107] Signing his lease in the early seventeenth century, the tenant of Oxford's dancing school promised to prevent damage to a neighbouring property from water cast from the school.[108]

'Our cottage . . . was musty, and most extremely rusty-fusty-dusty'[109]

Water ingress caused houses to become damp and smell musty. Saturated dunghills placed against external walls could encourage penetrating damp indoors, undermine structures and create the potential for flooding. Aware of these problems, the authorities tried to control the height of mounds, and to limit the amount of time they languished at the sides of properties. James Southern was ordered to remove his 'doung' from the side of Dorothy Bickseth's house in 1625.[110] Permission to keep a dunghill granted in 1590 for the occupier of a Manchester inn was rescinded in 1627 when the jurors were informed that the dunghill was now joined by a privy, and both damaged a nearby wall.[111] In the mid-eighteenth century Robert Grime from Manchester found that an inconsiderate neighbour had placed a dunghill against his wall. Water that channelled into the dunghill caused damage and annoyance. The problem continued for many months.[112] Heaps comprising other materials also caused structural damage. A pile of earth heaped against a house in St Dunstan-in-the-West caused damage in 1632.[113] In early seventeenth-century Manchester Charles Worsley was ordered by the manorial authorities to

43   Engraving, *Sawney in the Boghouse* (1745). Sawney is unfamiliar with the relative luxury of a privy. He puts his legs through the holes and urinates on the floor. His sword rests in the child's hole.

remove coal and timber from a neighbour's wall 'by w[hi]ch her walle ys rotted downe and her lighte stopped'.[114] In turn-of-the-century Manchester Henry Hardye's house suffered structural damage after one neighbour piled up coal against his property, and another heaped dung and timber.[115]

Citizens who situated their houses of easement against their neighbours' property could also trigger complaints and accusations of damage and nuisance. Waterclosets were not in widespread use during this period, but houses of easement or 'office' (also known as jakes, boghouses or privies) were often positioned in backyards and alleys. Some privies came with holes of various sizes, to cater to various ages (figure 43). Much of what we know about London's privies and houses of ease comes from unpleasant witness statements concerning gruesome discoveries of infants' corpses found among the filth. In the trial of Mercy Hornby for killing her newborn daughter we find details of the privy into which the child was cast. Newly constructed in the 1730s, it was six foot deep, with just over three feet of soil at the time of the incident. The seat was twenty-two inches broad with no crossbars within. The unpaved base was scattered with sand.[116]

Ideally, privies were located over running water, but in urban locations this was not often possible and so they were located above cesspits that needed to be emptied periodically.[117] Privies with cesspits or 'tubs' beneath them were best placed at the far end of properties, preferably in locations with rear access, to avoid the need to carry the waste through the house.[118] Cesspits were not watertight, enabling liquid waste to leak away and leaving just the solids to be collected by the nightmen.[119] The 'Stench and Ordure' made privies attractive only to flies and their maggots.[120] Some were topped with wooden lids to deter insects and reduce odour.[121] Those charged with cleaning them would have been well versed in the maxims 'he that wrestles with a turd is sure to be beshit' and 'the more you stir a turd the worse it stinks'.[122] This was surely the most rank of jobs. The tender-nosed Thomas Tryon got into a stew about privies, where he found the air to be 'very pernicious and baneful'.[123] The contemporary love of purgatives and the questionable source of some food supplies must have worsened the state of the privies.

The system of sewage collection and disposal was problematic, often relying on the conscientiousness of householders to keep the privies clean and the contents manageable and to stop them from overflowing. Lax care could cause stenches and fetid pollution, penetrating damp and the contamination of water supplies. The Manchester court leet heard cases of problem privies throughout the period. Some privies were described as 'noysome' and annoyed neighbouring properties.[124] One privy, at Smithy Door, was so decayed that it rotted down nearby walls.[125] In 1608, the watercourse that ran between two Manchester houses became clogged by waste from an ill-placed privy. The owner was ordered to clean it. When the privy still posed a nuisance two years later, he was ordered to remove it.[126] Another owner had the option of setting a 'tub' under his house of office, to better contain the effluent.[127] A makeshift privy located over a newly constructed 'puddle hoale' was used by a Manchester family in 1610, but annoyed the neighbours so much that the leet jurors demanded the hole and watercourse be filled in.[128] Robert Charnocke, also of Manchester, rubbed his neighbours' noses in the dirt in 1613. Not content with filling a 'Gynell or gutt[e]r' that lay between his and his neighbour's house with filth from his privy, he also kept his pigs there. These pigs 'by Rootinge' broke through into his neighbour's house. Charnocke was ordered to cease using the privy and remove his swine from the ginnel.[129]

Some privies were indoors, usually at ground-floor level. Flushing water closets, as promulgated by John Harington in his *An Anatomie of the Metamorphosed Ajax* (1596), did not prove to be popular.[130] The eighteenth century saw slightly more enthusiasm. The Duke of Chandos, updating St John's Hospital in Bath in the 1720s, requested John Wood to install water closets, but they leaked and the ensuing stench was so foul that privies were installed outdoors instead.[131] In 1770 Mr Melmoth epuipped his house in Bath with a water closet – but it was considered to be wasteful and his water supply was severed until he agreed to remove it.[132] Adjudicating over a case in King's Bench in 1705 Lord Holt pointed to the importance of keeping sound the wall separating an indoor privy from a neighbour's wall. Holt asserted that 'everyman . . . must keep in the filth of his house of office, that it may not flow in and damnify his neighbours.'[133] This was a matter close to Samuel Pepys's heart. On the morning of 20 October 1660 he stepped unto a 'great heap of turds' that had escaped from his neighbour's house of office and found themselves in Pepys's cellar. The mess was cleared up five days later, and the work charged to the Navy Treasury.[134]

'He lights his candle at both ends'[135]

Samuel Pepys suffered another annoyance during October 1660: as he stands in sewage he ponders the best location for a new window into his cellar 'in lieu of one that Sir W. Batten [a different neighbour] had stopped up'.[136] Pepys was not alone, and several nuisance cases of the period centred on building works that obscured neighbours' windows.[137] One citizen was fined for blocking the kitchen window of a Southampton town house by building a lean-to construction against his own property. Ordered to remove it, he was threatened with a further fine if he failed to comply. Four years later a tailor extended the front of his shop so far forward that neighbouring shops were shadowed by it.[138] A 1630s extension to the Oxford shambles on Queen Street obstructed traffic and cut light from 'fair houses' opposite.[139] Permission to enclose land in the centre of Bath, near the Abbey, was only granted on condition that the applicants did not erect a building there – nor a wall over seven feet high. Concern was expressed that the enclosure might 'obstruct or darken the lights of any house adjoining'.[140]

Legal opinion about the right to light was divided. In his *A briefe declaration for what manner of speciall nusance concerning private dwelling houses* (published posthumously in 1636) Robert Monson charted the arguments of four lawyers. One declared that an action could be had against a neighbour who blocks windows, preventing air from entering the house 'without which no man can live, and a house lacking light, is rather a dungeon then a house'. Another agreed, maintaining that 'no greater hurt, grieveance, or dammage can bee done to any mans Freehold, than to take away the light and ayre therof', and pointed out that light and air were commodities, stolen, in effect, by the new developer. This lawyer added the commonsense caveat that such proximate building would deny the householder an opportunity to repair the exterior of his house. Lawyers quibbled over the minimum numbers of obscured windows beyond which damage would be incurred. While some insisted that any loss of light represented a hurt and damage to the occupier, others argued that stoppages were only actionable if all windows were obscured. Worried about the consequences of an outright ban on window blocking, one lawyer argued for a need to infill between buildings when city plots were scarce and demand for housing high. Thus, in the interests of the 'maintenance of the City', some householders should accept the inconvenience of blocked windows to the sides of their properties. This lawyer cited civil laws that argued that two lights on the front and back of a house were sufficient for the entry of air and light. Another lawyer argued that to keep London 'the greatest City, and most populous in this Realm' more buildings were needed, so it was inevitable that some ancient windows would be blocked, in the name of progress.[141]

The occupants had a stronger case for appeal if the blocked windows formed part of a long-established or ancient house – 'erecting a shed so near a man's house, that it stops up his lights is not a nuisance for which an action will lie, unless the house is an ancient house, and the lights ancient lights,' noted Richard Burn in 1755.[142] William Blackstone sought to clarify the meaning of ancient and suggested, 'that is, have subsisted there time out of mind'.[143] A series of cases heard in King's Bench in the eighteenth century concerned a shed built by Mr Prior, situated so close to a property belonging to Mr Rosewell that 'it stopped up his lights'. This was a complicated case, as the defence argued that the plaintiff's house was not an ancient one (much discussion centred on what constituted the term 'time out of mind'). The court found for Rosewell, and with legal backing he proceeded to remove the nuisance by pulling down Prior's shed. Clearly the demolition got out of hand, as Rosewell was indicted for 'a riot in pulling down some part of a house, it being a nusance to his lights', and he was fined a nominal amount. The conflict did not end here, however, as a subsequent case revealed that the light continued to be blocked, and Rosewell sought redress for a continuation of the nuisance. However, by this time Prior's property had been leased to a tenant, so Rosewell sought clarification of the law, wondering whether Prior had transferred his property 'with the original wrong'.[144]

Even without the inconsiderate activities of neighbours, opportunities to enjoy natural light were limited by the Window Tax. This tax, first introduced in 1696, led to the bricking up of some existing windows and a reduction in the number of windows piercing new buildings, thus reducing opportunities for both light and air to enter rooms.[145] Tom Jones's landlady exclaimed, 'it is a dreadful Thing to pay as we do. Why now there is above forty Shillings for Window-lights, and yet we have stopt up all we could; we have almost blinded the House I am sure.'[146] The new box sash windows developed at the close of the seventeenth century meant that windows could be bigger and more elegant, helping to counter the dimming effects of the tax.[147]

The increasing sources of industrial and domestic air pollution would have further reduced available light. Georg Lichtenburg, visiting from Germany in 1775, mentioned in a letter to a friend that the street outside was 'enveloped in so thick a cloud of coal smoke' that he was 'writing by the light of a candle (at half past ten in the morning)'.[148] Artificial lighting was poor. Cheap yellow candles were made using inedible mutton or beef tallow collected from butchers and domestic kitchens. These gave a dim light.[149] Thomas Tryon noted that the first candles made in a batch were cleanest and finest, as the good tallow rose to the surface of the copper soonest. Candles made from the cruder tallow from the end of the dipping process did not burn clearly, and had a tendency to 'run and sputter'.[150] Tallow candles had a low melting point, and needed a thick wick to maximise output. The wick needed trimming regularly to prevent it getting soaked with fat and guttering (when tallow trickles down the candle shaft), or generating acrid smoke.[151] The girth of the wick was important: 'a great Candle with a little wick, will yield a dim and stupid Light for a long while together, and yet consume itself in the End.'[152] Rush lights, the poor man's candle, were made from soaked rushes dipped in animal fat, and could be lit at both ends (hence the phrase 'to burn the candle at both ends'). City dwellers used them but they were highly inefficient.[153] Cheap candles burnt very quickly or blew out in draughty locations, spawning the expression 'to wink like a farthing Candle and go out in a snuffe'.[154]

Robert Hooke proudly recorded his invention of a candlestick that kept the flame at the same height, thus reducing flicker, but few were able to utilise this invention as they could afford only minimal lighting gadgetry.[155] The constant flickering of candlelight was not conducive to the health of the eyes. Samuel Pepys mentioned eyestrain in his diary, and on one occasion excused his entry, written 'slubberingly', on account of his concerns that his candle would not last out.[156] The light cast by candles could be enhanced through the use of glass globes and mirrors (there is a reflecting sconce to the left of the scullion of Christ Church, Oxford, in John Riley's painting – see figure 26 on p. 73). Bernardino Ramazzini advised those who burned candles at both ends in their pursuit of study to avoid small and narrow rooms and splash out on wax candles or olive oil lamps that burned more brightly and slowly.[157] On moving to London in 1762 James Boswell resolved to burn wax candles, to take advantage of the 'finer light'. He also planned to lock them away when they were not in use.[158] James Woodforde was excited to receive the remains of the college altar candles on Boxing Day 1761, they 'being wax'.[159] In basement rooms, or chambers in narrow alleys and courts the opportunities for natural light were especially limited. These were commonly used as craftsmen's houses and workplaces. However, wax candles would have been prohibitively expensive for most craftsmen, who would have used the cheaper tallow ones. Describing working conditions in 1747, Mr Campbell noted of the tailor that 'he ought to have a strong sharp sight, which is much tried by working at Candle-light'.[160] Sugar-bakers and brewers worked many hours by candlelight, and were listed as major consumers of candles by the tallow-chandlers in the early eighteenth century.[161]

'All in on[e] gallroy called the Dark Entrey'

In order to maximise the light, buildings in cities were frequently only one room deep.[162] Ralph Treswell's survey of a complex of buildings on London's Monkwell Street (1612) shows a group of five houses on a one-room plan, in a court, each two storeys plus a garret high (see figure 44 on p. 148).[163] The shallow depth of these houses would have countered some of the darkening effects of being shoehorned into a small court. Building smaller properties in courts behind larger houses fronting the street would have created collections of dark little dwellings.

Expanding urban populations lead to cramped accommodation. When people lived cheek-by-jowl in these crowded courts the opportunities to annoy neighbours were considerable.[164] Giles Jacob presented a basic outline of the laws designed to protect people from the nuisances created by their neighbours. He included discharges from glasshouses, brewhouses and houses of office among the annoyances, and detailed the ways that the furnace of a tallow-chandler near an inn created a 'Stink' that annoyed the guests.[165] Neighbours near to houses in which beasts were kept or slaughtered would have endured stench and noise.[166] Jacob includes among his list of nuisances keeping pigs 'in a Hog-Stye near a Man's Parlour, whereby he loses the Benefit of it'. Such nuisances were actionable on the grounds of 'hindring of the wholesom Air, as well as for corrupting of it'.[167] A pigsty erected in the 'entrie'

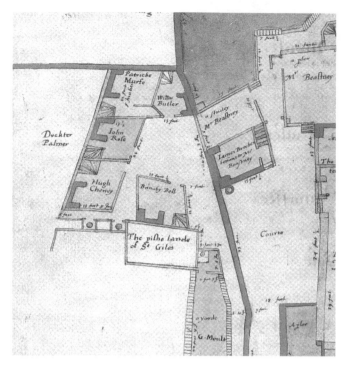

44   Five houses in a court off Monkwell Street – each property is one room deep. Detail from Ralph Treswell's survey of St James's Hermitage/Lambe's Chapel, Monkwell Street, 1612, Clothworkers' Company Plan Book, 37.

of a Manchester house was reported to cause 'great annoyance and danger of infection'.[168] Those living near Lewis Smart's huge piggery on London's Tottenham Court Road described how servants fell sick and resigned on account of the smell, which 'Drives thro' the walls of the houses'. Visitors to the house opposite were forced to hold their noses, and one neighbour explained how the fumes had dirtied newly laundered linen and tarnished plate. Properties were devalued by their proximity to the site, and even in Great Russell Street inhabitants could not use their front rooms due to the stench.[169] When space was scarce, infill building created courts of properties that shared facilities, party walls, boundaries, privies, chimneystacks and watercourses. Opportunities for conflict would have been legion.[170]

The houses that filled the spaces behind the finer houses fronting the central streets (where once stood orchards, yards and gardens) were also likely to be shabby and poorly constructed.[171] Many houses were built to resemble three boxes placed on top of each other: one room wide and one room deep on three storeys. The house on a one-room plan was more common than the surviving evidence suggests. One architectural historian has described it as 'an utterly standard form of housing' in the eighteenth century.[172] Small houses in dark courts would have provided unpleasant accommodation. Parishioners of St Margaret, Lothbury, complained in 1637 about a draper who owned five small tenements, 'all in on[e] gallroy called the Dark Entrey . . . being so noisome and unheathfull a place as few the like in London'.[173] The tenements down the dark, nasty, mean alleys and courts described by John Strype in his update of John Stow's *Survey* would have been dingy and poky.[174]

Richard Neve contrasted the light staircases, sash windows and high ceilings that were increasingly common in new buildings at the turn of the eighteenth century with the old properties with low ceilings and small openings for windows – 'Rooms built at random,' many steps between rooms, 'one would think the People of former Ages, were afraid of Light and good Air; or loved to play at hide and seek'.[175] Small properties were also common in other cities. As Oxford University expanded in the early seventeenth century new poor-quality properties were erected hastily to accommodate workers in the service economy.[176] Oxford Council expressed a disdain for one-roomed 'squabb houses' which made poor use of the available space, and gave streets a squalid and slummy feel.[177] In 1640 the university weighed in, blaming townsmen for building too many squab houses that were 'unseemlie to look to'.[178] John Wood bemoaned the poor quality of housing along Bath's Walcot Street: instead of finding it 'covered with Habitations for the chief Citizens, it is filled, for the most part, with Hovels for the Refuse of the People'. This formed a contrast with Horse Street (now Southgate), where a fire of 1726 had consumed 'the old thatch'd Hovels that formerly lined the Sides', allowing for finer replacements.[179]

Accommodation for the poorest urban dwellers was often gloomy and cramped. The first floor of a house of multiple occupation would have been the most desirable, 'rents falling as tenants rose or descended the staircases'.[180] While wealthier citizens occupied the better floors, poorer families and individuals crowded into dank basements and poky garrets. It is difficult to assess the extent of overcrowding, but clues suggest that cramped accommodation was quite common among the poor. A chamber of one of the properties surveyed by Ralph Treswell in 1612 was 'divided into diverse parcels wherein dwell diverse widows, 20' × 17''. In 1609 Sir John Parker divided a large house in London's Whitefriars into twenty tenements, bringing 'poor people' into the neighbourhood.[181] The central Millgate area of Manchester was very crowded – many houses were divided.[182] Not only were rooms shared; a share of a bed could be leased. Henry Fielding heard about houses 'accommodated with miserable Beds from the Cellar to the Garret, for . . . Twopenny lodgers' in the parish of St Giles-in-the-Fields. Beds were shared by men and women 'often Strangers to each other'. One property housed fifty-eight people 'the stench of whom was . . . intolerable'.[183] Three adults and a child shared a bed in a room above a ginshop in St John Wapping in the late 1730s.[184]

45 Engraving, William Hogarth, *The Distressed Poet* (1737). The poet's cupboard is bare, his garret room is dark and shabby, and his wig is itchy.

Live-in servants of the finer houses would have occupied the worst rooms – small garret rooms or spaces in the basement, near the kitchen, or even in outbuildings.[185] Garrets, basements and cellars were not comfortable spaces. Garrets were 'notoriously undesirable', being 'draughty, low-ceilinged and often unheated'.[186] According to one author, garrets were inhabited by 'married *Coblers, Porters*, and *Penny-Post-Men*' in the eighteenth century.[187] If the room had windows they would have been small and may have been partially obscured by a low parapet wall.[188] Garrets could be stifling hot and dry in the summer. They would also have been noisy in high winds.[189] Garret rooms with fireplaces would be most affected by smoke issuing into the room after being forced back down the chimney by winds.[190] Oxford saw a proliferation of cocklofts during the period.[191] These were tiny rooms in the roof space above the garret, usually accessed by a ladder. They were more exposed to the elements than other parts of the building and would not have had fireplaces, so would have been very cold.[192]

Rooms at the top of houses may have been uncomfortable, but rooms at the very bottom were worse. Basement storeys were increasingly sunk below ground in the expanding cities of early modern England.[193] The pit provided material for bricks, and the space made economical use of valuable city land.[194] An architect of the mid-eighteenth century acknowledged that these spaces were 'damp, unwholesome, and uncomfortable'.[195] Many were uninhabited and used only for storage. However, some of the poorest people were housed in basement spaces. Jonas Hanway described cellars as 'subterranean habitations of the poor'.[196] Even prestigious Oxford colleges had damp basements. One of Magdalen College's benefactors had provided four beds to give temporary shelter to 'any pore distressed people that are fitt to be pittied' in the basement of a building to the west of the tower. At the close of the sixteenth century this hostel was damp and unwholesome in the winter, rendering it unusable when there was greatest demand for accommodation. The beds were 'subject to rottennes', and eventually the chamber was boarded, the college records, remarking that this was to make it more comfortable for the poor and for the 'safetie of our beddes'.[197] Isaac Ware argued that when basement rooms were to be occupied by servants the rooms should be boarded – for the 'necessary care of these peoples healths'.[198] Basements were saturated by condensation, poor ventilation, rising damp and water ingress. They were stuffy and clammy on hot days, and cold and dank in the winter. Parts of Westminster were prone to flooding from the Thames. In March 1660 the inhabitants of cellars in King's Street were flooded out of their rooms.[199] In a petition of 1750 a gentleman appealed to the City to improve drainage, as some citizens were experiencing cellar flooding from springs in the Norton Folgate liberty. In the house of the petitioner's father there used to be three to four feet of water in the cellars: 'the servants used to punt themselves along in a washing tub from the cellar stairs to the beer-barrels to draw beer.'[200]

'No man will willingly bear with a smoky house'[201]

The location and layout of a dwelling were important factors influencing its cleanliness. Old wives warned, 'chuse not a house neere an inne, (viz for noise) or in a corner (for filth)'.[202] Houses in courts or alleys would have suffered from trapped influxes of dust and mud, pulled in by the wind. When houses were sufficiently large, smelly and dirty rooms such as kitchens could be located away from living areas, but most dwellings were too small for such elaborate layouts. Whatever the size of their house, householders struggled to keep their interiors smelling sweet and looking clean.

With open fires providing most of the heating, filthy discharges of soot and smut clung to interiors. Robert Clavering provided a troubleshooting guide for those who were affected by smoky fireplaces by explaining how chimneys drew air through houses.[203] He castigated negligent builders and sympathised that 'no situation in life can be more uncomfortable and unhealthy than residing in a smoky house: it is not only offensive to our sensations, but destroys all domestic enjoyment.'[204] Another expert argued that funnels needed to be perpendicular, and lofty enough to carry smoke away.[205] Clavering disagreed, asserting that a kink in some part of the funnel was 'absolutely necessary' as perpendicular chimneys were vulnerable to the absorption of 'great drops of hail, snow, and rain' which fell 'freely to the bottom, repelling the smoke a-long with it into the room'. Straight funnels carried a higher risk of soot deluge. Clavering identified clogged chimney pots as the cause of many smoky fireplaces, worsened by the sweep's fear of going high enough to reach the blockage, resulting in lackadaisical sweeping and increased smoking.[206]

Chimneys needed regular sweepings, to avoid the dual risks of sudden ash deluge and chimney fires. Anthony Wood had his chimney swept in May 1687 at a cost of threepence.[207] Chimney sweeps offered their services in the mid-eighteenth century, but some thrifty citizens tried to clean their own chimneys by deliberately setting them alight. In the mid-eighteenth century, fearful of fatal consequences, the Manchester authorities tried to extinguish this hazardous practice. The bellman was dispatched to broadcast a prohibition.[208] Clavering thought that chimney pots were overused and 'attended with a long train of disagreeable, and even dangerous circumstances'. He listed various examples of damage and injury caused by falling pots. In one case the sweep became stuck in a chimney pot and both fell into a pile of rubbish in the yard below. The sweep was hospitalised, the pot broke, and a maid who had been washing in the yard fell into an apoplectic fit.[209]

Coal was a dirty fuel option; it was more 'unctious and weighty' and the waste particles stuck readily to sides of chimneys and created more smoke than timber.[210] Coal had been an unpopular domestic fuel in the sixteenth century, initially used only as a last resort by the poorest citizens when timber supplies dwindled. However, as prices plummeted during the seventeenth century, domestic use increased; estimates suggest a twentyfold increase between 1580 and 1680.[211] The consequences of burgeoning coal use were dire. Coal dust smutted interiors, and ruined books, furniture and paintings. John Evelyn fulminated against the 'pernicious smoke . . . superinducing a sooty Crust or furr upon all that it lights, spoyling the moveables, tarnishing the Plate, Gildings and Furniture, and Corroding the very Iron-bars and hardest stone with those piercing and acrimonious Spirits which accompany its Sulphure'.[212] Smut got into all the nooks and crannies: however hard the owner tried to seal up their treasured collections in cabinets, they became besmutted 'as if it were the house of some *Miller*, or a *Bakers* Shop, where the *Flower* gets into their Cupboards though never so closely and accurately shut'.[213] On a tour of the Westminster Hall buildings Lodewijk Huygens found them all to be 'very dirty and grimy' and he dismissed the Abbey as 'narrow and very dirty'.[214] Little had changed half a century later, the Painted Chamber underwhelmed Zacharias Conrad von Uffenbach: the ceiling that gave this room its name could 'scarce be seen for the smoke', and his eye cast down at the 'uncommonly ugly and worn tapestries'. In the Upper Chamber he viewed tapestries 'so wretched and tarnished with smoke that neither gold nor silver, colours nor figures can be recognized'.[215]

'The taste of the kitchen is better than the smell', and in larger houses it would have been possible to put sufficient distance between kitchens and living areas to avoid kitchen smells and smeech from permeating the whole house.[216] The architect Roger Pratt advised that kitchens be placed at a distance from living quarters, so that the household would not be 'disturbed with the least noise or smell from them'.[217] The ideal kitchen layouts outlined in architectural works were inapplicable in the small spaces typically occupied by city tenants. The kitchen area was usually at the rear of the ground floor, or sometimes in the basement. Kitchens frequently had separate external entrances, for easy access to fuel supplies, water, yards and gardens, and were, as a consequence, sullied by the trampling of dirty feet and the ingress of street dust.[218] The kitchen would have been the sootiest room of the house. In his *Counterblast to Tobacco* (first published in 1604) King James I likened tobacco smoking to the kitchen – both were soiled and infected 'with an unctious and oylie kind of soot'.[219]

'Fine dressing is a usually foul house swept before the windows'[220]

Diligent householders fought a perpetual battle against dust, smut, soot and excreta. Foot scrapers were placed outside houses, but given the state of the streets much mire would have been carried indoors on footwear. One architect advised his client to use brown paving indoors rather than 'Portland or other White stone' in a city with few sedan chairs, as street dirt sullied and stained the stone, so the householder can 'never enjoy that beauty they purchase at excessive prices'.[221] Cleaning would have been a difficult task for some. The poorest citizens would not be able to afford to pay to be connected to a private water supply, and would need to fetch their water from public conduits or pumps located in courts and yards.

Thomas Tryon, an early compulsive cleaner, started a one-man mission to spread the cleaning gospel in the late seventeenth century. It is easy to visualise Tryon scrubbing the stoop and washing the pots. In *A Treatise of Cleanliness in Meats and Drinks* (1682) Tryon claimed that 'Cleanliness in House, especially in Beds, is a great Preserver of Health.' His argument ran thus: as beds are usually in the corners of rooms where dust and dirt collects, they are not subject to the refreshing powers of circulating air. 'In these shady dull Places, Beds are continued for many years, and hardly see the Sun or Elements.' Tryon maintained that beds in cities and large towns were especially prone to being unclean, due to the humid and sulphurous air. New clean linen was only the first step. Tryon also argued that beds should also be repositioned so they lay in circulating air, and windows be opened for most of the day. At night, Tryon advises keeping window and bed curtains open, to aid the passage of air and prevent the room becoming musty.[222]

Some householders were quite lax with their domestic chores. The fable of 'The spider and the gout' (1708) tells the tale of a spider finding comfortable accommodation in the hard lodgings of a 'poor Wretch' with a chaff-strewn floor. At home with a beggar she spreads her web in 'ev'ry Corner' and feeds handsomely on 'intangl'd Flyes'. The only breaches in her web are caused by the 'ruffing Air' of draughts.[223] Eliza Haywood's bustlingly bossy *A Present for a Servant-Maid* (1743) admonished the slutty idle maid who is neither 'thoroughly clean in her own Person nor the House'. Such a servant will sweep things under the carpet, and maintain a veneer of cleanliness, while putting off a thorough spring clean. Haywood warns that her actions will find her out in the end, as her task will become insurmountable and 'every thing infallibly shews the Slut'. Dismissal would follow.[224] John Clayton hectored the dirty poor in his *Friendly Advice to the Poor* (1755). He nagged that 'A Roof beset with Cobwebs, Walls bespattered with every Kind of filth, and Furniture covered with Dust and Dirt, is a nauseous loathsome Sight, a Matter utterly inconsistent with Reputation, and totally destructive of Health and Comfort.' Bemoaning how common such houses were, this author held that only charitably inclined respectable people would enter such squalid abodes, and argued that only half an hour of 'washing, sweeping and brushing' each morning would 'maintain the Face of Decency for the Day. And therefore the neglecting it bespeaks a Love of Filth, a beastly Delight in Wallowing in the Mire'.[225] Clayton would not have grubbied his hands with housework; maids would have cleaned for him.

Householders struggled to contain infestations of vermin. The Pepys household welcomed a cat at the end of 1660, the house being 'much troubled with mice'. The cat cannot have been the efficient mouser Pepys had hoped for. Just nineteen days later he purchased two mousetraps. Two years later, while he was adding an entry to his diary, a mouse scampered across his desk.[226] The gradual (or sudden in London's case) removal of timber-framed houses from the urban streetscape during the period made life slightly harder for vermin; even the toughest rat could not gnaw through the bricks separating houses. However, mice and rats did remain common features of city life. Foods were often stored high up in suspended containers, or in closed cupboards to keep them from vermin.

Insects proliferated too. John Southall, manufacturer of a liquor for killing 'Buggs and Nits', claimed to have based his product on a recipe learnt in Jamaica. The bugs Southall sought to eradicate were wood-boring beetles, and he claimed that London had suffered from increasing numbers of bugs for the sixty years preceding 1730. He attributed this growth to the imports of deal timbers, used widely to furnish interiors in houses rebuilt after the fire. Experimentation led him to observe that these bugs were choosy, and preferred deal timbers to the traditional oaks used previously. Arguing that bugs affected seaports more than inland settlements, Southall suggested they came from 'hotter climates'. Noting a need to tackle not just the bugs, but their eggs and larvae too, Southall considered the best time for action was winter. However, as this was the time they were least troublesome, many citizens did not take action then, and therefore did not maximise their efforts. In addition to applying liberal quantities of his product to fabrics and furniture, Southall made other suggestions about how to minimise infestations. He advised that all furniture be inspected for the tell-tale signs of holes and excreta. The laundress's baskets should be banished for ever from the house, as they harboured bugs in quantity. He suggested that the amount of paste and wood in houses be limited, and frowned upon the recycling of old wainscoting, doors and chimneypieces into new dwellings, a common practice among builders.[227] In 1756 *Harrop's Manchester Mercury* ran an advert for a book detailing how to rid houses of all manner of vermin. Its wide-ranging troubleshooting covered domestic infestations of 'Adders, badgers, birds, catterpillers, earwigs, flies, fish, foxes, frogs, gnats, Mice, otters, Pismires [ants], Pole-cats, Rabbits, Rats, Snakes, Scorpions, snails, spiders, Toads, Wasps, Weasles, . . . Moles, Worms in houses and gardens, Buggs, Lice, & Fleas &c.'.[228]

Despite legislation and technical developments, by 1770 many citizens lived in poor housing and in fear of fire. Comfort depended not only on the quality of the dwelling, but also on the location of the property and the allocation of space within it. Neighbours could add to the discomfort through their inconsiderate behaviour, or just by their close proximity. Some buildings were a danger to life and limb. Thomas Atwood, a Bath plumber and property developer, died in 1775 when the floor of an old house gave way.[229] More long-term health implications were attached to some poor-quality housing. Dampness, smoke and poor ventilation are now known to contribute to respiratory disease. The Duchess of Newcastle likened the body to houses 'that are musty, and fusty, and smoky, and foul, for want of Air to sweeten them, and full of Spiders, and Cobwebs, and Flyes, and Moths, bred from the dusty dirty filth therein, for want of Vent to purge them', especially in the winter months, when doors and windows are generally shut up.[230] The eminent physician Richard Mead argued that pestilential contagion was bred in the homes of the poor where they are 'stifled up too close and nasty'. Because 'nothing approaches so near to the first Original of *Contagion*, as Air pent up, loaded with Damps, and corrupted with the Filthiness that proceeds from *Animal Bodies*', Mead recommended that the overseers of the poor visited homes. He suggested that some poor be sent to 'better Lodgings', while others were encouraged to be 'more *cleanly* and *sweet*'. Mead reasoned that 'as *Nastiness* is a great source of *Infection*, so *Cleanliness* is the greatest Preservative: Which is the true Reason, why the Poor are most obnoxious to Disasters of this kind.'[231] Although they understood little about the means of infection, by the eighteenth century many people were aware of the dangers posed by poor sanitation, and were especially concerned about the risks of close contact during epidemics. Some lawyers even argued that the division of a town house to accommodate more poor people might be judged a common nuisance 'by reason whereof it will be more dangerous in the Time of Infection of the Plague'.[232] Eyes that were strained with the dim lighting could not fully perceive the dirt of accommodation that frequently failed to defend its occupants from the elements, failed to permit the entry of adequate lighting, and failed to 'preserve mans body in health'.[233]

CHAPTER 7

Busy

Plague epidemics temporarily depopulated London's streets and during one of the worst, in August 1665, the Reverend Thomas Vincent preached:

> Now there is a dismal solitude in London-streets . . . Now shops are shut in, people rare and very few that walk about, in so much that the grass begins to spring up in some places, and a deep silence almost in every place, especially within the walls; no rattling coaches, no prancing Horses, no calling in customers, nor offering Wares; no *London* cries sounding in the ears; if any voice be heard, it is the groans of dying persons, breathing forth their last, and the funeral knells of them that are ready to be carried to their graves.[1]

Both Samuel Pepys and John Evelyn remarked about the changes to street life caused by this epidemic. On 8 August Pepys wrote with dismay that the streets of London were 'mighty empty'.[2] A month later Evelyn described London and the suburbs from Kent Street to St James's as 'a dismal passage & dangerous, to see so many Cofines exposed in the streetes & the streete thin of people, the shops shut up, & all in mournefull silence'.[3] The following month Pepys found that although the Exchange was 'pretty full', the streets were empty and the shops were shut.[4] These passages are poignant. A city notorious for its bustle and noise had been stilled and silenced. Ordinary life fell into relief.

The city streets in the seventeenth and eighteenth centuries were usually heavily peopled during daylight hours. Occupants spilled out of their crowded homes and possessed the urban spaces. The streets rang with the broadcasting of municipal news, canvassing, debate and conversation. Doorstep tittle-tattle blended with rowdy banter and marketplace barter. The author of *Hell upon Earth: or the Town in an Uproar* (1729) described the hurly-burly: 'Citizens Wives, some at their Dram Bottles, and others criticising upon one another's Dress and Behaviour at Church, and throwing out little Portions of slander as a whet before Dinner'.[5] Street criers and hawkers strove to make their voices heard above the din. Edward Guilpin captured the scene in *Skialetheia* (1598):

> Heere scolds an old Bawd, there a Porter grumbles.
> Heere two tough Car-men combat for the way,
> There two for looks begin a coward fray,
> Two swaggering knaves here brable for a whore,
> *There brauls an Ale-knight for his fat-grown score.*

This 'hotch-potch of so many noyses' was occasionally surmounted by a crescendo – the fury of the mob, the clangour of bells, or the trundle of cartwheels.[6]

Daily life continued amidst a hubbub of activity. London was experiencing elephantiasis, constantly expanding its size, population and industrial output. Thomas Platter, visiting in 1599, noted that London was 'so populous . . . that one simply cannot walk along the streets for the crowd'.[7] Arriving in 1762 James Boswell noticed the 'hurry and splendour' of the city, with its 'dirty streets' and 'jostling chairmen'. He wrote of his journey to Fleet Street, 'the noise, the crowd, the glare of the shops and signs agreeably confused me . . . My companion [in the coach] could not understand my feelings. He considered London just as a place where he was to receive orders from the East India Company.'[8] During the eighteenth century the expanding northern towns were also becoming busy and overcrowded. The poet John Dyer described 'busy Leeds' where 'all . . . is in motion'.[9] Immigrants swelled the population and workforce. Arrival in the busy cities would have given the migrants a jolt. They would have needed to alter their spatial awareness in order to tolerate close proximity to other people.

Growth in trade, commerce and population meant more carts and coaches, a greater stress on the narrow central streets, and damage to the road surfaces.[10] Citizens strolling about needed to keep an eye on the traffic that filled the streets in increasing numbers. Pedestrians faced other hazards too – some paving was ankle-twistingly bad and deep puddles lurked on street corners. There was a weak demarcation between footway and carriageway: few pavements were raised, and posts were often ineffective and sometimes obstructive.

'Mingled with the jostling Crowd'[11]

The command of respect on the streets depended 'wholly upon Appearance'. If pavement decorum was observed the rich man (identified by his fine coat and 'nicely powder'd Wig, and lac'd Linnen'[12]) would have walked nearest the wall, and thus been saved from the ignominy of chamber pot splatter and carriage wheel spray (although he would have been more at risk of falling down unhatched cellars or over projecting steps). Decorum was not always observed. Tom Brown gave an exaggerated account of the disordered state of London's streets in *Amusements* (1700):

> Here a Sooty Chimney-Sweeper takes the Wall of a Grave *Alderman*, and a *Broom-Man* Justles the *Parson* of the Parish. There a Fat Greasie *Porter*, runs a Trunk full Butt upon you, while another Salutes your Antlers with a Flasket of *Eggs* and *Butter*. *Turn out there you Country Put*, says a *Bully*, with a Sword two Yards long jarring at his Heels, and throws him into the Channel.[13]

Matt Bramble found that in the crowds of Bath 'a very inconsiderable proportion of genteel people are lost in a mob of impudent plebeians, who have neither understanding nor judgement, nor the least idea of propriety.'[14] Another commentator saw 'Drunken Quarrels at all Corners of the streets amongst the Mob about precedency'.[15] These fictional accounts contain a kernel of truth.

The social classes mixed on the streets: the tattered and torn rubbed shoulders with the well-heeled rich. The hurry of the jostling city was discombobulating.[16] Bernard Mandeville remarked on the 'numberless swarms of People that are continually harassing and tramping' through the streets.[17] Lydia Melford, Matt Bramble's niece, was taken aback by the activity on London's streets. Surprised by the 'crowds of people that swarm in the streets', she thought that 'some great assembly was just dismissed, and wanted to stand aside till the multitude should pass'. Lydia soon realised that this was normal. Her uncle placed more stress on the sheer frenzy of the throng 'everywhere rambling, riding, rolling, rushing, jostling, mixing, bouncing, cracking, and crashing, in one vile ferment of stupidity and corruption – All is tumult and hurry.' Pedestrians 'run along as if they were pursued by bailiffs'.[18] Bramble does not see individual bodies, but rather an indiscriminate morass, a single beast – a heaving, sweating and stampeding crocodile.

Wealthy citizens were particularly unnerved by the way their body space was invaded on the streets. This was fuelled by fears of being dirtied. It was hard to keep ruffles clean and wigs spruce in the smutty city streets – especially when dirty artisans brushed past. Note the 'sooty' sweeper and the 'Greasie Porter' in Brown's account above. In the anonymous poem *The Diseases of Bath* (1737), the reader is taken on journey to the Pump Room in Bath where 'Tumult, Hurry, Noise and Nonsense blend, / T'annoy the Senses, and the Soul t'offend!' Here the poet twists contemporary concerns about the unwashed poor, and turns them against the unwashed rich. The throng is comprised of 'Foppish Slovens' who 'stink and shine' in their 'dirty Shirts and Tinsel' and ladies hot from their beds, stewing and steaming as 'Noisy as Goslings'. The walker is 'Forc'd to wade thro' a Mob of unwash'd Beaus / At th'ill Expense of elbows and of Cloaths'.[19]

The streets were the venues for commerce, entertainment and civic displays. Crowds formed quickly around street performers and spectacular salesmen, increasing the bustle and jostle. Street entertainments presented opportunities for time-wasting. Advising servant maids in the mid-eighteenth century, Eliza Haywood warned that 'a Croud gathered about . . . a Pedlar, a Mountebank, or a Ballad-singer, has the Power to detain too many of you.'[20] Others were more concerned about the obstacles to free passage presented by such performances. The constables of Middlesex were ordered to apprehend all persons 'driving and carrying wheelbarrows' or carrying gaming equipment such as dice, as these obstructed the way and hindered pedestrians.[21] The barrister William Hawkins explained that 'all common Stages for Rope-Dancers, and also all Common Gaming Houses, are Nusances . . . not only because they are great Temptations to Idleness, but also because they are apt to draw together great Numbers of disorderly Persons, which cannot but be very inconvenient to the Neighbourhood.'[22]

City authorities strove to limit crowds gathered without civic approval. The use of signalling equipment such as bells and drums, used by the civic officials when they needed to gather the citizens to disseminate important information, was carefully controlled.[23] A gentleman who rang the common bell of Liverpool in 1637 'whereby a great Rout was made' was given a hefty fine as an example to others.[24] A Portsmouth victualler got into trouble for 'riding through the town and Garrison at noonday with a trumpet sounding before him'.[25] Joseph Hambling, 'he being a Vagrant and a prize fighter going about the streets with a drawn sword in his hand & a drum beating thereby causing a great Mob and tumult', was put to labour in London in 1721.[26] In the same year two men, both 'comon shewers of poppet shows', were taken by the constable for 'beating of a Drum and playing on a violin in order to Entice and draw people together in a disorderly and Tumultuous manner'.[27]

Companies travelling the country seeking audiences for dancing bears, or gruesome or odd sights such as deformed people or mutant animals, would often try to attract attention to their spectacle using musical instruments. The authorities were quick to intervene. Humfry Bromely was permitted to show 'a strange Child with two heades' to Norwich audiences in 1616, but he was prohibited from sounding 'any Drumme' or using any other means to 'drawe company' besides displaying an image of the child. One week later their time was up, and Bromely and his wife were threatened with the Vagrancy Act and shooed out of the city. [28] In 1686 a Dutchman called John Angilgrove was given permission to show animals in Norwich, but he was ordered to desist from beating a drum or sounding a trumpet.[29]

The authorities were keen to limit the size of crowds and the frequency with which they gathered, because of the potential for outbreaks of mayhem. One elite member of Manchester society commented on the inevitability of bad behaviour when the rabble crowded together in vast numbers – to expect them to behave 'is a contradiction to the sence and experience of all mankind'.[30] The ordinary jostling and shoving of the market-day crowd could quickly swell into something more sinister; the streets were the breeding ground for mobs.[31] Those in power were rattled when groups of the powerless joined together. Henry Fielding described the mob as 'that very large and powerful body which form[s] the fourth estate in this community'.[32] A proverb warned, 'Take heed of the wrath of a mighty man, and the tumult of the people.'[33] Mobs were unpredictable – passers-by could get sucked into the vortex of distraction, and their combined might could threaten those in power. Conrad Von Uffenbach, visiting Tothill Fields to see the election of a Member of Parliament in 1710, was amazed by the behaviour of the crowds, and exclaimed that 'people behaved so wildly that one might have been in Poland . . . Since the tumult was so great . . . we remained in the coach . . . for we should else have been in great danger from the horses and scuffing that was going on.'[34]

Crowds and mobs offered anonymity for those wanting to voice criticism against the powerful, and a refuge for youthful high spirits. The discontented and the troublesome could retreat into the heart of the mob to avoid identification. A large reward was offered for information leading to the discovery of the 'idle people' who pelted the Duchess of Bedford with 'dirt and cabbage stalks' as she traversed Bath's Abbey Green in 1743.[35] The various civic fathers found that attempts to quash squib-throwing, whereby small fireworks were thrown at unsuspecting passers-by to shock them, absorbed much time.[36] In 1738 'several Rude and Disorderly Persons' threw 'Squibs, Serpents and other Fireworks' in Cheapside. To prevent future offences the Court of Aldermen set aside money to reward citizens who apprehended squib throwers.[37] Michael Dalton oulined the law: 'making, selling, Throwing or Firing Squibs, or other Fireworks in any Street, Highway or Passage, or into any House or Shop, shall be judged a common Nuisance.'[38]

The sedentary and slow experiences of the low-life mud-slinging mobs were thrown into great relief by the busy nature of the artisans, professionals and merchants. Among the fast-flowing and purposeful masses, people drifting with no ultimate location in mind, loitering on the street or begging in fixed locations, attracted the ire of the citizens. John Clayton rebuked the idlers who hung aimlessly about the Manchester marketplace while trades offered opportunities that they chose to ignore. Clayton whined about the multitudes of idle poor cluttering 'our Streets, our Markets, nay, our very Churches', crowding, wasting time, gazing and spectating. He wondered 'What swarms of Loyterers are to be met with upon every Occasion of publick Solemnity?' Clayton could not understand why, given the ample employment prospects of the town and the wealth of charitable institutions, the streets of Manchester 'still swarm with distressed Objects of every kind; Hunger and Nakedness, abject Misery, and loathsome Poverty may be found in every Neighbourhood.'[39]

Pickpockets and beggars profited in the jostle of the streets: 'Great assemblies are markets for the Cut-purse,' warned Nicholas Breton in 1607.[40] Thomas Jones was sentenced to death in 1750 after being found guilty of stealing a gold watch from General St Clair in a 'prodigious crowd of people'.[41] Beggars were attracted to areas of commerce, where passers-by might have ready money to spare, and crowds of beggars hoping to find a lucrative patch near the Royal Exchange annoyed Cornhill residents.[42] In 1755 a 'parishioner' from Newcastle railed against the shopkeepers 'who suffer their Doors to be daily besieged by Crowds of Beggars, to the great disquiet of many Customers'.[43]

'The rough pavement wounds the yielding tread'[44]

Pedestrians had other concerns beyond being obstructed, robbed, bedaubed, startled and distracted by the crowds on the streets. Pushing through the concourse the citizen might lose more than his purse and handkerchief – life and limb were at stake as well. The physician Richard Mead thought it was sensible to limit contact with the diseased, and advised his readers to 'avoid all *Crouds of People*'.[45]

There were further dangers underfoot. Before commissioners absorbed paving responsibilities after the mid-eighteenth century, citizens were supposed to pave and cleanse the street immediately outside their doors.[46] An MP highlighted the dangers and inconveniences of this custom, complaining that pavements were laid by individuals each 'consulting his own interest . . . without the least regard to order, or the safety or convenience of the public'.[47] Because such regulations were frequently ignored, trip hazards in the form of unlevel and poorly laid crazy pavements were common features of the street. Busy routes endured excessive wear and unless they were constructed of a uniform material the pavement wore away at different rates and created pits and rises underfoot – 'the rough pavement wounds the yielding tread.'[48] In 1678 the pavement along Manchester's Toad Lane was 'very uneven and very dangerous'.[49] Paving stones in front of a house in Southampton were reported to be so dangerous in 1624 that pedestrians could break their legs tripping over them.[50] The patrons of the Leg Tavern on Fleet Street would need to have trod carefully when they left the establishment, as the house next door but one was untenanted, and in 1740 the pavement was not attended to.[51] In 1751 the pitching outside Absolom Fuller's door in Bath was reported to be 'so shelving as to be very dangerous to those who walk or ride over the same'.[52]

The presence of kennels – channels that traversed the streets to carry away drain water – would have created further dangers underfoot, especially when they were silted or frozen. Where channels were misdirected, or pavements were particularly uneven, pockets of dirty water formed. The Bath Chamber was presented to the quarter sessions for making a dangerous gutter 'in a most public passage' at the upper end of Bath Market Place in 1756.[53] Holes left when water companies tore up the streets to lay pipes sometimes remained exposed, or were back-filled with insufficient materials.[54] These pits would fill with rainwater. Deep miry puddles were common nuisances on the city streets, although most were not of the size that engulfed Dr Foster in Gloucester. The Southampton leet jurors often recorded the presence of holes in the street that were dangerous or 'unseemly'.[55] In 1749 Edward Leech of Salford made a mudhole that was two yards deep in a foot passage in Manchester called the Sun Entry between the lower end of Market Street Lane and Cockpit Hill.[56] Two Leicester men, Thomas Toopots and Thomas Hastwell, dug a gravel pit in the city's Free School Lane at the end of the seventeenth century that was described as being 'soe big that horse and man may be spoyled at it'.[57] A deep pit near the Southampton farm of Sir John Jeffry, created when soil was taken to fill a void in another street, endangered lives in 1604. Many people had fallen into the filthy waters within, and it was feared that they could have drowned if others had not been at hand to fish them out. When the nuisance continued into the following year the scavengers were instructed to fill the hole in with night-soil.[58]

Buildings flanked most city streets. In order to protect their property many householders set up palisades, railings and posts outside their homes and businesses. These railings and posts narrowed the street, obstructed travellers and gave some streets a higgledy-piggledy lack of uniformity. The Oxford Council set about surveying posts and stones in 1657 in an attempt to curb their growth and identify candidates for removal. Finding unacceptable upright stones in Jesus College Lane and troublesome posts by the South Gate and on Grope Lane, the chamberlains engaged workmen to uproot them, and any other posts or stones 'thought offencive to the Inhabitants or Passengers'.[59] Obstructive posts, benches and spur stones were removed in Bath and Manchester too.[60] Other barriers formed a divide between the pathway and the carriageway. Posts that were over three foot high were common in the rebuilt portions of London, following the fire, but only on streets wide enough to accommodate them (see figure 46). Some streets just had a single bollard at the corner.

Some problems were caused by a lack of street furniture and railing. A cow died in 1607 when it fell down cellar stairs in a Manchester street, evidence of the need for stairs to be railed or covered.[61] John Harrison, a Manchester clothworker, occupied a cellar under the Exchange in Kings Street. In 1761 the rails to his steps and cellar were reported to be 'prostate and broken down and lye open to the great danger and common nusance' of pedestrians. Harrison was ordered to improve the railing.[62]

View of Ironmongers' Hall in Fenchurch Street................Vüe de la Halle des Marchands de Fer dans Fenchurch St.
London printed for Rob. Sayer Map & Printseller at the Golden Buck near Serjants Inn, Fleet Street?

46   John Donowell, *View of the Ironmongers' Hall in Fenchurch Street* (*c.*1750). The highway is separated from the pavement by tall posts. Railings create a divide between pavement and buildings.

The waste and detritus from city properties were channelled, swept and taken from the interiors to await sluicing or collection. There was increasing concern in the period about matter that held up pedestrians and vehicles. Complaints about street obstructions often concerned overly big or lolling dunghills. In 1600 a dunghill on Manchester's Fennel Street was described as 'not severed from the hye streete'.[63] Several citizens of Bath were presented to the quarter sessions in the 1750s for obstructing the pavements with timber, rubble and muck. The Corporation was also presented, for failing to remove a 'Prodigious Quantity of Rubbish' from Parsonage Lane, 'which renders the said lane almost impassable', and for leaving dirt from Cheap Street at Bear Corner.[64] Particularly noisome dunghills took up additional space as pedestrians gave them a wide berth.

As the urban population increased, new properties were constructed to accommodate the immigrants. While building work was being carried out, streets in the vicinity became storage yards for the construction materials. Pedestrians needed to manoeuvre around timber stacks, piles of bricks, stones and gravel. Timber heaped near a road in Southampton in 1603 was reported to remain 'to the great pesteringe the said place and verie daungerous to beast by day and children by night'. Eight were fined.[65] Street space was further reduced by scaffolding, props to unstable houses, and by the temporary use of streets as workshops for construction.[66]

47   John Robert Cozens (1752–99), *The Circus, Bath* (1733).

The chairmen of Bath were permitted to use the pavements as long as they did not 'stop, jostle, or rub against any Person walking singly close to . . . Houses or Walls'. Parked chairs could pose quite an obstacle, as the carrying poles were very long (see figure 47 above, figure 36 on p. 106 and figure 60 on p. 224).[67] In 1762 John Sherringham obstructed a London passageway with his sedan chair, while he waited for business. A witness stated that 'Nobody would walk where the chair stands', and this upset local shopkeepers.[68]

When the principal central streets were cluttered and crowded, pedestrians might also use narrow alleyways or passages known as snickleways, entries or ginnels. These were often just entries through houses, with rooms overhead. Some alleyways were insalubriously equipped with houses of ease, or acted as watercourses. In Bath these cut-throughs were called throngs – on account of 'the Difficulty of passing and repassing them'.[69] Posterns through city gates could also be narrow and uninviting. John Penrose, the mild-mannered vicar from Cornwall visiting Bath to relieve his gout, found himself in a scuffle over space in 1767 when he was walking through the West Gate postern, 'a narrow Pass not capable of two abreast, without some inconvenience'.[70] Whenever Jonas Hanway went near 'the narrow way by Craig's Court', a passage leading to the Houses of Parliament, he was reminded of age-old plans to widen the way, plans that hadn't come to fruition. He was most concerned about the safety and comfort of the elite gentlemen, such as judges, who had to wend their way through this inconvenient passage. 'It is surely an object of *great* importance', Hanway twittered, 'that their persons should not be in the least ruffled or discomposed' en route to their 'places of assembly'.[71]

Urban pedestrians also faced dangers and nuisances overhead – 'the low penthouse bows the walker's head'.[72] Low-hanging signs proliferated across towns and cities, until they were prohibited in piecemeal fashion by local authorities, while meat hung from butchers' stalls.[73] John Gay's pedestrian became entangled with poultry – 'strung in twines, combs dangle in thy face'.[74] Brackets and other fixtures for street lighting, waterspouts drawing water down buildings and nastiness decanted from chamber pots added to the head-level dangers that needed to be avoided in the slalom down the city streets.

'Great and violent Mastive Dogs'

Pedestrians slipping, bumping and tripping usually sustained only minor injuries, but a more serious menace also lurked on the streets. The dangers posed by loose dogs on city streets were manifold. Dogs carried parasites, and these would have been spread to humans via deposits of excrement. Dogs also caused fear as potential carriers of febrile diseases. Regarded as sources of the plague, dogs were rounded up and slaughtered in vast numbers during the various epidemics of the sixteenth and seventeenth centuries.[75] More than five hundred dogs were killed in the parish of St Margaret's, Westminster, in 1603.[76] It should also be remembered that rabies had not been eradicated from England at this time.[77] Hannah Glasse provided recipes to make cures for those bitten by mad dogs.[78] In 1754 Joseph Massie drew attention to the 'horrible Nuisance of MAD-DOGS', which had caused many deaths. Massie cynically pointed out that the authorities would not take this problem seriously until a 'very eminent or illustrious person' had fallen 'prey to its relentless Fury', and suggested that a tax might prevent owners letting their dogs roam free in the streets.[79] When the disease flared up in the winter straddling 1759 and 1760 owners were ordered to confine their dogs to their houses for one month.[80]

Mark Jenner has exposed the symbolic triggers that led to a concentration on dogs as vectors of disease, especially the plague, arguing that they were masterless and roaming, and 'a visible source of disorder in a way that rodents and lap-dogs were not'.[81] Additionally, unlike cats, pigs and rats, dogs had long been feared in the city streets for their occasional forays into the limbs and jugulars of unsuspecting passers-by. Dogs were probably a factor fuelling a fashion for walking sticks and canes in the period.[82] On his way to Greenwich in May 1663 Samuel Pepys was 'set upon by a great dog'. The dog bit into his garter, but Pepys took courage from the fact he had his sword with him.[83] Ned Ward thought that owners chose dogs that suited their own temperament. 'All Men, in short, that take delight / In surly Brutes that snarl and bite / Make choice, tho' to themselves unknown, / Of such whose Natures sute their own.' The worse behaved the owner, the more terrible the dog. Thus pretty ladies clutched delicate 'Lap-Dog Elves' who snarled and barked at all except those 'whom Madam favour shows'. Bailiffs and watchmen preferred dogs that growled at all 'but Rogues'. The drunken tinker kept a 'Mongrel of some ugly Breed / ... In whose sowre Aspect we may find / The Master's rough unpolish'd Mind'. Beggars' curs yapped at everyone.[84]

When stopping in Manchester during their tour of the country in 1725, three students remarked that 'the hounds here are of an uncommon bigness'.[85] One author made reference to a breed of dog common in Manchester 'that is enormously tall and large; and children frequently ride upon them in play'.[86] In 1668 Liverpool's inhabitants were ordered to tie or muzzle all 'dogs which can devour children or disturb others ... many having complained of such a crime'.[87] In the seventeenth century a dozen officers patrolled six areas of Manchester on the lookout for 'mastiffe dogs and bitches and greate Mungrell Curres th[a]t goe abroad in the streets'.[88] The number of officers patrolling Manchester increased during the eighteenth century; by 1756 there were sixteen.[89] The Manchester wig-maker Edmund Harrold explained to his diary that he had been fined for failing to attend the court leet to present cases in his capacity as a dog-muzzler in 1712. Perhaps he was put off by their 'uncommon bigness'.[90]

In 1677 several Manchester townsmen, including Oswald Mosely, were fined for keeping unmuzzled dogs. Mosely was fined again in 1684 for his mill guard dog.[91] In 1679 the owner of an unmuzzled dog that ran amok 'to the greate feare and Dread of his Neighbours' appeared among a list of five offenders.[92] Thirteen owners were fined in 1683 for causing 'greate Terror of theire Neighbours' by letting their dogs roam free.[93] In 1733 William Burgess, a clothworker, let his large unmuzzled bulldog terrorise the inhabitants. He was ordered to chain it up or enclose it.[94]

Butchers kept grizzly mutts to bait beasts prior to slaughter.[95] The butchers' dogs encountered by Ned Ward's 'Merry Travellers' were leering 'With vicious Eyes and Noses black' to mirror their masters' 'Rage and Cruelty'.[96] In 1637 a butcher called Thomas Wharmeby was among several fined in Manchester for keeping 'great and violent Mastive Dogs and bitches, and suffer them to goe abroad in the streetes' causing danger and terrorising the inhabitants.[97]

Dogs were not just annoying and frightening to pedestrians, they could also kill them. Again, children would have been especially vulnerable. Word spread to Samuel Pepys in 1662 that a child had been 'torn to pieces by two dogs at Walthamstow'.[98] Some cases involving aggressive dogs were heard in the Old

48   Engraving, William Hogarth, *The Four Stages of Cruelty* (1751), Plate II, 'Second stage of cruelty'. A horse has stumbled, overturning the coach. Cattle and sheep are driven to market through the streets; a bull runs amok in the background. A sleeping drayman is about to crush a boy under his wheel.

Bailey – where they were considered as a murder weapon. In the 1680s a 'dangerous' dog belonging to Thomas Jeffes terrorised the area around London's Coleman Street. The dog 'used to fly upon and bite People' and Jeffes had been ordered to hang it, but refused. In July 1684 the dog savaged a man, who died of his injuries.[99]

Dogs were not the only animals to scare and injure pedestrians. The citizens of Manchester were terrorised when a 'vitious Mule' ran amok and kicked people in the streets near Hyde Cross in 1748.[100] Commentators expressed concerns about the practice of driving cattle through the streets to market, or to be slaughtered in the back streets. Joseph Massie argued that driving live bullocks through the city streets to Smithfield Market was a 'dangerous Nuisance, gradually increasing, as the Town grows larger'. He claimed the practice led to frequent broken limbs and the occasional fatality. His proposed solution was to increase the number of animals slaughtered before they were brought to market.[101]

'A hurry of coaches and carts'

Across the country cities were at the forefront of an expansion of proto-industry. Increasing volumes of goods were manufactured and sold in England. In Manchester trade flourished due to unfettered commerce; Daniel Defoe described the town as industrious, and noted that even 'the smallest Children' were employed in the cloth trade.[102] The increase in trade caused a rise in the volume of wheeled traffic moving through and between cities. The need to accommodate an increasing number of wheeled vehicles in the densely packed networks of medieval streets was one of the greatest challenges facing the civic authorities. It was not often tackled successfully. Narrow and congested streets irked travellers and slowed the pace of trade.

When his character Sloth tries to enter London, Thomas Dekker notes that there is nowhere to sleep soundly in the afternoon: 'for in every street, carts and Coaches make such a thundring as if the world ranne upon wheeles . . . how then can Idlenes thinke to inhabit heere?'[103] The vast number of coaches was frequently the focus of letters and entries in travel accounts, diaries and civic records. Horatio Busino, a visitor to London in 1618, described the coaches and carts he saw and heard in London: 'there is such a multitude of them, both large and small . . . that it would be impossible to estimate them correctly.'[104] London traffic increased during the period. Members of various livery companies petitioned for a restraint of stagecoaches in 1671, and this petition was approved at a meeting of the Court of Aldermen.[105]

The inhabitants of Cornhill Ward, affected by traffic coming to and going from the Royal Exchange and the Bank of England, frequently called for hackney coachmen to be presented to the wardmote inquest.[106] The whole area was pestered with hackney coaches in such volumes that they hindered merchants and other travellers.[107] As the spaces in city streets were poorly demarcated, increasing volumes of traffic endangered pedestrians.

Horse-drawn vehicles are difficult to manoeuvre in tight spaces and are impossible to reverse. Carriages needed a wide turning circle. Horses do not always come to a halt when humans want them to. It would have been hard to control one or more horses in harness in a noisy, busy environment cluttered with overhanging signs, wheelbarrows and street furniture amidst 'a hurry of Coaches and Carts'.[108] A cart out of control could instantly scatter a crowd. Heavily laden carts would have been slow to draw to a halt and would have packed quite a punch on impact. Empty carts might have been easier to halt quickly, but might have been driven faster.

Various casualties of cart accidents are recorded in the Bills of Mortality for 1665.[109] In his update of John Stow's 1598 *Survey of London*, John Strype exclaimed that whereas the biggest danger to human life in Stow's time was 'Immoderate Quaffing' and fire, by 1720 it was encroachment on highways, and carts and coaches driven dangerously along the narrow streets.[110] Aiming to sort the traffic chaos around the Poultry and Cornhill areas in the eighteenth century, a warden was employed to move obstructions and keep the passage free. Unfortunately, in 1709 a warden was killed while performing his duty, dying after his leg was amputated following an accident. A successor complained of harassment from coachmen when he tried to move them on.[111]

It was not just the numbers of hackney coachmen that annoyed people in the Cornhill area of London, but also their temperaments. The drivers were reported to be 'evill natured' and disorderly, 'for the most part of them sweare curse [and] Quarell'.[112] In the face of extraordinary volumes of port traffic in Bristol, concern for the pavements had led to a ban on carts in the city. Traders used sledges instead to transport goods around. A student touring in 1725 found the drivers of these sledges to be 'remarkably rude' and that they had a tendency of 'running over people, unless they are very careful to get out of the way'.[113] A compiler of an eighteenth-century etiquette book even went as far as to suggest that there were dozens of London hackney coachmen who would 'with the utmost Pleasure and Satisfaction, drive over the most innocent Person whom they never knew . . . provided they could do it conveniently and safely, that is, *within the Verge of the Law*'.[114]

Children were especially vulnerable to traffic. They were shorter, and so less visible to drivers. Anthony Wood knew the dangers well. He was trampled by the horse of the Oxford University carrier when he was five, suffering bruising and short-term mental impairment.[115] Children might have been less wary of the traffic and more involved in play; they would have had inferior skills of visual judgement, and more fragile bodies. Of the seventy cases of cart, coach, dray and wagon accidents causing fatal injuries to other road users and pedestrians heard at the Old Bailey between 1679 and 1770, over half of the victims were children. In the cases where carts caused the fatalities, over two-thirds of the victims were children. Old Bailey reports detailing accident cases are sad and graphic. In 1691 Charles Collins accidentally killed a young girl called Sarah Smallnick by driving his brick cart 'over her Short Ribs'. Claiming he had not seen the child, Collins was acquitted on a murder charge.[116] A little boy 'was peeping at the Corner of the Post' shortly before he was trapped between the post and a cartwheel in 1696. He died of his injuries.[117] One child was killed as he knelt down to 'take some Mulberry Leaves off the Street when the Dray went over his Head, and broke his Skull'.[118] A toddler stooping to pick up gravel stones from the road in 1727 was felled by a cart.[119] Another child was hit while playing football in the street.[120] In one particularly tragic case a child was playing with straw on the road, and 'being cover'd with the same' was not spotted by a cart driver until it was too late.[121] One unfortunate boy was sitting on a Covent Garden bench when a dray pulled by two horses ploughed into him and 'wedged the Child's Head up against an Iron-Grate'.[122] Similar hazards faced the children of Manchester, where several deaths occurred in the mid-eighteenth century. An order was issued to decry the galloping of horses through the city.[123]

Many carters and coachmen involved in accidents were acquitted on chance medley (excused due to extenuating circumstances). Often the skittishness of the horses was cited in the driver's defence. Particularly nervous or young horses would be easily startled. A horse pulling a cart in Shoreditch in 1692 killed a little girl after it was frightened by drums.[124] In 1719 a young horse pulling a beer dray was startled by the pump of a fire engine and panicked, killing a man.[125] Witnesses for the defence of a coachman who had knocked down a milkmaid on the road between Shoreditch and Hackney in 1721 argued that 'the Horses were hot headed'.[126] Sometimes the victim was blamed for the accident. It was implied that Matthew Dun, an inmate of a workhouse, ended a drunken ramble in January 1728 under the wheels of a coach through his own carelessness.[127]

In a few cases the driver was found guilty of causing an accident by failing to pay due care and attention (see figure 48 on p. 168). The attitudes of the carters and coachmen were questioned. In particular, commentators complained about the lackadaisical way the drivers positioned themselves on their vehicles so that they could not easily see the road ahead.[128] It was recorded in 1692 that 'most of the carters, Carmen, and draymen that pass and repass with their several carts, carriages and drays through the public streets, lanes and places [of London and Middlesex] ... make it their common and usual practice and custom to ride negligently on their several carts.' Often nobody guided the horse, 'so that oftentimes their horses, carts, carriages and drays run over young children and other their Majesties' subjects, passing in the streets about their lawful occasions, whereby many lose their lives'.[129]

Other witnesses mentioned the speed with which vehicles careered down the streets. Many people described carters and coachmen as travelling extravagantly, fiercely, or 'furiously driving'.[130] A child was killed near Charing Cross in January 1684 when a coachman was driving at 'full speed . . . striving with another, to get a Fare, which called Coach'.[131] In 1721 two men from

London's Whitechapel area were found guilty of manslaughter after a hit-and-run incident that caused the death of a woman holding her child. The men had been driving an empty brick cart pulled by four horses 'very furiously along . . . as hard as they could'. In court the men were told they should not have been driving a cart down a public road, but should have been leading the horses on foot.[132] In 1770 two hackney coach drivers were seen jockeying along Bishopsgate Street, London. One of the coaches hit a pedestrian when the driver glanced backwards to check on his lead.[133] In 1717, a dray driver was found guilty of the manslaughter of a six-year-old girl after his 'Carelessness and hasty turning his Horses' crushed the child against a wall. The driver unsuccessfully argued that he was hard of hearing, and did not hear horrified witnesses warn him of the impending accident.[134] Some drivers were thought to be too drunk to drive safely.[135]

Clearly some drivers drove their vehicles in a reckless and dangerous fashion, but the road conditions were far from perfect and some accidents were unavoidable. The streets were shared spaces but few pedestrians enjoyed the luxury of a raised kerb or even a line of posts. Apart from newly cut ones, most streets were too narrow to accommodate them.[136] Street and market furniture cluttered the pathways and walkers were also forced to struggle past piles of refuse and stacks of goods and building materials. One evening in October 1761 a coach carrying four women and a child overturned in London's Arlington Street after it collided with some building rubble. The pile was not topped with a lantern, nor was it surrounded by a fence or guarded by a watchman. One woman was taken 'insensible' from the coach and died shortly afterwards.[137]

Street furniture added to the peril in some situations: in the cases detailed above one boy was trapped between a post and a wheel, and another was crushed against an iron grating. According to Jonas Hanway, posts were often too high and too narrow – he proposed they should be made stouter.[138] In 1692 an 'ancient Woman' was crushed against a stall by a dray at London's Pye Corner.[139] The paving surfaces were also poor. A Bath citizen was presented in 1753 for failing to pitch the way at Bear Corner, 'with so great a Descent as renders it very Hazardous to every Passenger especially on Horseback'.[140] Jonas Hanway identified open street gutters as a key peril to horses and cartwheels.[141] The continual heaping of matter to make road surfaces more solid also caused problems. In some parts of London the roads had been raised so substantially above their original height that carts were commonly overturned.[142] Ned Ward's 'Merry Travellers' slipped and slid on the 'greasy Stones', trying to avoid the 'Hackney Coach and Brewer's Dray'.[143] Carters and coachmen would have also slid about, especially on sharp gradients and odd cambers. The area around the Thames Quay in London, the location of 'landing places, laystalls, and wharves', was accessed 'by an inconvenient network of lanes, so narrow that the drays in their passage endangered houses and pedestrians, and so steep that the drays themselves were endangered every time a horse stumbled on the ascent'.[144]

Extenuating circumstances cited in defence of the drivers included the available light – some pleaded that they could not see their victims in the dusk or dark.[145] Anthony Wood reported that the fog was so dense in London one November afternoon in 1674 that 'people could not see a yard before them. Severall kill'd and wounded with carts and coaches.'[146] A crippled prizefighter ('a Lame old Man' with 'a Stick, or Crutches') was fatally injured when he was struck on a 'very Dark' night by the wheels of a dray in 1731, possibly after the horses had been frightened by noise made by 'empty Barrels on the Dray'.[147]

'Strait and narrow passages'[148]

As in most towns, the central commercial districts of London, Manchester, Bath and Oxford were labyrinthine. The medieval heart of each city was in need of a bypass – their narrow ventricles were blocked. Foot and vehicular travellers were held up by obstacles as they tried to reach their destinations. The busiest parts of each town were generally the oldest, most central streets – and these tended to have the narrowest thoroughfares and the greatest number of encumbrances such as rows of butchers' shops, and civic buildings and other structures. John Evelyn noticed that London's streets were narrowest in the 'very Center, and busiest places of Intercourse'.[149]

Edifices sited in the middle of the road also constricted traffic flow. Sometimes these obstructions were entire rows of cottages or shops, as in the cases of Middle Row in Oxford's Broad Street, and also Middle Row in Holborn, London. Roads were narrowed by encroachments on the building line.[150] In 1633 the foundations of a new building in the St Ebbe's parish of Oxford jutted so far into the street that they hindered pedestrians. The council unanimously decided to pull the structure down.[151] In Bath much traffic was funnelled through the Market Place, which was cluttered by the old Guildhall until it was relocated in 1777.[152] Even after the city compulsorily purchased properties to enlarge streets in the 1760s the streets of central Bath were very narrow; many could not easily accommodate two carriages at the same time.[153]

When Bath's Milsom Street was cut in the 1760s, the passage of traffic from the city centre to the Walcot area should have been eased, but the Bear Inn at the head of Stall Street stood in the way and held up traffic. The newly established uptown parts were badly connected to the old central heart of the city. Union Street was created (as an extension of Stall Street) but the large and imposing Mineral Water Hospital (built by John Wood in 1738) was an encumbrance.[154] Bath's High Cross was removed in 1783 after obstructing traffic for hundreds of years.[155] Anyone trying to turn from Manchester's

Shudehill in the mid-eighteenth century needed to negotiate around a 'hovel or stable' belonging to timberman James Wild. Wild also left timber, carts and dung along the road.[156] Joseph Massie thought that the Bank of England was 'situated in too narrow a street; where a perpetual conflux of Wheel-Carriages of all kinds, occasions very frequent Obstructions to Busness'. Rather than suggest traffic restrictions, Massie proposed the compulsory purchase of four houses fronting the gate, to give more room for manoeuvre. [157]

After the fire in 1666 the London Corporation was granted powers to make conduits smaller or remove them from busy thoroughfares.[158] In 1628 Manchester's ruinous conduit served only to hinder the traffic.[159] Oxford's conduit was positioned on Carfax and consisted of two great cisterns holding spring water collected from North Hinksey Hill through lead pipes (figure 49).[160] Completed in 1617, an upper cistern served the university, and a lower cistern taking the overflow from the upper served the town. Its location was swiftly identified as an obstruction, especially on market days.[161] Within two decades of erection the conduit was presented as a nuisance to the Chancellor of the University, Archbishop Laud. Despite continuing grumbles it remained in its central location until 1787.[162] Finding the overflow supply inadequate and unreliable, the town positioned its own cistern at Market Hill in Corn-market at the end of the seventeenth century, to be served with Thames water

49   Oxford University's obstructive conduit on Carfax.

drawn by a pumping station at Folly Bridge. Learning from the university's mistakes, the civic fathers insisted that it 'shall be artifically and ornamentally erected upon columns or pillars of the heighte of ten foote from the pavement, to the end that by the erecting thereof the market place may not be obstructed or narrowed, nor the inhabitants there any waies or prejudiced or hurt by the same'.[163] John Wood noted with regret how Bath's fancy conduits were replaced by taps on walls in the eighteenth century, to minimise traffic obstruction.[164]

City markets were necessarily sited in the most central locations, but their position frequently blocked passages when trading was underway. Much of the obstruction came from 'the Projection of Bulks and shew-Boards'.[165] At the close of the seventeenth century citizens living near to some of the London markets petitioned the House of Commons for tighter regulations for country folk bringing produce to sell on market days without having a pitch in a market. These farmers plied their produce on the common streets, 'under the Pent-Houses of the Neighbouring Houses'. They were out of the market's control and caused a 'great obstruction thereof' and a 'very great Nusance to Inhabitants'.[166] Stalls under Oxford's Carfax Church crept so far into the available foot space that the carts and passengers were reported to be unable to pass without danger (space was already at a premium due to the location of the conduit). Hucksters frequenting the area were moved on in an effort to maximise space.[167] Similar problems blighted the Bath street experience, with fishmongers and grocers singled out as key culprits in the mid-eighteenth century.[168] A dedicated vegetable market was built in 1762–3 to clear the market of the grocers' baskets and 'give Room for Carriages to stand and turn'.[169]

On rebuilding the Oxford butchers' shops following a fire in 1644 the council decreed that no stalls could be erected against the new shops. Trading could only continue within the premises. A century later one commentator described how the butchers' market spread over half of the High Street, and complained that 'the Farmers incumber the other principal streets with their Waggons and Corn.' He thought the whole enterprise was a 'great Nusance' that undermined the beauty of the city.[170] The Manchester butchers had slaughterhouses in the shambles in the marketplace, but they took up too much room and spread to outlying areas, causing congestion.[171] Manchester's corn market was cluttered by pot sellers and hucksters and it was reported that the citizens 'can neither pass nor repass with coach, waggon, wain, cart, horses loaden or unloaden, from Market Stead Lane to the Smith Door'. Fruit sellers were moved from the north side of the conduit to a new market in Hanging Ditch – and butchers spread into the spaces left.[172]

The livestock market at Smithfield supplied nearly half of the meat consumed in London in the early eighteenth century. Once purchased, the animals would be slaughtered nearby. When the market was first established it was located just beyond the built-up residential areas, outside the city walls. By the eighteenth century it was surrounded by residential developments. The movement of shoppers, sellers, vehicles and animals was intense, and the market area was busy and congested.[173] Wandering into Southwark Market, Ned Ward's 'merry travellers' 'squeez'd and jostl'd' their way through the crowds. Three decades later an Act of Parliament tried to bring order to the notoriously busy market, where the carts, stalls and stands formed a nuisance to all those living and working in the area. The location was to be moved from the common High Street 'which is a great Thoroughfare for all Carriages and Cattle' to 'The Triangle, abutting on a Place called the Turnstile, on the Backside of Three Crown Court Eastward, on Fowle Lane, Northward, and towards Deadman's Place Westward'.[174]

The Manchester potato market formed such an obstruction to pedestrians in 1748 that the inhabitants of Hyde Cross could not 'have Ingress or Egress to and from their Houses and shops without great Danger to their lives or Limbs'. The market was relocated shortly afterwards.[175] Hoping to alleviate traffic problems, the civic authorities in Bath embarked on a programme of market relocations in the early eighteenth century. The shambles were enlarged, absorbing space left by a house which was purchased and demolished by the council. The beast market was relocated to the Timber Cross, and a building called Noah's Ark was swept away to make room for a market for green produce.[176]

50   The East Gate, Bath, as seen from Boat Stall Lane.

51 Engraving by J. Skelton, showing the east side of the East Gate in Oxford.

It wasn't just the stalls and the materials for sale that held up the passers-by. Sometimes the traders tried to ply their wares a little too aggressively. In 1609 the New Exchange opened on the Strand. It was enshrined in the Exchange's rules that 'no man [was permitted] to call any man that is buying or selling from an other mans stall, or to pull or hale any man as he cometh by to buy or sell as hee is going along by his stall'.[177] This was a superior shopping experience – far removed from the normal tumult of the marketplace, where, Sundays excepted, citizens encountered pushy vendors and in-your-face hucksters who hustled amidst the bustle.[178] The transient sellers were not the only pushy traders. In 1680 several shopkeepers in Birchin Lane, Cornhill, were reported to 'shamefully & abuseively Ply and forceably pull in Passengers into their Shops to buy their Wares whereby many persons avoid this Lane which is a hinderance to the trade there'.[179] In *Hell upon Earth: or, the Town in an Uproar* (1729) vintners, victuallers and coffee-house proprietors stand 'eternally upon the *Watch* at their Doors and Windows, *hemming* after everyone that passes' to encourage them to 'propagate the Doctrine of Drinking'. These hems, issued from the threshold of the establishment, carried hints of challenge and temptation.[180]

Where traffic was channelled through a narrow city gate, or over a bridge, it would slow the pace of the traffic down, especially where the space only permitted single file.[181] The East Gate was Bath's narrowest bottleneck, at only seven foot wide, with head clearance of only nine foot (see figure 50 on p. 176). However, as this 'meanly built' gate only gave access to the quay, it survives to this day.[182] Oxford's East Gate (figure 51) was encrusted with a hotchpotch of buildings, creating a pinch point on the busy route to London. The council had tried, rather half-heartedly, to limit obstructions, and to this end one nearby house was demolished in 1634 to allow two coaches to pass under at once, but many buildings still encroached.[183] By 1770 increasing volumes of traffic squeezed on to a road that narrowed to just over twelve feet and the need for immediate action was identified.[184] The North Gate in Oxford was narrowed by the Bocardo, a notorious prison (see figures 53 and 54, pp. 190–1).[185] It was not just the medieval gates that caused concern: the newfangled turnpike gates also held up traffic if they were positioned badly.[186]

Road-widening schemes, although expensive, improved the free flow of traffic in cities labouring under the constraints of medieval street layouts. In Oxford the council had tried to enlarge the passage by the Bocardo a century earlier, by removing an encroachment, plus 'the pales and porch and stone and all other obstructions' along Bocardo Lane, but the congestion had continued.[187] Backed by Acts of Parliament, the Bath Council threw huge amounts of money into compulsory purchase schemes that included the demolition of three of the city's gates.[188]

Usually obstacles and pinchpoints simply held people up as they tried to go about their business. Sometimes blockages presented a danger to life. John Clark caused numerous annoyances to the citizens of Leicester in 1764. First, he left a laden cart on the street for many days, causing a 'publick Nusance'. On another occasion he blocked a road with his waggon and a 'large quantity of Muck'. On this occasion a funeral party was unable to pass by easily without risking falling into the cellar areas flanking the streets. Clark was also presented for having cellar windows that projected too far into the street and for letting the pavement outside his house remain damaged.[189]

In 1711 Richard Appleford at the Black Spread Eagle in Holborn erected posts in Gravel Lane that hindered carts.[190] There were similar problems in Hackney twenty years later when William Yelloly of Church Street put 'a large Stepping Stone in the Road'. When Jacob Upham came along in his coach he struck the stone and 'was flung from the Coach box', bruising his hip. The frightened horses ran away with the coach, causing it further damage.[191]

Abandoned and carelessly parked vehicles caused problems in all urban centres, especially at night. Many vehicles unloaded goods directly on to the streets. Woolpacks, milk drays, full and empty barrels and millers' sacks were all described as obstacles on the streets.[192] Further problems were caused by vehicles pausing for refuelling – straw and hay were strewn across the streets as the horses chomped.[193] Victualler Charles Rotten was presented to the Bath quarter sessions for allowing colliers to feed grains to their horses outside his house. During the same session, Gregory Atwood was presented for allowing colliers to unload and bed down their horses and break coals, obstructing the passageway to the Abbey Green.[194]

'Contesting for the way'

Due in part to rising living standards brought about by industrial developments, increasing numbers of citizens chose to travel around some cities by coach.[195] Although coach travel would have provided some protection from the irritations of the street, it was far from ideal, and not always the most comfortable option. Passengers in coaches would be 'cruelly shaken' by the ruts and pot-holes, and travel unsteadily along the narrow lanes.[196] The Royal College of Surgeons holds the leg bone of an eighteenth-century coachman that displays artery damage to the knee caused by travel over bumpy roads. Jostling along the street in a coach in December 1662 made Samuel Pepys's testicles hurt.[197]

Conversation in coaches could be awkward, stilted and frustrating. Crammed up close to strangers while being joggled about along the rutted tracks was some people's idea of a nightmare. Count Kielmansegge described the initial 'deep silence' among the passengers, which slowly fell away as conversation turned to the road conditions and the weather.[198] Thomas Sheridan's wife recalled a stagecoach trip she endured with a 'fellow . . . chattering away like a magpie'.[199] Conversation was difficult to maintain anyway, with the 'restless motion of wheels and Horses'.[200]

Some coaches were unable to travel down narrow passages, or streets that were encroached on by buildings and objects, and at times they became stuck in jams. Joseph Massie drew attention to one notorious point: the narrow part of Charing Cross 'where especially in *Parliament* and *Term* Time, Persons of high Rank are frequently seen closely hemm'd in, and imprison'd in their Coaches, by Stops, for a considerable Time'.[201] A spate of attacks on coaches in the late seventeenth century led to orders prohibiting the throwing of squibs and crackers into coaches. The Mayor and the aldermen were keen to ensure that 'all persons may pass in Coaches quietly and securely without harm or hindrance'.[202] Riding in a coach 'persons of quality' visiting from abroad were pelted with 'kennel dirt, squibs, roots, and rams-hornes' by children and apprentices.[203]

Faced with these conditions, the tempers of travellers and drivers could get frayed; some incidents were caused by deliberately driving one vehicle into another.[204] Many accidents occurred when drivers tussled for the right of way on the street.[205] Thomas Mace gave some thought to the road rage he witnessed in the late seventeenth century. He declared that drivers who failed to be orderly should be punished quickly to reduce the '*innumerable Controversies, Quarreling*, and *Disturbances*, which in that nature are *daily committed* in *contesting* for the way (which too often prove *mortal* or *very bad Consequence* to many)'. His plans aimed to tighten up road etiquette and thwart the actions of '*Uncivil, Refractory*, and *Rude Ruffian-like Rake-shames*, who too often make it their *business* and *boast*, thus to *disturb* and *abuse honest, quiet*, and *weary Travellers*; which is so great an *injury*, and an occasion to stir up, and *inflame* the *Spirits* of men, so *grosly abused*, that many times most *desperate mischiefs* immediately ensue'. Mace particularly disliked giving way to 'hundred of Pack-horses, Panniers, Whifflers, Coaches, Waggons, Wains, Carts', especially on market days on the outskirts of the city, and suggested a direction of travel on the right-hand side.[206] Count Kielmansegge described a quarrel over the right of way that took place between the driver of his coach and a carter. The carter eventually gave way, but only after the driver and some of the passengers had administered 'a good licking'.[207]

In the seventeenth and eighteenth centuries the urban streets were shared and busy. They were difficult to move along, both by foot and in a vehicle. Much discussion of the unpleasant environment on the city streets dwelt on the hazards and dangers created by the traffic, the free-ranging animals or the clutter of street and market furniture. City travel could be dangerous, time-consuming and frustrating. The body was jostled, shaken, jolted, shoved, twisted and tumbled by obstacles on the road – to the side, underfoot and from above. The increasing volumes of trade and traffic made the situation worse, despite attempts to improve the streetscape by those in positions of authority. Tempers could ignite in the rattle and din of fast-moving coaches and carts. Crowds could prove troublesome to pedestrians and coach travellers. Concern was devoted to the threat posed by the swinish multitude of disorderly and idle people. Those who loitered on the streets were viewed by the fast-walking, purposeful citizens as aesthetically unpleasing, morally corrupt, dirty, noisy, obstructive and threatening to the morals of minors and the property of adults. One commentator even blamed vagrants for the poor state of the city pavements,[208] which brings us to the subject of the next chapter.

CHAPTER 8

Dirty

Travellers hoping to find London streets paved with gold were disappointed. In reality, if paved at all, the streets were clad with stone and coated with dirt and mire. There was a wide variety of paving materials to choose from, including Purbeck stone, Kentish ragstone, cobbled setts, Guernsey pebbles, petrified kidney-shaped stones, compacted coal ashes, and gravel.[1] Comparing the streets of England with those of France, John Evelyn decided that the small squares of freestone covering Parisian suburbs did not 'molest the Traveller with dirt and ill ways as ours in England' and were easier underfoot than 'our pibbles of London'. However, he thought that the French surfaces were harder on hooves, slowing horses and lengthening journeys.[2]

During the mid-eighteenth century much discussion centred on the poor condition of some city streets. The Westminster Paving Act was passed in 1762,[3] twenty years after a similar bill had failed. At that time Lord Tyrconnel described the streets as rugged and filthy, and judged them to be a disgrace to the nation. They gave the indication that the people were

> a herd of barbarians, or a coloney of hottentots, The most disgusting part of the character given by travellers, of the most savage nations, is their neglect of cleanliness, of which, perhaps, no part of the World affords more proofs than the streets of London . . . [the city] abounds with such heaps of filth . . . as a savage would look on with amazement.[4]

In the years that followed, several men, including Jonas Hanway, proposed improvement schemes. Hanway even suggested the placing of water pipes in lamp standards, to be used for cleaning and fire-quenching.[5] The Act of 1762 also legislated for improvements in underground sewerage and better pipes from buildings, and prohibited certain encroachments and hanging shop signs.[6] The Act formed the basis of similar Acts, including the Bath Act of 1766 and the London Streets Act of the same year. Such legislation signalled a desire to get to grips with the state of urban streets.

'We must mend our ways'[7]

Responsibility for paving public areas such as markets, gates, the approaches to churchyards and other public spaces fell to the civic or parochial authorities. Newark's marketplace was first paved in the early seventeenth century. Initially this paving took the form of a six-foot-wide path cutting diagonally across the market and linking the civic chamber to the parish church. Its purpose was to prevent the muddying of ceremonial gowns.[8] The marketplace in nearby Nottingham was only paved on one side at this time; the other side remained 'very miry'.[9] Sometimes public paving was improved by crafty means. When an Oxford mason could not afford to pay for his freedom in 1651 the council let him provide his services instead, and set him paving 'soe much of the Court which lyeth against the office dore' with material from nearby Headington.[10]

Householders were expected to pave the ground that stood immediately in front of their own entrance door to the middle of the road. In 1754 an anonymous 'Gentleman of the Temple' highlighted the long-recognised limitation: that no standardisation in materials was stipulated. Paving was ad hoc and piecemeal. A hotch-potch of surfaces adorned each street; one neighbour might use small pebbles, another large ones, one might use rag-stones, another broken flint stones.[11] Many householders made botched and slapdash attempts using insubstantial materials such as scattered cinders.[12] The lack of uniformity was exacerbated by the inevitability that some citizens were too poor to pave properly, especially on broad streets lined with houses of low value. Demands on materials could not always be fulfilled. In 1691 the inhabitants of a street in Whitechapel were permitted to postpone their paving until a 'sufficiency of stones' could be procured. The scarcity of materials inflated costs, placing schemes beyond the pockets of 'fatherless children and widdows'.[13] As cities expanded, country lanes became newly paved streets as far as the buildings extended. With the vast increase in the number of new streets cut in the period came an increased demand not only for paving materials but also for the services of the paviors.

Some citizens displayed a lack of willingness to fulfil their paving obligations, with many householders ignoring the constant chivvying of the authorities. In 1617 Mr Thimblethorpe and Silvanus Wildblood were among several citizens in the vicinity of St Dunstan's Church, London, with defective pavements.[14] An apothecary, Edward Walker, was regularly fined by the court leet in the 1740s for persistently failing to repair his part of Market Street Lane in Manchester. In 1753 he was fined for the insufficiency of his repairs.[15] The same year, over in Bath, a tanner called Cornelius Parson was presented for failing to mend the pitching at Old House, Walcot Street. When he finally did get around to doing the job, Parson made the pitching too high. As this was 'a great Nusance to his Neighbours', he found himself presented to the quarter sessions again in 1755.[16] Poorly paved streets posed problems throughout the period in many cities. Surfaces that were not level would crack and collect pockets of water underneath them. The timing of the work was important; surfaces laid in rainy conditions were liable to sink and break up, especially if the substratum had been insufficiently compacted.[17] An additional hindrance to a finely finished street was the presence of vacant plots or abandoned and ruined houses, where no one claimed responsibility for street paving.[18]

In 1620 officials in Southampton despaired about the state of the city pavements, exclaiming that they were so decayed that to detail each particular default 'would fill upp this volume and wearie yo[u]r patience in reading'.[19] A keen observer of streetscapes, John Evelyn found Cambridge to be 'ill paved' when he visited in 1654.[20] Things were not much better in Manchester, where citizens created dangerous steps in the pavement by failing to lay their sections at a consistent level. In 1685 pavements in Old Millgate were found to be too high, with a steep descent to the gutter 'to the danger of all passengers'.[21] In 1602 the court leet had ordered that an entire street 'shalbe raised higher and new paved accordinge to the streets adjoyninge'.[22] The corners and junctions where two streets met were especially hazardous, as they were the most likely to be overlooked, with no householder taking responsibility for repairs, and they would also have borne the brunt of the stress when wheeled vehicles rounded them.[23]

The majority of cases presented to the wardmote inquest of the London ward of Portsoken between 1684 and 1760 centred on failures to mend pavements.[24] Likewise in St Dunstan-in-the-West much wardmote time was consumed considering defective pavements. The paving between the houses in Jack an Apes Lane, Lincoln's Inn Fields, was so broken and damaged that it was almost impassable.[25] Several cases of failure to mend the pavement in Bath were heard at the quarter sessions in the mid-eighteenth century. These involved institutions, such as the General Hospital, as well as citizens (including many prominent figures such as Lady Inchiquin, Doctor Harrington, Reverend Duel Taylor, the Mayor Thomas Atwood, and the Hon. Sir John Coxe).[26] Some civic authorities were also shown to be lax in paying attention to their paving responsibilities. In 1704 the London City Chamberlain was presented to the Portsoken wardmote inquest for neglecting the paving on Tower Hill.[27] The Bath Chamberlain was presented to the quarter sessions in 1753 for pitching oversights, and three years later for failing to repave the Town Acre, which was described as being in a 'dangerous Condition and requiring immediate inspection'.[28]

'Sweep before your own door'[29]

In central residential areas responsibility fell to the householders not only to pave the streets but also to ensure that they were swept and cleansed. These obligations were enshrined in bylaws. In 1615 Oxford's citizens were ordered to clean the street before their door each Saturday evening.[30] In London in the mid-seventeenth century the citizens were expected to sweep pavements each morning and leave piles of sweepings and dust vessels full of indoor waste to be collected by the soil-cart.[31] In the early seventeenth century some settlements established arrangements with existing elected or salaried officers such as bellmen and criers to manage waste disposal and clean the streets. The town crier of Southampton had the twice-weekly duty of cleaning the gutters and by-lanes. The crier was pulled up in 1605 for letting his standards slip when it was noticed that the streets 'Lyeth most fylthye'.[32] As the period progressed, larger towns and cities employed dedicated scavengers and rakers, known in London at the turn of the seventeenth century as 'Goungefermours' ('gunge-farmers'), to carry out or oversee the removal of waste and spoil, and to cleanse the public areas. As the period progressed the scavenger's role was increasingly one of supervisor; rakers or under-scavengers removed the waste.[33] London wards co-opted scavengers each year.[34] Oxford enjoyed the services of scavengers employed to keep 'sweete and cleanly the streets in the cittye walls and for carryinge awaye of all soyle, filthe and ordure in and aboute the streets and before men's houses and doores'.[35] A scavenger was appointed in Bath in 1615.[36] By 1615 Manchester had nineteen scavengers and two officers to keep the market streets clean.[37]

Scavengers would trundle their carts and tumbrels around the streets they could gain access to, warning citizens of their approach by bell, horn, clapper or cry.[38] The collected waste was either immediately spread on common ground or taken to laystalls (holding dumps), either at the urban fringe or, in the case of London, on the riverside. The 'water poet' John Taylor penned a mock dedication to a scavenger, describing him as 'Dominator of the Dunghils . . . Lord of the Soyle, and Privy Searcher of all Mixens, and Muckhills, simple or compound'. This 'Cleanser, clearer, and avoyder of the most Turpitudinous, Merdurinous, excrementall offals, muck and Garbadge' held court over the 'stinkards' and 'Turditanians' who populated the city. Taylor continued his dedication by describing the scavenger as 'Invader, Scatterer, Disperser, Consumer and Confounder of offensive unsavoury savors, smels, scents and vapours'.[39] The waste from the city and suburbs would be transported by barge to fertilise fields and market gardens.[40] One horticulturalist remarked that 'Horse-dung, and Kennel-Water, contribute beyond all belief to the forwarding of Plants.'[41]

There had been an attempt to centralise London street cleaning in the 1650s. John Lanyon made a contract with the Common Council to become 'surveyor-general' and to employ labourers to undertake the cleaning jobs previously carried out by the scavengers and rakers appointed by each ward. In the agreement it was stated that 'daily experience' had revealed the negligence of the scavengers whose duty it was to remove street dirt and smells. As a

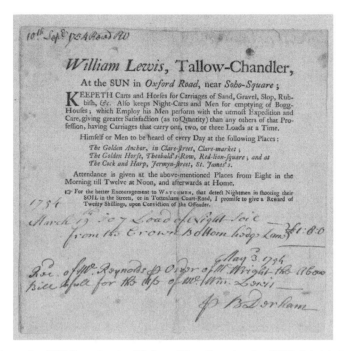

52 Trade card of William Lewis: 'Tallow-Chandler, At the SUN' (1754). Lewis also offers his services as a nightman.

consequence the streets were 'continually much pestered and made extreme offensive to the Inhabitants and Passsengers, with ashes, dust, dirt, rubbish and filth, and with noysome and unwholsome smels'. Lanyon agreed to survey the streets and check up on defaulters who had been presented at the various wardmote inquests. He would also oversee the collection and disposal of waste at a sufficient distance not to create a nuisance to the city.[42]

Carters, dustmen and chimney sweeps also set up private enterprises to carry away unusually disgusting or voluminous accumulations of waste, such as building debris or privy waste ('nightsoil'). William Lewis, a London tallow-chandler, rendered his services as a dustman in the mid-eighteenth century. His carriages could remove 'Sand, Gravel, Slop, Rubbish', and he kept 'Night-Carts and Men for emptying of Bogg-Houses'. Communities unsatisfied with civic sanitary provisions also employed such men. In 1703 the residents of Blue Anchor Alley in the London parish of St Giles-Without-Cripplegate clubbed together to pay a labourer to clean the alley and 'carry away the dirt and soil'.[43] In 1699 an entrepreneur, Edmund Heming, patented a machine for 'sweeping streets, greens and walks; loading the dirt, dust, or soil, also casks of all sorts, . . . repairing the highways so as to throw ridges into the ruts'.[44] History has not recorded the success or otherwise of this implausible contraption.

Urban waste disposal worked well if the householders carried out their duties, at the correct times, leaving neat orderly piles ready to be carted away. However, a sluttish observation of the rules and a complete failure to sweep were common. Not only did some streets remain unswept, but inappropriate dumping also occurred. There are numerous cases every year in the Manchester court leet records detailing the failures of the householders to carry out their street-cleaning duties and to manage their waste with due considera-tion to others. All areas of the town were affected. In 1684 John Traves, a barber, who had a shop in St Mary's Gate, was reported by the scavengers as not cleaning the street before his premises more than four times since they took office. It was also noted that Traves had verbally abused the scavengers and he was fined the substantial sum of three pounds.[45] In 1736 Ashton Marler of King Street was ordered to remove his dunghill from near the Queen's Entry. Three years later he was fined for not cleaning his part of Tibb Lane or removing his rubbish.[46] Streets across the country experienced similar degrees of slovenly care. In mid-seventeenth-century London the citizens needed to be reminded not to leave

any Seacole ashes, Oyster-shells, bones, horns, tops of Turneps or Carrets, the shells or husks of any Peas or Beanes, nor any dead Dogs or Cats, offall of Beasts, nor any other carion or putrid matter or thing, nor any Ordue or Excrements of Mankind or Beast, nor any manner of Rubbish, Dust, Dirt, Soile, Filth, nor any other filthy or noysome thing whatsoever.

This comprehensive list also included building materials such as lime, timber, broken plaster, bricks and wood, and also the scattering of ashes used to make soap, earth, straw, hay, weeds, stuffing, wares or victuals.[47] Part of the problem stemmed from the inaccessibility of crowded back alleys and courts to the scavenger's cart. This led to large-scale dumping of waste outside the (more prestigious) main frontage houses. The inhabitants of Ram Alley, off London's Fleet Street, made a pile of refuse in the side street in 1639. Ten years later the same problem was reported, and coal, ashes and other 'noysome filth and soyle' collected in Fleet Street 'before the Alley Gate'. A decade later the problem was still evident and other alley dwellers in the vicinity also contributed to the spoil.[48] Unoccupied properties presented a cleansing challenge as well as a paving problem, especially when whole rows of houses were abandoned. Rubbish gathered at 'a Parcel of old ruined Houses' in Woolpack Alley in the Houndsditch area of London.[49]

One of the biggest impediments to street cleansing was inadequate water supply and drainage (more on this later). The Southampton authorities, stressing the need for sanitation to combat disease, complained in 1601 that the town was 'verye fylthely kept'. Householders were ordered to sluice from their doorways and to clean gutters on Tuesdays, Thursdays and Saturdays.[50] John Wood noticed that the streets of Bath had a 'natural Declivity toward the River', giving the inhabitants a helpful sluice with each glut of rain. However, he whinged, this advantage was not taken in the mid-eighteenth century, unlike former times when 'the best of the Inhabitants would not lose the Opportunity of sweeping their Doors upon every hard Rainy Day'. Standards went down hill – street dirt did not.[51]

To work well, the system of waste disposal also needed the scavengers and rakers to fulfil their side of the bargain. Southamptonites in the neighbourhood of Biddles Gate complained in 1603 that the scavengers never arranged for the removal of filth left by local butchers, although they were paid to do so.[52] In London John Lanyon's centralising scheme was ill-fated. Complaints abounded and Lanyon was presented to the Cornhill wardmote inquest in 1656 when it was reported that Cornhill was 'noysome' and a dishonour to the city. After the scheme was abandoned the local scavengers and rakers resumed their responsibilities, with varying degrees of diligence. Robert Alsop, the Cornhill Ward raker, was presented for neglecting the streets in his patch in 1662. Alsop left 'great heapes of soyle sweepings and other noysome thinges' and was also pulled up for ignoring a dunghill outside the front of the Royal Exchange, to the 'great offence of the Inhabitants and of Merchants'.[53] The inhabitants of Church Lane in Wapping complained about the scavengers in 1682, arguing they had failed to employ any rakers to clean their lane. Furthermore, once out of office the scavengers added insult to injury by demanding money from the inhabitants to cover their services.[54] By the eighteenth century in the London parishes the scavengers were tradesmen with sufficient status and free time to oversee, organise, and gather funds for the cleaning. However, the post of scavenger was neither the most prestigious nor desirable of civic positions, and many co-optees were reluctant to fulfil their obligations.[55]

'Dung does no good till 'tis spread'[56]

Many waste products did not make it on to the piles, as they could be profitably reused elsewhere.[57] Neighbours would have salvaged large pieces of wood, cinders and building material. The pig, described by Gervase Markham as the best scavenger, 'for his food and living is by that which would else rot in the Yard', consumed much waste vegetable matter.[58] The 'black contaminated sulphurous substance called Greaves' left at the bottom of the tallow-chandlers' melting coppers could be fed to dogs. Fat that was cut from meat or that melted out during cooking was sold to tallow-chandlers to make candles.[59] Barges carrying London's refuse away were often refilled with bricks for the return journey. These bricks were in part made from reusable particles from the refuse, such as grit and ashes riddled from the street sweepings.[60]

If they nosed into the piles they shovelled up, the rakers would have found a variety of substances. A dunghill was a stinking morass of human and animal waste, rotten timber, friable plaster, rubble, carcasses, cinders and ashes, broken glass and crockery, clay pipes, spent bedding, feathers, straw, weeds, eel skins, fish heads, peelings, husks, stalks and cores, in various states of decay. They included items both accidentally and deliberately disposed of – including silver spoons and even, very occasionally, the bodies of infants.[61] These heaps, also known as muckhills, mullocks, middens and rammels, were an assault on the senses, especially in the summer months when they 'rotting smoakt and stunk away'.[62] In 1601 Raphe Hulme's dunghill on Manchester's Fennel Street was 'far out of good order' and 'noysome to the passers by'.[63] These piles annoyed on many levels; besides the stench emanating from them, they were unsightly and obstructive, and they undermined public health, attracting flies, vermin and swine. They were utilised at night by those needing to ease themselves.[64] The putrefying matter and liquid that leached from dunghills could damage street surfaces and public utilities.[65] As a consequence of scavenger and householder oversights piles often remained on the streets for longer than was desirable; they lolled, they leaked and they stank. They also became saturated in storms, or when water channelled into them.

Not all waste matter lay waiting for the raker. Some was deliberately stored for sale, or for spreading on to privately owned horticultural land. Horse dung, in particular, was a valuable commodity. In the seventeenth century the inhabitants of the Lancashire town of Prescot could temporarily store dung against their walls on payment of a fee.[66] Likewise, in Manchester piles of dung were sanctioned on the streets as long as they did not form an obstacle and did not become noisome.[67] In mid-seventeenth-century Liverpool 'middingsteads' (waste stored on the streets) were permitted as long as they were surrounded by a fence four foot high 'so they will not be a nuisance as they have been'.[68] Similar arrangements existed in Manchester, although the paling was supposed to be two yards high.[69]

Throughout the period a great deal of effort went into managing urban waste: it was a primary concern for all of the civic authorities, and their records attest to the pains the officers took in reminding the citizens of their duties, and punishing the lax. In each city there were areas blighted by stench and filth. At certain times (especially during epidemics) the authorities felt the need to coerce the citizens into action. In 1635 Cambridge householders were reminded not to dump dead dogs, pigs, rats, fowl, vermin or fish in the streets and churchyards.[70] When John Campe was employed to round up and kill all cats, pigs, dogs and tamed doves from the streets of Norwich in 1630 'because of the danger of Contagion', he was also instructed to bury the bodies.[71]

Fly-tipping was ubiquitous in the cities. Some citizens preferred not to soil their own patch, instead leaving their waste in churchyards, beside chapel walls, by gaols and prisons and in the centre of highways.[72] In 1679 a London carpenter was fined for dumping a hundred cartloads of rubbish on Bell Yard, a common highway to Lincoln's Inn.[73] Butchers wanting to get rid of stale meat and waste sometimes dumped rotting viscera. According to the burgesses of Westminster, butchers continually dumped the 'soyle and filth of their Slaughter houses and hogstyes' in the churchyard and the nearby passage. Two butchers caught dumping waste in St Clement's Churchyard in 1613 were ordered to take their waste to Lincoln's Inn Fields instead.[74] Six men from London's Whitechapel were indicted for nuisance in 1721 after throwing animal blood and excrement into the streets.[75] Ned Ward described the nocturnal actions of butchers who disposed of their 'stinking veal, and other meats too rank for Sale'.[76]

The contents of privy tubs and chamber pots were also dumped on to existing dunghills, splattered across the open streets or tipped over walls in the neighbourhood.[77] In 1682 a Manchester man was fined for annoying the neighbourhood by 'emptieinge Howse of office Tubbs upon the Middinge'.[78] In 1683 Mancunians were regularly reminded of the rule against carrying tubs of excrement through the streets in the morning. The poorer citizens were also warned against splattering the contents of their tubs on the bridge battlements. The following year, as an exemplary measure, five citizens were each fined five shillings for ignoring the prohibitions.[79]

Some areas became dumping grounds. In seventeenth-century Bath there was a 'mixon' just outside the East Gate. St Ann's Square in Manchester was built in the early eighteenth century on Acres Field. This had been the location of a big laystall.[80] Much of Oxford's waste was piled up at the city gates; the city council identified the area around the Bocardo in North Gate as the site of a huge dunghill (see figures 53 and 54).[81] By 1632 the council periodically employed a labourer to shovel the filth away. The limitations of the sanitary resources were highlighted when they were placed under great pressure. When Charles I held court in Oxford during the civil skirmishes it placed an unusual strain on the city infrastructure. The city authorities complained that the citizens and visitors were 'suffring the filth and dust to lie in the [streets], not onlie to the scandoll of the government of this place but allsoe to the great dainger of breeding an infeccon amongst us'.[82] The dreaded infection came with an outbreak of 'morbus campestris', a sort of gaol fever.[83] Four hundred and forty-four loads of dirt were carted from North Gate between 1642 and 1647.[84] Oxford's filth continued during the mid-century and in 1652 the streets were described as 'much annoyed with fylth, dunghills and other noisome rubbage by means whereof there hath bin a writt directed out of the Chauncery to command the Mayor and Bailiffs for the cleansing of the said streets and lanes'.[85] Preparations for a visit from James II in 1687 did not run smoothly. The High Street was 'laid thick with Gravell, that noe Horses or

53   Detail from Ralph Agas, map showing the North Gate, Oxford (1578).

Coaches could be heard tread'. However, the plans were scuppered by the weather. A deluge of rain turned the gravel to a quagmire, and it was hastily shovelled into North Gate Street.[86]

In the mid-eighteenth century there were also problem areas at London's gates. 'Nastiness', remarked Joseph Massie in 1754 was a particular problem at 'the Posterns of some of the City Gate: and (what is most scandalously shameful) Ordure, in Plenty, daily seen at *Noon-Day* and *'Change Time*, at the *North* Side of the *Royal Exchange*'. Massie expressed surprise that 'nobody had thought it worth their while to *Complain* of so *Loathsome* a Nuisance, and at a Place too, so much frequented by Foreigners, as well as Natives'.[87]

Some of the metropolitan laystalls were enormous. Various dump sites and the areas from which waste could be taken to them were established in the rebuilding legislation after the London fire of 1666.[88] Dung Wharf, a large dump next to Puddle Dock (now the site of the Mermaid Theatre), absorbed the waste from the wards of Farringdon Within, Castle Baynard, Aldersgate Within and St Mary's-le-Grand.[89] Another was located just a little to the west of this, at the end of Water Lane, a street described as being 'better built than inhabited, by reason of its being so pestered with Carts to the Lay-stall'.[90] 'Mount Pleasant' was the tongue-in-cheek name for a part of land near Gray's Inn. Originally a low and boggy patch of waste ground, a mount had built up

54   Bocardo prison, North Gate, Oxford.

through decades of dumping the soil of London. At the foundation was debris from the Fire of London. The entire area became rather unpleasant; the approach roads, including Little Gray's Inn Lane, were narrow, dank and squalid. By 1780 the heap covered eight and a half acres of ground, and could be approached via Laystall Street.[91]

'The small stone gives way first'[92]

Streets were the venue for an array of activities that placed excessive demands on the limited resources available to keep them well surfaced and clean. They were used for transport, manufacture and commerce, entertainment and minor husbandry and shared by humans, animals, street furniture and wheeled contraptions. The failure to adequately separate footways from carriageways resulted in large quantities of manure, rainwater and filth being sprayed directly on to the pavements with each passing vehicle, and run-off water from houses would trickle on to the roads. When wheels, feet and hooves churned up the streets the muddy substratum could break up and ooze through cracks. This created ruts and potholes in which dirty water collected. Further damage was caused by extreme weather conditions and rooting swine. Debris fell from carts, the wheels shed axunge (fat from the kidneys of geese or pigs) and horses pulling the carts, and cattle driven to market contributed dung.[93] John Evelyn noted that sooty deposits also added to the filth.[94] Some of the blame for poor and muculent pavements was placed at the feet of the paviors. In the 1670s bad paviorship took the form of gravel overuse (to fleece clients). This gravel would become displaced in sudden downpours and choke the kennels. The paviors were ordered to use only sufficient gravel to fill the joints between stones, and to ensure that they rammed and swept the gravel well.[95] Nearly a century later Jonas Hanway was complaining that some paviors, ignorant of the 'true principles of their art', did not use enough gravel to fill gaps between slabs.[96]

Traffic growth stressed the street surfaces, necessitating investment simply to prevent deterioration.[97] Recognising the damaging effects of carts on pavements, the Southampton authorities conceded that it was unfair for householders to pay for repairs because the iron wheels that had damaged the old surfaces had brought commerce and wealth to the town. A suggested solution was to consider providing the stone and gravel necessary for the repairs to each ward's streets at the manor's expense.[98] Bernard Mandeville also connected the condition of the streets to economic development and urban population increases, which in turn sucked in more raw materials and spewed out more waste products. All required heavier and more destructive vehicles.[99] Jonas Hanway stated frankly 'we must never expect good roads . . . where we draw great weights with narrow wheels.'[100] Many local bylaws were crafted to govern the types of wheeled vehicles permitted on different road surfaces. Iron-shod wheels were usually the focus of many prohibitions: they were narrow and heavy (especially when loaded with bricks, dung, liquids or grains) and caused much damage. The nails that fastened the iron rims to the wheel were not countersunk, exacerbating the potential for damage.[101] Destructive vehicles included the dung carts and tumbrels that needed to be wheeled to the outlying laystalls. Carts were barred entirely from some streets, and needed to pay a toll on some others.[102] Bylaws governing the streets of St Giles-in-the-Fields in the mid-seventeenth century prohibited carmen, brewers, brickmakers and water carriers from using iron-shod wheels.[103] Two men were presented to the Vintry Ward wardmote inquest in 1688 for using iron-shod wheels in prohibited areas. One of the men was a repeat offender, appearing in the minutes for 1694, and then yearly between 1696 and 1703.[104]

Thousands of jury orders across the country in the seventeenth century relate to wandering swine. Pigs were notorious mobile street nuisances; they poked their filthy snouts into grain sacks and discarded entrails, and grubbed through stinking dunghills. In Liverpool in 1664 all keepers of swine were ordered to house them in their backyards and gardens, until a swineherd could be engaged to supervise them on the commons. Any free-ranging pigs causing damage were to be confiscated and given to the injured party. Clearly the problem continued. In 1646 the residents of the churchyard area were ordered to stop keeping their pigs there. In 1655, a year after she was ordered to set up a door to her swineyard, Dorothy Bickerstaffe's swine spoilt the mayor's ground, and William Gardner piled his dung so high that his pigs escaped by using it to climb over a fence. Dead pigs caused nuisance, too, and the citizens were reminded to bury their carcasses.[105] The council eventually hired a man to impound trespassing swine: the pigs would be released on payment of a twelvepence ransom.[106]

Noisome abuses committed by swine figure regularly in the Manchester court leet records. The authorities tried to control the situation by establishing rules, setting fines, impounding pigs and ordering the removal of swine-related street furniture. Despite continual reissuing of orders and levying of fines the manor was unable to control the pig problem, and it remained one of the most common offences brought to book in the seventeenth century.[107] Although fewer offences were reported in the eighteenth century, some pigs were still present on Manchester's streets. As Richard Bostock's hogs wandered the streets of Manchester in 1738 they wiled away their time 'rooting in the Dung-hill and Midding steads', which was a 'great Annoyance to the Neighbour-hood'.[108] In 1740 swine belonging to Thomas Manyfolds sparked manifold complaints through their proclivity to 'ramble abroad and do mischief'.[109] A clampdown on pig activity in 1769 saw ten offenders booked, including a butcher, a tanner, a yeoman, a hatter and a carpenter.[110]

Pigs could be found in low-prestige courts and yards. Several of the inhabitants of the Bolt and Tun Yard in London kept hogs in the 1650s to the 'great Annoyance of neighbours & diverse Inhabitants dwelling in fleet street'.[111] However, by the eighteenth century the pig business had intensified and, apart from a few small-scale establishments, it was concentrated in large-scale establishments on the outskirts of the city, such as Bethnal Green to the east and Tothill fields to the west.[112]

Butchers' offal and bloody waste were particularly noisome features of the street environment. Each city made provisions to limit the dispersal of these unpleasant substances, for example by creating zones where butchery was permitted (often called the 'shambles'). Specific rules were crafted to deal with the disposal of butchery waste. In 1636 the Oxford butchers were expected to decant blood and filth into the street kennels.[113] By contrast Cambridge butchers would be fined if they failed to take 'paunches, guts, filth, entrall, and bloud of all their beasts' to the 'Pudding-pits, and the valley beyond the Castle-hills'.[114] Poor management of beast waste saw offal spewing across the streets. Three Southampton butchers were identified as the key offenders in the creation of some 'most noysome filth and durt ye[i]lding verie badd smells' in the year James I settled into the throne. George Barton ran a squalid butchery serving the citizens of Southampton. In 1604 his staff dumped offal and blood behind the Castle Gardens, and even lay it 'at mens back dores'. Barton was also fined for slaughtering sheep and calves in his house. A few years later another butcher was fined for throwing the 'very unseemly and noysome' refuse from his slaughterhouse at an unlucky man's door.[115] The problem of dirt lying under stalls was a common shortfall noted of the Manchester butchers.[116] In 1743 twenty-nine butchers were fined for that nuisance.[117]

Butchers trading in the London markets were expected to keep a tub hidden from view, into which they placed offal to be discarded. The offal was collected by the Beadle of the Butchers' Company and taken to the doghouse to feed the hounds of the common hunt. Before the mid-seventeenth century, butchers' waste from the East Cheap and Newgate markets fed the royal bears in Southwark Bear Garden.[118] London's Field Lane ran parallel to the Fleet Ditch and in 1720 was described as 'nastily kept', by virtue of 'being inhabited by Butchers and Tripe Dressers on the East side, by reason of the benefit of the Ditch that runs on the back side of their Yards and Slaughter Houses, to carry away their Filth'.[119]

Some areas were particularly badly affected by beast waste. Sited just beyond the city walls, Smithfield was London's key livestock market throughout this period. Many of the beasts traded at the market were slaughtered in the nearby lanes. By the eighteenth century, thanks to urban sprawl, this market that was once on the outskirts had been subsumed within the heart of the city and many people called for tighter regulation.[120] One 'gentleman of the Temple' argued that slaughter was carried out in inappropriate places, and believed the Corporation had let the streets become 'infested with this shameful Practice; the offensive Smells, the disagreeable Objects of bleeding Heads, Entrails of Beasts, Offals, raw Hides, and the Kennels flowing with Blood and Nastiness'.[121]

Although offal, entrails and blood were the most unpleasant waste products of the market, fishy waters and vegetable matter also contributed to the festering stew that littered the urban streets. At the end of the market day, debris such as hay, straw, vegetable leaves, legume shells and brassica stalks were supposed to be swept up and placed in vessels.[122] Three market traders in Manchester were fined for failing to remove the 'Husks' and other waste in 1752.[123] When the fruit and vegetable market moved from the west end of Cheapside to the north of St Paul's in 1657 a group of local goldsmiths complained about the dirt, smells and obstructions created. Sellers of peascods (peas in pods) remained on the original site and orders for them to sweep up discarded shells were reiterated regularly.[124] Such waste strewn on the streets did not just cause unsightly and smelly nuisances; they could also pose a hazard to the unwary. In London, one woman slipped on a 'Peas-cod-Shell', fracturing her 'crupper-bone' (coccyx) on the pavement.[125]

Manufacturers and construction workers also sullied and soiled streets with their waste products. The shortage of space meant that products were sawn, dried, draped and crafted in public spaces – sometimes even large items such as coaches.[126] Even seemingly benign trades could create a nuisance; feathers thrown into the air during upholstery generated neighbour complaints.[127] Debris from demolition, and dust from sawing, plastering and masonry created temporary nuisances around building sites.[128] Builders and roofers were expected to bring waste materials down from buildings in baskets or trays, rather than flinging them down on to the streets.[129] Although some of the rubble could be reused as hardcore, it was costly to transport away the unusable excess, and builders were sometimes reluctant to employ labourers to shift waste.[130] In 1676 a Manchester mason was twice ordered to remove stone and rubble from outside his house in Millgate.[131] Following the fire of 1666, rebuilding in London disturbed entire neighbourhoods. The Mercers' Company dealt with a complaint in 1674 from the tenants of a shop on the north side of the Royal Exchange, where masons reconstructing the Church of Bartholomew-near-the-Exchange (a casualty of the fire) were sawing stones 'to their [the tenants] greate p[re]judice, because the Dust Spoyles Some of their Comodities, and the Noyse offends all'.[132] A bricklayer's labourer working on a house in Elm Street, off Gray's Inn Lane, in 1732 set up a screen nearby to hide and contain construction and demolition rubbish. An argument with a neighbour turned nasty; a fight broke out and the neighbour was killed. The conflict was fuelled by the frustrations of living near a building site and centred on the storage of site rubbish. In her witness statement the neighbour's widow recalled him saying, 'it's hard that we can't stand at our own Door to take a mouthful of Air, but we must be choaked with your Dust.'[133]

'Every path hath a Puddle'[134]

Not all of the matter that blighted city roads was of a solid or dusty consistency; sludgy waters also created unsightly and smelly additions to the street surfaces. Most buildings were not connected to the various rudimentary urban subterranean sewerage schemes developing in the seventeenth and eighteenth centuries. Waste water combined with surface rainwater in street gutters and channels known as kennels. On wider roads there could be two kennels, each flanking the carriageway. On narrow streets one kennel sufficed, running down the centre of the street. The kennels flowed or trickled into ditches and streams, which in turn spewed into faster-flowing watercourses. In London the Thames was the main outlet for liquid waste. It was also a major source for the supply of water.

Much of the water carried via the kennels originated as rainwater on city roofs. Other liquids were issued from the interiors of domestic dwellings and business premises. The combined effects of waste water issuing from each house on a street could present a considerable challenge to urban drainage systems, especially in inclement weather. Basements were vulnerable to flooding if water was not carried swiftly from the streets. In the seventeenth century much water was carried from buildings via spouting gutters. These provided the pedestrians below with an unwelcome impromptu shower of dirty water. The London rebuilding legislation of 1667 after the fire prohibited spouting gutters on new buildings by insisting on the use of downpipes to convey the water down the side of the property and link up with the kennels.[135] By the mid-eighteenth century other cities were issuing similar instructions to the citizens. In Bath the council often stipulated the use of downpipes in leasing contracts for city properties, and the Bath Act (1757) ensured that from 1758 all new buildings had to be fitted with downpipes to carry water from rooftop to ground.[136] These downpipes would have ensured that the system of drainage worked more effectively, especially when they were connected to underground sewers.[137] However, many city streets were still blighted by overhead spouts in the mid-eighteenth century.[138] In Manchester a lead spout from an upper room poured dirty water and 'other nauseous matter' on to Hunts Back in 1754–5. The spout projected eight inches into street and was 'very inconvenient to passengers And in Summer Time especially occasions very unwholsome and naucious smells'.[139]

Domestic waste water would have been soapy and greasy, but more serious problems were presented when manufacturing crafts allowed waste to discharge on to the streets. The waste water from craftsmen such as dyers, tanners, soap-boilers and tallow-chandlers could have been noxious and offensive. Finding their streets regularly awash with water and soap suds, the neighbours of a Coventry feltmaker complained to the authorities, who presented him for nuisance in 1682.[140] Another feltmaker, Thomas Cawle of Southampton, created and maintained 'a filthie standynge puddle' from his suds in a lane that led to the marketplace. So bad and 'unseemelye' was this puddle that it was reported: 'people now cann hardlye passe by that waye w[i]thout durt or myre.' Both Cawle and his landlord were fined. That the Mayor's house stood along the path of this filthy puddle might have raised the profile of this case. Two years later the guilty landlord (now mayor himself) was again in trouble, this time for casting water into the road, which annoyed passers-by and damaged gardens.[141]

In theory the system of street kennels should have carried away the surface water. If urban drainage had any chance of carrying all the waste water away before the streets flooded or the water stagnated, kennels needed to be kept free from blockages.[142] Prohibitions were issued against the casting into kennels of carrion, rotting oranges and onions, rubbish, dung, sand, gravel and other substances liable to block the flow.[143]

Human waste was part of the gungy pottage that intermittently blocked the kennels. In Manchester Thomas Leigh cast excrement into a kennel outside a neighbour's house, blocking the water flow in 1686.[144] Many inhabitants of the Cock and Key Alley (between Fleet Street and Whitefriars) were presented to the annual wardmote inquest in 1617 'for not haveinge howses of office in their severall tenentes, by reason whereof they cast forth theire excrements into the highe streete and doe annoy the passengers'.[145] Different cities observed different rules concerning the disposal of human waste. Although in London in the early seventeenth century it was permissible to tip the contents of chamber pots directly into the kennel (not from a window), by the eighteenth century there was a greater expectation that citizens would collect their waste in privy pits and tubs to be collected by the night-soil men after dark.[146] Not every citizen went to the trouble of emptying their waste into the kennels. Londoner 'Widow Wall' was presented in 1638 for tipping chamber pots straight from her window, to the annoyance of her long-suffering neighbours in the St Dunstan's area.[147] In Manchester in the early seventeenth century the citizens were also permitted to decant chamber pot waste into the kennels, but not between four o'clock in the morning and nine o'clock at night.[148] There is also evidence of a shift in attitude there by the mid-eighteenth century. In 1768 John Smith was caught emptying his privy tubs in the public streets and fined for his offence.[149] It is possible that the authorities had decided it would be more appropriate for the townsfolk to empty their chamber pot waste directly into the River Irwell than into the kennels.[150] In Restoration Bath the citizens were ordered to prevent their children from doing 'theire easem[en]t or Ordure in any of the streets'. Reward money was set aside for those informing on miscreants.[151]

Citizens were expected to keep clean the kennels outside their door.[152] In Bath the council decreed in 1633 that citizens found to have swept street dirt into the kennel were to be fined (it should have been swept into orderly heaps, for collection).[153] The temptation to sweep into the kennels proved too strong for many. Cleansing orders were frequently flouted, and no less than eight householders were fined for sweeping dirt into the kennel at Manchester's Smithy Door in 1676.[154] Some years later various masters were fined for letting their servants sweep mire into the grate at Hanging Ditch, creating the potential for flooding in nearby cellars.[155] Despite the rules, clods of manure, clumps of straw, market waste and domestic sweepings blocked kennels across the country. In 1694 a dead baby lay concealed in the congealed silt of a Staines kennel after its mother 'prest it down with a spade to hide it'.[156] Once the course of water in a gutter or kennel became blocked its contents stagnated and stank, creating a fetid stew. Even when open sewers were covered over, problems could continue. The grate permitting water to enter the channel beneath Royal Exchange Gate became blocked in 1673, causing the 'continuall flowing and fowling the street with Foul water and offensive Mudd'.[157] The same problem was evident five years later, and it was reported that 'some persons have fallen and bin much damaged, and is very noysome'.[158]

'Cast no Dirt into the Well, that hath given you Water'[159]

Once it was dislodged, the waste matter clogging up the kennels would work into the system of ditches, rivers and streams that flowed through the cities. Jonathan Swift described waters bearing trophies such as dead cats, turnip-tops, 'Drown'd Puppies' and 'stinging Sprats, all drench'd in Mud' as they spewed into the ditches.[160] Large quantities of silty or chunky matter would block the watercourses. Oxford continued to rely on overland open sewers and ditches until the late eighteenth century. The 'Dunge' ditch near Binsey to the south-west was reportedly in need of cleansing in 1633, and the rivers and waters were 'much flundered and stopped for want of Clensing' the following year. The Commissioners of Sewers set about highlighting the defaults across the city and reported that the common waters were all dirty. A tax was levied on all freemen to pay for cleaning in 1652, but eight years later the river was 'flundered upp with mudde and filth' at Castle Mills and the blockage threatened to impede the mill wheels.[161] An open ditch to the east of New College had created a noisome nuisance in 1637 when it became 'floundered up with houses of office'.[162] In the 1670s it was 'overrun with mud and filth and is an occasion of stench and noysomness to the place'.[163]

The Southampton leet jurors tried to sort out the town's ditches in the early seventeenth century after they had become 'Chocked upp w[i]th weeds & filth and requier to be cleansed'. One of the town's butchers was fined for letting his stock graze along the banks of one of the ditches, which 'by multeringe downe the Earth have soe chocked upp the ditch that there cann no fish live there'. Pressure for action against this particular offender came from the Mayor, who enjoyed fishing rights and was deprived of his fish suppers. The butcher failed to undo the damage and was fined five pounds the following year. Other ditches in the town were the subjects of regular calls for scouring in the early seventeenth century, they lying 'fowle and filthie', or being 'noysome' or 'most filthie & unseemly'. Henry Lavender's ditch caused much concern in Southampton. In 1611 the Southampton jurors noted, somewhat wearily, 'we have manie tymes p[re]sented the fowle and filthie ditch Lyenge in the streat under the garden or orchard of henrye Lavender', and now 'findinge the same . . . Loathsome' recalled how Lavender had ignored a previous order to fill it up. By 1616 fears were expressed that this 'dangerous puddle' might take the life of a city child, but it continued to pose a threat for years.[164]

Bath's unattractively named Bum Ditch carried waste water along the rear of Horse Street (now Southgate). This open overflow drain presented a hazard to those nearby. After being presented at the quarter sessions in 1751 for keeping the ditch open, the council proposed that it should be filled up and pitched as soon as possible.[165] In London the Fleet Ditch (known as the 'Clocina') had started as a stream, but by the mid-seventeenth century it had become heavily polluted with waste from slaughterhouses and necessary houses that lined its path.[166] London's drainage system was improved as part of the rebuilding legislation following the fire in 1666.[167] By 1673 the Fleet had been widened and cleaned, and one portion had become the Fleet Canal.[168] In the decades that followed, the Fleet again became notoriously filthy and neglected. Rails around it decayed and 'many Persons perish'd, by falling therein by Night, and Beasts by Day'.[169] In 1722 an author, most likely to be Daniel Defoe, described the area around Field Lane as 'a Nauceious and abominable Sink of publick Nastiness'.[170] At the same time Pope was penning *The Dunciad*. He included a reference to the 'disemboguing streams' of the Fleet Ditch, as they roll a 'large tribute of dead dogs' to the Thames.[171] An Act of 1733 permitted the Corporation to fill the section of the ditch between Holborn Bridge and Fleet Bridge, which had become 'filled and choaked up with Mud . . . a grievous and abominable Nusance'. Work was complete in 1737 when the Fleet Market opened on the reclaimed ground.[172] The remaining waters were still murky and dirty. In 1749 the body of a man was dragged from the ditch. It was originally thought that he had been murdered, but on investigation he was identified as 'one who used to traverse the common sewer in search of dead dogs for the benefit of their skins'. It was supposed that in the course of his searches the man had been swept up by the tide in the covered section of the water.[173] In the 1760s the lower reach was also bricked over, and a road formed to connect with the newly opened Blackfriars Bridge.

Rivers received a rich stew from the cities – from domestic and trade sources, particles of earth, soot, sand, turds and rainwater. Silty liquid arrived via street kennels and open ditches. A small but increasing amount arrived via subterranean sewers. Some waste was discharged directly from waterside premises, such as the oily discharge from tanneries and the noxious and toxic waste products of the dyers' trade.[174] Whale, olive and rape oils used in soap-making would have polluted waters during manufacture and also when they were released during use.[175] Described as a 'a laborious nasty business', the making of soap involved boiling together lime, ashes and fats.[176] Bristol soap-boilers were ordered to halt their practice of casting waste ashes into the River Avon by the authorities, who feared it would lead to 'the utter decaie and destruction of the same river'.[177]

More solid particles of refuse were also cast into city rivers. Ordinary household waste could find its way into the waters: a notice was placed in the

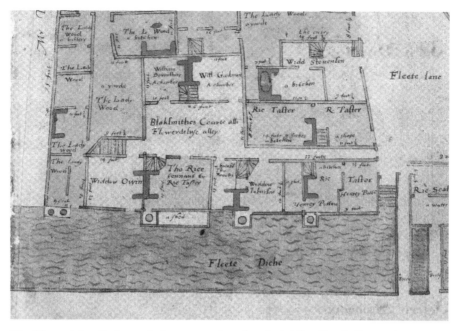

Various labels on the plan: *The Lady Wood*, *The L. Wood kitchen*, *The Lady Wood buttery*, *The Lady Wood*, *William Dowether A Chamber*, *Will Godman A chamber*, *The Lady Wood*, *Blaksmithes Courte als Flowerdeluse alley*, *The Lady Wood*, *The Lady Wood*, *Widdow Owin*, *The Rice tennant to Ric Taster*, *Ric Taster*, *R. Taster*, *Widd Stevenson*, *a kitchen*, *a shope*, *Widdow Tabues*, *Ric*, *Taster*, *Henry Potter*, *Henry Potter*, *Ric Scol*, *Fleete lane*, *Fleete Diche*

55 Five privies discharge their contents into London's Fleet Ditch. Detail from Ralph Treswell's survey of 1–6 Fleet Lane, 16–21 Farringdon Street, 1612, Clothworkers' Company Plan Book, 47.

Manchester Mercury warning people not to throw ashes, rubbish, dust or dirt into the River Irwell.[178] Most human excrement did not enter the basic sewage system because it was collected in cesspits to be removed by night-soil men for spreading on fields, but some solid human waste did reach the fluvial currents. Some privies were located above the Fleet. There were similar perches in Manchester where many discharged into a ditch that ran from Market Street Lane to Hanging Ditch.[179] A dozen citizens from London's Portsoken Ward had their 'houses of easement over the common shore' in 1692.[180] Most civic records of the period bear witness to the clandestine nocturnal dumping of offal and rotting meat into waterways. In 1728 the skins of several stolen sheep were tossed into the Thames.[181] Condemned meat was thrown into the waters by the authorities; in 1763 large quantities of meat confiscated from a butcher trading in Newgate Market were thrown into the Thames.[182]

By the eighteenth century some human effluent came to the river via underground sewers. In some cities, including Bath, the more wealthy citizens were presented with the opportunity to connect their homes up to underground sewers run by private initiative. In Bath this process began in July 1718, when Thomas Atwood and Walter Chapman drove a sewer ('a shoar') through the Upper Walks. This was not simply a drain for overflow water, as 'the Common House of Office in the said walks' discharged into it by order of the council. In December this shoar was also gathering waste from other houses of ease along its route. Gradually, a network of shoars developed incorporating Stall Street, the Duke of Chandos's new house near Cross Bath, Cox Lane and Cheap Street, Walcot Street and Westgate Street. Connections continued apace in the 1750s and 1760s.[183]

Although each city saw some developments in the quality and quantity of water supplies, with some households enjoying intermittent supplies on tap by the mid-eighteenth century, most citizens still relied on communal conduits, wells and pumps by 1770.[184] These sources were all vulnerable to pollution by the actions of others, or through their inappropriate locations. Many urban wells were positioned near privies or dirty trades and would have absorbed some of the matter from them. Inconsiderate actions compounded the problems – a gentleman was spotted abusing a well in Wigan in 1671 'by pisseing' into it.[185]

Conduits were vulnerable to pollution by the products washed at them, and by inconsiderate dumping nearby. In the cities rules were introduced limiting the types of activity permissible at communal sources of water, especially the conduits.[186] In the early seventeenth century the inhabitants of Manchester were prohibited from washing calves' heads, wooden vessels, meats, linen, wool and clothes, 'or any oth[e]r noysome thinge', at the conduit or any pump or well. It was asserted that such behaviour constituted a nuisance to 'so greate a treasure and Comoditie this towne hath'.[187] However, those giving the orders would not have been the residents expected to arduously carry water to the kitchens and yards across the city. It was reported that in 1603 the 'meaner sorte' of St Michael's parish in Southampton used to wash clothes and linen at the town conduits.[188] Poorer citizens washed at conduits because they did not have indoor space for the major upheaval of washday. Manufacturers also faced restrictions at the conduit: coopers were not permitted to hoop (that is to shrink the barrels into a watertight shape) in the water, and a butcher was fined after his maid had washed tripe and entrails 'at the trowes in houndwell howse'.[189] Officials concerned about the contamination and abuse of supplies protected Manchester's conduit.[190] In 1735 the local scavengers presented a Manchester butcher for allowing offal-ridden run-off pollute the water of a nearby well, following complaints from his neighbours.[191] A Coventry man was found emptying 'piss pots and other excrements' on the cistern over the Bull conduit.[192] In each city, the key water source was polluted with human effluent and domestic and trade waste. Matt Bramble gives his impression of the quality of the liquid to be obtained from the Thames:

> If I would drink water, I must quaff the maukish contents of an open
> aqueduct, exposed to all manner of defilement; or swallow that which comes
> from the river Thames, impregnated with all the filth of London and

Westminster – Human excrement is the least offensive part of the concrete, which is composed of all the drugs, minerals and poisons, used in mechanics and manufacture, enriched with the putrefying carcases of beasts and men; and mixed with the scourings of all the wash-tubs, kennels, and common sewers, within the bills of mortality.[193]

'Room for Improvement'[194]

The streets of each of the four cities had undergone changes between the years 1600 and 1770. Developments in Oxford and Manchester were not as dramatic as those in Bath and London. Major changes to the streets were not implemented in Oxford until the 1770s. The city's drainage and sewage disposal remained underdeveloped in the period. In 1764 one pamphlet complained that 'no City whose Streets are so spacious, and whose Public Buildings so magnificent, is so ill swept.' The pamphlet also drew attention to the citizens' habit of dumping waste outside public buildings, identifying the Clarendon Printing House as the key site – 'every Angle of which serves as a Reservoir for the Rubbish of the whole Neighbourhood'.[195] Following examples set elsewhere the Manchester authorities established a body of improvement commissioners in 1765 to oversee street cleaning and fire-fighting, and to consider nuisances. However, this body lacked energy and ceased to meet in 1776.[196] Most of the day-to-day care of the outdoor environment still rested with the co-opted manorial officers.

Bath's success as a visitor destination relied on having a pleasant outdoor environment. For this reason it is not surprising that by 1770 the streets of Bath were cleaner and better paved than Oxford and Manchester, and that the system of urban drainage was also superior. However, this had not always been the case. John Wood likened the mid-seventeenth-century streets to 'so many Dunghills, Slaughter-Houses and Pig-Styes', littered with 'Soil of all sorts . . . even Carrion'.[197] During the eighteenth century improved river transport ensured a steady supply of good-quality non-slip sandstone paving materials for society folk to promenade on.[198] In 1747 one visitor was impressed that he could walk from 'the End of the Parade, quite to the Pump-Room, on a fine Pavement' that kept him clean, even in inclement weather.[199] Visiting from his Cornish parsonage in 1766 the Revd John Penrose was impressed by the streets. He wrote, 'it is good walking here; for some of the Streets are all paved with flat Stones on each side of them, from which the Wet soon wears off.' [200] However, five years earlier Count Kielmansegge had damned the streets with faint praise, remarking that Bath had 'fairly good pavement (which appears to be better than it really is), compared with that of London'.[201] The Bath Act (1757) reiterated rules governing cleansing and paving, and gave stronger controls to vestries to oversee and enforce the rules.[202] A more significant

56 Purbeck paving slabs on King's Bench Walk, London.

57 Purbeck paving slabs at Hare Court, London.

Act of 1766[203] placed the duty of care for the streets on a body of commissioners. A regime of daily morning street-cleaning was outlined, and boxes for dust and litter were to be provided in public areas for the first time.[204] Bath did have some squalid areas, including a 'triangular piece of Ground before the Grand Parade', and a twelve-foot strip of land before South Parade where soil and ashes were regularly dumped, to be picked over by poor citizens hoping to salvage larger chunks of cinders to reuse or sell.[205] However, compared to Manchester and Oxford, the street experience in Bath was certainly a superior one.

A limitation of the old system based on householder responsibility was that pavements could not be guaranteed to have a consistency of height or a uniformity of materials. The most important development resulting from the Westminster Paving Act of 1762 was that responsibility for maintenance of the streets was taken from the householders and placed with a body of commissioners, who had powers of taxation. This ensured a greater degree of uniformity. Henceforth, Purbeck paving rather than pebbles were to be used on the streets, and the carriageway was to have a camber that would allow for side gutters rather than central channels. The eighteenth century had seen some efforts to tackle this but only on newly cut streets. A new street in London's Holborn, forming an extension of Red Lion Street, was assessed in 1706 to establish the paving requirements. It was decided that one part of the street was to be paved in stone, up to victualler Edward Izard's property, but that gravel would suffice further north (where it was presumably more sparsely populated or lightly trafficked).[206] In the 1740s the commissioners of sewers and pavements concluded that a major factor leading to the 'Badness of the Foot-ways in the narrow Streets' was the lack of uniform surfaces. Henceforth, they ordered, such streets will be 'new paved or repaired . . . with Purbeck Squares, or large broad flat Pebbles, two Foot in the Street, from the Curbs of the Cellar Windows, or Spurs or Steps of the Houses'. The report ended on a threatening point, that if the paviors and those who engage them do not carry out the orders, 'they will Answer the contrary at their Peril'.[207]

However, even after they had been granted similar improvement acts, London and other towns and cities in England still experienced particular street-related problems. It took many years to implement changes on existing roads and buildings. Many old buildings still sported projecting waterspouts rather than downpipes.[208] Littering continued in every urban centre, including loads shed from rakers' carts. Hanway thought that 'one of the greatest absurdities that ever prevailed' was that these carts were not equipped with a device to prevent them leaking en route, thereby resoiling freshly cleansed streets.[209] Although an increasing number of pavements were raised above the level of the carriageway, many were not, leaving them 'liable to be annoyed with Mud and Filth, and to be overflowed with water'.[210] Elevated pavements were difficult to accommodate on narrow roads, and where carts and coaches needed to turn into mews or stable blocks.[211] Pavements without raised kerbs could be divorced from the road by chunky bollards, but these took up a lot of pedestrian space.[212] Iron-shod wheels still damaged the road surfaces. Jonas Hanway suggested a solution – make the wheels broader, use larger stones and improve the substratum of the streets to make them more durable – but it was not until the nails on the rims were countersunk (in the 1770s) that improvements could be made.[213] Water companies still pitted and pot-holed the streets and failed to make good their repairs. [214] A key problem was one of enforcement: it was an expensive business to remedy nuisances through the legal system.[215]

CHAPTER 9

Gloomy

At the close of the sixteenth century a physician listed the four 'properties of wholesome aire'. First, air should be 'faire and cleare without vapours and mistes'. Second, it would be 'lightsome and open, not darke, troublous and close'. Third, 'not infected with carrian lying long above ground'. Finally, wholesome air would not be 'stinking or corrupted with ill vapours, as being neere to draughts, Sinckes, dunghills, gutters, chanels, kitchings, Church-yardes, or standing waters'.[1] The notion that air quality and environment were important to health stretched back to antiquity. If drawn into the body, bad airs were thought to cause internal corruption. In his manual of 1703 Richard Neve advised builders to chose locations with 'good Healthy Air', ruling out areas subject to 'foggy Noisomeness from Fens, or Marshes'. Neve also stipulated the need for gentle breezes 'which will Fan, and Purge the Air; the want of which would make it like a stagnated Pool, or standing Lake of Air (which is very unhealthy)'. Furthermore, the ideal location would not lack the 'sweet influence of the Sun-beams'.[2] This was a tall order on a small island.

'Nostrils stuff up with the tainted Air'[3]

Some city locations were blighted and drew the opprobrium of commentators. The air of Cambridge was notorious for its poor quality. John Evelyn found the city 'situated in a low dirty unpleasant place' and had thick air 'infested by the fenns'.[4] Even a Dutch traveller declared it to be unhealthily 'heavy and murky' in summer, due to 'the vapours from the bog lands'.[5] In the 1740s John Wood bemoaned the poor press that Bath's air had endured, complaining that 'Popular Prejudice and Ignorance' had 'Decreed this eminent Place to be a City standing in a Hole, and built on a Quagmire; to be Impenetrable to the very Beams of the Sun . . . that People can hardly . . . Breathe or Converse beyond the Smell of their own Excrements'. He attempted to quash such 'false and malicious Representations'.[6] Some believed that the health-giving qualities of the hot springs countered any disadvantage of the low situation of the city.[7] Others dismissed them as giving off 'sickly, crude, offensive Vapours'.[8]

Some cities were wafted through with health-giving breezes and without fenland murk. A wholesome air cleansed Nottingham, a city positioned on a sandstone bluff a convenient distance from the fast-flowing River Trent. The citizens avoided the 'crude, chilly, aguish vapours' commonly suffered by those living near slow-running rivers.[9] Oxford in the 1650s suited the needs of itinerant German scholar Henry Oldenburg, partly due to its 'healthful air'.[10] Nearly a century later the seasoned traveller Thomas Salmon largely concurred; but added that Oxford's record of good health was blemished in the winter. Waters that flooded the meadows stagnated, releasing 'vapours . . . that are not very Salutory: It is observable also, that these Meadows lie chiefly on the South and West part of the City, from which points the Winds usually blow, and consequently the Air of the Town must be very moist.'[11]

Homes were heated by burning timber and coal, generating soot, dust and billowing clouds of smoke. Initially coal had been unpopular due to its acrid smell, but falling prices seduced thrifty consumers.[12] Coal remained unpopular among those who could afford to burn wood. Dudley Ryder thought that English coal was especially smoky, and had a particularly foul smell and unsavoury taste.[13] Despite the rising use of coal to heat dwellings, John Evelyn did not think that domestic fires were the primary cause of smoke pollution, remarking that they contributed 'little, or nothing in comparison [with the] . . . foul mouth'd Issues' of certain trades (a modern expert has queried this assertion). Evelyn claimed that the city smoke blanket thinned on Sundays, when these establishments were closed.[14] Urban craftsmen such as maltsters, brewers and hammersmiths used smoky ovens, furnaces and forges.[15] Abraham Shakemaple, a Finsbury smith, filled Grub Street with 'filthie smoke' in 1612, and smoke from a goldsmith working in London's Fleet Street engulfed all passers-by whenever his forge was fired up.[16]

Cities consumed increasing quantities of building material as they expanded, and much fuel was burned in the manufacture of lime mortar and bricks. Lime kilns surrounded London, burning chalk lime from the nearby hills.[17] A citizen of Bath created a 'nuisance to this City by his Lime Kiln' at the end of the seventeenth century.[18] Bricks were expensive to transport so they were manufactured in or around urban developments. Brick kilns were frequently cited as sources of annoying smoke, and the stench coming from them was described as being 'exactly like carrion, to such a degree as to excite nausea'.[19] Evelyn singled out several areas of London as suffering from extreme smoke pollution, including Bank-Side near the Falcon (the location of brick kilns and breweries) and St Paul's.[20] In the 1760s smoky gusts from the Chelsea waterworks and nearby brick kilns blew across Queen's Palace (now Buckingham Palace).[21] The effects of materials manufacture even irritated the plutocrats of urban expansion. Property developer the Duke of Chandos moaned that his exclusive house in London's Cavendish Square was 'poisoned with the brick kilns and other abominate smells which infect these parts'.[22]

'Leave the smutty Ayr of London, and com hither to breath sweeter'[23]

Some cities managed smoke through zoning activities, others were assisted by favourable topography. One of the advantages in Manchester was the welcome 'strong gust' of wind that regularly blew the town 'clear of the mingling wreath of smoke that curled up from its modest chimneys'.[24] Although Nottingham was surrounded by areas of clay land and had numerous brick-kilns, these were established 'at a Distance sufficient to give no Annoyance'.[25]

As a general rule, the western side of any town or city was (and still is) the most salubrious part, and therefore home to the most desirable and fashionable areas. Prevailing westerly winds carried industrial and domestic effluvia across to the east, and prevented carriage of fumes and dust from those parts. Many affluent Londoners chose to settle in the west during the suburban boom of the seventeenth and eighteenth centuries. In Sir William Petty's words, they sought to escape 'the fumes, steams and stinks of the whole Easterly Pyle, which where seacoal is burnt is a great matter'.[26] Winds carried noisome air to the poorer suburbs in the east. According to Henry Fielding, Ealing had the best air 'in the whole Kingdom', being high and exposed to the south and 'guarded from the smells and smoak of London by its distance'.[27] Queen Square, 'which is Held by Me', boasted John Wood, was built in the north-west of Bath 'on a High, Airy, and Healthy Spot of Ground'. It became one of the city's most exclusive addresses.[28]

However, smoke was generally not easily or quickly carried away from the cities and towns, especially as they became increasingly built up and industrial.[29] John Evelyn found Leicester pestered with chimney flues 'like so many smiths forges'.[30] The atmosphere was so smoky in some areas that people near to house fires often perceived them by hearing crackling sounds, rather than smelling smoke. The Finnish botanist Pehr Kalm was in London in March 1748 when a fire engulfed houses near London's Royal Exchange. Few people were aware of the fire, because 'thick and voluminous smoke' commonly floated 'over the town'.[31]

London's air was indeed blighted; a letter in *The Spectator* mentioned living 'within the Smoke of London'.[32] In September 1676 Robert Hooke was riding on a jolting horse. Pausing to nurse his bruised testicles he observed the cloud of smoke over London. The consummate measurer estimated the mass to be half a mile high and over twenty miles long.[33] During a visit to Hampton Court in 1652 Dutchman Lodewijk Huygens cast his eye back to the capital.

He was surprised that St Paul's Cathedral and the bell tower were 'too much obscured by smoke' to pick out.[34] Georg Lichtenberg described 'the cloud of smoke which hangs perpetually over immeasureable London, which is round about a German mile distant'. Smoke-induced mid-morning gloom forced this continental tourist to write his travel account by candlelight.[35] In the opening gambit to his *Fumifugium* (1661) John Evelyn stressed the unpleasant visual aspects of the smoke around Whitehall. This was probably calculated to appeal to the aesthetic concerns of Charles II, to whom his book was dedicated. Evelyn illustrated how the area was invaded and 'infested' with this smoke 'to such a degree, as Men could hardly discern one another for the Clowd'. He described the smoke of London as a 'prodigious annoyance' and a 'pernicious *Nuisance*', painting an emotive image of a proud and stately city with her head wrapped 'in Clowds of Smoake and Sulphur, so full of Stink and Darknesse'.[36]

The smoke did more than spoil the views. The unpleasant, choking smog spoilt food, smutted linen and buildings and suffocated vegetation. It also suffocated the citizens. As early as 1610 a surveyor complained that the chimneys proliferating in the country 'raise so many duskie cloudes in the ayre [which] . . . hinder the heat and light from the Sunne from earthly creatures'.[37] John Graunt conducted early analyses of London's bills of mortality and published his results in *Natural and Political Observations* (1676). Graunt asserted that a low life expectancy among Londoners was due to 'Fumes, Steams, and Stenches' creating an environment 'less healthful that that of the Country'. It was hard to endure 'the smoak of *London*, not only for its unpleasantness but for the suffocations which it causes'.[38] Thomas Tryon raged against the 'unwholesome Airs' of built-up areas, the 'stinking, gross sulphurous Smoaks' that proved 'very often Pernicious to Mankind, by Infecting the common Air with terrible Pestilences and Distempers'.[39] John Evelyn's key concern was for the health of citizens forced to breathe 'nothing but an impure and thick Mist, accompanied with a fuliginous and filthy vapour, which renders them obnoxious to a thousand inconveniences, corrupting the Lungs and disordering the entire habit of their Bodies; so that Catharrs, Phthisicks, Coughs and Consumptions, rage more in this one City, than in the whole Earth besides . . .' Evelyn cursed the '*Coughing* and *Snuffing*' heard in '*London* Churches and Assem[b]lies of People, where the Barking and Spitting is uncessant'.[40] Spluttering congregations were so commonplace by 1732 that a chemist advertised an 'Inestimable, Angelical Electuary' to ward off disease in consideration of the 'daily Disturbance in churches, by continual coughing'.[41]

Proffering advice about how to purge the smoggy air, Evelyn proposed that smoky trades should be removed from the centre and sited about five miles away, especially those trades that consumed much sea coal (that is, coal imported by sea from Newcastle), including brewers, dyers, soap and salt boilers, and lime burners. Evelyn also suggested that London be ringed with a green belt of fragrant plants – although not cabbages, as their 'rotten and perishing stalks have a very noisom and unhealthy smell'.[42]

Some citizens took a country home in order to escape from the harmful conditions in the city and breathe in the ambrosial 'country air'.[43] Others needed to be content with occasional trips into the countryside. In the early eighteenth century money was raised to repair Bath's Lansdown Road so that invalids could travel by sedan chair up the hill to take the airs beyond the city. After the road was turnpiked residents and visitors wishing to take the air were reimbursed their toll on return to the city.[44] In seeking to limit the fees set by chair carriers in 1739 the Bath authorities were keen to ensure that sick visitors 'may be carried at a reasonable Rate into a Region free from Smoak and Smell of the City; since the Invalids [may wish to] take the Benefit of the fresh Air'.[45]

'What serves Dirt, if it do not stink?'[46]

Smoke mingled with other smells in the semi-industrial cities. Areas were immersed in cocktails of odours from combinations of animals, minerals and plants. Districts became associated with their particular stenches. London's Southwark was the centre of various manufacturing trades, including the dyers, brewers, lime-burners and makers of glass and saltpetre, all of which polluted the air, water and land nearby.[47] Paint-making, described by Campbell as 'an odious stinking Business', was concentrated away from the City, also in Southwark.[48] London's hat-makers plied their stinking trade in the Bridewell area (Thomas Tryon served his apprenticeship there).[49] The fumes produced in the workshops of craftsmen such as apothecaries, horners, jersey-combers and sulphur workers were so prodigious that they could not be contained within the premises. Odours leaked readily from their draughty workshops. Gilders risked being dazed, deafened or made dumb by breathing the vapours of their trade, while the fumes inhaled by pewterers were thought to make them paralytic.[50] Indeed, in order to have any chance of survival during the worst processes, workers would have needed good ventilation. Throwing open doors and windows, they would have dispersed the noxious vapours across the neighbourhood.

Woad balls, used by dyers to create blue hues, emitted such a disgusting sulphurous stench when fermenting that Queen Elizabeth banned woad processing within five miles of a royal residence.[51] In the early seventeenth century labourers employed by Southampton dyer Philip De la Mote were fined for casting woad and water from the dye house into the back part of the street, 'w[hi]ch is most unseemelye & Causeth unsavorie smells to the people passinge bye, and therefore not sufferable'.[52] This nuisance continued after De la Mote's death, when the business passed into the control of his widow. Mrs De la Mote was given increasingly steep fines for the pollution.[53] Industrial enterprises like the De la Motes' were backyard affairs; others were on a grander scale. The Wapping alum works established in 1626 caused consternation to neighbours disgusted by the pong from the furnaces for boiling urine. Local brewers discovered that the waste discharge had corrupted their water supply from wells. The pollution was so bad that the Privy Council issued a closure order in 1627. Despite this, the works were still operating two years later.[54]

The pungency of plants and minerals combined with the odours thrown off in the heating or treatment of animal fats and skins. Of particular concern was the vile smell created when tallow was melted. Mr Campbell warned that breathing is difficult 'near the Scent of a Tallow-Chandler's Work-House'.[55] The smell was thought to be sufficiently potent to induce hysteria.[56] During an outbreak of the plague in 1625 the Oxford authorities ordered chandlers to remove their melting houses from the High Street and forbear melting tallow in the open streets within the walls during the hot summer months.[57] William Ackland was presented to the Portsoken wardmote inquest in 1723 'for melting of Rough Tallow in the Day time to the great Annoyance of the Inhabitants'.[58] Pondering the possible motivations that led Susanna Garner to set fire to her own house on Charles Street (near Downing Street in London) in 1769, one witness suggested it could have been an act of revenge against her immediate neighbour, a tallow-chandler, Mr Wells. The witness claimed that at the time of the arson attack Garner had been lamenting the loss of a child, and was reported to have said that 'the stink of Mr Well's tallow was the death of her child . . . she would be revenged'.[59] The smell is hard to imagine now, but anyone who has smelt one tallow candle burn might have some idea of what this acrid stench might be like if it was multiplied on an industrial scale.

Tanners working hides endured the stench of both the raw product and the solutions used to make it pliable and smooth, such as urine, lime, alum and bark. Council officials sniffed out 'diverse and sundry corrupt and unvendible skinnes' at the houses of two Oxford furriers in 1617.[60] Streets around the tanneries worked by several Manchester men were frequently strewn with 'Stinking raw Hides' awaiting treatment in the eighteenth century.[61] An interesting case heard in the 1730s concerned the stench from tanning pits in Tooting Lane, Wandle. The case centred on the appropriateness of the location of the pits, and the manager was accused of infecting and corrupting the air nearby. The defendant was found guilty and fined one hundred pounds for a public nuisance.[62]

It is clear when comparing contemporary reactions to smoke pollution with smells created by noxious substances such as rancid fats and street dirt that more concern was paid to the latter than the former. Indeed, such was the ambivalence surrounding the issue of smoke that some thought it would even protect against diseases such as the plague.[63] In Nottingham during an outbreak of the plague it was noted that the most badly affected lived on the higher ground. One street, known as 'Narrow Marsh', lay at the foot of the sandstone cliff and was thought to be immune from the outbreak. There were nearly fifty tanneries in that area at the time and wealthy Nottingham folk, seeking protection in the form of smoke from 'burning moist Tanners Knobs', crowded into it, mingling with the indigenous tanners.[64]

Despite John Evelyn's efforts at enlightenment, it was not respiratory disease that caught the medical limelight, but the ill-effects of infectious airs, polluted by rotting or stagnating matter. Fearing for the health of citizens, Thomas Tryon echoed popular concerns by fretting about 'gross stinking Foggs, Scents and Vapours' that he thought unclean and damaging to the mind and body, especially to the young, with 'their tender, fine spirits'. Tryon included slaughterhouses and butchers' shops, and other trades using the by-products of the meat industry such as the tallow-chandlers, among the chief culprits in the production of bad air. Musing about the odours in animal dung, Tryon worried most about horse manure – a substance so offensive that it put people off their food and 'infects them with sundry Diseases'. On inhalation of such 'gross or foul smells', Tryon advised his followers to open their mouths, sending the noxious particles immediately back out of the body. [65]

A strong belief in the harmful effects of bad airs – or miasmas – prevailed throughout the period. It was thought that the corrupt air itself caused and spread diseases when it was breathed in. Memories of the dreadful Oxford Assize fever of 1577, which killed hundreds 'by a poysonous Steam', lingered long.[66] In 1750 the Old Bailey was similarly affected (with fewer mortalities, although including Mayor Samuel Pennant and two judges), after disease spread from the nearby Newgate Prison. Reports noted 'a very Noisome Smell' and blamed the 'putrid *Effluvia* which the Prisoners bring with them in their Cloaths, &c. especially where too many are brought into a crowded Court together, may have fatal effects on People who are accustomed to breath better Air' (in reality both outbreaks were likely to have been caused by typhus, a disease spread by lice).[67] Miasmas were thought to drift up from corpses and carcasses, stagnant gutters and ditches, dunghills, privies and any other festering matter. Miasmatic fears were heightened during epidemics.[68] It was considered desirable to place the diseased away from the populace, and, if possible, in the fresh air. During a plague outbreak in 1609 the Oxford Council stipulated that cabins should be erected for the afflicted 'if a convenient place may bee gotton'. Eventually the decision was made to site them near Port Meadow, to the north-west of the city.[69] A pesthouse was constructed at Port Meadow Gate in 1641. It was removed four years later, and the timber stored in the Guildhall, to be re-erected in 1665, owing to 'the present siklyness of the

Season'.[70] Miasmatic theory was still informing medical knowledge in 1720 when Richard Mead, a fellow of the College of Physicians and of the Royal Society, conducted an inquiry into how the air was made infectious by the 'Stinks of stagnating waters' and 'the Corruption of dead Carcasses'.[71] Even by the end of the eighteenth century such views were presented as self-evident. 'It is well known', remarked a fumigator, 'that foetid smells, stagnated and putrid Air, are in general the Cause of many Dreadful Diseases; such as Malignant Fevers, putrid sore Throats, the Plague, &c, &c.'[72]

Matter, including air, which was considered to be 'infectious' and was supposed to cause disease could be treated as a public nuisance. The civic authorities stressed this notion when issuing fines and warnings to nuisance creators. A significant case heard in 1610 clarified the legal position on infectious odours. In Harlesdon, Norfolk, Thomas Benton had set up a pigsty in his garden, creating a fetid stench. The smell of the sty was annoying to his neighbour, William Aldred. Benton argued that no one should be so tender nosed that they could not tolerate the smell of pigs. Presiding, Chief Justice Wray ordered that the case was actionable because the air was infected and corrupted; wholesome air had been stopped.[73] When in 1624 the fouling at the De la Mote establishment in Southampton resumed, the authorities voiced their concerns that it 'might bring infectious disease'.[74] Rotting offal fed to dogs by Abraham Alsopp, a Hackney hound and beagle keeper, was feared to corrupt and infect the air nearby.[75] In 1733, Lewis Smart, a distiller who lived near Tottenham Court Road, kept several hundred pigs. Accused of a public nuisance for letting his sty become constantly offensive, his defence argued unsuccessfully that his pigs were a 'public convenience', as they consumed the waste products of his trade. His product was good for the citizens in general, and therefore he could not be judged a public nuisance. Lewis also argued that his piggery was well sited, as the area was already blighted by the stench of cows, nightmen's pits, common laystalls and a ditch. The defence even tried to shift the blame on to these other sources and argued that the neighbours were little troubled by his pigs. They also argued that a few should tolerate any nuisance for the sake of the public good. However, this was an extreme nuisance: householders fell sick and were deserted by their servants. The value of local properties declined, linen was discoloured and silver tarnished. Lewis's neighbours presented such a convincing olfactory picture of dangerously odiferous swine that he was found guilty on the basis that his sty caused infection.[76] In each of these cases it was the potential to spread disease, rather than annoy the senses, that captured attention.

For the same reasons that pesthouses were kept at a distance from the populace, noxious trades were also zoned to some degree in the towns. Trades such as candle-making, brewing, pig-keeping and dog-breeding were often clustered in particular areas. Because of the stench, and the associated fire risks of melting tallow, chandlering had long been prohibited from particular areas in cities.[77] 'It hath been holden', wrote the eighteenth-century barrister William Hawkins, 'that it is no common nusance to make Candles in a Town, because the Needfulness of them shall dispense with the Noisomness of the Smell.' However, Hawkins questioned this, arguing that they could be made anywhere, and 'surely the Trade of a Brewer is as necessary as that of a Chandler, and yet it seems to be agreed, That a Brew-house, erected in such an Inconvenient Place, wherein the Business cannot be carried on without greatly incommoding the Neighbourhood, may be indicted as a common Nusance. And so in the like Case may a Glass-House or Swineyard.'[78] Another legal writer, William Blackstone, noted that tanners, tallow-chandlers and similar trades, although 'lawful and necessary', should be 'exercised in remote places'.[79] John Evelyn held long-cherished hopes that chandlers and butchers would be completely expelled from London to avoid exposure to 'horrid stinks, *niderous* and unwholsome smells which proceed from the Tallow, and corrupted Blood'.[80] Evelyn argued that freshly slaughtered meat and candles should be carted into the city. This would avoid livestock being driven through narrow streets, creating noisome smells in the crowded city centre. In 1760 the stench from the slaughterhouse of a butcher in London's Cannon Street was so noisome that it caused a slump in rents. A house once let at twenty-five pounds per year became fit only for the poorest subtenants.[81] Smells from slaughterhouses near Bath's Pulteney Bridge triggered complaints in the 1750s. Citizens called for their removal in the 1770s.[82]

'It is an ill Air, where nothing is to be gained'[83]

There were still many tracts of open space in many city centres. The Manchester of the seventeenth century still had bosky woods close to town, providing opportunities for fishing and strolling. Oxford colleges retained large green spaces for water meadows, orchards and walled gardens. Magdalen College occupied a large plot of land: it was the most expansive green area in Oxford with an edge-of-city location that abutted Shotover Forest. The river and fence enclosures kept animals in and the great unwashed out. In 1609 Magdalen engaged workmen to form a footpath in St Clement's Street to 'divert the inconvenient multitude of peasants, and to turn away the idle rabble of the poor of the city of Oxford'.[84] Even though they were often denied access, the citizens would have benefited from the trees and greenery in private gardens, which reduced airborne pollution. Part of the attraction of Bath for visitors was the spaces available for open air promenading. In the 1720s and 1730s the council bore the costs of removing the palisades and pillars which had stood between the Upper and Lower Walks in Bath, and to repair the Walks and slope the ground, making them 'fit for people to walk in and made into one ground'.[85] Even London had a sufficient amount of open spaces to impress the German traveller Conrad von Uffenbach in 1710.[86]

However, open spaces were shrinking in all of the cities as the period progressed. Some increase in population was accommodated by outward spread. Virgin land and peripheral wastes were clawed away by the fingers of development.[87] Swineherding had been carried out on Collyhurst waste in Manchester since 1567, but it was abandoned in 1616 when only forty acres were left due to building and enclosure.[88] This probably led to an increase in the numbers of pigs prowling the town centre. As cities expanded beyond their walls the distance to green open space beyond the town also grew.

In 1630 fellows of the College of Physicians were invited by the Privy Council to consider ways to prevent further outbreaks of the plague. In their report the physicians pointed to conditions that gave opportunities for disease to multiply, including the effects of building to accommodate newcomers, who depleted the quantity and quality of air.[89] The notion that extra bodies would consume available air adds another dimension to the understanding of air in the period. Yet even while the physicians were making their suggestions, London and other cities were expanding and infilling. The availability of fresh air was regarded as an indicator of the quality of life. In the countryside the 'wholsome Air suspends the Doctors Bills', quipped Ned Ward.[90]

Such was the pace of expansion in London that in 1613 it dawned on the bewigged Society of Lincoln's Inn that their nearby stamping ground of Lincoln's Inn Fields would not escape development for much longer. The Society worried that developers would 'fill upp that small remaynder of Ayre in those partes with unnecessary and unprofittable Buildinges, which have been found the greatest meanes of breedinge and harbouring Scarcity and Infection'. The petitioners claimed that such building would be a nuisance, 'to the generall inconvenience of the whole Kingdome'. Hoping to frustrate potential construction they asked for this expansive marshy tract to be drained and converted to a recreation ground – treatment recently undertaken at Moorfields. Despite some consideration and surveying, the walks did not materialise, and the prospect of building loomed. During Charles I's reign the Society petitioned the Privy Council. Building, they argued, would deprive the lawyers of fresh air, and annoy them with 'offensive and unhealthful savors' and disquiet their studies. Their bid was largely unsuccessful; although the central area was kept free for walks, buildings multiplied around the periphery.[91]

The remarks of the Lincoln's Inn petitioners show a dread of contaminated and close air. Although other concerns are evident in their petitions, what comes through sharply was the desire to preserve spaciousness and fresh air. The ability to live in an environment where goods could ventilate and air circulate easily was seen as health-giving. Crowding brought dankness and dinginess. Other bodies bought noise, dirt, inconvenience and disease. With increased densities came corrupt and unwholesome air – and this bothered people more than the curtailment of visual and aural privacy. When they petitioned Parliament in 1645 the Society complained that their walks had become littered with thousands of loads of dung and dirt, and a common horse pool, remarking that they were 'quite deprived of their former liberty of Walking, Training, drying of Cloathes, and recreating themselves in the said fields'. Nearly a century later, in the preamble to an Act for enclosing the fields (1735)[92] Lincoln's Inn Fields was described as having 'for some years past lain waste and in great Disorder, whereby the same has become a Receptacle for Rubbish, Dirt and Nastiness of all Sorts'.[93] The 'Bog Houses' on the fields had even gained notoriety as a homosexual pick-up point.[94] The Society's fears were vindicated.[95]

'Airy Habitations for Merchants and Gentlemen of Taste'

As space for fine developments became increasingly hard to find, some commentators looked to areas already established as residential but which housed the poorer citizens as places fit for redevelopment. John Wood singled out the high strand of land which lay near the curve of the River Avon, at Stall Boat Quay and Boat Stall, as a good plot to build upon, but was dismayed that 'instead of finding it covered with Habitations for the chief Citizens, it is filled . . . with Hovels for the Refuse of the People'.[96] At the same time, over in London, Joseph Massie was eyeing up the area of Lower Moorfields, 'where the Brokers of Household Goods live'. He suggested that another (less desirable) plot be found 'for the Internment of *Lunaticks*' (the Hospital of St Mary's of Bethlehem, otherwise known as Bedlam), and the demolition of the slums in Blackfriars and Whitefriars. He proposed that a square be established in each place, and advised the creation of 'airy Streets', which would make 'pleasant and airy Habitations for Merchants and Gentlemen of Taste'.[97]

Great ingenuity was needed to accommodate migrants into popular cities, especially walled cities with rules against suburban development. Buildings that had formerly sheltered just one family were split into houses of multiple occupation. Houses were also extended upwards (sometimes with the addition of cocklofts). Pockets of small-scale development saw the spaces between buildings utilised. Infilling the established urban fabric was common in towns with narrow medieval burgage plots. Backyard space was increasingly squeezed by extending buildings backwards, or by erecting new buildings in yards and on the backs of houses. Such developments continued until small groups of court houses gathered together, becoming gradually more integrated with the properties fronting the street. The infill started early in London: Ralph Treswell's surveys of the turn of the seventeenth century show the cramped living quarters of many Londoners, 'creating architectural conglomerates characterised by a confusing complexity' (see figure 44 on p. 148 and figure 55 on p. 200).[98] By the mid-eighteenth century desirable houses that fronted the principal city streets often had several neighbours to their rear, accessed via narrow alleyways and dark entries.[99]

The increased density of buildings in central Oxford becomes apparent when contrasting Ralph Agas's map of 1578 with David Loggan's map, drawn a century later. Loggan's map shows a city that has burst through its walls, and demonstrates the scale of wasteland development. Demand for space was high at the time, with college developments often absorbing much of the central land; residential plots were squeezed. Several city wall towers were converted into dwellings.[100] The erection of a row of cottages down the side of a rear garden was common in Oxford from the seventeenth until the early nineteenth century.[101] Such developments are evident in Holywell Street, Swan Passage off the High Street, Bliss Court off Broad Street, Ship Street, George Street and Gloucester Green. The effect of this infill was to reduce land available for storage yards, gardens and orchards, to reduce light from interiors by blocking windows, and to increase urban population densities. Infill placed greater pressure on amenities; as one physician put it, 'the more pent-up the Houses, the lower and closer the Rooms, the narrower the Streets, the smaller the Windows, the more numerous the Inhabitants, the unhealthier the Place.'[102]

'Crouding up the streets to an unseemly and inconvenient narrowness'

The sense of being squeezed was not particular to crowded courts and alleys; it was evident on the main streets too, and was especially noticeable in claustrophobic narrow medieval streets. Urban wasteland was common ground not in use.[103] Over the years, much central urban wasteland was nibbled away by building. These encroachments usually took the form of small additions, such as cellar stairs, shop signs, bow windows, horse blocks or pigsties. The encroachments were often part of retail or service establishments, extended to allow for expanding business. To provide storage space for increasing quantities of stock shopkeepers banged up lean-tos against walls and erected sheds, stalls, 'bulks' and 'pentices' in the streets.[104] Bowed windows helped shop sellers to entice customers by providing enclosed and protected spaces in which to display their wares. By adding such a window on to a property, the shopkeeper could gain an advantage over neighbouring traders by over-shadowing their properties.[105]

The City of London licensed 'purprestures', private encroachments on the street, usually for a small fine and yearly rent.[106] In Oxford the council owned the waste and controlled encroachments upon it (although not to the satisfaction of the university). Many Oxford encroachments were viewed as a regular form of income; the constructor would pay rent on land taken from the city – a 'languable' ('land-gavel').[107] An Oxford baker sought retrospective permission for his 'pretty porch' and 'small window' in 1625, promising an annual peppercorn rent and offering a one-off payment. His insistence that he was 'not willing to have an eyesore to any man' might have swung his case, and the council accepted his deal.[108]

As the population of Oxford expanded in the seventeenth century central urban wasteland contracted. The civic authorities often tolerated encroachments as long as they were not excessively large or inconvenient. These irregularly built structures were often misaligned to the street and disregarded a uniform building line. Some of the citizens went too far in their developments; chandler John Toldervey's massive encroachment jutted far into Oxford High Street in 1624.[109] Where the city saw opportunities to maximise civic income through leasing wasteland, the university saw 'unsightly and obstructive jetties, chimneys and shop signs'. In response the city claimed to permit only those encroachments that did not deface the street.[110] Anthony Wood highlighted the hypocrisy of town complaints about the university's conduit (see chapter 7 above, 'Busy'), when town-sanctioned encroachments nearby posed a greater nuisance. Wood blamed 'greedy officers of the towne court' desiring money from languables, against the long-term interests of the city.[111] In the 1630s the university identified various unacceptable Oxford encroachments and tried to gain Privy Council help to oversee their destruction.[112] When Mr Loveday, the proprietor of Oxford's Blue Boar Inn, made a great encroachment on the street in 1660 the council rather weakly expressed hope that he would make some modifications.[113] Four years later Oxford was so pestered by encroachments that the council declared that such excrescences detracted from the beauty, and derogated the honour, of the city. The city viewers were asked to report back to the council with recommendations.[114] Complaints about encroachments had reduced by the end of the seventeenth century, as the population levelled and the demand for land fell.[115]

Problematic encroachments were common in Bath in the following century. Before major suburban developments the citizens crowded into the 'small Compass of the City'. Defoe complained that Bathonians 'croud up the Streets to an unseemly and inconvenient Narrowness'.[116] Bath Corporation officials investigated building work contracted by the poet and milliner Mary Chandler in 1738. Chandler was ordered to make good damage to the town wall that occurred when she constructed a new lodging house between the Orange Grove and the abbey, abutting the city wall. She was also fined ten shillings, plus five guineas for stones she had filched from the city wall.[117] Demand for land was also quickening in Manchester by the mid-eighteenth century; vacant street fronts were filling up quickly and jetties were underfilled to maximise city space. Small encroachments proliferated like verrucas along the town's medieval-plan streets. In 1747 one man erected a 'Hovel to grind Razors in'.[118] When Robert Oldham of Hanging Ditch erected a small building in the public street two years later he was given a month to remove it. Samuel Mellor promised to shave ten inches from the steps to his house at Smithy Door (this was a cramped location) and nine inches from his horse block in 1753.[119] Showing some desperation in 1770 the constables paid James Bancroft of Toad Lane more than two pounds to leave his land clear of building 'to make the King's highway more open'.[120]

'To make the King's highway more open'

Encroachments had become such a problem in London by the mid-eighteenth century that Joseph Massie, clamouring for reform, accepted that most would have to be 'lamented' rather than 'remedy'd'.[121] Massie drew particular attention to building creep, whereby front walls were advanced 'several Inches . . . into the Street, beyond their old Foundations, and the Front-walls of their next Neighbours'. Massie thought it was time to end this 'evil', arguing that by 'this surreptitious way of contracting and darkening the Streets, the Publick has long been injured'. Areas he identified where this was common included the north side of Lincoln's Inn Fields. Massie also wished for an end to the

58   Robert West, *The South East Prospect of the Church of St Dunstan in the West* (1756). The church is encrusted with shop buildings.

practice of placing shop sheds against London church walls, especially in the most public or narrowest streets. He singled out shopkeepers near St Dunstan's on Fleet Street as some of the worst offenders, describing the constructions as 'indecent and inconvenient' (see figure 58).[122] This was no novel concern – more than half a century before Massie produced his tract, these shops appeared as nuisances in the wardmote inquests.[123]

A squeaking overhanging sign could be hazardous: 'in high Winds often proves dangerous, and in Rainy weather always an Annoyance to Foot-Passengers'. The signs darkened the street by casting shadows and made pavements feel more constricted. It was complained that a sign could obstruct 'the free circulation of the Air . . . and at Night more or less intercepts the Light of the Lamps'.[124] Among numerous proposals to improve the street environment was one to limit the size of signs to two foot square, to prevent some dwarfing others 'whereby they obscure, not only their next Neighbours, but do also darken the Streets'.[125] In the engraving *The Beaux Disaster* (see figure 33 on p. 90) overhanging signs narrow the Strand and project a surprising distance from the building.

Streets narrowed by signs, posts and encroachments were thought to hinder the free flow of air, which would create an unwholesome environment. Increasingly, the higgledy-piggledy mix of houses along labyrinthine street networks were regarded as signs of a lack of urban sophistication and social refinement. 'There was a close correlation', argues a modern historian, Rosemary Sweet, 'between dark and narrow streets, filled with Gothic and medieval structures, and the extent to which the spirit of politeness and improvement had penetrated . . . The confined spaces, irregularity, gloom and dirt were the physical manifestations of all that was contrary to the polite ethos.'[126]

The civic authorities recognised the need to declutter the central areas. Part of the motivation was to improve traffic flow through the streets, but the desire to create more airy environments also provided an impetus for change. The removal of obstructive buildings, walls and gates widened streets in many cities in the eighteenth century. In an uncharacteristically present-centred comment, the historian Penelope Corfield has described the removal of city walls and gateways as 'blithe destruction'.[127] The streets were becoming intolerably pinched – the medieval design suited medieval volumes of traffic, but were a problem for the citizens of the eighteenth-century city. Severe localised congestion evident in Bath suggests that the removal of the North and South Gates in the 1750s and West Gate in 1776 was not done blithely.[128] Backed by Acts of Parliament, the Bath Council allocated huge amounts of money in the 1750s and 1760s for compulsory purchase schemes in order to extend the Pump Room, and widen streets and walks in the centre of the city.[129] Visitors to Nottingham entering via Hollow Stone (the narrow passage cut through rock, which formed the southern entrance to the city) around the time of the civil wars would travel past 'a Parcel of little Rock-houses [and] (if the wind was Northerly) [be] saluted with a Volley of suffocating smoke, caused by the burning of Gorse and Tanners knobs'. This main southern entrance to the town pinched traffic to a single file. A century later, the Corporation of Nottingham sought permission from the Duke of Kingston to demolish a house in his possession at this entrance, in order to fulfil a widening scheme at 'The Hollow-Stone'.[130]

The various widening schemes allowed the city authorities to create more spacious areas in the city centres and these found favour and adulation from visitors and inhabitants alike. In Bath the ability to promenade in comfort was a crucial aspect of the city's tourism industry. Commodiousness made areas seem attractive; three students delighted in the 'very spacious & beautifull' marketplace in Nottingham during their tour in 1725.[131] St Giles, a very wide street in Oxford, was held to be a glory of the city by one commentator, who described it as having 'all the Advantages of Town and Country, it is broader than the High Street, well planted with Elms on each side'.[132]

Prized civic landmarks such as fine churches were enhanced by spacious and airy surroundings. During the rebuilding of Kensington parish church at the end of the seventeenth century the decision was made to move the watch house and whipping post from the vicinity, and make the churchyard and passages to it 'more large and convenient'.[133] As part of his discussion about 'open areas of Bath' John Wood complained that properties in Stall's Church Yard were 'not only mean in themselves, but they clogg up that Part of the City which should be the most Free and Open for Use, as well as Ornament'. He proposed a major design, with many properties removed to create an 'open Place in the Middle of the City', which would draw the appropriate attention to the abbey and the Pump House.[134] When General George Wade (MP for Bath 1722–48) built his house near to the abbey in the 1720s he also cleared a pathway (Wade's Passage) through properties to the north of it in an attempt to prevent the abbey being used as a pedestrian rat run.[135] People continued to use the abbey as a thoroughfare, and in 1756, by a narrow margin, the council voted to remove the shop in front of the Abbey House in order to make the passage from the churchyard to the Abbey Green more commodious.[136]

Unfortunately, some spacious central areas were still approached through unpleasant passages and entrances. In the mid-eighteenth century the entrances to St Ann's Square in Manchester were cramped and grotty (see Map 6 and figure 60). Vehicles drove through a narrow gate under the Old Coffee House. In 1772 a Manchester old-timer recalled that the entry to the square could only accommodate a single cart 'and to make ill worse, there was a wooden staircase on one side to a room above, under which was a cobbler's stall, to work in, that no room might be lost'.[137] This gloomy, dark and dirty passage took the pedestrian through a small court to then burst out into the

59   A figure stands in the 'Dark Entry', far right. 'Coffee house, Manchester' (*c*.1776).

splendour of the square (see figure 1 on p. 14).[138] These tunnel-like, muggy and dirty passages contrasted strongly with the more spacious areas they funnelled into.[139]

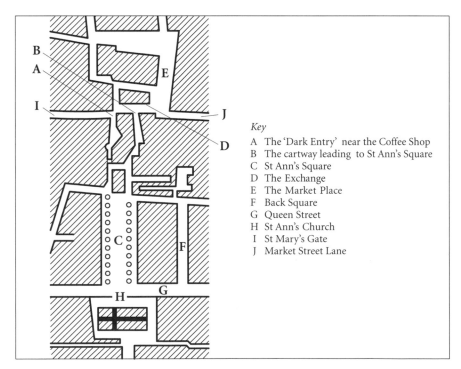

Key

A   The 'Dark Entry' near the Coffee Shop
B   The cartway leading to St Ann's Square
C   St Ann's Square
D   The Exchange
E   The Market Place
F   Back Square
G   Queen Street
H   St Ann's Church
I   St Mary's Gate
J   Market Street Lane

Map 6 The area around Manchester marketplace in the eighteenth century, showing the 'Dark Entry' and the cartway leading to St Ann's Square.

'He that runs in the dark may well stumble'[140]

As the gloaming turned to night a dingy blanket spread across the city streets.[141] The civic authorities did have some measures in place to light the way of pedestrians and passengers at night, but these would not have cast much light on the streets. In 1614 Oxford householders were instructed to hang a candle in a lantern between six and nine in the evening 'in darke nightes . . . for the better direction and lightening of passages'.[142] In an effort to reduce the householder burden the Cambridge authorities demanded that townsfolk hang a candle and lanthorn from five o'clock until eight o'clock each winter evening on a rota basis, with every fourth house taking turns.[143] Similar obligations making householders directly responsible for lighting the street outside their home were habitually neglected across the country. Clearly some Oxford householders were a little lax in their attention to lighting, and in 1615 the bellman was given the additional duty of crying the instruction to hang lanterns on winter nights to chivvy them.[144] In 1688 defaulters in Oxford were reported to the Council and fined sixpence per night.[145]

The tallow candles used in street lanterns did not give off a sufficiently bright or enduring light to make a difference to the ease of movement after dark. Illumination was most needed after nine at night, when most shops and businesses had closed. However, candles had often extinguished by then. Superior oil-burning lamps were developed and used increasingly in cities in the 1680s. The entrepreneur and inventor Edmund Heming got a patent to use his 'Lamps with Convex Glasses' (to magnify the light) on one in ten houses on moonless nights, starting on Kensington Road.[146] Heming personally oversaw the lighting and cleaning of the lamps under his charge, 'and himself never went to Bed all the Winter, till Twelve or One a Clock, and was constantly up again at Four or Five in the Morning, to Trim and Order the Lights'.[147] Competition came from Heming's nemesis, John Vernatti, who installed convex lights in the Cornhill area.[148] Self-interested tallow-chandlers, horners (who made the semi-transparent sides of the lanthorns), tin men and cotton spinners (they supplied candle wicks) brought attention to the greater costs involved in using oil lamps.[149] Despite the opposition the lamps remained.

By the end of the 1680s the Middlesex and City authorities were so impressed by convex oil lamps that they allowed citizens to contract out their lighting obligations.[150] In London by 1694 a fine was set at two shillings for all lantern defaulters, unless they had opted instead to join a scheme run by various lamp patentees.[151] By an Act of 1736 the streets of London were illuminated by one thousand oil lamps.[152] The number of lights across the city multiplied rapidly, and lamps also spread to other cities where the authorities encouraged citizens to transfer their responsibilities to a lighting scheme.[153]

Corporations also installed lights on city properties. The Mayor of Bath oversaw the installation of ten convex lamps in 1702 as part of the preparations for Queen Anne's visit.[154] A notice appeared in the *Manchester Mercury* in July 1767 from the Clerk to the Commissioner inviting proposals 'to undertake the putting up, cleansing, finding Men, Oil and other Materials, lighting, maintaining, upholding, and delivering in good condition, 300 Lamps' in time for the winter gloom.[155]

60   Engraving, William Hogarth, *The Rake's Progress* (1737), Plate IV, 'The Arrest'. The distracted lamplighter, who is aloft his ladder, spills his oil.

Street lamps were high maintenance (Heming made himself ill with their upkeep).[156] The lighters needed to carry ladders and other apparatus.[157] Contractors topped up the reservoirs with oil, trimmed wicks and lit the lamps at specified hours.[158] Robert Campbell, the sole employee of a female lamplighter in London, stole and sold on the oil he was supposed to use to refuel the lamps on his rounds. Suspicions were aroused in his mistress after she had been informed that her lamps burnt out by eleven o'clock in the evening, 'I knowing I allow'd a sufficiency of oil, suspected the prisoner made away with the oil'. Her son was dispatched on a covert surveillance mission, and he reported that Campbell only filled the lamps halfway, and siphoned the remainder into a bladder.[159]

Although clearly an improvement on the old candle and lanthorn, these globular lamps were fuelled with crude animal oils and their light would have been intermittent and fairly dim.[160] The lamps might have impressed country hicks like the Revd Penrose, who, visiting Bath in 1766, marvelled that the streets were 'well illuminated in the night with Lamps, that you may walk about as well as by Day', but they were rapidly seen as inadequate by the citizens.[161] Witnesses were often asked if a crime scene had been light enough for certain identification.[162]

Although the number of lamps erected steadily increased, the citizens and authorities were not always satisfied. Several types of lighting erected by various privately run schemes lit streets in the Spitalfields area of London. In 1705 the Middlesex authorities sought to control an increasingly chaotic system, whereby some inhabitants falsely claimed they contributed to a rating scheme.[163] Parishioners in St Dunstan-in-the West argued that their lamps 'are badly lighted and that in general there is a Want of a greater Number'.[164] Some contractors were accused of placing lamps too far apart to be effective.[165] While acknowledging that lighting improvements had done much for the 'Honour and safety' of London by the 1750s, Joseph Massie thought that their coverage could be more widespread. Duck Lane, near Smithfield Market, was such a dim street 'that the Citizens are forced to grope their Way through Darkness'. Massie also highlighted the case of Long Lane (also near Smithfield), where the north side was lit at regular intervals, but the south side was not illuminated at all.[166]

Lamps were vulnerable to theft and damage. In 1718 James Withy stole '25 Fountains of Lamps of the Convex-Lights'.[167] Thirty years later several lamps were stolen from sheep pens in Smithfield.[168] Lamps were also the targets of rakish rampages: an Oxford Regius Professor of Physic was reported to have removed the lamps from his house in response to 'nocturnal Rioting frequent in our Streets'.[169] Bath was plagued by the behaviour of 'evil-disposed Persons . . . wilfully destroying or extinguishing lamps' in the mid-eighteenth century.[170] In 1753 the Manchester town attorney was asked to 'discover the persons who broke the Lamps in Town'.[171]

Given the inadequacy of mounted lighting, citizens still carried lanterns, or engaged linkboys who carried links – torches of rope stiffened with fat, pitch or resin – to light their path on moonless nights.[172] In Hogarth's nocturnal image the drunken barber works by candlelight, one candle per window square, as does the tapster filling his beer barrel, beneath a smoke-filled night sky (see figure 61). The path of the freemason and his steward (staggering arm in arm) is lit by their lantern, and a linkboy crouches at the bottom left, blowing his torch into a flame while he waits for a paying customer. Samuel Pepys often

61   Engraving, William Hogarth, *The Four Times of the Day* (1738), Plate IV, 'Night'.

journeyed around the dark streets of London with a linkboy to light his way.[173] To keep the linklight bright the charred parts needed to be removed by rubbing them on the wall. Some householders installed and painted shaped slabs of stone into their exterior wall, by the entrance door, for the linkboys to use to avoid smeared and singed brickwork. Other paraphernalia, such as extinguishers and link rests, were fixed to iron palisades.[174] It was commonly feared that a miscreant linkboy, exploiting his client's vulnerability, might blow

62   Lighting paraphernalia adorns the exterior of Alfred House, Alfred Street, Bath.

out his link and commit an offence. They would 'knock down Gentlemen in Drink, and lead others out of the Way in to Dark and remote Places'. Defoe suggested a linkboy badge scheme, to reassure pedestrians in need of nocturnal illumination.[175]

Darkness caused many problems for citizens. Streets that were bemired and slippery in the day became even more hazardous by night. The potential for pedestrians to slip was increased by their inability to spot lolling dunghills, broken pavements, discarded pea shells and unfenced stairs.[176] On his way home in the dark on the evening of 16 September 1660 Samuel Pepys saw a gentleman have 'a great and dirty fall over a water pipe that lay along the Channell' in Poultry.[177] 'He that runs in the Dark', warned the old adage, 'may well stumble.'[178] Pedestrians walking near Manchester's collegiate church needed to tread carefully in the seventeenth century, as a cellar continued to remain open despite repeated calls for it to be railed.[179]

Citizens abroad at night were also at risk from muggers and fraudsters: 'Twilight and the first Darkness are the proper Hours for the thief and Robber,' warned a chaplain of Manchester's collegiate church.[180] The Earl of Chesterfield, hoping to teach his illegitimate son about life, warned him to think of the night not just as a time for repose, but also as the time 'for the commission and security of crimes; such as robberies, murders and violations, which generally seek the advantage of darkness, as favourable for the escapes of the guilty'.[181] Francis Quin was mugged shortly after falling over rubbish in Wild Street, off London's Drury Lane, on a dark winter's evening in 1745.[182] Many markets, shops and hawkers were still operating after nine o'clock. Purchases were always governed by 'caveat emptor', but in the dark the hapless customer could not easily judge the quality of goods traded outside the hours controlled by market officials. The feeble illumination made it difficult to do anything in the dark – everything was rendered unfamiliar. This was particularly apparent to strangers new to the town. When a man from Oxfordshire was attacked after going drinking in Charing Cross, London, in 1726 he found himself lost and confused in an alien environment that was 'mortal dark'.[183]

Carriage drivers were forced to make quick manoeuvres to avoid obstacles in their path. A practical reason to prohibit carts from parking on the streets at night was that other vehicles or pedestrians could not see them. Two men were presented by the Manchester scavengers in 1744 for leaving a cart in St Ann's Square at night 'over which severall persons have fall[e]n and been hurt'.[184] In 1686 the authorities of Manchester were concerned about carts being left on the dark streets without illumination. Acknowledging that some public houses did not have convenient spaces for their patrons' wagons, in the mid-eighteenth century the Manchester jurors conceded that carts could remain on the streets at night if they were set with a lamp or light all night.[185] Piles of refuse and materials also needed to be illuminated. Building rubble stacked up in Arlington Street, London, caused a fatal coach accident at night in 1761.[186] Part of the case built against Samuel Lucas for laying large quantities of rubbish in the Manchester marketplace centred on his failure to place a lamp or light atop the rotting piles.[187]

In 1764 William Huddesford penned *An address to the Freemen and other inhabitants of the city of Oxford*. In this pamphlet Huddesford complained that the '*Tradesmen of Oxford love Darkness, rather than Light*'. As a consequence the city streets had dim illumination, causing the occasional gownsman to 'run his Head against a Post'.[188] In response an Oxford 'Citizen' wrote up the results of his own nocturnal lighting survey and concluded that 'the illuminations of the *Town* are greatly superior to those of the *University*.' He singled out the High Street as being 'extremely well illuminated', except for the vicinity of Queen's College. 'Though the Grand Entrance appears calculated to attract the Eye, a Stranger who has just the Opportunity in a Winter's Night of hurrying down the principal Street, after the Arrival of the Stage Coaches, finds no friendly Aid to gratify his Curiosity by a Contemplation of the noble Statue of her late Majesty, placed in the Dome over the Entrance.' The porters' lodge at Queen's was cast in 'utter darkness'. Likewise, Brasenose, 'though a very *polite* Society, are wholly in the Dark, exclusive of the Assistance afforded by oblique Glances from the Radclivian Lamps, on that *Distinguished Nose*, placed upon their Gates'. The entrances of Exeter and Jesus colleges both shared the dim light cast by a single lamp. Trinity College lacked 'a single taper' and Balliol only had one 'badly supplied' lamp for the four hundred paces occupied by the college site. [189]

The quality of the air was different in each part of each city. To be able to breathe fresh air a citizen would need to live away from noxious and smoky industries, near open spaces and along spacious streets. Most citizens did not enjoy such luxuries, especially the poorest. City air was generally smoky and noisome, but more attention was paid to the smell of infectious matter than smoke – because more concern was paid to contagious disease than respiratory problems. Nuisances focused on stinking animal and vegetable matter, rather than discharges caused by minerals. Good air equated to good ventilation – healthiness came with spaciousness. The eighteenth century saw street-widening schemes in the cities, especially in the showcase central areas. At the same time, urban infill behind the principal streets created increasingly fetid and close environments in the mean alleys and festering courts, where, Dr John Coakley Lettsom noted in 1773, the majority of febrile diseases occurred.[190] City streets were dark, not just in the night, but also, thanks to the blanket of smoke, in the daytime. At night, where lit at all, the streets were lit badly. The final verdict on the university's contribution to lighting in Oxford given by the 'Citizen' was that it was 'extremely absurd, and of little Utility to the Publick; being frequently, during this Perambulation, obliged to *grope my Way*'. [191]

CHAPTER 10

'Such things as these . . . disturb human life'

By considering the dislikes and distastes of English citizens and visitors to cities, this book has shown that all of the senses could be upset, or even disgusted, by nuisances and irritants encountered at home, at work and on the streets. We have considered bodies in their immediate environment, hearing reactions to uncomfortable clothes, skin conditions, grease and dirt. We have seen the revulsion experienced when eyes were exposed to ugly sights, and the irritation when ears heard unpleasant noises. We have regarded bodies in their wider environments, as part of the streetscape and affected by the atmosphere.

The complaints have revealed divergences of opinion and a great diversity of lifestyles in the seventeenth and eighteenth centuries. However, the historian's challenge is to draw multiple experiences into a coherent picture. There are some broad themes that unite the responses expressed by the contemporary citizens. First, and perhaps most obviously, experiences depended in part on the wealth and status of the individual. There was a gulf between the lives of the rich and those of the poor. This is reflected in different attitudes to nuisances, and the allocation of blame for the creation of unpleasant situations. These differences cannot be expressed in simple terms: the rich did not always have it easy, and their lives were not necessarily more comfortable than those of poorer citizens. Indeed, a person's outlook seemed to guide their path to contentedness (or unhappiness) just as much as their wealth or status. Some people were less sensitive to annoying situations and upsetting circumstances than others. Some were naturally more laid-back, or too busy to notice things or to complain about them.

Secondly, the senses were most likely to be upset when experiences did not match expectations. Consensual norms guided the citizens. Moderate behaviour and reactions that were consistent with a person's rank, station, gender and age comforted the senses and put observers (or listeners, or smellers) at ease. Likewise, usual tastes and textures relaxed people; unusual ones vexed them. Extreme or unfamiliar actions, sights, smells and sounds or forms of behaviour annoyed people, on both a physical and an emotional level.

Thirdly, reactions changed as society and the environment changed. This is no simple story of progression; it is not a Whiggish tale. The citizens do not seem to have become more contented as their environment improved (which most cities did between 1600 and 1770). Despite developments in the transportation of food, in architecture and housing, in streetscape design and in clothing, the chuntering and grumbling continued. Bodies and minds swiftly became used to improved conditions and wanted more. Previously overlooked nuisances were noticed as the threshold of decency changed. Many people also harked back to fabled days a couple of generations back when life was idyllic and people were better behaved. Some developments did create a more unpleasant environment. For example industrial expansion led to greater exposure to pollutants in many urban areas. This raises a question: why did citizens remain in cities that gave them so many opportunities for dissatisfaction and irritation? I make some suggestions, before concluding with a summary of the state of the four cities of London, Oxford, Bath and Manchester as we leave them in 1770.

'Rich Men feel Misfortunes, that fly over poor Men's Heads'[1]

Inevitably, the accounts and portraits presented in this book are skewed – they highlight the views of the relatively rich, literate, male minority. It is certain that more notice was paid when 'diverse' of the 'best qualitye' complained, and we risk doing the same thing here.[2] Richer citizens were generally less tolerant. Those who complained the loudest were often not those who suffered the most.

The citizens who were exposed to the worst nuisances would have been the less vocal poor. Extremes of poverty were most evident in the rain. The poorest were doomed to trudge through the mire, their darned stockings soaking up water admitted though their leaking shoes. Wheels of carriages holding richer citizens splashed the threadbare coats of the street-level poor. However, on a daily basis both rich and poor endured discomfort – the rich in the name of fashion, the poor out of necessity. While the rich donned itchy ruffles and cumbersome wigs for show (scrubbed and powdered by the hired help), the ragtag poor wore patched clothes for warmth and protection.

Quality of life depended largely on what a person did for a living. The trades of the butcher and the tallow-chandler were notoriously dirty and unpleasant. Horners were relatively lucky: the smell of horn was thought to keep them chipper.[3] Apothecaries were also in a happy place (as long as they were not preparing ointments of marshmallows, which might set them to vomiting). How wonderful, pondered Bernardino Ramazzini, were the powerful odours of their trade, which 'according to our idiosyncrasie . . . produce marvellous effects'.[4] The apothecaries may have been stoned, but the painters were dazed and confused. Their workshops smelt like privies, and some painters lost their sense of smell after years of handling toxic substances.[5] The delicate-nosed Robert Hooke did not last long as a painter's apprentice. Society ladies encountered similar toxins in their toiletries and lotions.

The wealthy had greater opportunity to move to cleaner and quieter areas, or make the most of grim locations with architectural developments that increasingly divorced domestic space from civic space. Access to space was the key to privacy, comfort and cleanliness. When the poor did inhabit finer houses, they usually did so as servants or subtenants, and were placed in the least comfortable rooms – in basements and garrets.[6] Dirty fuel supplies smutted their homes, and they also had fewer opportunities to bake their own food, and less time to implement Thomas Tryon's cleaning tips. Generally, the poorest citizens lived in the least salubrious parts of town, shoehorned into dark lanes and grotty courts – unconnected to water supplies and inaccessible to the scavenger – often within zones colonised by noxious tradesmen.[7]

Discomfort about unwanted contacts between the well-heeled and the down-at-heel are evident.[8] Thoughts of the scabby, mangy hands of servants and cooks infecting food also worried polite society. Cooks preparing salads with unwashed hands after visiting the necessary house or after handling raw meat were a concern expressed in Jonathan Swift's *Directions to Servants* (1745).[9] Some conduct books included rules for the attendants at dinner. They were ordered to desist from scratching their heads 'or any other part of their Body', and called on to keep their hands 'in open view, neat and clean'. They should take special care not to sneeze over food as this 'breeds a Jealousie [in the diners] that some Nastiness may have happened into what they eat or drink'.[10] In chapter 4 we heard Matt Bramble's distaste about strawberries 'soiled and tossed' by greasy and beastly hands. Worst still, Bramble horrified himself with the thought of a 'dirty barrow-bunter' rubbing the dust off fruit with spit, and shivered at the idea of a 'fine lady of St James's parish' eating cherries 'which had been rolled and moistened between the filthy, and, perhaps, ulcerated chops of a St Giles's huckster'.[11] Fears about the contaminating effects of other people are evident in the many commentaries about the waters of Bath. In *The Diseases of Bath* (1737), after pushing through 'a Mob of unwash'd Beaus' the anonymous author reaches the pump. He waits his turn until 'some Clown' before him had 'rudely swill'd his Potion up', but is disgusted to see a 'slobber'd' glass 'with all his Drivel fraught'. The glass is rinsed before reuse, but this leaves 'foul Finger-prints', thus adding to the contaminants on the cup. The shoving continues, the beaker slips – the experience does not heal, it unsettles.[12]

To some, the destitute and street filth were synonymous – to cleanse the environment the authorities needed to expunge both. The acclaimed physician Richard Mead lumped beggars with dunghills when contemplating the stuff that obstructed and dirtied streets trod by the goodly citizens. Both, Mead argued, should be 'taken up' and moved away to prevent pestilential contagion.[13] A colleague went further. William Buchan argued that it was not sufficient for a person to maintain good levels of personal hygiene if his neighbour wallowed in filth. 'If dirty people cannot be removed as a common nuisance,' he noted with chagrin, 'they ought at least to be avoided as infectious. All who regard their health should keep at a distance even from their habitations.' Especially harmful were streets smeared with 'the excrements of the diseased'.[14]

In 1755 John Clayton, the chaplain of the Collegiate Church in Manchester, wrote a distinctly unfriendly pamphlet entitled *Friendly Advice to the Poor*. His advice amounted to little more than 'stop being poor', and Clayton claimed that the poorest citizens were habituated to poverty and wilfully refused work or help because they were 'so familiarized to Filth and Rags, as renders them in a Manner natural; and have so little Sense of Decency, as hardly to allow a Wish for it a Place in their Hearts'. 'Methinks,' he snorts, 'there is nothing very amiable in Rags and Tatters, Filth and Grease, that can make them desirable.'[15] Joseph Massie, a commentator on trades, was scarcely more understanding: 'The Swarms of BEGGARS and VAGRANTS, in our Streets,' he snarled 'is a most disgraceful and baneful Nuisance; more especially considering our enormous POOR-RATE.'[16]

A letter in *The Spectator* considered what looks 'ill, and is offensive to the Sight'. The author concluded that the 'Worst Nusance of which kind methinks is the scandalous Appearance of the Poor in all Parts of this wealthy City. Such miserable Objects affect the compassionate Beholder with dismal Ideas, discompose the Chearfulness of his Mind, and deprive him of the Pleasure that he might otherwise take in surveying the Grandeur of our Metropolis.'[17] This may be tongue-in-cheek, but it mirrored (or parodied) some contemporary views. Just as the unfashionable and messy pre-Georgian housing and street layouts were subject to criticism, the splattered, sweaty, dusty and noisy poor clashed with the fashionable taste for clean and frilly things. Sight was not the only sense to be offended: the cries of the hawkers were deafening, the rooms of the poor stank and the bodies of beggars reeked.

Different types of citizen endured different types of discomfort. They also perceived the causes of nuisances and annoyances differently. People in other groups were derided, feared and loathed. This was partly triggered by jealousy – as Nicholas Amhurst noticed, it is 'natural for us to rail at what we do not possess . . . an ugly old hag hates a pretty young woman'.[18] Bernard Mandeville put a slightly more positive spin on this, suggesting that 'the Chaste Man hates Fornication, and the Drunkenness is most abhorr'd by the Temperate.'[19] Things that a person disliked, or was disgusted by, depended on who they were, where they lived and what they did. Citizens from different backgrounds ordinarily had different degrees of choice in the way they lived their lives. Extraordinary events temporarily brought all citizens down to the same level. Only in these unusual circumstances, when there was no choice, did the rich not complain. In a neat passage contrasting the ordinary lives of the rich with those of the poor, Anthony Wood considered the temporary effects of the Fire of London:

> Those that were this day riding wantonly in coaches, were, the next, glad to ride in dung carts to save their lives. Those that thought the ground too unworthy to be touched by their feet, did run up to the knees in dirt and water to save themselves from the fury of fire or the falling of houses. Those that faired deliciously this day . . . were within few days following glad of a brown crust . . . [20]

Ultimately many of the problems encountered in this book and many of the dislikes expressed stemmed from a clash between people who spent most time indoors and those who spent most time outdoors. Wealthier citizens vilified the travelling repairmen and the salesfolk peddling second-hand goods who inhabited the rookeries in areas such as St Giles-in-the-Fields. Menders and service providers such as knife-grinders and tinkers were portrayed as being driven by a love of idleness and waste.[21] 'Tinkers and cobblers' were thought to be the 'best ale drinkers'.[22] Efforts to shift traders of second-hand clothes from London's Tower Hill area in the eighteenth century revealed a divergence of priorities between rich and poor.[23] In 1700 a high constable of the Tower division was called on to suppress a riotous assembly 'held and kept in the public highway and streets in and about . . . Rosemary Lane' in the Whitechapel area. Crowds had gathered to buy clothes and other goods from hawkers and barrow-men depicted in the records as purveyors of substandard or stolen goods.[24] These sales presented opportunities for traders with no access to sheltered premises to make a simple living. They also channelled affordable, cast-off goods to needy members of society. Service providers allowed poorer citizens to extend the life of their precious possessions. However, to the rich, ad hoc salespeople caused obstructions on account of the large numbers of 'disorderly persons' congregating at their barrows. It should be noted that these traders undermined new sales and thereby affected the manufacturers and sellers of new goods, so we must be careful not to completely swallow the views of those who filled the civic posts and left the records. Holders of rummage stalls might have created a temporary nuisance, but the charge of being 'highly injurious to the Neighbourhood in General' stretches credulity.[25]

'He that makes his Bed ill, must be contented to lie ill'[26]

Second-hand sales presented the poor with opportunities to buy into recent fashions. However, the rich did not like the emulation they perceived among their social inferiors – many expressed the hope that the poor would be content with their lot and not be tempted by durable or edible luxuries. In addition to concerns about their own contamination from mangy hands and pawed comestibles, some commentators worried about the effects that fine foods and other titbits might have on the morals of their social inferiors. Eliza Haywood thought maids had no business munching on such trifles as cakes and nuts, and suggested they might suffer damage by them. Broken victuals were often a perk of service, but one Lady reputedly dispatched her maid to the Bridewell for eating a slice of leftover pudding.[27] An eighteenth-century historian bemoaned the proliferation of luxury foodstuffs among the humble workers of Nottingham, whinging that 'almost every Seamer, Sizer, and Winder, will have her Tea . . . even a common Washer Woman thinks she has not had a proper Breakfast without Tea and hot buttered white Bread.' This author was horrified by the sight of a 'ragged and greasy Creature' at the grocer's with her two children, asking for a 'Pennyworth of Tea and a Halfpennyworth of Sugar' and claiming to be unable to live without 'drinking every Day a little Tea'.[28] In a similar vein, John Clayton berated miserable ragged families for taking tea 'in a wretched Garret, or more loathsome Cellar, fooling away a precious Hour, and spending more Money over this confessedly hurtful Food'.[29] Both men were concerned by what they perceived to be a lack of priorities, and Clayton also extended his argument to criticise the poor for their tippling. 'It is surprising', he exclaims, 'that the hungry, with neither wholesome beds nor clothes should indulge in junketing and riot.'

The key to not offending anyone was to act according to your station, gender, age and occupation – if a person did not, they might upset others and suffer the consequences of doing so. Margaret Cavendish, Duchess of Newcastle, noted this in 1655: although 'it is the nature of mankinde to run into extreams', the route to happiness lay in the path of moderation. Immoderation led to an early death and caused offence to other people.[30] Quietness was the ideal state of women, the poor and neighbours. Disquiet was a state of mind and body, and what disturbed the quiet of the citizens has been the focus of this book. In a society where balance was proper, extremes courted criticism. 'The *Medium* between a *Fop* and a *Sloven* is what every Man of Sense should endeavour to keep, and not be Ambitious of transgressing in either kind,' argued a 'Gentleman' in 1715.[31] Didactic literature reflected ancient medical concepts still current at the time – a happy body depended on achieving balance. In turn, balanced bodies created a happy society. While moderation was good, excess was not. Food that was too salty, too sweet or too decayed upset the balance in the body. People who were too drunk, too shabby, too seedy, too loud, too smelly, overly hirsute, too poor or too rich upset society.

The language used to describe behaviour frequently revealed a blurring between perceptions of physical and moral matters. The language of the senses gave an account of the whole world of perception; the senses did not just perceive material things in the environment, they also judged human behaviour. Words used to describe physical decay and putrefaction were commonly deployed when describing the moral degeneration of others. Immoral behaviour and dishonesty could be smelt, metaphorically at least, like physical corruption. A canny person could 'smell a Rat'.[32] Foulness, impurity and corruption could be moral or physical. Dirty, insipid matter percolated to the bottom of the environment. This notion was adapted to apply to society: the immoral sank like sediment to the bottom of the social hierarchy. A sink was a pool for collecting waste water, a sort of cesspit. The word also had a contemporary application to describe places where people gathered to engage in corrupt or immoral behaviour.[33]

Dishonour had a fetid odour. In a poem about sexually deviant acts committed by Venus it was noted that her 'Honour smelt worse than a stinking Red-herring'.[34] Connections were frequently made between open sewers and rotting dunghills and poor moral standards. Women who wore patches and beauty spots were described by one purist as 'sorrily adorned', their appearance suggesting that they 'tumble in some filthy kennell . . . sinne is called mire, filth, folly, a blot, polution, dung . . . &c.'[35] Paracelsus (full name Theophrastus Philippus Aureolus Bombastus von Hohenheim Paracelsus), a controversial early chemist, was described by a fellow of Corpus Christi College, Cambridge, as 'a walking Dunghil (so offensive and corrupt his life)'.[36] 'How vile it is', warned Caleb Trenchfield in his didactic manual, 'to bury our selves in a dunghil, and make the stench of our corruption more noisome than otherwise it would be, by an unprofitable life.' Trenchfield warned that care should be taken of one's reputation, gained through past family endeavour and concern. It should 'run in the purest channel, where no soyl nor mud defile it; but that you may recieve [sic] it, as uncontaminated from others'.[37] In this mud-slinging society, an individual needed to work hard to avoid being 'bespattered' with scandalous rumours.[38] A 'court Baud' was likened to a common sewer – both took in filth, and issued forth a foul smell.[39] 'The 'water poet' John Taylor likened the bawd to a 'tumbrel or barrow' for the 'conveyance of mans luxurious nastinesse, and sordid beastiality'. These women are cast as voluntary scavengers, picking out a living from the 'dunghill of our vices'. Raking up the garbage and 'noysome excrements', they grow fat with 'the merdurinous draffe' of man's excesses.[40] Such comparisons abound in the period. The author of *The London Jilt* (1683) described prostitutes as 'filthy, nasty, and stinking

Carcasses . . . A Whore is but a close-stool to Man, or a Common shoar that receives all manner of Filth.'[41] Other matter that polluted the urban environment was also compared to the morally filthy. Sex and soot entwined in smuttiness.[42] Just as one could carry the whiff of dishonour, credit and honour could also be tarnished, stained or infected.[43] A 'Town-fop' was described as leaving 'a *stench*, if not *infection* behind him; he is too often the *stain* of a good Family, and by his debaucht life blots the noble *coat* of his Ancestors.'[44] Past sins could be dug up like rubbish, or 'left unstir'd' like 'the nauseous Muck-hill rot'.[45] These were the stains that could not be washed off.

'Tis the Men, not the Houses, that make the City'[46]

In the seventeenth century the civic authorities showed their concern about various unpleasant aspects of the urban environment. Their officers tackled suppliers of putrid foods, those who polluted the water supplies, and people who soiled the streets. These priorities should be placed into context. The city fathers were fearful of a return of the dreaded plague and did what they could to reduce the threat to the urban economy. By the eighteenth century the concern of authorities was less about stench and infection and more about passage and obstacles. The authorities saw opportunities to maximise output by attracting entrepreneurs in manufacturing, improving trade and enticing visitors. In Manchester presentments for street-cleaning offences and nuisance pig-keeping dwindled during the century, to be replaced with an increasing number tackling obstructions.[47] A harder line was taken with dangerous open cellar doors and pushy bow windows.[48] By the mid-eighteenth century some commentators started to consider the aesthetics of the urban sphere, putting forward proposals to improve approaches to cities and entrances to major public spaces, and to sweep away encroachments, street clutter and ill-matched and tawdry street furniture. Some of the motivation was to improve the beauty of the city centres – their concern was for civic pride rather than public health.[49] This suggests that there was some degree of satisfaction with the various improvement acts already implemented in the cities. In an essay written in 1754 a writer on trade and economics mapped out the order of priorities towards civic pride. First, nuisances should be removed. Next, inconveniences and inelegancies would be removed. Finally tasteful designs would ornament and embellish the cities.[50] By 1770, in parts of some cities, the citizens could start to consider the last of these three priorities. Despite rises in population and an expanding built environment, many urban centres were more pleasant places in which to live and work in the mid-eighteenth century than they had been throughout the seventeenth century. At the least, in each city there were areas that had become significantly more salubrious.

Citizens were increasingly expected to make financial rather than physical or practical contributions to keep the urban environment functioning well: householders became ratepayers. The machinery established to collect rates was more effective than previous measures to cajole apathetic householders into personally mending and illuminating their streets to a sufficiently high standard. In 1648 the Liverpool scavengers had complained that 'they cannot prevaile with the Inhabitantes for clenseing of the streets but are abused and much affronted in the Execution of their office'. The civic authorities ordered the scavengers to hire labourers to undertake the cleaning, giving them the power to confiscate goods to cover costs.[51] Eventually more cities moved towards systems whereby commissioners gained powers to remove nuisances and improve lighting and streets.[52] Improvement acts multiplied after the mid-eighteenth century. Rates to pay for scavengers and lighting schemes created an extra tier of local government involved with finances, but the public works were carried out to a consistently higher standard.[53] When paving a whole section of street, the substratum could be levelled and compacted to the same density; this had not been possible with the piecemeal crazy paving of yore.

Not all cities enjoyed these developments. Cambridge citizens were unusual in rejecting plans to apply for an improvement act in 1769.[54] Concern was expressed that the costs of putting the Bill through Parliament and under-taking the work would fall on the overburdened pockets of the underprivileged tradesmen and 'middling Sort of People'. It was decided that an enforcement of the existing rules would be a more cost-effective solution. Citizens voiced concerns that new laws might damage trade and discourage building works – leaving the improved streets 'disgraced with bad Houses'. Burdens would fall on the tenants (mostly townsmen), not the landlords (colleges and Corpora-tion members). Such a scheme would, it was feared, rob the respectable poor to 'gratify the Rich'.[55] It was feared that properties would need to shrink to accommodate wider streets and reduce encroachments. Consequently the streets of Cambridge remained 'wretched', especially the gutters. Plans to improve illumination in the city also received a 'lukewarm' reception from the university, as many college heads feared that brighter nocturnal streets would spark increased town/gown violence and tempt the undergraduates to smash the lamps.[56]

Much of the impetus for urban change came from the professionals and other members of the 'middling sorts'.[57] Paul Langford has noted how the propertied urban citizens became united by 'a spirit which sought improve-ment not in potential panaceas but in highly specific remedies'.[58] A quest for respectability and order among these citizens spurred actions against squalor, dirt and chaos. Activities took various forms, including lobbying and raising funds for parliamentary Acts, active vestry membership, holding civic office, being members of commissions and bestowing individual philanthropy and advice or running turnpike trusts. Some entrepreneurs developed private enterprises to improve street cleaning and lighting, or to establish water supplies.

'The wealthy Cit grown old in trade now wishes for a rural shade'[59]

At the end of the seventeenth century, the compiler of *The Country Gentleman's Vade Mecum for his Comparison for the Town* had advised his country-dwelling correspondent that leaving the country for the town would be foolish. 'What? Leave the endearing Sweets of a Country Life, for a little dull Noise, and rude Justlings and Confusion.' Directly comparing the 'Content, Happiness, and Quiet of the Country', which bestows a 'quiet easie life', with the 'Disturbance, Hazard and Noise of the City', which leads to 'a Life of Noise, Vexation and Disappointment', this author's allegiance is clear: country life was more pleasant than city life.[60] In contrast to the crowded noisy urban scene, the country appeared more idyllic, and improved transport by both road and water would have made it more accessible. Carl Estabrook has shown that the seventeenth-century accounts of the rural idyll depicted 'an idealised moral metaphor, not a place of habitation', but the mid-eighteenth century 'urbane rusticators . . . actually took up residences outside cities'.[61] Some of the wealthiest citizens, especially those who could bear to be at a distance from their city-centre businesses, relocated to the countryside, or held both urban and rural residencies. Robert Lloyd's 'The wealthy Cit, grown old in trade' wished instead 'for a rural shade'.[62] The umbrella-wielding philanthropist Jonas Hanway thought that most people wished to flee from all towns, preferring the rural scene, where one can 'suck in the ambrosial air . . . delight the ear with the melody of birds, and the eye with shady groves'.[63] Later, while staying in the Wiltshire village of Wylye, his displeasure at the inelegance of his accommodation was compensated for by its location: 'being free from noise and hurry it was more comfortable to me than the inns in great towns.'[64] In September 1749 William Hogarth moved from London to the furthest fringe of the sleepy village of Chiswick. A high wall surrounded his new house, and all of the windows faced away from the city. Hogarth, like many other affluent professional citizens, moved out to seek respite from the sordid, dirty and noisy capital – the very place that had inspired most of his finest works.[65] Bath could be seen as the ideal retirement spot – offering both urban and rustic delights – but not for Mary Chandler. Later editions of her *Description of Bath* were coupled with short pastoral pieces that indicated the poet's desire to seek relief from the bustle of the city in the landscaped gardens of country estates. Her ultimate wish would be for a house in the country 'at an easy distance from the Town'.[66]

London of the seventeenth century was not a city of palaces; these were located in more idyllic and bucolic spots. Many of the grand mansions lining the Strand were demolished after the Restoration, never to be rebuilt.[67] Discussing the proclivity of Londoners to be 'skirters' of the city in the seventeenth century – to avoid it as much as commit to it – the medical historian Margaret Pelling has noted that the English did not erect town palaces 'but rather ... inns which looked like palaces – that is, urban accommodation which provided status and comfort, but on a temporary basis'.[68] 'Think what London would be, if the chief houses were in it, as in the cities in other countries, and not dispersed like great rarity plums in a vast pudding of a country!' exclaimed Horace Walpole when he considered large erections of the past in a letter written in 1743. However, Walpole was writing at something of a turning point; some urban areas were becoming quite desirable locations for larger residences. Walpole remarked on the recent improvements in London houses, which had become much more grand. Previously 'the nobility had contracted themselves to live in coops of a dining-room, a dark back room with one eye [i.e. window] in a corner, and a closet'.[69] Commentators felt confident that city-centre improvements focusing on creating new open spaces through compulsory purchase and road widening would attract gentry sons to city living and make 'pleasant and airy Habitations for Merchants and Gentlemen of Taste'.[70]

At the same time, richer householders distanced themselves from gore and excrement within the home. Chamber pots were whisked away down the servants' stairs, and meat was skinned and gutted by the maids in the kitchens.[71] They also distanced themselves from the polluted urban centres by establishing exclusive suburban areas and desirable squares. Suburban living, although not entirely novel to the period, was booming. Eight large houses in Leeds were replaced with grander ones between 1743 and 1757. From 1767 the pace of building in segregated and enclosed areas on the western edge of Leeds intensified, leading to the establishment of genteel areas within commuting distance of businesses and the social hub of the city, but at a distance from the dirty hoi polloi.[72]

New fashionable squares offered safe and clean containment; they were the modern gated communities of the day. John Wood's Queen Square in Bath was designed like a Palladian rural retreat (1729–36). The houses were of uniform appearance, and uniformity of behaviour was expected from the residents: 'all kinds of private nuisances are prohibited in the building leases of the houses fronting Queen Square.'[73] Exclusive squares often had private rating schemes for cleansing and lighting, and fenced and gated central gardens with formal planting or paving. Many squares also prohibited advertising graffiti.[74] In London the Strand may have been declining, but St James's Square heralded West End developments with squares at their heart.[75]

The desire to flee to the countryside or the more desirable squares and suburbs was not noticeable in all cities, or among all citizens. We have seen that Nottingham was unusually blessed with good air, fine foods and solid buildings. During the seventeenth and early eighteenth centuries the number of workers in dirty trades such as smithery and tanning fell dramatically in the city. As the relatively clean manufacture of lace became a primary occupation in the city, there was a greater incentive for the more wealthy citizens to stay in central locations. Consequently, at least for a while, Nottingham bucked the trend. In the words of Charles Deering, a physician who relocated to the city in the 1740s, whereas other large commercial settlements 'seldom gave Gentlemen great Encouragement to be fond of settling in them', gentlemen flocked to Nottingham, building lofty and stylish mansions along the central streets.[76]

'We will bear with the Stink, if it bring but in Chink'[77]

Some questions arise at this point. Why did cities continue to grow and attract visitors if the buildings were poor, the food bad, the roads congested and dirty, the air impure and smoky and the behaviour of many of the citizens was ugly? Why, despite their complaints, did most people remain once they had settled into a town or city – even those who complained about the conditions? Crucial was the ability of humans to adjust to difficult environments. Also, for many individuals the benefits attached to city living outweighed the nuisances. Additionally, a fairly poor understanding of the health hazards attached to living in a city might have encouraged citizens to tolerate smog and mire.

Humans generally cope. People often get used to difficult situations or unpleasant experiences and no longer notice or comment on them. Those born into the roar and filth of the city would have become acclimatised to it during their childhood. Incomers gradually became habituated to the hustle and bustle of the urban environment. Bodies got used to their immediate surroundings in time – they became accustomed to particular tastes and smells; just as 'each Mans own Bed does not stink or smell strong to himself, because he is accustomed to it . . . the greatest Slut in the World does hardly smell her own House or Bed stink'.[78] Bodies adjusted to particular types of fabric and ergonomic stresses. One physician observed that craftsmen and husbandmen, 'although they be old and weake, can doe that which stronger and younger men, being not so inured, may not do'.[79] Contemporary views of the body were still guided by ancient notions. Sir Thomas Pope Blount recognised that 'Custom we know is of so great account among Physicians, that according to the great Hippocrates, there is no one thing ought more to be regarded: Nay says he, whatsoever a Man is us'd to, altho' it be bad, is less harmful than what we are not accustomed to.'[80] Blount noted the effect of custom on the 'outward senses' – that the eyes are dazzled when they go from a very dark to a very light environment, but that they gradually recover. He extends his discussion to consider 'those several Tradesmen whose Noise displeases us so much, and who dwell in Mills and Forges, *Custom* has made it so familiar to them, that they are no ways disturb'd with this constant Clattering, but rest and sleep as quietly with the Noise, as others do without it'.[81] Nuisances would have been most intrusive when they were first encountered. Through experience the mind often manages to filter out the unpleasant features of an environment. Afflicted neighbours often got used to noises and smells in time.

While many contemporary commentators saw acclimatisation as a good thing, others were ambivalent. The physician Bernardino Ramazzini noted that tallow-chandlers, up to their elbows in animal fat all day, suffered from a 'chronic lack of apetite and loathe food'.[82] Thomas Tryon believed that 'all persons that are accustomed to stinking places . . . become dull, foul and gross' – so much so that they stop smelling 'those horrible Scents and pernicious Fumes that old Tallow sends forth when it is melted'. Years of exposure to noxious odours allowed tallow-chandlers and butchers to continue at their work and become habituated to the 'thick, dreadful Fumes thereof', but at a cost to themselves.[83] There was, however, room in Tryon's philosophy for some optimism. For Tryon (as a good scholar of Galenic humoralism), most things came down to achieving a balance fit for each body. He believed that the food a person consumed prepared their body for the particularity of their immediate environment, and that the constitutions of most habituated (or hardened) city dwellers permitted them to thrive among the 'gross Scents and thick Vapours' that hung about in cities. Thus, 'as few Dye [*sic*] in them as in the Country . . . notwithstanding the cleanness and goodness of the Air.' Indeed, to Tryon, the poor, ill-prepared diets of the rural folk cancelled out any health benefits accrued by the inhalation of 'Brisk Lively Spirits' in the air.[84] There were consolation prizes for those citizens prepared to put up with congested roads and grimy houses. The prospect of finding secure employment, with the opportunity to specialise and diversify, attracted migrants to the cities and induced them to settle, despite the risks and squalor.[85] Thomas Tryon was evidently concerned about the hazards of urban life. Nonetheless he lived in London, his adopted city, for most of his adult life, and continued for much of this time in a notoriously stinking trade. By living in London Tryon maximised his opportunities for trade – and he would also have found it easier to establish himself as an author.

People concerned about the state of the urban realm were aware of the need to make trade-offs. 'Muck and money go together' and 'We will bear with the Stink, if it bring but in Chink' rang the contemporary proverbs.[86] Bernard Mandeville noticed how this philosophy extended down to the lowest members of society: 'the Smell of Gain was fragrant even to Night-Workers' (i.e. night-soil men).[87] For Mandeville luxury came with a murky underbelly:

'dirty Streets', he asserted, 'are a necessary Evil inseparable from the Felicity of *London*.'[88] A dour writer about trades noted that the black cloud cast by the gin industry which lowered moral standards and sparked 'national drunkenness' carried a silver lining in the form of tax revenues.[89] There was a practical, almost utilitarian notion alive in the cities – fuelled by a hope for even more riches to come. One builder remarked that 'in cities and large towns, business is more regarded than pleasure; there we are obliged to do what we can, not what we chuse, particularly if cramped for room'.[90] This balance could be precarious. Cities experiencing increased trade and commerce became more economically prosperous. However, some were doomed by their own success. In Bath, increases in traffic, bustle and pollution eventually deterred the richest society folk. While trade and proto-industry boosted the fortunes of some cities, a few languished. As a whole, however, the country was entering a period of rapid urbanisation and the largest towns were those with the most opportunities for entrepreneurial activity.

Bound up with the commercial hustle and bustle were the obvious pleasures of society living and leisure facilities. These factors attracted migrants and visitors alike to the city. Thomas Tryon remarked that 'the Citizen can rarely be long easie in the Country, but complains he's melancholly for want of Company, and knows not how to spend his time.'[91] While the German physicist Georg Lichtenberg found London's smog and gloom oppressive, he also rationalised that 'One could certainly not endure it were it not for other consolations which far outweigh that.'[92] John Brewer and Peter Borsay have explored these consolations in majestic detail.[93] The money, the opportunities, the social interactions, the arts and cultural scene: the cities were the place to be for those wanting to make and spend money. For these obvious pleasures people would put up with the manifold nuisances of a busy urban existence. Even Matt Bramble recognised that a 'companionable man will, undoubtedly, put up with many inconveniences for the sake of enjoying agreeable society. A facetious friend of mine used to say, the wine could not be bad where the company was agreeable.' However, Bramble was not a companionable man and London was too extreme for him; the company was not so good that the city should 'mortify my senses, and compound with such uncleanness as my soul abhors'.[94] The fourth Earl of Chesterfield was more positive about the pleasures. On building Chesterfield House in the 1740s in the West End of London (South Audley Street) he reasoned that 'congenial society is, in the end, the greatest joy in life, and it can be found only in capitals. It is on this principle that I am at present in the process of ruining myself by building a fine house here.'[95]

The various laws and bylaws aimed at controlling, punishing and reforming nuisances between 1600 and 1770 did not hold back the development of proto-industrialisation in English cities. The laws governing nuisances were insufficiently encompassing or powerful to halt industrial pollution and developed little in the period. Judges considering industrial nuisances made compromises that increasingly favoured manufacturing developments.[96] Cities became increasingly smutted, polluted, gloomy, smelly, dusty and, in many respects, unhealthy. The very fact that English cities were able to fall into conditions that shocked European travellers used to more salubrious surroundings might have been one of the factors that pushed England to the fore in the massive industrial expansion to come in the nineteenth century. Some towns even held their smoke as evidence of their industrial might.[97]

A few people would need to suffer some upset for the greater glory of the city and the nation. The lawyer Edmund Plowden justified new buildings blocking the windows of existing properties – because 'it would not be beautifull that Cities should have any voyd places in them and it would be most honourable that they should be populous'.[98] Others also recognised a need to share space with a mind to maximise the number of new habitations rather than protect the condition of existing ones. Some argued that a cheek-by-jowl city scene was the most desirable. Another sixteenth-century lawyer asserted that 'If one house should not bee adjoining unto another, it would bee a great deformity, and if *Cheapside* were so built, it would be a strange *Cheapside* . . . This City is the greatest City, and most populous in this Realme, and the more populous the more honourable, & the more buildings the more populous and honourable will it be.'[99] For many people the economic health of the nation took priority over the comfort of the citizens.

People might have thought differently if they had a better understanding of the damage inflicted on their health by the grim, dark and dirty city environment.[100] A lack of genuine concern about pollution and contamination (in food, water and the environment) was evident throughout the period. John Evelyn's plans to clean up the city came to nothing, even after the fire had created an opportunity for his designs. Medics were slow to link pollution to ill-health. Despite Evelyn's efforts, little attention was paid to the harmful effects of smoke. Many citizens, including John Wood and Tobias Smollett, suffered from asthma and emphysema. The concerns that drove some improvements seemed to have a basis in trade or aesthetics rather than health. The cities became more visually pleasing, suggesting there was a degree of satisfaction with the practical changes already implemented to improve lighting, cleansing and paving. Many narrow medieval streets seen as claustrophobic and constricting, impolite and ugly were widened and made more uniform. There was no room for the higgledy-piggledy rows of twisted mismatched houses in a city about to give birth to the stuccoed symmetry of Regent's Park. Shabby was not chic; flush facades and straight building lines were in vogue, and uniform streets were easier to keep clean and maintain. Many local Acts of Parliament aimed at improving the urban realm cited the need for purely visual improvements as well as practical developments.[101] Roads were widened to help keep traffic moving, streets were cleaned and paved to reduce dangerous obstacles. Attention was paid not just to road and entrance widths, but also to the overhead restrictions. Jetties had been banned in rebuilding in London, and they were becoming less common in other cities too. The days of the hanging sign were also drawing to a close. In London and Bath they were prohibited during the 1760s, to be replaced by flat signboards attached to the walls of properties.[102] The Revd John Penrose noticed the change on his return visit to Bath in 1767.[103] Manchester and Oxford followed in the early 1770s.[104] The clutter of signs, posts and other street furniture was rejected; the 'confined spaces, irregularity, gloom and dirt were the physical manifestations of all that was contrary to the polite ethos'.[105]

Health was not a prime concern in the contemporary discussions. City improvement acts of the mid- to late eighteenth century were designed to remove the dirt and clutter that held people up and soiled their shoes: that the dirt also spread disease was rarely noted before the second half of the eighteenth century.[106] Perhaps here again we risk slipping into E. P. Thompson's 'hypocrisy of hindsight'. It was not until after the 1770s that public health started to become a priority among civic leaders and medics. Building on the London 'Bills of Mortality', Dr Thomas Percival collated statistics, published as *Observations on the state of population of Manchester* in 1774, and this highlighted the effects that a poor environment had on the health of the citizens.[107] Doctors and academics started to think in a more 'scientific' manner; Lazzaro Spallanzani discovered bacteria in the 1770s. Nearly one hundred and eighty years after John Harington tinkered with the flushing toilet, the first patent was taken out to resolve the problem of closing the closet with a valve. This invention, by a London watchmaker Alexander Cumming, combined with the U-bend, represented the true birth of functional domestic plumbing.[108] Modern-style hospitals were built in the larger cities: Oxford's Radcliffe Infirmary opened in 1770, the Manchester Infirmary in 1752. The first local Board of Health was established in Manchester in the 1790s.[109]

By 1770 only two of our characters were still alive, and Tobias Smollett was only just – he died from an intestinal disorder in September 1771. James Woodforde was to die in 1803. Samuel Pepys, Robert Hooke and Thomas Tryon had all died a century earlier, within six months of each other. Before he died Hooke had been responsible for many developments of modern living. A jack of all disciplines, he developed timepieces, coined the word 'cell', publicised the merits of microscopy, and he had even worked on the sash window that changed the face of city buildings.[110] Thomas Tryon had died a rather apposite death for a man reluctant to use the privy – succumbing to 'the Strangury or Retention of Urine'.[111]

The urban centres of Bath, Oxford, Manchester and London were very different places in 1770 to those they had been in 1600. The four cities changed in appearance; all had grown bigger and burst through their walls (if they had them) and gates. Infrastructural developments allowed the cities to cope with expansions in trade and commerce. In London two new bridges were erected to supplement London Bridge (itself repaired and decluttered in the 1750s). Westminster Bridge opened in 1750, and Blackfriars Bridge was completed eighteen years later. The Pulteney Bridge spanning the River Avon in Bath was built between 1769 and 1771. Markets were moved and improved. The covered market opened in Oxford in 1774 to reduce congestion on the road now called Queen Street and parts of the High Street around Carfax. In 1768 the Manchester pig market moved from the central marketplace to a patch of wasteland to the east, near the potato market (itself moved in 1748 after causing problems in its original location around the Exchange) at Shudehill.[112]

On the whole London was becoming a cleaner, healthier and, some argued, more polite place. Bernard Mandeville breathed his last breath in 1733, just as London's notorious Fleet Ditch was being partially covered, and the city was becoming slightly more salubrious. Medics noted the positive effects of the airy and paved streets, and improved water provisions.[113] Commenting in 1776, one author thought 'the rabble, or those who compose the mob' had become 'much mended' within the last fifty years.[114] The historian Dorothy George has described London in the 1780s as 'not the London of Fielding and Hogarth, its dirt and insecurity were no longer worthy of a medieval town'.[115] The author John Noorthouck thought that the improvements brought about by the London Streets Act (1766),[116] modelled on Westminster's Act, were even more dramatic, as the conditions had been worse.[117]

Bath as explored by Matt Bramble in the second half of the eighteenth century was experiencing a decline of fortunes, and had become significantly less popular among the society beaux and belles.[118] Critics were noting dirt piling up on the streets, and the notoriously smoky Somerset coal was smutting newly constructed buildings.[119] However, at the same time the city was starting to function better. The citizens of Bath enjoyed developments brought about by the Improvement Act of 1766. Properties that restricted the movement of traffic were subjected to compulsory purchase orders and taken down. The leaking and tumbledown Guildhall was destined to be shifted from its stranded location in the middle of the highway, and the market stalls that clustered limpet-like around the building were relocated in the 1760s.[120]

In 1770 Oxford was careworn, tatty, dark and dirty, but major regeneration beckoned. With the Mileways Act (1771), long overdue reforms radically transformed the city. Following decades of decline Oxford's Magdalen Bridge, on the main highway to London, was rebuilt in 1779.[121] Just as in Bath and

London (where various city gates were demolished in the 1760s and 1770s), the crumbling and constricting northern and eastern gates were demolished as part of road-widening schemes. New and wider roads and bridges were developed, the obstructive conduit at Carfax was removed, a clutter of buildings in the central area was razed, signs were positioned flush with the walls, and street paving, cleaning and lighting were reorganised by commissioners. James Woodforde was most impressed with the ongoing developments in 1771.[122]

There were still, of course, pockets of misery and industrial blight in each of the urban settlements. In the more desirable residential locations problems such as street dirt and smells were tackled through the combined efforts of public and private initiative. The areas less touched by such developments were generally those avoided by the commentators whose records have survived. Improvement acts of the mid-eighteenth century largely concerned showcase areas in each city. Overall, the improvements were impressive and brought order to cleansing and lighting. However, these were not Acts for social regeneration; they rarely helped the poorest citizens in the poorest neighbourhoods. In a telling comment about the contrast brought about by the improvements of the 1760s, Noorthouck claimed that London 'no more resembles what it was fifty years ago, than the best part of Westminster now resembles the worst part of Wapping'.[123] While in some parts of some cities people were stumbling over carcasses and slipping in stinking kennels, in fashionable areas efforts centred on aesthetic developments. Rebuilt, cleansed and well-lit parts of each city abutted poky and dirty areas. New developments built on higher ground attracted the richer citizens and new arrivals to the city, while more central low-lying properties decreased in desirability and value.[124] When conducting his survey of the state of Bath's streets in the mid-eighteenth century, John Wood complained that the fifty-one houses along Avon Street had 'fallen into an Irregularity and meanness not worth describing'.[125] Bath's improvement schemes left little mark on this street, the Georgian red-light district where the 'nymphs' plied their trade.[126] John Penrose took a long detour in May 1766 to avoid going down this 'Street of ill Fame', and arrived sweating and with aching feet at his lodgings.[127] There was increased lighting provision on the street, but this just served to highlight the grime and squalor. The *Bath Chronicle* drew attention, in its edition of 17 July 1777, to the rising disquiet about this notorious area of the city. A letter by 'Civis' expressed hopes that some plan might be formed 'for restraining, not only the practice of easing nature on the pavement in almost every corner', but also the hurling of chamber pot contents from windows and cinders from doors.[128]

Samuel Johnson argued that to get a true sense of the magnitude of London, the visitor should not look to the great streets, but 'must survey the innumerable little lanes and courts. It is not in the showy evolution of buildings, but in the multiplicity of human habitations which are crowded together that the wonderful immensity of London consists.' If they looked into the mean alleys visitors would find London 'perplexed with narrow passages . . . embarassed [*sic*] with obstructions, and Clouded with smoke'.[129] Other areas of blight lay on the outskirts of the cities, or in non-places such as riversides and floodplains. Ribbon developments spreading out of London were frequently the location of noisome trades.[130] Ringed by muck-heaps and smoking brick-kilns, London's edge was an embarrassment. In 1706 the ditches which flanked the approach roads were 'so full of Nastiness and stinking Dirt, that oftentimes many Persons, who have occasion to go in or come out of Town, are forced to stop their Noses'.[131] Sixty years later Jonas Hanway claimed that the inhabitants of the capital 'had taken pains to render its environs displeasing both to sight and smell. The chain of brick kilns that surrounds us, like the scars of the smallpox, makes us lament the ravages of beauty.'[132]

As the city footprint grew, the previously remote places were remote no more. In his ambitious but naive plans for a verdant green belt, Evelyn had allowed little room for further city expansion. It might have surprised Evelyn to know that the area reserved for his sylvan idyll is now at the heart of the central metropolis. The city was constantly expanding over, and towards, its own filth. The case of *Rex vs. Burrell* (1757) centred on a dog kennel where stinking horsemeat and the stench of burning bones were said to infect the nearby air. An apothecary described the establishment as unwholesome, adding 'The smell makes me ready to vomit.' Horses riding past were frightened by the stench. In an interesting comment for the defence it was noted that 'the town is come to the dog kennel'. Urban creep meant that a once rural and isolated business was perceived to be obnoxious to recently arrived citizens. This did not persuade the judge, and the defendant was found guilty.[133]

By 1770 the focus of urban expansion shifted northwards – towards the industrialising cities of Manchester, Nottingham, Oldham and Leeds. The Manchester Streets Act (1776) made the central parts of Manchester more pleasant, bringing about the much-needed widening of St Mary's Gate (the passage between the Exchange and St Ann's Square) and the cutting of a new road to the east of Old Millgate.[134] Until then the court leet had struggled to deal with overcrowding around the Exchange on market days. However, the Act did not improve lighting, and many streets were still not flagged by the end of the eighteenth century, making 'the walking in them, to strangers, very disagreeable'.[135] While London seemed to be becoming more pleasant and welcoming, even the once highly praised city of Nottingham was slipping into filth and became increasingly crowded.[136]

Manchester was on the cusp of a meltdown. The city struggled to cope with rising numbers of migrants brought in to work in the factories and mills. Erstwhile peruke-maker Richard Arkwright set up Cromford Mill in Derbyshire in 1771, heralding the dawn of a new era. Arkwright brought his inventions to Manchester in the early 1780s, building the Miller Street cotton mill near Shudehill. The cheap cotton products churned out by these new methods were prized for their robust and washable qualities, but their intensive manufacture created even dirtier urban environments, changing the sounds of manufacture, and the working conditions of many people. The manorial authorities failed to cope with the increasing discharges of liquid and particulate waste.[137] Mill workers shrouded in smutted shawls made their way to the factory gates from crowded houses and dingy cellar rooms with 'shattered windows' in 'narrow back streets'.[138] Some immigrant workers even moved into uncompleted properties.[139] At the end of the eighteenth century a doctor worried about workers crowded into 'offensive, dank, damp, and incommodious habitations, a too fertile source of disease!'[140] Infrastructure began to fail to cope with a mushrooming population, the crude sanitary facilities were overburdened and febrile disease raged in some parts. Thomas Percival, a fellow of the Royal Society, recalled the epidemic of an 'Ulcerous Sore Throat' that killed many in 1770.[141] Alexis de Tocqueville viewed developments in Manchester in the early nineteenth century. 'Here', he exclaimed, 'humanity attains its most complete development and its most brutish.' He was struck by the inescapable noise, bustle and filth – just as many visitors to London had noticed the like in the seventeenth century.[142]

So what *did* upset the senses of our seventeenth- and eighteenth-century city dwellers? What, to borrow a phrase from James Boswell, 'disturbed human life' in the period? The weather played a part; rain permeated clothing, puddled the streets and dribbled onto pedestrians' heads. Most citizens put the blame for much of their discomfort at the feet of other people – delaying their fellow citizens through their inconsiderate use of the street, vexing them with their noises, and annoying with their smells. Nuisances provoked different reactions. Matt Bramble and Morose were misanthropic caricatures. John Clayton carped and whinged, but he was not in their league. The ingenious few (such as Robert Hooke) designed their way to a more comfortable future. Some (such as the Elizas Smith and Haywood, and the slightly deranged Thomas Tryon) told their readers how to cope. Ned Ward and William Hogarth cuttingly satirised their experiences. But many, like the indomitable Samuel Pepys, saw opportunity and excitement in their dirty, noisy and smelly cities, even with their shoes mired in turd. Indeed, it could have been worse. They could have been stranded in the countryside, with crude, turnip-eating 'clownish, lubberly, untaught, barbarous, ignorant, blundering, plain . . . rude, slovenly, absurd, boysterous, blustering' rustic fools.[143]

Bibliographic Abbreviations

BCL   Bath Central Library

BRO   Bath Record Office

CLRO   Corporation of London Record Office

Court Leet Records (Southampton) F. J. C. Hearnshaw and D. M. Hearnshaw (eds), *Court Leet Records, Volume I, Part III A.D. 1603–1624*, Publications of the Southampton Record Society, 4 (Southampton, 1907)

Evelyn, *Diary* E. S. de Beer (ed.), *The Diary of John Evelyn* (6 vols, Oxford, 1955)

GL   Guildhall Archives, Guildhall Library, London

Hooke, *Diary* Henry W. Robinson, and Walter Adams (eds), *The Diary of Robert Hooke F.R.S., 1672–1680* (London, 1935)

LMA   London Metropolitan Archives

OBSP   *Old Bailey Sessions Papers*

ODNB   *Oxford Dictionary of National Biography* (Oxford, 2004)

Oxford Council Acts 1583–1626 H. E. Salter (ed.), *Oxford Council Acts 1583–1626*, Oxford Historical Society, 87 (Oxford, 1928)

Oxford Council Acts 1626–1665 M. G. Hobson and H. E. Salter (eds), *Oxford Council Acts 1626–1665*, Oxford Historical Society, 95 (Oxford, 1933)

Oxford Council Acts 1665–1701 M. G. Hobson (ed.), *Oxford Council Acts 1665–1701*, Oxford Historical Society, n.s., 2 (Oxford, 1939)

Pepys, *Diary* William Matthews and Robert Latham (eds), *The Diary of Samuel Pepys* (11 vols, London, 1970–83)

Ryder, *Diary* W. Matthews (ed.), *The Diary of Dudley Ryder, 1715–1716* (London, 1939)

VCH Oxon, IV *The Victoria History of the County of Oxford IV*, ed. A. Crossley (Oxford, 1979)

Notes

Sources are given in full here if they are cited only once; full details of other sources are in the Select Bibliography.

1. 'The City in a Hubbub'

1 For example, Brewer, *Pleasures of the Imagination*; Borsay, *English Urban Renaissance*; Langford, *A Polite and Commercial People*.
2 'Disgust for all its visceralness turns out to be one of our more aggressive culture creating passions'. William Ian Miller shows how disgust helps people to structure their environment, in *Anatomy of Disgust*, p. xii and passim.
3 *Jacobellis v. State of Ohio*, 378 U.S. 184, 197 (1964), cited in Evelyn Brooks Higginbotham, 'African-American women's history and the metalanguage of race', *Signs: Journal of Women in Culture and Society*, 17:2 (1992), pp. 251–74 at p. 253.
4 Kames, *Elements of Criticism*, I, p. 338. Hans Rindisbacher points out that the senses lead to a distrust and uncertainty: 'As the suppliers of an experience that is unalienably personal, they contain an anarchic potential that cannot easily be yoked to social utility.' Rindisbacher, *The Smell of Books*, p. 1.
5 Miller, *Anatomy of Disgust*, p. 18.
6 J. Douglas Porteous, *Landscapes of the Mind: Worlds of Sense and Metaphor* (Toronto and London, 2001), p. 61.
7 Pepys, *Diary*, I, p. 192, and n2, p. 200.
8 Pepys, *Diary*, II, p. 25.
9 C. S. Knighton, 'Pepys, Samuel (1633–1703)', *ODNB*. For further details of Pepys's life and career see Claire Tomalin, *Samuel Pepys: The Unequalled Self* (London, 2002). The best version of his diary is the one edited by William Matthews and Robert Latham, *The Diary of Samuel Pepys*.
10 Clark, *Life and Times of Anthony à Wood*, I, p. 43.
11 Graham Parry, 'Wood, Anthony (1632–1695)', *ODNB*.
12 Clark, *Wood's City of Oxford*, p. 24.
13 For a fuller account see Whitaker, *Mad Madge*.
14 James Fitzmaurice, 'Cavendish [née *Lucas*], Margaret, duchess of Newcastle upon Tyne (1623?–1673)', *ODNB*.
15 Pepys, *Diary*, VIII, pp. 186–7.
16 See Lisa Jardine's biography for a fuller account of Hooke's life and work, *The Curious Life of Robert Hooke: The Man Who Measured London* (London, 2003).
17 Hooke, *Diary*.
18 Hooke, *Diary*, pp. 17, 33, 74, 188.
19 Richard Waller's introduction in Hooke, *Posthumous Works*, pp. xxvi–xxvii.

20 Patri J. Pugliese, 'Hooke, Robert (1635–1703)', *ODNB*.
21 Virginia Smith, 'Tryon, Thomas (1634–1703)', *ODNB*; Tryon, *Memoirs*, pp. 17–18.
22 James Sambrook, 'Ward, Edward [Ned] (1667–1731)', *ODNB*; see also H. W. Troyer, *Ned Ward of Grub Street: A Study of Sub-literary London in the Eighteenth Century* (Cambridge, Mass., 1946).
23 John Harland presented a rather prudish edition of part of Harrold's diary in 'Diary of a Manchester wig-maker'; Craig Horner is currently preparing an edited version of Harrold's diary for publication. Chetham's Library holds the original – Mun A.2.137.
24 Chetham's Library, Mun A.2.137, for example see fol. 2v (p. 4).
25 David Lemmings, 'Ryder, Sir Dudley (1691–1756)', *ODNB*.
26 Ryder, *Diary*, p. 331.
27 M. M. Goldsmith, 'Mandeville, Bernard (bap. 1670, d. 1733)', *ODNB*.
28 R. L. Winstanley, 'Woodforde, James (1740–1803)', *ODNB*.
29 Hargreaves-Mawdsley, *Woodforde at Oxford*, p. xi.
30 Shuttleton, 'Mary Chandler's *Description of Bath* (1733)', pp. 173–4.
31 Ibid., p. 174.
32 Prescott and Shuttleton, 'Mary Chandler', p. 32; Janine Barchas, 'Chandler, Mary (1687–1745)', *ODNB*.
33 Shuttleton, 'Mary Chandler's *Description of Bath* (1733)', p. 179.
34 Smollett, *Humphry Clinker*, I, p. 99.
35 Ibid., I, p. 62; II, p. 12.
36 Ibid., II, p. 11.
37 John F. Sena, 'Smollett's persona and the melancholic traveler: an hypothesis', *Eighteenth-Century Studies*, 1:4 (1968), pp. 353–69.
38 Kenneth Simpson, 'Smollett, Tobias George (1721–1771)', *ODNB*.
39 'Although Bramble has some un-Smollettian characteristics, in his views on society he is very much his master's voice.' Lewis, *Tobias Smollett*, pp. 77, 153.
40 William Camden (first written in Latin in 1586), *Britain, or a Chorographicall description* (London, 1637), p. 567.
41 Mare and Quarrell, *Lichtenberg's Visits*, pp. 98–9.
42 Evelyn, *Diary*, III, pp. 122, 131.
43 Whitaker, *Mad Madge*, p. 241.
44 Figures from Chalklin, *Rise of the English Town*, p. 77; Porter, 'Cleaning up the Great Wen', p. 66; Power, 'The East London working community', p. 103; Roger Finlay and Beatrice Shearer, 'Population growth and suburban expansion', in A. L. Beier and Roger Finlay (eds), *London, 1500–1700, the Making of the Metropolis* (London, 1986), pp. 37–59 at p. 38.
45 Stow, *Survay of London*, p. 220 (some mispagination occurs at this point, where two consecutive pages are numbered 220 – this is the second p. 220).
46 Schofield, 'The topography and buildings of London', pp. 297, 315.
47 Alexander Pope, 'The alley', in *Works*, III, p. 188.
48 Sheppard, 'London before the L.C.C.'; Manchée, *Westminster City Fathers*, p. 145.
49 Massie, *Essay*, p. 23; see chapter 5, 'Noisy', for the confusion shown in the Niblett case.
50 *The Journeys of Celia Fiennes*, introduced by John Hillaby (London, 1983), p. 50.
51 Crossley, 'City and university', pp. 106–7.
52 *VCH Oxon*, IV, pp. 74–6, 181; Crossley, 'City and university', pp. 106, 129–30,.
53 Amhurst, *Terrae Filius*, II, p. 258.
54 See *VCH Oxon*, IV, pp. 130–40.
55 Salter, *Oxford City Properties*, p. viii; *Oxford Council Acts 1583–1626*, pp. 71, 135, 142; *Oxford Council Acts 1665–1701*, pp. 14, 34, 59, 176, 287–8. Some of the viewers worked in the construction industries, such as carpenters and masons – *Oxford Council Acts 1583–1626*, p. 302; *Oxford Council Acts 1626–1665*, p. 233.
56 Crossley, 'City and university', pp. 110–14; *VCH Oxon*, IV, pp. 155–9, 168–71, 350–2; *Oxford Council Acts 1626–1665*, p. 273.

57 I. G. Philip, 'The Court Leet of the University of Oxford', *Oxoniensia*, 15 (1950), pp. 81–91.
58 Henry Chapman, *Thermae Redivivae: The City of Bath Described* (London, 1673), pp. 2–3.
59 Evelyn, *Diary*, III, p. 102.
60 Chalklin, *Provincial Towns*, p. 74; McIntyre, 'Bath: the rise of a resort town', p. 204.
61 Jean Manco, 'Bath and the great rebuilding', *Bath History*, 4 (1992), pp. 25–51 at p. 48.
62 Ward, 'A Step to Bath', p. 166.
63 Figures from McIntyre, 'Bath: the rise of a resort town', p. 214; Chalklin, *Rise of the English Town*, p. 78; Chalklin, *Provincial Towns*, p. 74.
64 *The Bath and Bristol Guide*, p. 4.
65 Fawcett, *Bath Administer'd*, pp. 31, 35.
66 Ibid., p. 25.
67 Richard Wright Procter, *Memorials of Bygone Manchester* (Manchester, 1880), pp. 373–4.
68 (Figures exclude Salford.) Rounded figures, based on a table in Horner, 'Proper persons to deal with', pp. 46–7; G. B. Blackwood, *The Lancashire Gentry and the Great Rebellion 1640–1660* (Manchester, 1978), p. 8; Alfred P. Wadsworth and Julia De Lacy Mann, *The Cotton Trade and Industry: Lancashire 1600–1780* (Manchester, 1931), p. 510.
69 Chalklin, *Provincial Towns*, p. 89.
70 BCL, MS B914–238, p. 51.
71 John J. Parkinson-Bailey, *Manchester: An Architectural History* (Manchester and New York, 2000), pp. 4–5.
72 William Stukeley, *Itinerarium Curiosum, or, an Account of the Antiquities, and Remarkable Curiosities in Nature or Art, Observed in Travels through Great Britain* (2 vols, London, 1776), I, p. 58.
73 Defoe, *A Tour Thro' Great Britain*, III, p. 219.
74 For a good account of the powers of the manorial court see Redford, *History of Local Government in Manchester*, I, esp. p. 150.
75 Aikin, *Description of Manchester*, p. 191.
76 Rupert C. Jarvis, 'The Manchester constables: 1745', *Transactions of the Lancashire and Cheshire Antiquarian Society*, 71 (1961), pp. 75–89 at p. 75.
77 Earwaker, *Court Leet Records of Manchester*, II, pp. 159–62; VIII, pp. 128–32.
78 H. D. Rack, 'The Manchester Corporation project of 1763: legend or history?', *Transactions of the Lancashire and Cheshire Antiquarian Society*, 84 (1987), pp. 118–42 at pp. 118, 136.
79 Aikin, *Description of Manchester*, p. 191.
80 Tryon, *Tryon's Letters*, p. 6.
81 Gerard, *Essay on Taste*, p. 213.
82 *The Manchester Mercury and Harrop's General Advertiser*, no. 590, 21–28 Aug. 1759, p. 4; see also Ryder, *Diary*, p. 261.
83 For the more interesting accounts see D. Lowe, *History of Bourgeois Perception*, pp. 7, 15, 24; D. R. Woolf, 'Speech, text, and time: the sense of hearing and the sense of the past in Renaissance England', *Albion*, 18 (1986), pp. 159–94; Martin Jay, *Downcast Eyes: The Denigration of Vision in Twentieth-Century French Thought* (Berkeley, 1994), pp. 21–82. For the early modern period see Noel Chomel, *Dictionnaire Oeconomique, or the Family Dictionary* (2 vols, London, 1725), I, s.v. 'Ear'; Henry Peacham, *The Garden of Eloquence* (London, 1577), sig. B3v; Brathwaite, *Essaies upon the Five Senses*, p. 6; Robert Burton, *The Anatomy of Melancholy* (Oxford, 1621), p. 34; Thomas Tomkis[?], *Lingua; or, the Combat of the Tongue* (London, 1607).
84 See Cockayne, 'Experiences of the deaf', p. 495.
85 Rindisbacher, *The Smell of Books*, p. 1 – because words do not convey experiences well in texts, 'whole chunks of experience escape. They remain dangling outside the

structures of verbal communication in a world of unincorporated individuality.' David
Chidester argues that debates about the sensory hierarchy reveal only the bias of the
commentator: David Chidester, *Word and Light: Seeing, Hearing and Religious
Discourse* (Urbana, Ill., 1992), p. x. An earlier, similar view was expressed in Grose, *The
Olio*, p. 258. See also Jonathan Rée, *I See a Voice: A Philosophical History of Language,
Deafness and the Senses* (London, 1999).

86 Anthony Nixon, *The Dignitie of Man* (London, 1616), p. 64.
87 See Cockayne, 'A cultural history of sound', pp. 37–41.
88 Tryon, *Tryon's Letters*, pp. 31, 119.
89 Tryon, *Memoirs*, p. 112.
90 Tryon, *Tryon's Letters*, pp. 1–3, 6, 10–11, 16.
91 Evelyn, *Diary*, III, p. 67.
92 Tryon, *Tryon's Letters*, pp. 1–4.
93 Ibid., p. 7.
94 Ray, *Compleat Proverbs*, p. 60.
95 Ibid., p. vii.
96 *Hell upon Earth*, cover page.
97 Byrom [?], *A Serious Disswasive*, pp. 5, 24.
98 Ray, *Compleat Proverbs*, p. 136.
99 Pottle, *Boswell's London Journal*, p. 284.
100 Earwaker, *Court Leet Records of Manchester*, III, p.10.
101 Chandler, *Liverpool*, p. 153; Power, *Liverpool Town Books*, pp. 150, 242.
102 Thomas Pennant, *British Zoology* (4 vols, London, 1768–70), I, p. 41.
103 Monson, *Briefe Declaration* (1639), p. 15.
104 Fielding, *The Intriguing Chambermaid*, p. 28.
105 Otter, 'Cleansing and clarifying', p. 46.
106 Blackstone, *Commentaries*, III, p. 218.
107 Brenner, 'Nuisance law', p. 403.
108 Blackstone, *Commentaries*, III, p. 216.
109 Ibid.; Burn, *Justice of the Peace*, II, p. 155.
110 Dalton, *Country Justice* (1742), p. 156; *Rex v. Smith* (1725), in Strange, *Reports of
     Adjudged Cases*, I, p. 704; England and Wales, *The Statutes at Large* (1706), III, pp.
     1945–6.
111 Burn, *Justice of the Peace*, II, pp. 156–7.
112 Dalton, *Country Justice* (1742), p. 156.
113 Baker and Milsom, *Sources of English Legal History*, p. 493; In an interesting case, *Rex
     v. Pappineau* (1726), an appeal hinged partly on the inappropriateness of a fine for a
     common nuisance – see Strange, *Reports of Adjudged Cases*, I, pp. 686–9.
114 Blackstone, *Commentaries*, III, pp. 219–20; Burn, *Justice of the Peace*, II, p. 155.
115 For example, GL, MS 12,071/6, fol. 121r (1744), following investigations into
     complaints that foot passages were being obstructed the culprit was 'to be prosecuted
     by the clerk of this Company at the Companies Expence in order to prevent the like
     nusance for the future'.
116 Brenner, 'Nuisance law', pp. 420–1.
117 For more details here see Langford, *Public Life*, pp. 448–55.
118 Power, *Liverpool Town Books*, p. 266.
119 Earwaker, *Court Leet Records of Manchester*, VIII, p. 87.
120 Blackstone, *Commentaries*, III, p. 216; Burn, *Justice of the Peace*, II, p. 155;
121 Dalton, *Country Justice* (1742), p. 156.
122 Hawkins, *Pleas of the Crown*, I, pp. 197–200.
123 Blackstone, *Commentaries*, III, pp. 5, 220: Burn, *Justice of the Peace*, II, p. 156.
124 Great Britain, Court of King's Bench, *Reports of Cases*, II, p. 248.
125 Blackstone, *Commentaries*, III, pp. 220–2.
126 Brenner, 'Nuisance law', p. 406.

127 See Earwaker, *Court Leet Records of Manchester*, II, p. 131 for rules for dealing with 'any special annoyance betwixt neighbour and neighbour' made in 1597.
128 Brenner, 'Nuisance law', p. 406.
129 Jacob, *Every man his own lawyer*, p. 39.
130 Blackstone, *Commentaries*, III, p. 217.
131 Cited in Baker and Milsom, *Sources of English Legal History*, p. 258.
132 Hamlin, 'Public sphere to public health', p. 193.
133 Baker and Milsom, *Sources of English Legal History*, p. 492.

2. Ugly

1 Cavendish, *Worlds Olio*, p. 91.
2 *Wits Cabinet*, pp. 28–9.
3 Isobel Grundy, *Lady Mary Wortley Montagu: Comet of the Enlightenment* (Oxford, 1999), pp. xviii, 99–102.
4 Pat Rogers, 'Samuel Johnson (1709–1784)', *ODNB*.
5 Clark, *Life and Times of Anthony à Wood*, I, p. 199.
6 *OBSP*, 7–10 Sept. 1720, p. 3; *OBSP*, 6–13 July 1774, p. 365.
7 *OBSP*, 7–12 Dec. 1692, p. 3.
8 Cox, *Spitalfields*, pp. 23–4, 85–90.
9 Ray, *Compleat Proverbs*, p. 2.
10 Gilman, *Making the Body Beautiful*, p. 88.
11 Helen Berry, 'An early coffee house periodical and its readers: the *Athenian Mercury*, 1691–1697', *London Journal*, 25:1 (2000), pp. 14–33 at p. 27.
12 *The Weekly Journal, or The British Gazetteer* (4 Feb. 1727), from Rictor Norton, *Early Eighteenth-Century Newspaper Reports: A Sourcebook*, 'Cleanliness', at www.infopt.demon.co.uk/grub/soap.htm (accessed 12 Sept. 2005).
13 Smith, *Complete Housewife*, p. 256.
14 Parkinson, *The Journal of John Byrom, Volume I, Part I*, pp. 356–7.
15 Ramazzini, *De Morbis Artificum*, p. 393.
16 John Aubrey, *Brief Lives and Other Selected Writings*, ed. A. Powell (London, 1949), p. 344.
17 Ward, *Hudibras Redivivus* (1722), p. 24 [part II, canto II]; Pope, 'The alley', in *Works*, III, p. 187.
18 Mildmay Fane, Earl of Westmorland, *Otia sacra optima fides* (London, 1648), p. 138; see also *Twelve Ingenious Characters*, p. 38
19 Smollett, *Humphry Clinker*, II, p. 5.
20 Piper, *The English Face*, pp. 125–7.
21 'Miso-spilus', *A Wonder of Wonders*, sig. A2 (p. 3); N. F. Lowe has written about the significance of beauty spots in Hogarth's work: 'The meaning of venereal disease'; also Lowe, 'Hogarth, beauty spots, and sexually transmitted diseases'.
22 Hall, *Loathsomnesse of Long haire*, pp. 118–19.
23 John Gauden, *Several Letters Between Two Ladies; Wherein the Lawfulness and Unlawfulness of Artificial Beauty in a Point of Conscience, Are nicely Debated* (London, 1701), p. 87.
24 Cleland, *Memoirs*, I, p. 38.
25 Philip Bliss (ed.), *Athenea Oxonienses, an Exact History of all the writers and bishops who have had their education in the University of Oxford . . . By Anthony à Wood* (4 vols, London, 1813–20), IV, p. 119.
26 Ryder, *Diary*, pp. 341, 343.
27 Ibid., p. 68
28 Phillips, *Mysteries of Love and Eloquence*, sig. H2v-H3r.
29 Ramazzini, *De Morbis Artificum*, p. 135.
30 Wecker, *Cosmeticks*, pp. 116–17.

31 Cavendish, *Worlds Olio*, p. 89 and frontispiece.
32 Ward, 'The Merry Travellers' (1729), p. 28 [pagination restarts with each part in this work].
33 Sander L. Gilman, *Fat Boys: A Slim Book* (Lincoln, Nebr., 2004), pp. 88, 90–3, 95–7.
34 Davies, *Thomas Raymond*, p. 29.
35 Ward, 'The Merry Travellers' (1729), pp. 11–12, 23.
36 Uglow, *Hogarth*, pp. 453–4.
37 Richard Waller's introduction to Hooke, *Posthumous Works*, pp. xxvi–xxvii.
38 Thomas Tryon, *A Treatise of Dreams and Visions*, 2nd edn (London, 1695), frontispiece; Tryon, *Memoirs*, p. 64.
39 BCL, MS B914–238, p. 117.
40 Ryder, *Diary*, p. 241.
41 Furnivall, *Stubbes's Anatomy*, part I, p. 188.
42 Cavendish, *Worlds Olio*, p. 137.
43 *A certaine Relation of the Hog-faced Gentlewoman called Mistris Tannakin Skinker, who was borne at Wirkham* (London, 1640); *A monstrous shape. Or a shapelesse monster. A description of a female creature borne in Holland, compleat in every part save only a head like a swine* (London, 1639).
44 Galloway, *Norwich 1540–1642*, p. 146.
45 Todd, *Imagining Monsters*, pp. 147, 157.
46 Evelyn, *Diary*, III, p. 132.
47 Pepys, *Diary*, V, p. 243; Clark, *Life and Times of Anthony à Wood*, II, p. 226.
48 Clark, *Life and Times of Anthony à Wood*, II, p. 445.
49 Todd, *Imagining Monsters*, pp. 47–8.
50 *The Gentleman's Magazine and Historical Chronicle*, vol. 16, May 1746, p. 270.
51 Gowing, *Common Bodies*, p. 127.
52 Clark, *Life and Times of Anthony à Wood*, II, p. 54.
53 Cavendish, *Worlds Olio*, p. 85.
54 Nicholas Bowden, *Be it known unto all men, that I Nicholas Bowden chirugion, cutter of the stone, and also occultest, curer of the ruptures without cutting, with the helpe of almightie God, can cure and helpe these sicknesses and infirmities following . . .* (London, c.1605).
55 Fuller, *Gnomologia*, p. 111.
56 George, *London Life*, p. 205.
57 Wilson, *Surgery, Skin and Syphilis*, p. 34.
58 J[ohn] B[ulwer], *Anthropometamorphosis: Man Transform'd: or, the artificiall changling* (London, 1653), p. 432.
59 Brathwait[e], *Whimzies*, p. 90.
60 Ramazzini, *De Morbis Artificum*, pp. 49, 53, 67, 281.
61 Daniel Defoe, 'The pacificator', in *A Second volume of the Writings of the Author of the True Born Englishman. Some Whereof never before printed. Corrected and enlarged by the author* (London, 1705), p. 161; Playford, *Wit and mirth*, p. 139.
62 Smollett, *Humphry Clinker*, II, p. 156.
63 Kames, *Elements of Criticism*, I, p. 340.
64 Gilman, *Making the Body Beautiful*, pp. 49–51, 68; see also Claude Quétel, *History of Syphilis* (London, 1990), p. 21.
65 Lowe, 'The meaning of venereal disease', p. 169.
66 Gilman, *Making the Body Beautiful*, pp. 60–1.
67 Blackwell, '"Extraneous bodies"', p. 27; see Lowe, 'The meaning of venereal disease', pp. 171–5.
68 Haywood, *Present for a Servant-Maid*, pp. 13–14.
69 O. P. Sharma, 'Alexander Pope (1688–1744): his spinal deformity and his doctors', *European Respiratory Journal* (Nov. 1999), pp. 1235–7 at p. 1235.
70 Pepys, *Diary*, I, p. 295.

71 Kielmansegg, *Diary of a Journey*, p. 49.
72 Clark, *Life and Times of Anthony à Wood*, II, p. 140.
73 Exwood and Lehmann, *William Schellinks' Travels*, p. 33.
74 Bachrach and Collmer, *The English Journal: Huygens*, p. 147.
75 Trenchfield, *A Cap of Gray Hairs*, pp. 113–15.
76 Mary Chandler, 'A true tale', attached to *The Description of Bath*, pp. 81–5.
77 Doughty, 'A Bath poetess', p. 420; Shuttleton, 'Mary Chandler's *Description of Bath* (1733)', p. 174.
78 Cavendish, *Worlds Olio*, pp. 90, 92.
79 Francis Bacon, *The essaies of Sir Francis Bacon Knight, the Kings Atturney General. His Religious meditations. Places of perswassion and disswasion. Seene and allowed* (London, 1624), sig. D6.
80 Ward, *Nuptial Dialogues and Debates* (1710), II, p. 122.
81 Cited in Gowing, *Common Bodies*, p. 78.
82 Pepys, *Diary*, III, p. 16.
83 Tryon, *Memoirs*, p. 87.
84 Fuller, *Gnomologia*, p. 158.
85 Edward Ward, *Matrimony unmask'd; or, The comforts and discomforts of marriage display'd* (London, 1714), pp. 45–8.
86 *The art of governing a wife*, pp. 153–4.
87 *The Bath and Bristol Guide*, p. 11.
88 Cox, *Spitalfields*, p. 93.
89 Susannah R. Ottaway, *The Decline of Life: Old Age in Eighteenth-Century England* (Cambridge, 2004), p. 33; Alexandra Shepard, *Meanings of Manhood in Early Modern England* (Oxford, 2003), p. 45.
90 Clark, *Life and Times of Anthony à Wood*, II, pp. 163–4.
91 Thane, *Old Age*, p. 90.
92 Ward, *Nuptial Dialogues and Debates* (1710), I, pp. 349–52.
93 Saltonstall, *Picturae Loquentes*, sigs B7v–B8r.
94 Overbury, *Overburie His Wife* (1611), sigs D4r–v.
95 Nicholas Breton, *The Wil of Wit, Wits of Will, or Wils Wit, chuse you whether. Containing five discourses, the effects whereof follow* (London, 1606), sig. F3v.
96 Cleland, *Memoirs*, 1, p. 38
97 Edward Ward, *Labour in Vain: or, what signifies little or nothing* (London, 1700), pp. 7–8.
98 Ward, *Nuptial Dialogues and Debates* (1710), I, p. 44.
99 *The art of governing a wife*, p. 147.
100 Fuller, *Gnomologia*, p. 233.
101 Ramazzini, *De Morbis Artificum*, pp. 397–9.
102 *Coma Berenices*, p. 18.
103 Ward, *Hudibras Redivivus* (1715), II, p. 23 [canto II].
104 *The art of governing a wife*, pp. 153–4.
105 Ryder, *Diary*, p. 298.
106 Mitchell and Penrose, *Letters from Bath*, p. 29.
107 *The Grub-Street Journal*, 2 Sept. 1731, from Rictor Norton, *Early Eighteenth-Century Newspaper Reports: A Sourcebook*, at www.infopt.demon.co.uk/grub/lowlife3.htm (accessed 12 Sept. 2005).
108 Bachrach and Collmer, *The English Journal: Huygens*, p. 74.
109 Jones, *Man of Manners*, p. 10.
110 Ray, *Compleat Proverbs*, p. 116.
111 *Hell Upon Earth*, pp. 32–3, 39.
112 Cooper, *Annals*, III, p. 280.
113 Clark, *Life and Times of Anthony à Wood*, I, p. 509; see also, II, p. 96.
114 Pepys, *Diary*, II, p. 66.

115 Philip Carter, *Men and the Emergence of Polite Society: Britain 1660–1800* (Harlow, 2001), pp. 124–56.
116 [John Evelyn], *Tyrannus, or the Mode: in a Discourse of Sumptuary Lawes* (London, 1661), p. 18.
117 Byrom [?], *A serious disswasive*, pp. 17–18.
118 *Satan's Harvest Home*, pp. 50–1.
119 Atherton, 'The "mob"', p. 52: the butcher is easily identified as 'a burly fellow in jacket or shirt, generally a kerchief or cap on his head, with his steel, knife and marrowbone'.
120 Ward, *Field Spy* (1714), pp. 33–4.
121 Ward, 'The Merry Travellers' (1729), pp. 13–14.
122 Tryon, *Tryon's Letters*, p. 78.
123 Campbell, *London Tradesman*, p. 281.
124 Willis and Hoad, *Portsmouth Sessions Papers*, pp. 98, 137.
125 Hardy, *Middlesex County Records 1689–1709*, pp. 13, 157.
126 Fawcett, *Bath Commercialis'd*, p. 19
127 Clark, *Life and Times of Anthony à Wood*, II, p. 68.
128 Heywood, *Philocothomista*, pp. 3–6.
129 BL Harleian MS 2027, fol. 320v. In N. W. Alcock and Nancy Cox, *Living and Working in Seventeenth Century England: An Encyclopedia of Drawings and Descriptions from Randle Holme's Original Manuscripts for The Academy of Armory (1688)* CD Rom, The British Library, 2000. John Hart, *The Dreadfull Character of a Drunkard* (London, 1663).
130 Bury, *England's Bane*, pp. 4–5.
131 Willis Bund, *Worcester Quarter Sessions Rolls*, pp. 52–3; J. R. Bloxam (ed.), *Magdalen College and King James II 1686–1688: a series of documents, with additions*, Oxford Historical Society, 6 (Oxford, 1886), p. 71.
132 Bury, *England's Bane*, pp. 10–11.
133 *OBSP*, 12–15 Oct. 1726, p. 2; *OBSP*, 12 Oct. 1743, pp. 288–91; Willis and Hoad, *Portsmouth Sessions Papers*, p. 77.
134 Fuller, *Gnomologia*, p. 136.
135 Clark, *Life and Times of Anthony à Wood*, III, p. 135.
136 Ryder, *Diary*, p. 115.
137 Cooper, *Annals*, III, pp. 26–7.
138 Great Britain, *A Collection of all the Statutes Now in Force, Relating to the Duties of Excise in England* (London, 1764), p. 355.
139 Chetham's Library, Mun A.2.137, fols 7r–8r (pp. 13–15); see also Chetham's Library, Mun. C.7.20, bundle 12 (2), V. Bailey's Paper.
140 Campbell, *London Tradesman*, p. 261.
141 Clayton, *Friendly Advice to the Poor*, pp. 17–19.
142 Bury, *England's Bane*, p. 25.
143 Campbell, *London Trademan*, pp. 265–7, 280.
144 Jean Manco, 'Bath and the great rebuilding', *Bath History*, 4 (1992), pp. 25–51 at p. 39. There would also have been taverns and alehouses.
145 King, *Beer has a History*, p. 87; see also *Oxford Council Acts 1626–1665*, p. 19.
146 Clark, *Life and Times of Anthony à Wood*, II, p. 404.
147 Davies, *Thomas Raymond*, p. 117.
148 Hargreaves-Mawdsley, *Woodforde at Oxford*, pp. 40, 116.
149 Clark, *Life and Times of Anthony à Wood*, III, p. 3
150 Ibid., II, pp. 6, 25.
151 Ibid., III, pp. 354–5; with additional information from Robin Darwall-Smith, the archivist at University College, Oxford.
152 John Rouse Bloxam, *A Register of the Presidents, Fellows, Demies, Instructors in Grammar and in Music, Chaplains, Clerks, Choristers, and other members of Saint Mary Magdalen College in the University of Oxford, from the foundation of the College to the present time* (8 vols, Oxford, 1853–85), III, p. 39.

153 See Jessica Warner, *Craze: Gin and Debauchery in the Age of Reason* (New York, 2002), and Patrick Dillon, *The Much Lamented Death of Madam Geneva: The Eighteenth-Century Gin Craze* (London, 2002).

154 Mandeville, *Fable of the Bees* (1724), pp. 86–8.

155 *OBSP*, 12–15 Apr. 1738, pp. 77–8.

156 Fielding, *Works*, IV, p. 546.

157 *A satyr upon old maids*, p. 11.

158 Manchée, *Westminster City Fathers*, pp. 112–13.

159 Hardy, *Middlesex County Records 1689–1709*, p. 300.

160 *OBSP*, 12 Oct. 1743, pp. 288–91.

161 Oldys, *The London Jilt*, 'To the reader', sig. A4.

162 Bailey, *An Universal Etymological English Dictionary* (1742), s.v. 'fustilugs (FU–FY).

163 Gowing, *Domestic Dangers*, p. 80.

164 Stubbes, *Anatomie of Abuses*, sig. G2.

165 Hall, *Loathsomnesse of Long haire*, pp. 101–2.

166 Charles Gildon, *The post-boy rob'd of his mail* (London, 1692), p. 24.

167 Dunton, *Voyage*, p. 145.

168 Earwaker, *Court Leet Records of Manchester*, VIII, p. 39.

169 Mandeville, *Fable of the Bees* (1714), p. 90.

170 Ward, *The Insinuating Bawd* (1700), pp. 11–12.

171 Lowe, 'The meaning of venereal disease'.

172 Overbury, *Overburie His Wife*, sig. G6v.

173 Breton, *The Good and the Badde, Or, Descriptions of the Worthies and Unworthies of this Age* (London, 1616), p. 29.

174 Brathwaite, *Essaies upon the Five Senses*, pp. 134–5, 138.

175 Brathwait[e], *Whimzies*, pp. 173–85. See also *The art of governing a wife*, p. 154.

176 *The Spectator*, no. 209, 30 Oct. 1711 [Addison].

177 *Poor Robin's True Character of a Scold* (London, 1678), p. 3.

178 Brathwaite, *Essaies upon the Five Senses*, pp. 136, 138.

179 Ibid., pp. 135–6; *Twelve Ingenious Characters*, p. 23.

180 *The Merry Dutch Miller and New Invented Windmill* (London, 1672), frontispiece and title page.

181 A '*virulent scold* is her Neighbours perpetual disquiet', *Twelve Ingenious Characters*, p. 23; Earwaker, *Court Leet Records of Manchester*, III, p. 31

182 Hardy, *Middlesex Quarter Sessions*, II, p. 182. See also III, p. 126.

183 GL, MS 2649/1 (unfoliated), presentments for 1710.

184 *Court Leet Records* (Southampton) pp. 381, 401.

185 *Oxford Council Acts 1626–1665*, pp. 146, 432.

186 Earwaker, *Court Leet Records of Manchester*, VII, p. 70.

187 Ibid., II, p. 178; III, pp. 12, 138, 283; VI, pp. 72, 121 – the stool was repaired again in 1679, but out of use in 1681; Earwaker, *Constables' Accounts*, II, pp. v, 59, 64; Bradshaw, *Origins of Street Names in Manchester*, p. 6; Harland, 'The old market place in 1772', p. 210.

188 Bury, *England's Bane*, pp. 7, 25.

189 Hanway, *Journal of Eight Days Journey*, p. 222.

190 *The art of governing a wife*, pp. 145, 159.

191 Ray, *Compleat Proverbs*, p. 17

3. Itchy

1 Ray, *Compleat Proverbs*, p. 12.

2 Phillips, *Mysteries of Love and Eloquence*, p. 162 (sig. M1v).

3 Pelling, 'Appearance and reality', pp. 89–90.

4 It returned for an encore in 1763. Hargreaves-Mawdsley, *Woodforde at Oxford*, pp. 53–4, 67, 87–91, 116; see also Pepys, *Diary*, I, p. 46.

5 Tryon, *Tryon's Letters*, p. 53.

6 Linda E. Merians, *The Secret Malady: Venereal Disease in Eighteenth Century Britain and France* (Lexington, KY, 1996); Daniel Turner, *Syphilis: A Practical Dissertation on the Venereal Disease* (London, 1717).

7 For example, see Phillips, *Generosi Ludentes* (appended to his *Mysteries of Love and Eloquence*), pp. 36, 47 (sigs Y2v and Y8).

8 Ward, *Hudibras Redivivus* (1715), II, p. 24.

9 Pottle, *Boswell's London Journal*, pp. 55, 85, 142, 147–8; see also p. 238.

10 Pepys, *Diary*, I, pp. 215–16, 270, 276, 279; II, pp. 96, 98; IV, pp. 347, 379, 382–6.

11 Tryon, *Wisdom Dictates*, p. 102.

12 Smith, *Complete Housewife*, p. 283.

13 *OBSP*, 14–19 Jan. 1732, p. 56.

14 Ward, *Hudibras Redivivus* (1715), II, p. 20.

15 *Harrop's Manchester Mercury and General Advertiser*, 15–22 June 1756 (no. 220).

16 Southall, *Treatise of Buggs*, p. 33.

17 Exwood and Lehmann, *William Schellinks' Travels*, p. 35.

18 Herbert, *Outlandish Proverbs*, sig. B5v (no. 343).

19 Victor Houliston, 'Moffet, Thomas (1553–1604)', *ODNB*; [Thomas Muffet's contribution to] Edward Topsell, *The History of Four-footed Beasts, Serpents, and Insects* (London, 1658), pp. 1101–2; see also pp. 1090–4 for his description of lice.

20 Southall, *Treatise of Buggs*, p. 30.

21 Tryon, *Cleanliness in Meats*, p. 7.

22 Tryon, *Wisdom Dictates*, p. 21.

23 Tryon, *Cleanliness in Meats*, pp. 5–7

24 Pepys, *Diary*, I, p. 19 and n4; IV, p. 65; V, pp. 11, 55, 62.

25 Haywood, *Present for a Servant-Maid*, pp. 72–6.

26 I. C. Tipton and E. J. Furlong, 'Mrs George Berkeley and her washing machine', *Hermathena*, 101 (1965), pp. 38–47 at p. 44.

27 Clayton, *Friendly Advice to the Poor*, p. 32.

28 Tryon, *Wisdom Dictates*, p. 21.

29 Tryon, *Cleanliness in Meats*, pp. 6–11.

30 Ray, *Compleat Proverbs*, p. 30.

31 Lawrence Stone, *The Family, Sex and Marriage in England, 1500–1800* (London, 1977), p. 159.

32 Thomas, 'Cleanliness and godliness', pp. 57–9, 62–5.

33 Holme, *Academy of Armory*, book III, p. 128.

34 Pottle, *Boswell's London Journal*, p. 82.

35 Parkinson, *Private Journal of John Byrom, Volume I, Part II*, pp. 356, 611–12.

36 Pepys, *Diary*, III, p. 188; see also p. 73; IV, p. 165; V, p. 320; VI, pp. 21, 44; VII, pp. 172, 206.

37 McLaughlin, *Coprophilia*, pp. 38, 42–3.

38 Cogan, *Haven of Health*, p. 77.

39 Tryon, *Wisdom Dictates*, p. 102.

40 Hooke, *Diary*, p. 39; see also p. 22.

41 Evelyn, *Diary*, III, p. 87.

42 Joseph Browne, *An account of the wonderful cures perform'd by the cold baths* (London, 1707), p. 50.

43 Ryder, *Diary*, pp. 79, 89, 190, 194, 201, 203–6, 219, 229.

44 Lewis, *Tobias Smollett*, pp. 148–9.

45 Ramazzini, *De Morbis Artificum*, pp. 443, 97, 227, 231, 233, 237, 257.

46 Campbell, *London Tradesman*, p. 328.

47 Shesgreen, *Criers and Hawkers of London*, p. 114.

48 Cunnington and Lucas, *Occupational Costume*, p. 122; Ramazzini, *De Morbis Artificum*, p. 233.

49 Francis Spilsbury, *Free Observations on the scurvy, gout, diet and remedy*, 2nd edn (Rochester, 1783), p. 110.

50 Campbell, *London Tradesman*, pp. 104, 107–8, 164, 190; Ware, *Complete Body of Architecture*, p. 86.

51 Sheila O'Connell, 'London 1753 at the British Museum', *History Today*, 53:6 (June 2003), pp. 4–5.

52 *Manchester Magazine*, 1 Apr. 1746, cited in Horner, 'Proper persons to deal with', p. 65.

53 Jonas Hanway, *The State of the Master Chimney-Sweepers, and their journeymen* (London, 1779), p. 10.

54 Chesterfield, *Letters to his son*, II, p. 60.

55 Baker, *Plants and Civilization*, pp. 163–4.

56 Clark, *Life and Times of Anthony à Wood*, III, p. 156.

57 Evelyn, *Fumifugium*, p. 14.

58 Earwaker, *Constables' Accounts*, II, p. 7.

59 British Library, 551.a.32, 'Proposals for selling the Swimming Girdles', in 'Advertisements [a collection of 231 advertisements, etc., chiefly relating to quack medicines. The greater part English, the rest German.], 1675–1715, no pagination.

60 Exwood and Lehmann, *William Schellinks' Travels*, p. 106.

61 Pepys, *Diary*, IX, p. 233.

62 Ward, 'A step to Bath' (*c.* 1701), p. 157; Smollett, *Humphry Clinker*, I, p. 92.

63 *The Diseases of Bath*, pp. 14–15.

64 Thomas Shadwell, 'The humorists', in *The Dramatick Works of Thomas Shadwell, Esq* (4 vols, London, 1720), I, p. 138.

65 Isaac Watts, *Catechisms: or, instructions in the principles of the Christian Religion* (London, 1730), p. 184.

66 *The Spectator*, no. 631, 10 Dec. 1714 [Tickell].

67 David Hume, *A Treatise of human nature: being an attempt to introduce the experimental method of reasoning into moral subjects* (3 vols, London, 1739–40), III, p. 265.

68 Buchan, *Domestic Medicine*, pp. 124–5, 131.

69 Smith, *Complete Housewife*, p. 287.

70 Wecker, *Cosmeticks*, pp. 115–16.

71 Cavendish, *Worlds Olio*, pp. 84–7.

72 Piper, *The English Face*, p. 142.

73 Campbell, *London Tradesman*, p. 329; Chetham's Library, Halliwell-Phillips Collection, HP 1239.

74 Cavendish, *Worlds Olio*, pp. 84–7

75 Exwood and Lehmann, *William Schellinks' Travels*, p. 90.

76 Smollett, *Humphry Clinker*, I, p. 135.

77 Samuel Wesley, 'Snuff', in *Poems on Several Occasions*, 2nd edn (Cambridge, 1743), p. 124.

78 Edward Ward, *Battel without bloodshed: or, martial discipline buffon'd by the City-Train-Bands* (London, 1701), pp. 4, 12, 16; Ward, *Hudibras Redivivus* (1715), II, part III, canto III, p. 8; Ward, *London-Spy* (1709), I, p. 103; II, p. 16. See also McLaughlin, *Coprophilia*, p. 90. Unfortunately, of the several books recently published about English masculinity in the period, few historians have considered the smell of men.

79 Fuller, *Gnomologia*, p. 207.

80 Mayer Lewis, *An Essay on the Formation, Structure and Use of the Teeth* (London, 1772), p. 22.

81 Ryder, *Diary*, pp. 97, 117, 195, 205, 221, 244, 276, 295.

82 Cogan, *Haven of Health*, pp. 70–1, 81.

83 *Weekly Journal, or The British Gazetteer*, 6 Nov. 1725, from Rictor Norton, *Early*

Eighteenth-Century Newspaper Reports: A Sourcebook, 'Haemorrhoides, hernia, bad teeth and other ailments', at www.infopt.demon.co.uk/grub/hernia.htm (accessed 28 Dec. 2003).

84 *Wits Cabinet*, p. 30.

85 Cogan, *Haven of Health*, pp. 78, 189.

86 Tryon, *Treatise of Cleanliness*, p. 20. The Earl of Chesterfield advised his son to use a sponge with warm water to clean his teeth. Chesterfield, *Letters to his son*, II, p. 60.

87 *The Manchester Mercury and Harrop's General Advertiser*, 7–14 June 1757, p. 3; also 2 June 1767, p. 3; *OBSP*, 11–13 Apr. 1716, p. 6.

88 *Weekly Journal, or The British Gazetteer*, 6 Nov. 1725.

89 Blount, *Glossographia*, s.v. 'Dentiscalp' ('an instrument to scrape the teeth, a tooth picker').

90 Tryon, *Cleanliness in Meats*, pp. 17–18.

91 Paul Hentzner, *A Journey into England: By Paul Hentzner* (Twickenham, 1757), pp. 48–9, 88; see also Sidney Mintz, *Sweetness and Power: The Place of Sugar in Modern History* (New York and London, 1985), pp. 92–5; *The London Chaunticleres: A Witty Comedy Full of Various and Delightful Mirth* (Anon.) (London, 1659), p. 13.

92 Thomas Baker, *Tunbridge-Walks: Or, The Yeoman of Kent; a comedy* (London, 1703), p. 45.

93 Frederick Slare, *Experiments and observations . . . to which is annex'd Vindication of Sugars* (London, 1715), p. 5 (of *Vindication of Sugars*).

94 Ryder, *Diary*, pp. 119, 142.

95 Blackwell, '"Extraneous bodies"', pp. 21–68.

96 *OBSP*, 11–13 Apr. 1716, p. 6.

97 Fuller, *Gnomologia*, p. 1.

98 See Pelling, 'Appearance and reality', esp. pp. 89–95.

99 Pepys, *Diary*, III, pp. 91, 97.

100 For example, the tinker, and the 'old shoes for new brooms' trader; Cunnington and Cunnington, *English Costume*, p. 96.

101 Ward, *Field Spy* (1714), p. 26.

102 *Oxford Council Acts 1665–1701*, p. 63.

103 Chetham's Library, Mun. A.2.137, p. 12 (fol. 6v).

104 Hibbert Ware, *Life and Correspondence*, pp. 32–3.

105 Neale, *Bath 1680–1850*, p. 56.

106 Mitchell and Penrose, *Letters from Bath*, p. 181.

107 Phillips, *Generosi Ludentes* (appended to his *Mysteries of Love and Eloquence*), p. 13 (sig. V7).

108 Pepys, *Diary*, III, p. 96; Jonathan Swift, *The Lady's Dressing Room* (London, 1732), p. 5.

109 Chetham's Library, Mun A.2.137, p. 9 (fol. 5r).

110 Ibid., p. 5 (fol. 3r) and p. 25 (13r).

111 Ibid., p. 2 (fol. 1v).

112 Ibid., p. 20 (fol. 10v).

113 Harland, 'Diary of a Manchester wig-maker', p. 197.

114 Pointon, *Hanging the Head*, p. 121.

115 Pepys, *Diary*, VI, p. 210.

116 *Coma Berenices*, pp. 19, 22–3, 37.

117 Richard Richardson, *A declaration against wigs or periwigs* (n.p., 1682), pp. 3–4.

118 *An Extract of the Rev. Mr. John Wesley's Journal, from February 16, 1755, to June 16, 1758* (Bristol, 1761), p. 36.

119 John Mulliner, *A Testimony against Periwigs and Periwig-Making* (London, 1677), esp. pp. 3, 8; see William Gibson, '"Pious decorum": clerical wigs in the eighteenth century', *Anglican and Episcopal History*, 65:2 (1996), pp. 145–61 at pp. 148–154.

120 Henry Peacham, *The Truth of our Times: Revealed out of one Mans Experience, by way of Essay* (London, 1638), p. 74.

121 Campbell, *London Tradesman*, p. 203.
122 Chetham's Library, Mun A.2.137, p. 9 (fol. 5r) and p. 11 (6r).
123 Pepys, *Diary*, IV, pp. 130, 290, 358; see also IX, p. 322.
124 Pointon, *Hanging the Head*, pp. 107–40; Campbell, *London Tradesman*, p. 203.
125 Piper, *The English Face*, p. 143.
126 Pointon, *Hanging the Head*, p. 117.
127 Macray, *A Register of Magdalen College*, IV, p. 165.
128 Piper, *The English Face*, p. 125.
129 Ibid., p. 143.
130 David Lemmings, 'Dudley Ryder (1691–1756)', *ODNB*.
131 [John Clubbe], *A letter of free Advice to a young Clergyman* (Ipswich, 1765), p.15.
132 Cunnington and Cunnington, *English Costume*, p. 91.
133 Piper, *The English Face*, p. 143.
134 Ibid., p. 125.
135 Cunnington and Cunnington, *English Costume*, p. 255.
136 Pointon, *Hanging the Head*, p. 128; Piper, *The English Face*, p. 144.
137 Janet Arnold, *Perukes and Periwigs* (London, 1970), p. 7.
138 Chetham's Library, Halliwell-Phillips Collection, HP 1239.
139 Cunnington and Cunnington, *English Costume*, p. 96.
140 Ward, *Field Spy* (1714), p. 21.
141 Pointon, *Hanging the Head*, p. 121.
142 Fuller, *Gnomologia*, p. 127.
143 *The Spectator*, no. 129, 28 July 1711 [Addison].
144 Hargreaves-Mawdsley, *Woodforde at Oxford*, pp. 4, 10, 12.
145 Amhurst, *Terrae Filius*, II, p. 97.
146 Cunnington and Lucas, *Occupational Costume*, pp. 82–5, 102, 115–16, 123, 137–8, 289, 328.
147 Cunnington and Cunnington, *English Costume*, p. 99.
148 *Essays and Letters on Various Subjects*, p. 133.
149 Jones, *Man of Manners*, pp. 4–5.
150 Edward Hawkins (ed.), *Travels in Holland, the United Provinces, England, Scotland, and Ireland, 1634–1635, by Sir William Brereton, bart.*, Chetham's Society, o.s., 1 (Manchester, 1844), p. 186.
151 Clark, *Life and Times of Anthony à Wood*, II, p. 300.
152 Ryder, *Diary*, p. 55.
153 *OBSP*, 16–21 Sept. 1761, p. 360.
154 Haywood, *A Present for a Servant-Maid*, p. 22.
155 Defoe, *Every-Body's Business is No-Body's Business*, pp. 4–5, 15–16.
156 *OBSP*, 7–12 Sept. 1743, p. 258.
157 Ryder, *Diary*, p. 184.
158 *OBSP*, 22–27 Feb. 1749, p. 55.
159 *OBSP*, 1–2 June 1682, pp. 2–3.
160 *OBSP*, 6–9 July 1748, pp. 225–6; *OBSP*, 30 June–5 July 1714, p. 6.
161 *OBSP*, 17–20 Apr. 1765, p. 140–1.
162 Ward, *Nuptial Dialogues and Debates* (1723), pp. 34–5.
163 Defoe, *Every-Body's Business is No-Body's Business*, p. 5.
164 Thomas Nashe, *Lenten Stuffe* (London, 1599), sig. A4v, 'I had as lieve have . . . no cloathes, rather than wear linsey wolsey.'
165 Hardy, *Middlesex County Records 1689–1709* p. 218; *OBSP*, 14–17 Oct. 1696, p. 2.
166 *OBSP*, 2–5 July 1766, p. 233; *OBSP*, 15–18 Oct. 1740, p. 276. Margaret Spufford draws attention to the varieties of qualities concealed in the name of a fabric: some were fine and some were coarse, some were durable, some were delicate. Spufford, 'Fabric for seventeenth-century children', p. 51. An expert in trades explained that the linen draper's skill 'consists in a perfect Knowledge of the Linen Manufacture in

general, the Difference between the different Fabricks, and the Properties of the Linens of all different Countries'. Campbell, *London Tradesman*, p. 282.

167 Spufford, 'Fabric for seventeenth-century children'.
168 Stubbes, *Anatomie of Abuses*, sig. E1r.
169 Hardy, *Middlesex County Records 1689–1709*, p. 60.
170 Ibid., p. 300.
171 Peter Earle, *A City Full of People: Men and Women of London, 1650–1750* (London, 1994), p. 256.
172 Fuller, *Gnomologia*, p. 37.
173 Earwaker, *Court Leet Records of Manchester*, III, pp. 78, 88; VI, pp. 29, 31, 48, 112, 133, 157, 166, 196, 212, 248; VII, p. 19, see also pp. 64–5.
174 Mayhew, *London Labour and London Poor* (1861–2), cited in Woodward, '"Swords into ploughshares"', p. 177.
175 Elizabeth C. Sanderson, 'Nearly new: the second-hand clothing trade in eighteenth century Edinburgh', *Costume*, 31 (1997), pp. 38–48 at p. 38.
176 Hargreaves-Mawdsley, *Woodforde at Oxford*, p. 117.
177 See, for example, *OBSP*, 4–7 Apr. 1733, p. 116.
178 *OBSP*, 10–15 Dec. 1735, pp. 32–3.
179 Hargreaves-Mawdsley, *Woodforde at Oxford*, pp. 11, 24, 52, 124, 125.
180 Earwaker, *Constables' Accounts*, II, p. 10.
181 Miles Lambert, '"Cast-off wearing apparell": the consumption and distribution of second-hand clothing in northern England during the long eighteenth century', *Textile History*, 35:1 (2004), pp. 1–26 at p. 2.
182 *Bath Chronicle*, 29 Nov. 1764, cited in Fawcett, *Voices of Bath*, p. 30.
183 GL, MS 2649/1 (unfoliated), presentments 1737.
184 *OBSP*, 14–16 May 1719, p. 4; *OBSP*, 25–29 May 1732, p. 136.
185 Lemire, 'The theft of clothes'.
186 *OBSP*, 17–20 Jan. 1724, p. 5.
187 Pepys, *Diary*, IV, p. 28.
188 *OBSP*, 25–29 May 1732, pp. 130–3.
189 *OBSP*, 5–8 Oct. 1733, p. 11; *OBSP*, 5–10 July 1749, p. 113; *OBSP*, 8–10 Dec. 1756, p. 9; Lemire, 'The theft of clothes', pp. 262–3.
190 Ward, *The Insinuating Bawd* (1700), p. 12.
191 Brathwait[e], *Whimzies*, p. 134.
192 *The Tatler*, no. 68 (1709); *The Spectator*, no. 150, 22 Aug. 1711 [Budgell].
193 Fuller, *Gnomologia*, p. 150.
194 John Bancks, 'A description of London', in *Miscellaneous Works in Verse and Prose by Mr John Bancks*, 2nd edn (London, 1739), pp. 337–8 at p. 337.
195 Parkinson, *Journal of John Byrom, Volume I, Part II*, pp. 604–7; see also Lucas, *Kalm's Account*, p. 37.
196 Swift, 'Description of a city shower', in *Miscellanies*, p. 408.
197 William Sangster, *Umbrellas and their History* (London, 1871), pp. 21–2.
198 Cunnington and Cunnington, *English Costume*, p. 179; Brimblecombe, *The Big Smoke*, p. 64.
199 Evelyn, *Fumifugium*, 'To the reader', sig. A2r.
200 Earwaker, *Court Leet Records of Manchester*, VII, pp. 236, 239; some London properties still had these spouts in the 1760s – Corporation of London, *To the Commissioners of the Sewers*, p. 9.
201 Sheppard, *A sure guide for Justices of Peace*, p. 193.
202 Mitchell and Penrose, *Letters from Bath*, p. 83.
203 Fawcett, 'Chair transport in Bath', p. 123.
204 Mandeville, *Fable of the Bees* (1714), p. 219.
205 Pepys often grumbled about getting daubed or wet on the streets – for example, see Pepys, *Diary*, II, p. 189.

206 Hooke, *Diary*, p. 181.
207 Jones, *Man of Manners*, p. 44.
208 Hanway, *A letter to Mr. Spranger*, p. 38.
209 *The Gentleman's Magazine*, I. 8, Aug. 1731, p. 332. Kennels were street gutters. A 'kennel-dash' was a splash of drain water.
210 One woman slipped on a 'Peas-cod-Shell', fracturing her 'crupper-bone' (coccyx) on the marble pavement: Wilson, *Surgery, Skin and Syphilis*, p. 35.
211 Defoe, *A Tour Thro' Great Britain*, II, p. 275.
212 Holme, *Academy of Armory*, book III, p. 14.
213 Hooke, *Diary*, p. 156.
214 Cunnington and Cunnington, *English Costume*, p. 173.
215 Huddesford, *An address*, p. 10. Some of these sharp cobbles remain in Oxford and are avoided by pedestrians who skirt the Radcliffe Camera.
216 Ward, 'The Merry Travellers' (1729), p. 29 [pagination restarts with each piece in this volume].
217 *OBSP*, 28–30 June 1733, pp. 172–3.
218 *OBSP*, 24–27 Feb. 1725, p. 7.
219 John Ray, *A Collection of English Words, not generally used* (London, 1691), p. 95.
220 Swift, *Directions to Servants*, pp. 9–10, 53.
221 Tryon, *Tryon's Letters*, p. 29.

4. Mouldy

1 Stephen Mennell, *All Manners of Food: Eating and Taste in England and France from the Middle Ages to the Present* (Oxford, 1985), p. 3.
2 Richard Thomas and Martin Locock, 'Food for dogs? The consumption of horseflesh at Dudley Castle in the eighteenth century', *Environmental Archaeology: The Journal of Human Palaeoecology*, 5 (2000), p. 83; Brathwait[e], *Whimzies*, p. 120.
3 Cogan, *Haven of Health*, pp. 182, 185.
4 Ibid., pp. 29–33.
5 Fuller, *Gnomologia*, p. 247.
6 Ray, *Compleat Proverbs*, p. 123.
7 Fuller, *Gnomologia*, p. 21.
8 Ibid., p. 107.
9 Ibid.
10 Clark, *Life and Times of Anthony à Wood*, III, p. 437.
11 Tryon, *A Pocket-companion*, pp. 22–3.
12 Edward Ward, 'A dialogue between a botcher and his wife, after his return from the ale-house', in *The Fourth Volume of Writings* (London, 1709), p. 12.
13 *OBSP*, 17–23 Dec. 1766, pp. 4–8.
14 *OBSP*, 14–17 July 1756, p. 239.
15 Drummond and Wilbraham, *The Englishman's Food*, p. 187.
16 Campbell, *London Tradesman*, pp. 277–9.
17 Ryder, *Diary*, p. 33.
18 Parkinson, *The Private Journal John Byrom, Volume I, Part II*, p. 342.
19 E. P. Thompson, *The Making of the English Working Class* (London, 1963), p. 12.
20 Cogan, *Haven of Health*, p. 210.
21 Ibid., pp. 26–7, 98.
22 Hooke, *Diary*, esp. pp. xiv, 6, 92, 105, 172, 217, 226, 272, 330.
23 Tryon, *A Pocket-companion*, p. 7.
24 Hooke, *Diary*, p. 100.
25 Shesgreen, *Criers and Hawkers of London*, p. 158.
26 Fuller, *Gnomologia*, p. 112.

27 Evelyn, *Fumifugium*, pp. 7, 14.
28 Ray, *Compleat Proverbs*, p. 3; Herbert, *Outlandish Proverbs*, sig. A5v.
29 Lane, *Jane Austen and Food*, p. 13.
30 Thomas Tryon, *A New Art of Brewing Beer, Ale and other sorts of Liquors, so as to render them more healthful to the Body, and agreeable to Nature, and to keep them longer from souring, with less Trouble and Charge than generally practised, which will be a means to prevent those torturing Distempers of the Stone, Gravel, Gout and Dropsie* (London, 1690), pp. 132.
31 Drummond and Wilbraham, *The Englishman's Food*, p. 185.
32 Mace, *Profit*, p. 21.
33 Deering, *Nottinghamia*, p. 15.
34 Drummond and Wilbraham, *The Englishman's Food*, p. 186.
35 Overbury, *Overburie his Wife*, sigs K6r–K7r.
36 Langford, *Public Life*, p. 170.
37 Sheppard, *The Offices of Constables*, sigs H3v–H4r.
38 Jones, *The Company of Poulterers*, p. 99; Jones, *The Butchers of London*, pp. 132–6.
39 Earwaker, *Court Leet Records of Manchester*, II–VIII; there are yearly entries in each volume detailing the number and names of the officers. Dearth and escalating prices (and riots) in the 1750s saw an increase in the number of officers checking bread supplies.
40 Andrew Clark (ed.), *Register of the University of Oxford, Volume II (1571–1622), Part 1: Introductions*, Oxford Historical Society, 10 (Oxford, 1887), p. 255.
41 Earwaker, *Court Leet Records of Manchester*, VII, p. 70; see also pp. 78, 118.
42 Ibid., V, pp. 8–9.
43 *The Spectator*, no. 362, 25 Apr. 1712 [Steele].
44 For example, Earwaker, *Court Leet Records of Manchester*, VI, p. 219; see VII, p. 121 for a long list of butchers not cleaning stalls.
45 Ward, *Hudibras Redivivus* (1715), II, p. 19 [part II, canto II].
46 Jonas Hanway, *A Journal of Eight Days Journey from Portsmouth to Kingston upon Thames*, 2nd edn (2 vols, London, 1757), II, contents page.
47 Cox, *Spitalfields*, p. 56.
48 Earwaker, *Court Leet Records of Manchester*, VII, p. 241; VIII, p. 2.
49 *Court Leet Records* (Southampton), p. 392; see also Chandler, *Liverpool*, p. 193.
50 Chandler, *Liverpool*, p. 301.
51 Holme, *Academy of Armory*, III, ch. 3, sec. 3, p. 86.
52 Cogan, *Haven of Health*, p. 33.
53 Ellis, *The Country Housewife's Companion*, p. 22.
54 Sachse, *Minutes of the Norwich Court of Mayoralty*, p. 97.
55 Drummond and Wilbraham, *The Englishman's Food*, p. 188; Filby, *Food Adulteration*, pp. 80–4; Ronald Sheppard and Edward Newton, *The Story of Bread* (London, 1957), p. 73.
56 Drummond and Wilbraham, *The Englishman's Food*, p. 188; Filby, *Food Adulteration*, pp. 84–5.
57 Earwaker, *Constables' Accounts*, II, p. 359.
58 'Sampson Syllogism A Baker', *A Modest Apology in Defence of the Bakers* (London, 1757); Emanuel Collins, *Lying Detected; or, some of the most frightful untruths that ever alarmed the British Metropolis, fairly exposed* (Bristol, 1758).
59 Collins, *Lying Detected*, p. 5.
60 *An Essay on Bread* (1758), cited in Drummond and Wilbraham, *The Englishman's Food*, pp. 189–90; see also Filby, *Food Adulteration*, pp. 96–8.
61 Smollett, *Humphry Clinker*, II, p. 7.
62 Swift, *Journal to Stella*, I, p. 581.
63 Paston Williams, *The Art of Dining*, p. 212.
64 Emily Lorraine de Montluzin, *Daily Life in Georgian England as reported in the*

Gentleman's Magazine, Studies in British and American Magazines, 14 (Lampeter, 2002), p. 52.

65 *The Spectator*, no. 251, 18 Dec. 1711 [Addison].

66 Shesgreen, *Criers and Hawkers of London*, p. 192.

67 Evelyn, *Fumifugium*, p. 25; Evelyn, *Acetaria: A Discourse of Sallets*, 2nd edn (London, 1706), p. 17.

68 Cogan, *Haven of Health*, p. 100.

69 Ibid., p. 110.

70 Clark, *Life and Times of Anthony à Wood*, II, pp. 198, 253.

71 Smollett, *Humphry Clinker*, II, p. 9.

72 Shesgreen, *Criers and Hawkers of London*, p. 138.

73 Ibid., p. 84.

74 Smollett, *Humphry Clinker*, II, p. 10.

75 Ibid., p. 194.

76 Fuller, *Gnomologia*, p. 152.

77 *OBSP*, 27 Feb.–4 Mar. 1751, p. 119.

78 *OBSP*, 8–13 Dec. 1736, p. 8.

79 Lane, *Jane Austen and Food*, p. 12.

80 Smith, *The Complete Housewife*, p. 1; Haywood, *A Present for a Servant-Maid*, pp. 51–2.

81 Haywood, *A Present for a Servant-Maid*, p. 52; see also Worcester Quarter Sessions Rolls 1/1/109 1667–8 – butchers from Shipton upon Stour had 'blowed the said calves with human breath' – www.a2a.org.uk (accessed 28 May 2005).

82 Jones, *Butchers of London*, p. 140.

83 Ibid., p. 134.

84 Cogan, *Haven of Health*, p. 133.

85 *The Lady's Companion: or, an Infallible Guide to the Fair Sex*, 4th edn (London, 1743), p. 303.

86 Noshir H. Wadia and Gagandeep Singh, 'Taenia solium: a historical note', in Sudesh Prabhakar and Gagandeep Singh, *Taenia Solium Cysticercosos: From Basic to Clinical Science* (Chandigarh, 2002), pp. 157–68.

87 Stead, 'Necessities and luxuries', p. 74.

88 Evelyn, *Fumifugium*, pp. 12–13; see Stead, 'Necessities and luxuries', p. 74.

89 Haywood, *A Present for a Servant-Maid*, p. 53.

90 Cogan, *Haven of Health*, pp. 131–2.

91 Haywood, *A Present for a Servant-Maid*, p. 52.

92 Ibid., pp. 52–3.

93 Cook, *Professed Cookery*, p. 195.

94 Haywood, *A Present for a Servant-Maid*, p. 56. This was previously mentioned in an anonymous work, *The Whole Duty of a Woman: or, an infallible guide to the fair sex* (London, 1737), p. 638.

95 Ward, 'The Merry Travellers' (1729), p. 16.

96 Jones, *Butchers of London*, p. 138.

97 *The History and Antiquities of the City of York from its origin to the present times* (3 vols, York, 1785), II, p. 108.

98 Jones, *Butchers of London*, p. 135.

99 John Fitzherbert, *The Boke of Husbandry* (London, 1533), fol. 37v; Earwaker, *Court Leet Records of Manchester*, IV, p. 51n.

100 The surviving records for the eighteenth century start in 1731.

101 Earwaker, *Court Leet Records of Manchester*, IV, pp. 51, 68, 288; V, pp. 41, 161, 170; VI, p. 16.

102 Ibid., IV, p. 135; V, p. 11; VI, pp. 15, 49.

103 Ibid., V, p. 20.

104 Ibid., VII, pp. 86, 96, 185, 101.

105 Ibid., VII, pp. 17, 98, 248.
106 Ibid., IV, p. 16.
107 Ibid., V, p. 55.
108 Ibid., VII, p. 205.
109 Ibid., VIII, p. 96.
110 Ibid., VII, pp. 6, 37, 67, 101, 154, 162, 166, 215, 226, 248; VIII, pp. 6, 27, 97.
111 Ibid., VII, pp. 10, 86, 98, 127, 140, 154, 162; VIII, p. 103.
112 Ibid., VII, pp. 80, 140, 146, 173, 205, 226; VIII, pp. 6, 9.
113 Ibid., VII, pp. 19, 25, 34, 37, 63, 80, 90, 98, 120, 127, 131, 140, 148, 154, 162, 166, 188, 205, 226.
114 Ibid., VII, pp. 37, 146, 166, 188, 205, 215.
115 Ibid., VII, pp. 47, 68, 111, 117, 120, 121, 127, 140,148; VIII, pp. 6, 59, 110.
116 Ray, *Compleat Proverbs*, p. 107.
117 Fuller, *Gnomologia*, pp. 46, 153.
118 Brathwait[e], *Whimzies*, p. 12.
119 Haywood, *A Present for a Servant-Maid*, pp. 53–4.
120 Stead, 'Necessities and luxuries', p. 69.
121 Cogan, *Haven of Health*, pp. 161, 165, 168.
122 Pepys, *Diary*, III, p. 120.
123 Earwaker, *Court Leet Records of Manchester*, IV, pp. 31, 68, 243, 259; V, pp. 32, 55; VI, p. 210.
124 Ibid., V, p. 32; VI, pp. 210, 256; VII, pp. 140, 205, 219, 220, VIII, p. 49.
125 Ibid., VII, pp. 184, 205, 219, 244; VIII, p. 49.
126 Ibid., VII, p. 220; see also p. 10.
127 Ibid., VII, p. 7.
128 Fuller, *Gnomologia*, p. 37.
129 Stout, 'Three centuries of London cowkeeping', p. v; Sheppard, *The Offices of Constables*, sig. F3r; Drummond and Wilbraham, *The Englishman's Food*, p. 191.
130 Smollett, *Humphry Clinker*, II, pp. 10–11.
131 Fussell, *English Dairy Farmer*, p. 44; Edward Lisle, *Observations in Husbandry* (2 vols, London, 1757), II, p. 102.
132 Stout, 'Three centuries of London cowkeeping', p. ix; Drummond and Wilbraham, *The Englishman's Food*, p. 193.
133 Lane, *Jane Austen and Food*, p. 12.
134 Fussell, *English Dairy Farmer*, p. 306.
135 Paston Williams, *The Art of Dining*, p. 216; Fussell, *English Dairy Farmer*, p. 306.
136 Quarrell and Mare, *London in 1710*, p. 12.
137 Deborah Valenze, 'The art of women and the business of men: women's work and the dairy industry, *c.* 1740–1840', *Past & Present*, 130 (1991), pp. 142–69 at p. 149.
138 Fussell, *English Dairy Farmer*, p. 287.
139 Ibid., p. 284; Stow [updated by Strype], *Survey of London*, II (book V), p. 210.
140 Smith, *Complete Housewife*, pp. 3–4.
141 Thomas Tryon, *The Way to get wealth: or, A New and Easie Way to make Twenty-Three sorts of Wine* (London, *c.*1701), p. 107.
142 Haywood, *A Present for a Servant-Maid*, p. 57.
143 Cogan, *Haven of Health*, p. 183.
144 Fussell, *English Dairy Farmer*, pp. 224–5.
145 Haywood, *A Present for a Servant-Maid*, p. 57.
146 Phillips, *Mysteries of Love and Eloquence*, p. 182 (sig. N3v).
147 Glasse, *The Art of Cookery*, p. 161.
148 Campbell, *London Tradesman*, p. 281.
149 Fuller, *Gnomologia*, p. 153.
150 Stead, 'Necessities and luxuries', p. 96.
151 Smith, *Complete Housewife*, p. 4; also Haywood, *A Present for a Servant-Maid*, p. 57.

152 Glasse, *The Art of Cookery*, p. 117; see also p. 128; Stead, 'Necessities and luxuries', pp. 86–8.
153 Stead, 'Necessities and luxuries', p. 95.
154 Glasse, *The Art of Cookery*, p. 130.
155 Cook, *Professed Cookery*, p. 68.
156 Ellis, *Country Housewife's Companion*, p. 109; Cook, *Professed Cookery*, p. 63.
157 Stead, 'Necessities and luxuries', p. 68.
158 Fuller, *Gnomologia*, p. 65.
159 Stead, 'Necessities and luxuries', p. 95.
160 Glasse, *The Art of Cookery*, p. 12.
161 Pepys, *Diary*, I, p. 291.
162 Sara Pennell, '"Great quantities of gooseberry pye and baked clod of beef": victualling and eating out in early modern London', in Griffiths and Jenner, *Londinopolis*, pp. 228–49 at p. 230; Manchée, *The Westminster City Fathers*, p. 72.
163 Woodward, '"Swords into ploughshares"', p.183.
164 Nancy Cox, '"A Flesh pott, or a brasse pott, or a pott to boile in": changes in metal and fuel technology in the early modern period and the implications for cooking', in Moira Donald and Linda Hurcombe (eds), *Gender and Material Culture in Historical Perspective* (London, 2000), pp. 143–57 at p. 150.
165 Ward, *Nuptial Dialogues and Debates* (1710), I, pp. 168–70.
166 Stead, 'Necessities and luxuries', p. 82.
167 *Serious Reflections on the dangers attending the use of copper vessels* (Anon.) (London, 1755).
168 *OBSP*, 14–19 Jan. 1732, p. 41.
169 Edwina Erhman et al., *London Eats Out: 500 Years of Capital Dining* (London, 1999), p. 58.
170 *A True and perfect Relation of that execrable & horrid Fact, Committed in White-Lyon-Yard near Nortonfolgate, near the Spittle, by some malicious, diabolical-sperited persons, for the poysoning the whole neighbourhood dwelling there . . .* (London, 1674), p. 2.
171 Ward, *Nuptial Dialogues and Debates* (1710), I, p. 171.
172 Ray, *Compleat Proverbs*, p. 18.
173 Ward, *Nuptial Dialogues and Debates* (1710), I, p. 171.
174 Peter Brears, 'Pots for potting: English pottery and its role in food preservation in the post-mediaeval period', in C. Anne Wilson, *Waste Not Want Not: Food Preservation from Early Times to the Present Day*, Papers from the Fourth Leeds Symposium on Food History and Traditions, April 1989 (Edinburgh, 1991), pp. 32–65 at p. 37.
175 Ivan Day (ed.), *Eat, Drink and be Merry: The British at Table, 1600–2000* (London, 2000), p. 43.
176 Glasse, *The Art of Cookery*, p. 73.
177 *OBSP*, 9–10 Oct. 1689, p. 4.
178 Phillips, *Mysteries of Love and Eloquence*, p. 164 (sig. M2v).
179 Haywood, *A Present for a Servant-Maid*, p. 8.
180 Swift, *Directions to Servants*, pp. 32, 42, 45–6.
181 Pepys, *Diary*, IV, p. 108.
182 'Silver exhibits good anti-bacterial properties': D. P. Dowling, K. Donnelly, M. L. McConnell, R. Eloy and M. N. Arnuad, 'Deposition of anti-bacterial silver coatings on polymeric substrates', *Thin Solid Films*, 398–9 (2001), pp. 602–6, at p. 602. A discussion about how silver kills food-borne pathogens appeared on 'Footsore Britain', *Connect*, BBC Radio 4 (broadcast 9 July 2003), presented by Quentin Cooper, produced by Alison Ayres.
183 Haywood, *A Present for a Servant-Maid*, p. 57.
184 Smollett, *Humphry Clinker*, II, pp. 2–4.

5. Noisy

1 James Gibbs, *Book of Architecture, containing designs of buildings and ornaments*, 2nd edn (London, 1739), p. vi, plates XVI–XXI.

2 D. H. Allen (ed.), *Essex Quarter Sessions Order Book, 1652–1661*, Essex County Council Record Office Publications, 65 (Chelmsford, 1974), p. xvi; 'Essex Shire Hall and Gaol. Petitions on the state of the very old buildings and the suitability of the present situation', abstract on www.bopcris.ac.uk/bop1700/ref14681.html (accessed 7 Dec. 2004).

3 E. Bennett, *The Worshipful Company of Carmen of London* (London, 1982), p. 26.

4 *The Tatler*, no. 9, Apr. 1709 [Steele]; *The Spectator*, no. 376, 12 May 1712 [Steele]; Swift, *Miscellanies*, p. 405.

5 William King, *The Art of Cookery; in imitation of Horace's Art of Poetry* (London, 1708), pp. 100–1.

6 Shesgreen, *Criers and Hawkers of London*, pp. 36–8.

7 *The Spectator*, no. 251, 18 Dec. 1711 [Addison]; Grose, *The Olio*, pp. 210–11.

8 *The Spectator*, no. 251.

9 John Captain Stevens, *A new Spanish and English dictionary* (London, 1706), s.v. 'ruydo'.

10 Fuller, *Gnomologia*, p. 159.

11 Pepys, *Diary*, I, pp. 17–18.

12 GL, MS 3018/1, fol. 106r.

13 Ibid., fols 15v, 101v. For similar incidents see fols 61v, 90r, 244r, and LMA, MJ/SR/541, recognizance no. 22.

14 Herbert, *Jacula Prudentum*, p. 330, no. 286.

15 GL, MS 3018/1, fol. 27v.

16 Brown, *Amusements*, p. 20.

17 [Thomas Legg], *Low-Life; or one half of the world knows not how the Other Half Live . . . in the Twenty-four Hours, between Saturday-Night and Monday-Morning. In a true Description of a Sunday, as it is usually spent within the Bills of Mortality*, 3rd edn (London, 1764), pp. 3, 22, 95.

18 Hardy, *Middlesex County Records 1689–1709*, p. 346.

19 LMA, typed calendars of Middlesex Book and Orders of Court 1732–47 – Calendar for 1008–1016 ('Orders of the Court vol. V', MJ/SBB/1008–1016, book 1014, fol. 38r–38v).

20 *Oxford Council Acts 1626–1665*, p. 171.

21 LMA, MJ/SR/1252, recognizances 129–31, 135, 137–8, 140–4; see also CLRO, Misc. MSS –58/35.

22 *Court Leet Records* (Southampton), p. 414.

23 Ward, *Nuptial Dialogues and Debates* (1723), I, p. 259; see also Hardy, *Middlesex County Records 1689–1709*, p. 119, 'watchmen being often overtaken in drink'.

24 Smollett, *Humphry Clinker*, II, pp. 5–6.

25 Ward, *Nuptial Dialogues and Debates* (1723), I, p. 259.

26 Fuller, *Gnomologia*, p. 263.

27 Jonson, *Epicoene*, esp. sigs A4v, B3v, B4v, C4r, G2r–v, H2v–H3r.

28 According to Keith Wrightson, neighbourliness in the early modern period involved 'a degree of normative consensus as to the nature of proper behaviour between neighbours'. Wrightson, *English Society*, pp. 51–3.

29 Bacon, *The Essayes or Counsels*, sig. 2L1v.

30 Pepys, *Diary*, VI, p. 39.

31 Herbert, *Outlandish Proverbs*, sig. A6v.

32 Richardson, *Sir Charles Grandison*, VI, p. 119.

33 Herbert, *Outlandish Proverbs*, sig. D8r.

34 Power, 'The East London working community', p. 113.

35 LMA, MJ/SBR/1, fol. 420.

36 Hatcher and Cardwell Barker, *History of British Pewter*, p. 119.

37 Stow, *Survay of London*, p. 220 (some mispagination occurs at this point: two consecutive pages are numbered 220 – this is the second p. 220).

38 John Evelyn, *London Revived* (1666), cited by Wall, *Literary and Cultural Spaces*, p. 44.

39 Blount, *Blount's Essays*, p. 111.

40 Ramazzini, *De Morbis Artificum*, pp. 231–3; Fuller, *Gnomologia*, p. 146.

41 Sachse, *Minutes of the Norwich Court of Mayoralty*, p. 48; *A View of the Penal Laws Concerning Trade and Trafick, Alphabetically disposed under proper Heads* (London, 1697), p. 52.

42 Jonson, *Epicoene*, sig. B3r.

43 Ward, *The London-Spy* (1709), I, p. 3; Charles Coffey, *The Devil to Pay; or, the Wives Metamorphos'd. An opera* (London, 1731), p. 23.

44 Jonathan Swift, *The Works of Dr Jonathan Swift, Dean of St Patrick's, Dublin* (8 vols, Edinburgh, 1761), VI, pp. 297–8.

45 Campbell, *London Tradesman*, p. 264.

46 CLRO, Rep. 126, fols 473–4, 494. There are no references to Niblett's noise in the wardmote inquest minutes for Cornhill Ward, GL MS 4069/2. In 1724 Niblett was fined for having too many apprentices and he was elected as an assistant of the company at the same meeting. Four years later Niblett was given a week to pay a fine of three pounds for non-attendance at meetings. He was elected Master in 1732. GL, MS 12,071/5, fols 59, 92v.

47 Francis Bacon identified the discovery of whether hot or cold brass sounds loudest when struck with a hammer as a future line of enquiry in 'The history and first inquisition of sound and hearing', in Basil Montagu (ed.), *The Works of Francis Bacon, Lord Chancellor of England* (16 vols, London, 1825–36), XV, p. 233.

48 W. C. Roberts-Austen, *An Introduction to the Study of Metallurgy*, 5th edn (London, 1902), p. 18.

49 Ramazzini, *De Morbis Artificum*, p. 437.

50 Hatcher and Cardwell Barker estimate that in the seventeenth century there were about a dozen free coppersmiths in the Pewterers' Company (*History of British Pewter*, p. 272); nine master coppersmiths signed a petition of 14 Feb. 1615 – GL, MS 7090/4; C. Welch, *History of the Worshipful Company of Pewterers of the City of London* (2 vols, London, 1902), II, p. 117.

51 Henry Hamilton, *English Brass and Copper Industries to 1800*, 2nd edn (London, 1967), pp. 279, 290; Daniel Defoe, *A Plan of the English Commerce. Being a compleat prospect of the trade of this nation, as well the home trade as the foreign* (London, 1728), pp. 290–1.

52 Bruce R. Smith, *The Acoustic World of Early Modern England: Attending to the O-Factor* (Chicago and London, 1999), pp. 49–71.

53 See, for example, *An Essay upon Harmony* (London, 1729), p. 19; Holme, *Academy of Armory*, II, p. 388; Cotgrave, *Dictionarie*, s.v. 'noise'; John Kersey, *A New English Dictionary* (London, 1702), s.v. 'noise'; Bailey, *An Universal Etymological English Dictionary* (1721), s.v. 'noise'; Johnson, *Dictionary*, s.v. 'noise'; *The Tatler*, no. 1, 12 Apr. 1709 [Steele].

54 Holme, *Academy of Armory*, II, pp. 134, 388.

55 Johnson, *Dictionary*, s.v. 'noisy' and 'noisiness'; see also Bailey, *Dictionarium Britannicum*, s.v. 'noisy'.

56 I am adopting a tighter definition than Peter Bailey used for 'Breaking the sound barrier', p. 50. In the dictionaries, the word 'clamorous' reveals this meaning more obviously than the word 'noise'. See, for example, John Kersey, *Dictionarium Anglo-Britannicum: or, a general English Dictionary* (London, 1708), s.v. 'clamour'; Robert Cawdrey, *A Table Alphabeticall* (London, 1604), s.v. 'clamarus'.

57 Colvin and Newman, *Of Building*, pp. 10–11. See also Augustus Jessopp (ed.), *The Autobiography of Hon. Roger North* (London, 1887), pp. 40–1, 106–7.

58 Robert Hooke, 'A curious dissertation', transcr. in Penelope M. Gouk, 'The role of acoustics and music theory in the scientific work of Robert Hooke', *Annals of Science*, 37 (1980), pp. 573–605 at p. 605.

59 Dylan M. Jones and Anthony J. Chapman (eds), *Noise and Society* (Chichester, 1984), p. 3.

60 Bailey, 'Breaking the sound barrier', p. 50.

61 Magalotti, *Travels of Cosmo*, p. 245. See also Ralph Thoresby's reaction to celebrations which went on too long in 1702: Joseph Hunter (ed.), *The Diary of Ralph Thoresby FRS, Author of the Topography of Leeds (1677–1724)* (2 vols, London, 1830), I, p. 390.

62 Clavering, *Essay on Chimneys*, pp. 97–8.

63 Clark, *Life and Times of Anthony à Wood*, III, p. 81; see also p. 451.

64 Hargreaves-Mawdsley, *Woodforde at Oxford*, p. 96.

65 Wood, *Essay*, II, p. 417.

66 *Martin v. Nutkin et al.* (1724): see William Peere Williams, *Reports of Cases argued and determined in the High Court of Chancery* (3 vols, London, 1740–9), II, pp. 266–7.

67 J. H. Baker, *An Introduction to English Legal History*, 2nd edn (London, 1979), pp. 357–60.

68 *Gaunt v. Fynney* (1872), see R. A. Buckley, *The Law of Nuisance*, 2nd edn (London, 1996), p. 72.

69 *Jeffrey's Case* (*c*.1560), see Baker and Milsom, *Sources of English Legal History*, p. 592.

70 Helena M. Chew and William Kellaway, *The London Assize of Nuisance, 1301–1431*, Publications of the London Record Society, 10 (London, 1973), pp. 160–1. The Assize of Nuisance investigated a London armourer whose neighbours were disturbed by his hammering. The landlords of the armourer argued that men of any craft 'viz. goldsmiths, smiths, pewterers, goldbeaters, grocers, pelters, marshals and armourers' are all at liberty to trade anywhere in London and to adapt their premises to suit their purposes. They maintained that ancient custom stipulates that any man may lease property to craftsmen using great hammers, and that the neighbours have no right to complain because their messuage was built in a fashion which exaggerated any nuisance. The result of this case is unrecorded. Patricia Basing, *Trades and Crafts in Medieval Manuscripts* (London, 1990), p. 63.

71 CLRO, COL/SJ/27/465; J. S. Loengard, *London Viewers and their Certificates*, Publications of the London Record Society, 26 (London, 1989), p. xlii.

72 Corporation of London, *Lawes of the Market*, sig. A7r–v.

73 Ibid., sig. A6v.

74 Salter, *Oxford City Properties*, p. 240.

75 Salter, *Surveys and Tokens*, p. 119.

76 Ryder, *Diary*, p. 57 and n3.

77 *Oxford Council Acts 1626–1665*, pp. 81, 320.

78 Bold, 'The design of a house, 1724', p. 76.

79 J. A. Sharpe, 'Crime and delinquency in an Essex parish, 1600–1640', in J. S. Cockburn (ed.), *Crime in England, 1550–1800* (London, 1977), p. 102; Keith E. Wrightson, 'Alehouses, order and reformation', in Eileen Yeo and Stephen Yeo (eds), *Popular Culture and Class Conflict, 1590–1914* (Brighton, 1980); Wrightson, *English Society*, p. 167.

80 Dalton, *The Countrey Justice* (1618), p. 25.

81 Willis Bund, *Worcester Quarter Sessions Rolls*, pp. 567, 648, 657.

82 R. F. B. Hodgkinson (ed.), 'Extracts from the Act Books of the Archdeacons of Nottingham', *Transactions of the Thoroton Society*, 30 (1926), pp. 11–57, at p. 55.

83 *Rex v. Smith* (1725): see Strange, *Reports*, I, p. 704; Hawkins, *Pleas of the Crown*, I, p. 198.

84 *OBSP*, 12 Oct. 1743, pp. 288–9.

85 It is typical that there is no mention of noise in a work by a 'Gent. of the Temple'

entitled *Public nusance considered*. Other works, such as Monson's *A Briefe Declaration* display a similar lack of interest. The nuisances discussed in these works include light deprivation caused by overshadowing, dunghill creation, blocked and diverted watercourses and excess smoke. See also Blackstone, *Commentaries*, III, p. 122.

86 GL, MS 3018/1, fol. 106r; likewise, other citizens who complained in the same year to the Court of Aldermen about poultry stored in 'Storyes yard' at the east end of Christchurch detailed not only the noise of the fowl, but also the stench of their ordure and offal: Jones, *The Company of Poulterers*, pp. 83–4.

87 LMA, MJ/OC/V, fols 38r–v. See also LMA, MJ/OC/V, fols 85v–86r.

88 Jonson, *Epicoene*, B4r–v.

89 Porter, *The Great Fire of London*, pp. 22–45; Evelyn, *Diary*, III, p. 453.

90 See Wall, *Literary and Cultural Spaces*, pp. 5–6, 189.

91 C. F. Innocent, *The Development of English Building Construction* (Cambridge, 1916), p. 150.

92 Although this act was not the first to be concerned with wall thickness, it was the most far-reaching. C. C. Knowles and P. H. Pitt, *The History of Building Regulation in London, 1189–1972* (London, 1972), pp. 20–33.

93 Platt, *The Great Rebuildings*, pp. 151–2; Wood, *An Essay*, II, A2r–A3r.

94 Michael Reed, *Age of Exuberance 1550–1700* (London, 1986), pp. 339–40.

95 Matthew Johnson, *Housing Culture: Traditional Architecture in an English Landscape* (London, 1993), pp. 106, 128; Platt, *Great Rebuildings*, pp. 23, 151.

96 Walter Ison, *The Georgian Buildings of Bath from 1700 to 1830* (Bath, 1980), p. 100.

97 *OBSP*, 7–10 Apr. 1725, pp. 1–2; see also *OBSP*, 17–23 Dec. 1766, pp. 4–8; *OBSP*, 4–6 Apr. 1722, pp. 3–4.

98 *OBSP*, 14–19 Jan. 1732, pp. 34–41, esp. p. 35; *OBSP*, 6–11 Sept. 1738, pp. 138–40.

99 Colvin and Newman, *Of Building*, p. 69.

100 Seaton, *Conduct of Servants*, pp. 171, 177.

101 Colvin and Newman, *Of Building*, pp. 89–90.

102 Gunther, *Architecture of Sir Roger Pratt*, pp. 27, 63–4.

103 Bold, 'The design of a house, 1724', p. 79.

104 Mark Girouard, *Life in the English Country House* (Harmondsworth, 1980), p. 138.

105 Important research on privacy conducted by Tim Meldrum has forced historians to take more care when describing room use, and not rely solely on the architectural evidence. Meldrum, whose work focuses on privacy, argues that although an architect might have intended the space to be used in a particular way, future occupants were at liberty to utilise their space as they wished. Thus, more research needs to be carried out, using a variety of sources, before one can assert with authority how developments in room use might have reduced or enhanced noise movement through buildings. Meldrum, 'Domestic service'.

106 Breton, *Fantasticks*, sig. C4v.

107 Power, 'East London working community', p. 103.

108 Earle, *Micro-cosmographie* (1628), sig. I11r–K1r; Evelyn, *Diary*, III, p. 638.

109 John Houghton, *A Collection For Improvement of Husbandry and Trade*, IV, no. 95, 25 May 1694. My thanks to Natasha Glaisyer for this reference.

110 Pepys, *Diary*, I, p. 309; II, pp. 7, 106; V, p. 165: VIII, p. 169; IX, p. 310.

111 John Dryden, 'Of Dramatick Poesie, and Essay' (1668), in W. P. Ker (ed.), *Essays of John Dryden* (2 vols, Oxford, 1900), I, p. 84.

112 H. George Hahn, 'Country myth and the politics of the early Georgian novel', in Hahn (ed.), *The Country Myth: Motifs in the British Novel from Defoe to Smollett* (Frankfurt, 1990), pp. 16–17.

113 Brown, *Amusements*, p. 20.

114 John Gay, *Rural Sports: a Poem* (London, 1713), p. 1.

115 Smollett, *Humphry Clinker*, I, pp. 64–5.

116 E. Arber (ed.), *John Earle Micro-cosmographie (first edition 1628, plus Characters from the*

fifth edition 1629 and sixth edition 1633), facs edn, English Reprints (London, 1869), p. 88; Fuller, *Gnomologia*, p. 63.

117   Cockayne, 'Cacophony', p. 40.

118   John Grubb, *The British Heroes* (London, 1707), p. 6.

119   Athanasius Kircher, *Musurgia universalis* (1650), cited in Thomas L. Hankins and Robert J. Silverman, *Instruments and the Imagination* (Princeton, NJ and Chichester, 1995), p. 73.

120   Wood, *Essay*, II, p. 417; Christopher Anstey, *The New Bath Guide: or, memoirs of the B-r-d family*, 4th edn (London, 1767), p. 45.

121   Geoffrey Holmes, *Augustan England: Professions, State and Society 1680–1730* (London, 1982), pp. 3–18; Rosemary O'Day, *Professions in Early Modern England, 1450–1800: Servants of the Commonweal* (London, 2000). Anna Bryson notes that a key development of the early modern period was the growth of London as the centre of gentlemanly conduct: *From Courtesy to Civility: Changing Codes of Conduct in Early Modern England* (Oxford, 1998), p. 281.

122   Paul Griffiths, *Youth and Authority: Formative Experiences in England, 1560–1640* (Oxford, 1996), pp. 139–47.

123   Cockayne, 'Cacophony', pp. 35–47.

124   Shesgreen, *Criers and Hawkers of London*, pp. 128–9.

125   *The Spectator*, no. 251; Swift, *Journal to Stella*, I, p. 581.

126   *The Spectator*, no. 251.

127   For example, tinkers, knife-sharpeners, sow gelders, card match sellers, hobby horse sellers and small coals men.

128   Hugh De Quehen (ed.), *Samuel Butler: Prose Observations* (Oxford, 1979), p. 127.

129   LMA, MJ/SR/1663, indictment no. 19; also MJ/SBB/424, Sessions of the Peace Book, 1684–5, fol. 51r; Jeaffreson, *Middlesex County Records*, IV, pp. 283–4.

130   Sean Shesgreen raised this idea in *Criers and Hawkers*, p. 168.

131   Francis Bacon, *Sylva Sylvarum* (1627), in James Spedding, Robert Leslie Ellis and Douglas Denon (eds), *The Works of Francis Bacon* (14 vols, London, 1857–74), II, p. 561.

132   Fielding, *The Intriguing Chambermaid*, p. 28.

133   Jeaffreson, *Middlesex County Records*, IV, p. 285.

134   A. L. Beier, *Masterless Men: The Vagrancy Problem in England, 1560–1640* (London, 1985), pp. 90–1. Thomas Overbury remarked that 'if he scape Tiburne and Banbury, he dies a beggar', *Overburie His Wife*, sig. F8r; *A New Tale of an Old Tub: or, the Way to Fame. An odd sort of a story* (London, 1752), p. 14. See also E. B. [Edward Bysshe?], *A Trip to North Wales: being a description of that country and people* (London, 1701), p. 11.

135   *The Spectator*, no. 251, 18 Dec. 1711 [Addison].

136   See Westerfield, *Middlemen in English Business*, p. 316; Danby Pickering, *The Statutes at Large* (42 vols, Cambridge, 1762–99), X, p. 168, 'An act for licensing hawkers and pedlars' (1697).

137   R. B. Manning, *Village Revolts, Social Protest and Popular Disturbances in England, 1509–1640* (Oxford, 1988), p. 159.

138   Breton, *Fantasticks*, sig. C4v.

139   Burnaby, *The Reform'd Wife*, p. 26.

140   Margaret Cavendish, 'Loves adventures', in *Playes written by the Thrice Noble Illustrious and Excellent Princess The Lady Marchioness of Newcastle* (London, 1662), stage direction, p. 13.

141   Gomme and Norman, *Lincoln's Inn Fields*, p. 9; see also chapter 9, 'Gloomy', below.

142   Public Record Office, PRO 30/26/74/5 fol. 26r; 74/11 fol. 36r – Estates . . . at www.british-history.ac.uk/report.asp?compid=8404&strquery=noise (accessed 19 May 2005).

143   Fielding, *The Temple Beau*, p. 37.

144   *The Spectator*, no. 175, 20 Sept. 1711 [Budgell]. In Jonson's *Epicoene*, Clerimont

informs the audience that Morose has chosen to live in a narrow street which will not accommodate 'coaches nor carts nor any of these common noises', sig. B3r.

145 Mare and Quarrell, *Lichtenberg's Visits*, p. 42.
146 *The Burwell Lute Tutor. Facsimile edition with an introductory study by Robert Spencer* (Leeds, 1974), fol. 40v. My thanks to Stewart McCoy for this reference.
147 Chetham's Library, Mun. A.2.140, p. 2 (fol. 1v).
148 For a discussion of a later quest for quiet see John M. Picker, 'The soundproof study: Victorian professionals, work space, and urban noise', *Victorian Studies*, 42:3 (2000), pp. 427–53, esp pp. 434–5.
149 Schofield, *Surveys of Ralph Treswell*, p. 21.
150 Jenni Calder, *The Victorian Home* (London, 1977), p. 15.
151 Sean Shesgreen has written an evocative account of the aural aspects of this image, in *Images of the Outcast*, pp. 110–13.
152 Uglow, *Hogarth*, pp. 300–2.
153 L. Jenkins, 'Child's play', *Early Music Today*, 5 (1997), pp. 5–6 at p. 6.
154 Uglow, *Hogarth*, p. 300.
155 Henry Fielding, *The Journal of a Voyage to Lisbon, by the Late Henry Fielding, Esq.* (London, 1755), p. 49–50.
156 Paulson, *Hogarth*, II, p. 114.
157 Cynthia Wall argues that disasters such as conflagration disturb and dislocate patterns and structures of life: *Literary and Cultural Spaces*, pp. 5–6, 189.
158 Mandeville, *Fable of the Bees* (1714).

6. Grotty

1 Beresford, 'East End, West End', p. 32. Early brick houses still had wooden frames.
2 *A Description of England and Wales. Containing a Particular Account of each County* (10 vols, London, 1769–70), VIII, p. 125.
3 BCL, MS B914–238, p. 80.
4 Ray, *Compleat Proverbs*, p. 108.
5 George, *London Life*, p. 74.
6 Ayres, *Building the Georgian City*, p. 104; Guillery, *Small House*, p. 70.
7 Neve, *The City and Countrey Purchaser*, p. 42.
8 Pierre Jean Grosley, *A Tour to London; Or, New Observations on England, and its inhabitants*, trans. by Thomas Nugent (2 vols, London, 1772), I, p. 77.
9 *Court Leet Records* (Southampton), p. 589.
10 Tryon, *Tryon's Letters*, pp. 51–2.
11 Reddaway, *Rebuilding of London*, p. 285.
12 Guillery, *Small House*, p. 49: 'Legislation did not *ipso facto* alter behaviour, and London's house builders had for decades been accustomed to ignoring building regulations . . . There was much poor workmanship.'
13 Cited in Downes, *Hawksmoor*, pp. 241–2.
14 John Evelyn, preface to Roland Freart, *A Parallel of the Antient Architecture with the modern, in a collection of Ten Principal Authors who have written upon the Five Orders*, 2nd edn (London, 1707), p. 5, 'Back matter, to the reader'.
15 Neale, *Bath 1680–1850*, p. 135.
16 Joseph Moxon, *Mechanick Exercises: or, the doctrine of handy-works, applied to the Art of Bricklayers-works* (London, 1700), pp. 21–2.
17 John Woodforde, *Georgian Houses for All* (London, 1978), p. 44.
18 Cruickshank, *Georgian Town Houses*, p. 181.
19 Ibid., p. 2.
20 Guillery, *Small House*, p. 69.
21 Neve, *The City and Countrey Purchaser*, p. 71.

22 Ware, *A Complete Body of Architecture*, p. 291; see also Cruickshank, *Georgian Town Houses*, p. 3.
23 Crossley, 'City and university', p. 133.
24 Ware, *A Complete Body of Architecture*, p. 292.
25 Fuller, *Gnomologia*, p. 152.
26 Cruickshank, *Georgian Town Houses*, p. 36.
27 Ware, *A Complete Body of Architecture*, p. 110.
28 Guillery, *Small House*, p. 161.
29 Ibid., p. 65.
30 Ware, *A Complete Body of Architecture*, p. 111.
31 Pantin, 'Fisher Row', p. 125.
32 Davis and Bonsall, *Bath*, p. 39.
33 Ray, *Compleat Proverbs*, p. 15.
34 Meldrum, 'Domestic service', p. 37; Pantin, 'Fisher Row', p. 122.
35 Porter, 'The Oxford fire of 1644', pp. 291, 293, 296; Clark, *Life and Times of Anthony à Wood*, I, p. 111.
36 Porter, 'The Oxford fire of 1644', pp. 291–4.
37 Earwaker, *Court Leet Records of Manchester*, III, p. 7; see also p. 176.
38 Ibid., III, p. 8; for a Coventry example at the close of the seventeenth century see Fox, *Coventry Constables' Presentments*, p. 37.
39 GL, MS 3018/1, fols 99v–100r.
40 CLRO, Rep. 79, fol. 111r.
41 GL, MS 4069/2, fol. 205v; see also fol. 16v.
42 GL, MS 3018/1, fol. 224r.
43 *Court Leet Records* (Southampton), pp. 378, 400.
44 Earwaker, *Court Leet Records of Manchester*, II, pp. 307, 308.
45 Ibid., VI, pp. 64, 96.
46 Ibid., II, p. 288.
47 BRO, Council Minutes Book 1, p. 57 (22 Apr. 1633).
48 *Oxford Council Acts 1626–65*, p. 40; see also p. 128.
49 *Oxford Council Acts 1665–1701*, p. 74.
50 Porter, 'The Oxford fire regulations of 1671'.
51 *Orders agreed upon by the Heads of Houses for the Preventing and Quenching of fire* (Oxford, 1671).
52 Clark, *Life and Times of Anthony à Wood*, II, pp. 221–2.
53 Wood, *Essay* (1749), 1, p. 232.
54 Fawcett, *Voices of Bath*, p. 31.
55 Strange, *Reports*, II, p. 1167.
56 Bold, 'The design of a house, 1724', pp. 78, 80–1.
57 Herbert, *Outlandish Proverbs*, sig. B5v.
58 Fuller, *Gnomologia*, p. 136.
59 Salter, *Cartulary, volume III*, pp. 329–30.
60 Salmon, *Present State of the Universities*, pp. 29–30.
61 Ibid., p. 27; see also Kielmansegg, *Diary of a Journey*, p. 96.
62 Pantin, 'Domestic architecture in Oxford', p. 133.
63 Ray, *Compleat Proverbs*, p. 204.
64 BRO, Council Minutes Book 2, p. 332 (29 Dec. 1662).
65 *Oxford Council Acts 1583–1626*, p. 71.
66 *Oxford Council Acts 1626–1665*, p. 18.
67 Salter, *Oxford City Properties*, p. 169.
68 *Oxford Council Acts 1626–1665*, p. 213; see also p. 252.
69 For Southampton cases see *Court Leet Records* (Southampton), p. 465; see also p. 406. See also Sachse, 'Minutes of the Norwich Court of Mayoralty', p. 48.
70 Earwaker, *Court Leet Records of Manchester*, VI, p. 45; see also II, p. 175; VI, p. 44.

71 *Oxford Council Acts 1626–1665*, pp. 262–4.
72 Fuller, *Gnomologia*, p. 158; Holme, *Academy of Armory*, book II, p. 388.
73 *Oxford Council Acts 1626–1665*, p. 18.
74 Graunt, *London's Dreadful Visitation*, no pagination, 7–14 Feb. 1664.
75 Guillery, *Small House*, p. 31 and passim.
76 Samuel Johnson, *London: a Poem, In Imitation of the Third Satire of Juvenal*, 2nd edn (London, 1738), p. 4.
77 Nicholas Hawksmoor, 'Letter to George Clarke at All Souls College, 17 February 1715', cited in Downes, *Hawksmoor*, p. 242.
78 GL, MS 3018/1, fol. 224r.
79 Mare and Quarrell, *Lichtenberg's Visits*, p. 113.
80 Massie, *Essay*, pp. 12–13.
81 GL, MS 3018/1, fols 237r–238r, 228v–229v.
82 Hanway, *A Letter to Mr. Spranger*, p. 58.
83 GL, MS 2649/1 (unfoliated), presentations for 1768.
84 Massie, *Essay*, pp. 12–13.
85 Fuller, *Gnomologia*, p. 253.
86 Monson, *A Briefe Declaration*, p. 1.
87 Brimblecombe, *The Big Smoke*, pp. 23–4.
88 Ralph Treswell's surveys suggest that even the smallest London houses enjoyed heat in at least half the rooms. John Schofield notes that this was atypical of English cities: Schofield, *The Surveys of Ralph Treswell*, p. 17.
89 Salmon, *Present State of the Universities*, p. 32.
90 Wood, *Essay*, II, sig. A2r–v (Preface).
91 Cited in Neale, *Bath 1680–1850*, pp. 131–4.
92 Pepys, *Diary*, III, p. 32.
93 Clark, *Life and Times of Anthony à Wood*, III, p. 321.
94 Ryder, *Diary*, p. 328.
95 Magdalen College Archives, Liber Computi, 1622; Clark, *Life and Times of Anthony à Wood*, I, pp. 431–2.
96 Earwaker, *Court Leet Records of Manchester*, II, p. 267; see also p. 326.
97 *Court Leet Records* (Southampton), p. 416; see also Chandler, *Liverpool*, p. 306.
98 Blackstone, *Commentaries*, III, pp. 216–17; Dalton, *The Country Justice* (1742), p. 156; *Court Leet Records* (Southampton), p. 573.
99 See, for example, a case mediated by the London Company of Armourers and Braziers involving water falling from a shed and damaging the foundation of a house in Thames Street. As the company leased both the shed and the house it became involved in the discussions. GL, MS 12,071/6, fols 128v, 129v, 130r, 131v.
100 BRO, Council Minutes Book 3, p. 397 (1 Jan. 1705).
101 Pepys, *Diary*, I, p. 304.
102 Fox, *Coventry Constables' Presentments*, pp. 37–8; see also Earwaker, *Court Leet Records of Manchester*, II, pp. 276, 295; VII, p. 183.
103 *Court Leet Records* (Southampton), p. 580.
104 Ibid., p. 445; see also Earwaker, *Court Leet Records of Manchester*, VII, p. 65.
105 Earwaker, *Court Leet Records of Manchester*, III, p. 61.
106 GL, MS 3018/1, fol. 106r.
107 Earwaker, *Court Leet Records of Manchester*, VI, p. 115.
108 Salter, *Oxford City Properties*, p. 240.
109 John Taylor, *A New Discovery by Sea, with a wherry from London to Salisbury* (London, 1623), sig. A7v.
110 Chandler, *Liverpool*, p. 118; see also Earwaker, *Court Leet Records of Manchester*, III, p. 13.
111 Earwaker, *Court Leet Records of Manchester*, III, p. 130; see also pp. 21, 62, 80, 138.
112 Ibid., VII, pp. 184, 187–8.

113 GL, MS 3018/1, fol. 120v; see also fols 106r, 159v.

114 Earwaker, *Court Leet Records of Manchester*, III, p. 20.

115 Ibid., II, pp. 165, 169, 175.

116 *OBSP*, 24–26 Apr. 1734, pp. 108–9. See also *OBSP*, 12–15 Oct. 1726, pp. 3–4 and *OBSP*, 13–15 Apr. 1743, pp. 149–53.

117 See the privies located over the Fleet Ditch: Schofield, *Surveys of Ralph Treswell*, plate 10, between p. 22 and p. 23.

118 Ibid., pp. 23–4, 139.

119 Eveleigh, *Bogs, Baths and Basins*, p. 10.

120 Henry Brooke, *The Fool of Quality, or, the history of Henry Earl of Moreland. In four volumes* (5 vols, Dublin, 1765–70), IV, p. 308.

121 Eveleigh, *Bogs, Baths and Basins*, p. 8.

122 Ray, *Compleat Proverbs*, p. 172; James Howell, *Paroimigraphia Proverbs* (London, 1659), p. 24; see Ramazzini, *De Morbis Artificum*, pp. 95–7 for the working conditions of these labourers.

123 Tryon, *Tryon's Letters*, p. 118.

124 Earwaker, *Court Leet Records of Manchester*, II, pp. 197, 234; III, p. 100; VI, pp. 35, 165, 183.

125 Ibid., III, p. 87.

126 Ibid., II, pp. 234, 247, 252.

127 Ibid., VI, p. 232.

128 Ibid., II, p. 252.

129 Ibid., II, p. 287.

130 John Harington, *An Anatomie of the Metamorphosed Ajax* (London, 1596); see Jason Scott-Warren, *Sir John Harington and the Book as Gift* (Oxford, 2001), esp. pp. 57–9; Jonathan Kinghorn, 'A privvie in perfection: Sir John Harrington's Water Closet', *Bath History*, 1 (1986), pp. 173–88.

131 Neale, *Bath 1680–1850*, p. 135. Indeed, the whole joint venture between the Duke of Chandos and Wood was a little inauspicious. The development was cramped and poorly lit as well.

132 Wright, *Clean and Decent*, p. 94.

133 Cited in Brenner, 'Nuisance law', p. 406.

134 Pepys, *Diary*, I, pp. 269, 274.

135 Fuller, *Gnomologia*, p. 77.

136 Pepys, *Diary*, I, p. 269, see also p. 273.

137 See, for example, CLRO, COL/SJ/27/465, esp. fols 5v, 10r and 22v.

138 *Court Leet Records* (Southampton), pp. 507, 580; see also p. 593.

139 Crossley, 'City and university', p. 132; *Oxford Council Acts 1626–1665*, p. 332.

140 BRO, Council Minutes Book 4, p. 338 (30 Mar. 1724).

141 Monson, *A Briefe Declaration*, esp. pp. 2, 11–13, 21–4.

142 Burn, *Justice of the Peace*, II, p. 156.

143 Blackstone, *Commentaries*, III, p. 217.

144 *Reports of Cases adjudged in the Court of King's Bench; with some special cases in the Courts of Chancery, Common Pleas and Exchequer*, 6th edn (3 vols, London, 1795), II, pp. 459–60.

145 George, *London Life*, p. 77.

146 Henry Fielding, *Tom Jones. The History of a Founding* (London, 1749), p. 180.

147 Wood, *Essay*, I, p. 225.

148 Mare and Quarrell, *Lichtenberg's Visits*, p. 111.

149 Dillon, *Artificial Sunshine*, p. 42. For a sense of the level of darkness reached inside buildings at night see Melville, 'The use of domestic space', p. 83.

150 Tryon, *Tryon's Letters*, pp. 89–90.

151 Dillon, *Artificial Sunshine*, p. 45.

152 *Hell upon Earth*, p. 12.
153 Dillon, *Artificial Sunshine*, pp. 39–40; Hargreaves-Mawdsley, *Woodforde at Oxford*, p. 96.
154 Theodore de la Guarden, *Mercurius Anti-Mechanicus, Or the simple cobblers boy* (London, 1648), p. 43.
155 Hooke, *Diary*, p. 182.
156 Pepys, *Diary*; for references to Pepys's eyestrain see IV, p. 50; V, pp. 19, 108, 142, 285, 290; VII, pp. 168, 182, 406, 426; VIII – many references throughout the year. He writes 'slubberingly' in October 1662: III, p. 236.
157 Ramazzini, *De Morbis Artificum*, pp. 139, 403.
158 Pottle, *Boswell's London Journal*, p. 302.
159 Hargreaves-Mawdsley, *Woodforde at Oxford*, p. 67.
160 Campbell, *London Tradesman*, p. 193.
161 Chetham's Library, Halliwell-Phillips Collection, HP 2182.
162 Cited in Guillery, *Small House*, p. 60.
163 Schofield, *Surveys of Ralph Treswell*, pp. 97–8.
164 A goldsmith's furnace and forge caused problems to a shop in Fleet Street: 'the smoake and steame arising . . . doth . . . annoy the said Mrs Banner in her shoppe', CLRO, Rep. 78, fol. 306v.
165 Jacob, *Every man his own lawyer*, pp. 38–9.
166 GL, MS 2649/1 (unfoliated), presentments for 1699 and 1700; *Court Leet Records* (Southampton), p. 407; Jones, *The Company of Poulterers*, p. 84; Manchée, *Westminster City Fathers*, p. 76.
167 Jacob, *Every man his own lawyer*, p. 39; see also Blackstone, *Commentaries*, III, p. 217; the seminal case here is *Aldred v. Benton* (1610).
168 Earwaker, *Court Leet Records of Manchester*, III, p. 125.
169 Harris, *The Life of Lord Chancellor Hardwicke*, I, pp. 268–9. For more on this, see chapter 9, 'Gloomy', below.
170 Lena Cowen Orlin, 'Boundary disputes in early modern London', in Orlin, *Material London*, pp. 344–76 at p. 345.
171 Guillery, *Small House*, p. 52.
172 Ibid., pp. 50–2; Guillery and Herman, 'Deptford houses 1650–1800', p. 69.
173 George, *London Life*, p. 77.
174 Stow [updated by Strype], *A survey of London*, II, pp. 28, 31, 449; Dr Lettsom also argued that tenants in 'narrow courts and alleys' were more likely to fall victim to 'fevers of a putrid tendency': Lettsom, *Medical memoirs*, pp. 33–4.
175 Neve, *The City and Countrey Purchaser*, p. 71.
176 Porter, 'The Oxford fire of 1644', p. 289; a Dutch traveller dismissed Oxford's town houses in 1652 as being 'very small and dirty': Bachrach and Collmer, *The English Journal: Huygens*, p. 111.
177 *Oxford Council Acts 1583–1626*, p. lxi; Pantin, 'Fisher Row', p. 125.
178 Porter, 'The Oxford fire of 1644', p. 290.
179 Wood, *Essay*, II, pp. 331–3.
180 Meldrum, 'Domestic service', p. 36.
181 Walter George Bell, 'Wardmote inquest registers of St Dunstan's-in-the-West', *Transactions of the London and Middlesex Archaeological Society*, n.s., 3 (1914–17), pp. 56–70 at pp. 64–5.
182 Marnie Mason, 'Manchester in 1645: the effects and social consequences of plague', *Transactions of the Lancashire and Cheshire Antiquarian Society*, 94 (1998), pp. 1–30 at p. 24.
183 Henry Fielding, *An inquiry into the causes of the late increase of robbers, &c, with some proposals* (Dublin, 1751), pp. 70–1.
184 McLaughlin, *Coprophilia*, p. 114; *OBSP*, 12–15 Apr. 1738, pp. 77–8.
185 Meldrum, 'Domestic service', p. 34; Bold, 'The design of a house, 1724', p. 76.

186 Guillery, *Small House*, p. 31.

187 *Hell upon Earth*, p. 5.

188 Apart from the wide and shallow windows of weavers' garrets, common in some parts of the East End of London. Parapet walls conceal the garret windows in Bath's Circus Buildings (built by John Wood Sr and Jr, 1754–8).

189 Clavering, *An Essay on Chimneys*, p. 98; Samuel Johnson, *The Rambler* (6 vols, London, 1752), IV, p. 149.

190 Clavering, *An Essay on Chimneys*, p. 46.

191 Pantin, 'Domestic architecture in Oxford', pp. 143–5.

192 Pantin, 'Fisher Row', pp. 122–4; Salter, *Oxford City Properties*, p. 240.

193 See for example BRO, Council Minutes Book 2, p. 122 (1 Jan. 1655); Book 3, p. 273 (27 Mar. 1699), p. 547 (27 June 1710).

194 George, *London Life*, p. 89.

195 Ware, *Complete Body of Architecture*, p. 346.

196 Hanway, *A Letter to Mr. Spranger*, p. 23.

197 William Dunn Macray, *Notes from the Muniments of Magdalen College* (Oxford, 1882), pp. 82–6.

198 Ware, *Complete Body of Architecture*, p. 347.

199 Pepys, *Diary*, I, pp. 93, 93n.

200 McLaughlin, *Coprophilia*, p. 109.

201 James Kelly, *A complete collection of Scotish [sic] proverbs* (London, 1721), p. 44.

202 Herbert, *Outlandish Proverbs*, sig. B3v.

203 Clavering, *An Essay on Chimneys*, p. 1; Samuel Pepys and Woodforde were both blighted with smoky chimneys: Hargreaves-Mawdsley, *Woodforde at Oxford*, p. 114; Pepys, *Diary*, II, p. 22.

204 Clavering, *An Essay on Chimneys*, pp. 7, 14.

205 William Salmon, *Palladio Londinensis; or, the London art of building* (London, 1734), p. 126.

206 Clavering, *An Essay on Chimneys*, pp. 9, 45, 95–6.

207 Clark, *Life and Times of Anthony à Wood*, III, p. 219.

208 Earwaker, *Court Leet Records of Manchester*, VII, p. 186.

209 Clavering, *An Essay on Chimneys*, pp. 2, 95–7.

210 Ibid., p. 4.

211 Brimblecombe, *The Big Smoke*, pp. 30–5.

212 Evelyn, *Fumifugium*, p. 6.

213 Ibid., pp. 7, 12; see also Clavering, *An Essay on Chimneys*, p. 1.

214 Bachrach and Collmer, *The English Journal: Huygens*, pp. 41, 46.

215 Quarrell and Mare, *London in 1710*, pp. 74–5.

216 Fuller, *Gnomologia*, p. 206; Port, 'West End palaces', p. 30.

217 Gunther, *The Architecture of Sir Roger Pratt*, p. 63; see also pp. 27–8.

218 Guillery and Herman, 'Deptford houses 1650–1800', p. 75; Sara Pennell, '"Pots and pans history": the material culture of the kitchen in early modern England', *Journal of Design History*, 11:3 (1998), pp. 201–16, at p. 206.

219 *James I King of England his Counterblast to Tobacco* (London, 1672), p. 11; Holme, *Academy of Armory*, book III, p. 293: 'The Maukin is a foul and dirty Cloth hung at the end of a long Pole, which being wet, the Baker sweeps all the Ashes together therewith, which the Fire or Fuel in the heating of the Ovens hath scattered all about.' See also Cotgrave, *A Dictionarie*, s.v. 'Patrouille'.

220 Fuller, *Gnomologia*, p. 58.

221 Bold, 'The design of a house, 1724', p. 81.

222 Tryon, *Treatise of Cleanliness*, pp. 5–7, 14.

223 'The spider and the gout', in Aesop, *Truth in Fiction: or, morality in masquerade*, trans. Edmund Arwaker (London, 1708), pp. 188–91.

224 Haywood, *A Present for a Servant-Maid*, p. 7.

225 Clayton, *Friendly Advice to the Poor*, p. 32.
226 Pepys, *Diary*, I, p. 325; II, p. 19; III, p. 158.
227 Southall, *Treatise of Buggs*, p. 36.
228 *Harrop's Manchester Mercury and General Advertiser*, no. 230, 3–10 Aug. 1756, p. 3.
229 Ayres, *Building the Georgian City*, p. 187.
230 Cavendish, *The Worlds Olio*, p. 186.
231 Mead, *Pestilential Contagion*, pp. 40–1, 48.
232 Hawkins, *Pleas of the Crown*, I, p. 199.
233 Monson, *A Briefe Declaration*, p. 1.

7. Busy

1 Thomas Vincent, *God's Terrible voice in the City* (London [?], 1667), p. 36.
2 Pepys, *Diary*, VI, p. 186.
3 Evelyn, *Diary*, III, pp. 417–18.
4 Pepys, *Diary*, VI, p. 282.
5 *Hell upon Earth*, p. 6.
6 Edward Guilpin, *Skialetheia. Or, A shadowe of truth, in certaine epigrams and satyres* (London, 1598), sig. D5r.
7 Evelyn, *Diary*, IV, p. 382; Williams, *Thomas Platter's Travels*, p. 174.
8 Pottle, *Boswell's London Journal*, pp. 51, 96, 174.
9 John Dyer, 'The fleece' (1757), in *Poems by John Dyer, L.L.B. Viz. I Grongar Hill. II The Ruins of Rome. III The Fleece in four books* (London, 1770), pp. 139–40.
10 Bernard Mandeville noticed these developments in *Fable of the Bees* (1714), sig. A6v.
11 'Person of Abingdon', in *Trifles in rhyme, or the Berkshire Miscellany* (Oxford, 1761), p. 7.
12 Jones, *Man of Manners*, p. 3.
13 Brown, *Amusements*, p. 21.
14 Smollett, *Humphry Clinker*, 1, pp. 71–2.
15 *Hell upon Earth*, p. 10.
16 Corfield, 'Walking the city streets', p. 143.
17 Mandeville, *Fable of the Bees* (1714), sig. A6v.
18 Smollett, *Humphry Clinker*, I, pp. 186, 192–3.
19 *The Diseases of Bath*, p. 13.
20 Haywood, *A Present for a Servant-Maid*, p. 8.
21 Hardy, *Middlesex County Records 1689–1709*, p. 198.
22 Hawkins, *Pleas of the Crown*, I, p. 158.
23 See Cockayne, 'A cultural history of sound', pp. 157–88.
24 Chandler, *Liverpool*, p. 220.
25 Willis and Hoad, *Portsmouth Sessions Papers*, p. 154.
26 LMA, MJ/SR/2363, House of Correction List for 12 Apr. 1721.
27 LMA, MJ/SR/2376, House of Correction List for 4 Dec. 1721.
28 Galloway, *Norwich 1540–1642*, pp. 146–7.
29 Water Rye (ed.), 'Extracts from the Court Book of the City of Norwich 1666–1688', *Norfolk and Norwich Archaeological Society*, extra parts, 2 (Norwich, 1905), pp. 97–205 at p. 180.
30 Byrom [?], *A Serious Disswasive*, pp. 6–7.
31 Atherton, 'The "mob"'.
32 Henry Fielding, 'The Covent-Garden Journal', in *The Works of Henry Fielding, Esq; with the life of the author*, 2nd edn (8 vols, London, 1762), VIII, pp. 189–323 at p. 269.
33 Herbert, *Jacula Prudentum*, p. 68; see Cockayne, 'A cultural history of sound', pp. 189–226 for a broader discussion of the sounds of aggression and conflict.
34 Quarrell and Mare, *London in 1710*, pp. 146–7.
35 Fawcett, *Bath Administer'd*, preface; see also Wood, *Essay*, pp. 414–15.

36 See, for example, CLRO, Rep. 121, fol. 382r; see also LMA [typed calendar, early 20th century, 'Books and Orders of Court numbers 850–877'] Apr. 1727–Dec. 1729, Westminster Order of Court, I, fols 123r–v; vol II, fols 63r–v.

37 CLRO, Rep. 142, fol. 570r. There was a long battle against squib throwing, see also Rep. 79, fol. 421r.

38 Dalton, *The Countrey Justice* (1742), p. 157; see also *OBSP*, 8–11 Dec. 1697, p. 2.

39 Clayton, *Friendly Advice to the Poor*, pp. 3, 7, 13.

40 Nicholas Breton, *Wits Private Wealth stored with choise Commodities to content the Minde* (London, 1607), sig. C4v; see also B3r. See also J[ohn] D[avies] and C[hristopher] M[arlowe], *Epigrammes and Elegies* (1599), sig. C4v.

41 *OBSP*, 28 Feb.–7 Mar. 1750, pp. 47–8.

42 GL, MS 4069/2, fol. 487.

43 'A parishioner', *An address to the ministers, churchwardens, and parishioners of Newcastle upon Tyne* (Newcastle, 1755), p. 12.

44 Gay, *Trivia*, p. 54.

45 Mead, *Pestilential Contagion*, p. 51.

46 See chapter 8, 'Dirty', below.

47 C[harles] W[alcot], *Considerations for the more speedy and effectual Execution of the Act, for Paving, Cleansing and Lighting the city and Liberty of Westminster, and for Removing Annoyances therein* (London, 1763), pp. 6–7.

48 Gay, *Trivia*, p. 54.

49 Earwaker, *Court Leet Records of Manchester*, VI, pp. 66–7.

50 *Court Leet Records* (Southampton), p. 601.

51 GL, MS 3018/1, fol. 224r.

52 BRO, Quarter Sessions Book 1743–1776, (unfoliated), 9 Sept. 1751.

53 Ibid., 2 Apr. 1756, 1 July 1756.

54 In 1709 the Burgess Court of Westminster received complaints about a water company breaking the pavements and not repairing the damage – cellars flooded and the citizens were faced with the task of undertaking the repairs themselves. Manchée, *Westminster City Fathers*, p. 135; see also 'Gentleman of the Temple', *Public nusance considered*, p. 3.

55 *Court Leet Records* (Southampton), pp. 374, 501. The nursery rhyme about Dr Foster reads 'Doctor Foster went to Gloucester/ In a shower of rain./ He stepped into a puddle/ Right up to his middle/ And never went there again.'

56 Earwaker, *Court Leet Records of Manchester*, VII, p. 184; see also II, p. 323; III, p. 34; Chandler, *Liverpool under Charles I*, pp. 122, 243–4.

57 Chinnery, *Borough of Leicester 1689–1835*, p. 35.

58 *Court Leet Records* (Southampton), pp. 407, 428, 505.

59 *Oxford Council Acts 1626–65*, pp. 220, 227; see also *Oxford Council Acts 1665–1701*, pp. 49, 139: pales, stones and other obstructions were removed from Bocardo Lane in 1671, and stones positioned against doors along Magpie Lane were removed in 1681.

60 BRO, Council Minutes Book 2, p. 218 (24 Aug. 1659); Book 7, p. 223 (3 Oct. 1757); Book 8, p. 36 (28 Dec. 1761); see also Earwaker, *Court Leet Records of Manchester*, VI, p. 224.

61 Earwaker, *Court Leet Records of Manchester*, II, p. 231.

62 Ibid., VIII, p. 58; see also BRO, Quarter Sessions Book 1743–1776 (unfoliated), presentments for 2 Apr. 1756 – Mr Reed of Bath's Parade was presented for not putting a sufficiently high rail on his kitchen steps.

63 Earwaker, *Court Leet Records of Manchester*, II, p. 157.

64 BRO, Quarter Sessions Book 1743–1776 (unfoliated), presentments for 9 Sept. 1751, 6–19 Nov. 1753.

65 *Court Leet Records* (Southampton), p. 388; see also pp. 390, 488, 430, Earwaker, *Court Leet Records of Manchester*, VI, pp. 9, 43, 190, 229; see also II, pp. 175, 305; VI, 149; see also 206; GL. MS 12,071/6, fol. 121r (1744).

66 GL, MS 68, fol. 79v.
67 Fawcett, 'Chair transport in Bath', p. 123.
68 Oldham, *The Mansfield Manuscripts*, II, pp. 901–2.
69 Wood, *Essay*, II, p. 326.
70 Mitchell and Penrose, *Letters from Bath*, p. 187.
71 Hanway, *A Letter to Mr. Spranger*, pp. 10–11.
72 Gay, *Trivia*, p. 54.
73 When he was travelling through the Newgate Shambles in 1662 Samuel Pepys became embroiled in a fracas with some butchers after his coach accidentally 'plucked down two pieces of beef into the Dirt': Pepys, *Diary*, III, p. 283.
74 Gay, *Trivia*, p. 55.
75 Jenner, 'The great dog massacre'.
76 Ibid., p. 49.
77 Peter Shaw, *A Treatise of Incurable Diseases* (London, 1723), pp. 27–8.
78 Glasse, *The Art of Cookery*, p. 166.
79 Massie, *Essay*, pp. 15–16.
80 Charles Warren, 'Dogs in London', *Contemporary Review*, 51 (Jan. 1887), pp. 104–11 at p. 107.
81 Jenner, 'The great dog massacre', p. 55.
82 Cunnington and Cunnington, *English Costume*, p. 100.
83 Pepys, *Diary*, IV, p. 131.
84 Ward, 'The Merry Travellers' (1729), pp. 20–3 [pagination restarts with each piece in this volume].
85 BCL, MS B914–238, p. 55.
86 John Whitaker, *The History of Manchester. In four books*, 2nd edn (2 vols, London, 1773), II, p. 66.
87 Power, *Liverpool Town Books*, p. 231.
88 Earwaker, *Court Leet Records of Manchester*, III, p. 4.
89 Ibid., VII, p. 4; VIII, p. 4.
90 Harland, 'Diary of a Manchester wig-maker', p. 201. Unfortunately the court leet records for this period are missing.
91 Earwaker, *Court Leet Records of Manchester*, VI, pp. 35, 206.
92 Ibid., VI, p. 103.
93 Ibid., VI, p. 178.
94 Ibid., VII, p. 20.
95 Jenner, 'The great dog massacre', p. 52.
96 Ward, 'The Merry Travellers' (1729), p. 20.
97 Earwaker, *Court Leet Records of Manchester*, III, p. 260.
98 Pepys, *Diary*, III, p. 205.
99 *OBSP*, 3–5 Sept. 1684, p. 3.
100 Earwaker, *Court Leet Records of Manchester*, VII, p. 166.
101 Massie, *Essay*, p. 15; see also Evelyn, *Fumifugium*, p. 21.
102 Defoe, *A Tour thro' the Whole Island of Great Britain*, 4th edn (4 vols, London, 1748), III, pp. 246–7. See also appendix to Richard Procter Wright, *Memorials of Bygone Manchester* (1880), 'A description of the town of Manchester and Salford', p. 355.
103 Thomas Dekker, *The Seven deadlie Sinnes of London: Drawne in seven severall Coaches, Through the seven severall Gates of the Citie. Bringing the plague with them* (London, 1606), pp. 25–6.
104 Peter Razzell (ed.), *The Journals of Two Travellers in Elizabethan and Early Stuart England. Thomas Platter and Horatio Busino* (London, 1995), p. 155.
105 CRLO, Rep. 78, fol. 3r.
106 GL, MS 4069/1–3, various. The rules determining the numbers and use of hackney coaches are included in *A View of the Penal Laws Concerning Trade and Trafick* (Anon.), (London, 1697), pp. 46–8.

107 GL, MS 4069/2, fols 3v, 7r, 11r and passim.
108 *OBSP*, 6–8 June 1717, p. 4.
109 Graunt, *London's Dreadful Visitation*, no pagination, bills for 10–17 Jan., 14–24 Jan., 14–21 Mar., 16–23 May, 23–30 May and 4–11 July.
110 Stow [updated by Strype], *A Survey of London*, I, p. 242.
111 At www.bopcris.ac.uk/bop1700/ref14341.html (accessed 7 Dec. 2004); *OBSP*, 6–9 Sept. 1710, pp. 1–2; GL MS 4069/2, fol. 209r (1709).
112 GL, MS 4069/2, fol. 88r, see also fols 205r, 389r; see Jenner, 'Circulation and disorder', p. 44.
113 BCL, MS B914–238, p. 122.
114 Jones, *Man of Manners*, pp. 43–4.
115 Clark, *Life and Times of Anthony à Wood*, I, p. 46.
116 *OBSP*, 9–12 Sept. 1691, p. 2.
117 *OBSP*, 8–13 July 1696, p. 2.
118 *OBSP*, 12–15 Oct. 1715, p. 2.
119 *OBSP*, 30 Aug.–1 Sept. 1727, p. 5.
120 *OBSP*, 19–21 Apr. 1721, p. 8.
121 *OBSP*, 2–10 Mar. 1709, p. 3.
122 *OBSP*, 25–29 May 1732, p. 138.
123 Earwaker, *Constables' Accounts*, II, pp. 7, 16, 108, 140.
124 *OBSP*, 12–15 Oct. 1692, pp. 1–2.
125 *OBSP*, 4–7 Oct. 1719, p. 2.
126 *OBSP*, 12–17 Jan. 1722, p. 5.
127 *OBSP*, 28 Feb.–5 Mar. 1727, p. 5.
128 *OBSP*, 11–14 Sept. 1745, p. 215; *OBSP*, 1–10 Sept. 1686, p. 4.
129 Hardy, *Middlesex County Records 1689–1709*, p. 64; see also p. 85.
130 *OBSP*, 11–13 Oct. 1732, p. 244; *OBSP*, 22–25 Feb. 1737, p. 59; *OBSP*, 11–14 Oct. 1721, p. 6; *OBSP*, 27–28 Feb. 1684, p. 2.
131 *OBSP*, 27–28 Feb. 1684, p. 2.
132 *OBSP*, 11–14 Oct. 1721, p. 6.
133 *OBSP*, 24–29 Oct. 1770, pp. 386–7.
134 *OBSP*, 6–8 June 1717, p. 5.
135 *OBSP*, 11–18 July 1770, pp. 310–11.
136 Ayres, *Building the Georgian City*, p. 95; Fawcett, *Voices of Bath*, p. 168; Hanway, *A Letter to Mr. Spranger*, p. 20. Hanway worried that if raised kerbs were introduced on roads too narrow for them, the pedestrians would be liable to slip off into the path of oncoming traffic.
137 Oldham, *The Mansfield Manuscripts*, II, p. 901.
138 Hanway, *A Letter to Mr. Spranger*, p. 21.
139 *OBSP*, 16–19 Jan. 1693, p. 3.
140 BRO, Quarter Sessions Book 1743–1776 (unfoliated), presentments for 19 Nov. 1753.
141 Hanway, *A Letter to Mr. Spranger*, p. 14.
142 Laugero, 'Infrastructures of enlightenment', p. 49.
143 Ward, 'The Merry Travellers' (1729), p. 11.
144 Reddaway, *Rebuilding of London*, p. 221.
145 *OBSP*, 18–20 Apr. 1694, p. 3; *OBSP*, 3–5 Sept. 1719, p. 5.
146 Clark, *Life and Times of Anthony à Wood*, II, p. 298.
147 *OBSP*, 13–15 Oct. 1731, p. 12.
148 Stow [updated by Strype], *Survey of London*, I, p. 230 (ch. XXVIII).
149 Evelyn, *Fumifugium*, 'To the reader', sigs a1v–a2r.
150 See chapter 9, 'Gloomy', below.
151 *Oxford Council Acts 1626–65*, pp. 51–2. The workmen employed by the council to pull the foundations down were indemnified against any legal repercussions.

152 Fawcett, *Bath Administer'd*, pp. 54, 129.

153 Samuel Derrick, *Letters written from Leverpoole, Chester, Corke, the lake of Killarney, Dublin, Tunbridge-Wells, and Bath* (2 vols, Dublin, 1767), II, p. 65; Borsay, *English Urban Renaissance*, pp. 62–3. The narrowness of the streets fuelled the fashion for sedan chairs in Bath. Fawcett, 'Chair transport in Bath'.

154 Fawcett, *Bath Administer'd*, p. 129; McIntyre, 'Bath, the rise of a resort town', pp. 228–34.

155 Christopher Woodward, '"O Lord! Bath is undone, 'tis undone; 'tis undone!" Bath and the pre-history of architectural conservation', *Bath History*, 7 (1998), pp. 7–26 at p. 12.

156 Earwaker, *Court Leet Records of Manchester*, VII, p. 163.

157 Massie, *Essay*, p. 21.

158 Reddaway, *Rebuilding of London*, p. 79.

159 Earwaker, *Court Leet Records of Manchester*, III, p. 150.

160 *Oxford Council Acts 1583–1626*, p. 253 – the City granted permission for the university to lay pipes.

161 *VCH Oxon*, IV, p. 87.

162 Cole, 'Carfax conduit', pp. 144, 147, 150; Clark, *Wood's City of Oxford: City and Suburbs*, p. 63.

163 Salter, *Oxford City Properties*, pp. 355–6; Cole, 'Carfax conduit', p. 149.

164 Wood, *Essay*, II, pp. 272–4.

165 London, *To the Commissioners of the Sewers*, p. 8; see also p. 10.

166 Chetham's Library Archives, Halliwell-Philips Collection, HP 2122.

167 *Oxford Council Acts 1626–1665*, p. 10; *Oxford Council Acts 1583–1626*, p. 258.

168 BRO, Quarter Sessions Book 1743–1776 (unfoliated), 4 Nov. 1754.

169 Fawcett, *Bath Administer'd*, p. 129.

170 *Oxford Council Acts 1626–1665*, pp. 215, 219, 221; Salmon, *Present State of the Universities*, p. 28.

171 Earwaker, *Court Leet Records of Manchester*, IV, pp. 272–3; VI, pp. 8, 11–12; VII, pp. 122, 228.

172 Redford, *Manchester Local Government*, I, pp. 137–8; Earwaker, *Court Leet Records of Manchester*, VI, pp. 8, 11–12.

173 Westerfield, *Middlemen in English Business*, p. 194; Robey, '"All asmear with filth"', p. 1.

174 28 Geo II ch 28, *The Statutes at Large, From the Twenty-fourth Year of King George the Second To the Thirtieth Year of King George the Second, inclusive* (6 vols, London, 1758), VI, p. 269.

175 Earwaker, *Court Leet Records of Manchester*, VII, p. 172.

176 BRO, Council Minutes Book 5, p. 287; Book 8, pp. 18, 246; see also Book 9, p. 19.

177 T. N. Brushfield, 'Britain's Burse, or the New Exchange', *Journal of the British Archaeological Association*, n.s., 9 (1903), pp. 90–4 at p. 93.

178 Charles Gildon, *The Post-boy rob'd of his Mail, or, The pacquet broke open consisting of five hundred letters to persons of several qualities and conditions, with observations upon each letter* (London, 1692), book I, letter II, p. 23. In 1708 three men kept stalls under the front of the Royal Exchange, selling papers and pamphlets, annoying the shopkeepers and merchants at the Exchange: GL, MS 4069/2 fol. 460v; see also fol. 474v.

179 GL, MS 4069/2, fol. 88v (1680).

180 *Hell upon Earth*, p. 11.

181 The main southern entrance to Nottingham pinched traffic to a single file: Deering, *Nottinghamia*, pp. 4, 16.

182 Wood, *Essay*, II, p. 322.

183 *Oxford Council Acts 1626–1665*, pp. 53–5; *Oxford Council Acts 1583–1626*, p. 223; Salter, *Oxford City Properties*, p. 335.

184 Salter, *Cartulary, Volume 1*, illustration on pull-out map no. 1 at the end of the book.

185 Skelton, *Oxonia Antiqua Restaurata*, p. 76.

186 Turnpike trusts were semi-autonomous administrative bodies established by local initiatives with the backing of local Acts of Parliament. Each unit collected tolls and used funds to improve and maintain the surface. They were often a local inconvenience but the turnpikes did improve the general road conditions. Laugero, 'Infrastructures of enlightenment', pp. 45, 48.

187 *Oxford Council Acts 1626–1665*, p. 84; *Oxford Council Acts 1665–1701*, p. 49.

188 BRO, Council Minutes Book 7, pp. 101–12 (17 and 24 June 1754); John Wood had called for this action in the 1740s, remarking that it was necessary 'in order to render the streets and avenues in and to this city more extreme and commodious': *Essay*, II, p. 340.

189 Chinnery, *Borough of Leicester 1689–1835*, pp. 116–17.

190 GL, MS 2649/1 (unfoliated), presentments 1711.

191 Hackney Petty Sessions Book 1734 (nos 695–1778), *British History Online*, 709, 713, at www.british-history.ac.uk/report.asp?compid=38828 (accessed 19 May 2005).

192 Earwaker, *Court Leet Records of Manchester*, VI, p. 251; VIII, p. 80; VI, p. 249; VII, pp. 7, 26, 103, 131, 236; Power, *Liverpool Town Books*, p. 184.

193 Earwaker, *Court Leet Records of Manchester*, VI, p. 190; VII, p. 45.

194 BRO, Quarter Sessions Book 1743–1776 (unfoliated), presentments for 8 May 1753.

195 See Jenner, 'Circulation and disorder'. Unlike in London, few of the wheeled vehicles in Manchester were owned or used by the merchants, who preferred sedan chairs: 'About 1720 there were not above three or four carriages kept in the town.' The first hackney coach stand was not established until 1750: Aikin, *Description of Manchester*, pp. 187, 191.

196 See César de Saussure's experiences: Muyden, *A Foreign View of England*, p. 166.

197 Pepys, *Diary*, III, p. 301.

198 Kielmansegg, *Diary of a Journey*, p. 255.

199 Pottle, *Boswell's London Journal*, p. 91.

200 Phillips, *Mysteries of Love and Eloquence*, p. 2.

201 Massie, *Essay*, p. 43.

202 Corporation of London, Lord Mayor, *By the Mayor, to the Alderman of the Ward of [blank]* (London, 1684).

203 John Evelyn, *A Character of England as it was lately presented in a letter to a noble man of France* (London, 1659), p. 8.

204 *OBSP*, 7–12 Sept. 1743, pp. 247–8; *OBSP*, 11–13 Oct. 1732, p. 244.

205 *OBSP*, 31 Aug.–2 Sept. 1692, p. 2.

206 Mace, *Profit*, pp. 1–5.

207 Kielmansegg, *Diary of a Journey*, p. 256.

208 'Gentleman of the Temple', *Public nusance considered*, pp. 1–2.

8. Dirty

1 Chetham's Library, Halliwell-Phillips Collection, HP 2106; James Granger, 'Old streets of Nottingham', *Transactions of the Thoroton Society of Nottinghamshire*, 11 (1907), pp. 67–87 at p. 69; Ayres, *Building the Georgian City*, pp. 97, 100; Corporation of London, *To the Commissioners of the Sewers*, p. 13.

2 Evelyn, *Diary*, II, pp. 94, 135.

3 2 George III, ch. 21: for details see Great Britain, *Statutes at Large* (1768–70), VIII, p. 639.

4 L. W. G. Malcolm, 'Early history of the paving of London', *The Newcomen Society*, 14 (1935), pp. 83–94 at p. 89.

5 Hanway, *A Letter to Mr. Spranger*, p. 33.

6 Porter, *London*, p. 125; Ogborn, *Spaces of Modernity*, pp. 93–7.

7 Hanway, *Journal of Eight Days Journey*, p. 314.

8 M. Barley, 'Excavations in Newark market place 1965', *Transactions of the Thoroton Society of Nottinghamshire*, 69 (1965), pp. 77–8 at p. 77.

9 Deering, *Nottinghamia*, pp. 16–17.

10 *Oxford Council Acts 1626–1665*, p. 181.

11 'Gentleman of the Temple', *Public nusance considered*, pp. 3–6.

12 Court of Common Council (London), *Act of Common Councel 1655*, p. 7.

13 Hardy, *Middlesex County Records 1689–1709*, pp. 53, 74.

14 GL, MS 3018/1, fol. 98v.

15 Earwaker, *Court Leet Records of Manchester*, VII, pp. 98, 102, 109, 111, 147, 149, 157, 227.

16 BRO, Quarter Sessions Book 1743–1776 (unfoliated), for example see Benjamin Axford not pitching by door at Bear Corner, 21 Apr. 1752.

17 Hardy, *Middlesex County Records 1689–1709*, pp. 53, 58, 85.

18 GL, MS 3018/1, fols 224r, 228v; 'Gentleman of the Temple', *Public nusance considered*, p. 3; Hardy, *Middlesex County Records 1689–1709*, pp. 49, 230.

19 *Court Leet Records* (Southampton), p. 572.

20 Evelyn, *Diary*, III, p. 140.

21 Earwaker, *Court Leet Records of Manchester*, VI, p. 219; see also VII, p. 6.

22 Ibid., II, p. 185.

23 Massie, *Essay*, p. 12.

24 GL, MS 2649/1.

25 GL, MS 3018/1, fol. 135r; see also fols 98v, 105v, 144r. Concerns about poor paving seemed to increase as the period progressed; there were a huge number of presentments in 1751 (fol. 236r).

26 BRO, Quarter Sessions Book 1743–1776 (unfoliated): see for example entries for 25 Apr. 1751, 9 Sept. 1751, 21 Apr. 1752, 20 Mar. 1753, 8 May 1753, 21 Sept. 1753, 6 Nov. 1753, 21 Mar. 1754, 1 Aug. 1754, 4 Nov. 1754, 25 Feb. 1755, 26 Aug. 1755, 11 Dec. 1755, 2 Apr. 1756, 1 July 1756, 28 Sept. 1756, 1 Mar. 1757, 9 June 1757.

27 GL, MS 2649/1 (unfoliated) presentments for 1704; see also 1718.

28 BRO, Quarter Sessions Book 1743–1776 (unfoliated), 8 May 1753, 28 Sept. 1756.

29 Fuller, *Gnomologia*, p. 183.

30 *Oxford Council Acts 1583–1626*, p. 243.

31 London, *Act of Common Councel 1655*, p. 10; An Act of Parliament – Westminster and Middlesex 1690/1 – determined that on Wednesdays and Saturdays citizens were to sweep and heap the refuse from the street outside their houses, and retain all dusty and noisome materials indoors, or in their yards until it would be collected; cited in Bond, *Compleat Guide*, pp. 238–43.

32 *Court Leet Records* (Southampton), p. 430; see also pp. 443–4.

33 Hardy, *Middlesex County Records 1689–1709*, p. 73; Thomas Baker, *An Act at Oxford. A Comedy* (1704), p. 42.

34 For example, see GL, MS 2649/1 (unfoliated), officer lists for 1734; GL, MS 3018/1, fols 70v, 89v, 105v.

35 *Oxford Council Acts 1583–1626*, pp. 297, p. 305; *VCH Oxon*, IV, p. 352.

36 BRO, Council Minutes, transcription of volume I by Rev. Shickle, pp. 5–6 (17 Jan. 1615).

37 Earwaker, *Court Leet Records of Manchester*, II, pp. 303–4.

38 Hardy, *Middlesex County Records 1689–1709*, p, 27; GL, MS 4829, fols 92, 99v, 111, 169 (1729 and passim); *A Compendious library of the Law, necessary for all degrees of persons and professions. In two parts* (London, 1740), p. 27; Jeaffreson, *Middlesex County Records*, III, p. 228; *A new and compleat history of London*, p. 260.

39 John Taylor, *Nonsence upon Sence: or Sence upon Nonsence: chuse you either, or neither* (London, 1651), p. 13.

40 BRO, Council Minutes, transcription of volume 1, pp. 5–6; BRO, Council Minutes Book 1, p. 31 (22 Apr. 1614); see also p. 192 (27 Feb. 1644).

41 Pierre Le Lorrain (Abbé de Vallemont), *Curiosities of nature and art in husbandry and gardening* (London, 1707), p. 268.

42 Court of Common Council (London), *Act of Common Councel 1655*, pp. 5–6, 11–13. For further discussions of Lanyon's scheme see Weinstein, 'New urban demands', p. 31; Mark Jenner, 'Another epocha? Hartlib, John Lanyon and the improvement of London in the 1650s', in Mark Greengrass, Michael Leslie and Timothy Raylor (eds), *Samuel Hartlib and Universal Reformation: Studies in Intellectual Communication* (Cambridge, 1994), pp. 343–56, esp. pp. 343–5, 356.

43 Hardy, *Middlesex County Records 1689–1709*, p. 255.

44 Woodcroft, *Index of Patentees*, p. 264 (patent 364).

45 Earwaker, *Court Leet Records of Manchester*, VI, p. 212.

46 Ibid., VII, pp. 48, 87.

47 Court of Common Council (London), *Act of Common Councel 1655*, pp. 7–8.

48 GL, MS 3018/1, fols 127r, 134v, 135r, 142r.

49 *OBSP*, 6–11 Dec. 1732, p. 8.

50 *Court Leet Records* (Southampton), p. 409.

51 Wood, *Essay*, II, p. 352.

52 *Court Leet Records* (Southampton), p. 385. The Liverpool scavenger was presented for neglecting his duties in 1651: Power, *Liverpool Town Books*, p. 22.

53 The raker employed by the ward in 1680 was presented for being 'notoriously deficient', following numerous complaints: GL, MS 4069/2 (part 1), fols 14r, 30v, 88r; see also fol. 94r.

54 Hardy, *Middlesex County Records 1689–1709*, p. 73.

55 Ibid., pp. 71, 284, 312.

56 Fuller, *Gnomologia*, p. 147.

57 Woodward, '"Swords into ploughshares"'.

58 Gervase Markham, *Cheape and good Husbandry* (London, 1614), p. 87.

59 Tryon, *Tryon's Letters*, p. 90.

60 Ayres, *Building the Georgian City*, p. 61; for more details see chapter 6 above, 'Grotty'.

61 *OBSP*, 24–27 Feb. 1725, p. 1; *OBSP*, 15–17 Oct. 1746, pp. 277–8; *OBSP*, 7–10 Sept. 1748, p. 258;. A servant had been accused of stealing spoons from a public house. However, after 'a raven was seen to carry a tea-spoon . . . and bury it in a laystall', the servant was released: *The annual register, or view of the history . . .* , 2nd edn (London, 1778), p. 76.

62 *The Oak and the Dunghill. A Fable* (London, 1728), p. 1.

63 Earwaker, *Court Leet Records of Manchester*, II, p. 167, see also p. 189.

64 *OBSP*, 28–30 June 1733, p. 168.

65 Dung posed a hazard to the foundations of Manchester's Mill Bridge in 1624: Earwaker, *Court Leet Records of Manchester*, III, pp. 78, 85.

66 King, 'How high is too high?', p. 449.

67 Earwaker, *Court Leet Records of Manchester*, II, p. 168; III, pp. 13, 198; VII, pp. 91, 98. In 1763 a man living on Millgate kept a 'stinking' dunghill in his yard. This was declared to be a common nuisance, and he was ordered to remove it: VIII, p. 72.

68 Power, *Liverpool Town Books*, p. 81.

69 Earwaker, *Court Leet Records of Manchester*, II, pp. 157, 190; III, pp. 12, 61, 92, 210.

70 City of Cambridge, *Whereas divers disordered people . . .*

71 Sachse, *Minutes of the Norwich Court of Mayoralty*, p. 61.

72 Earwaker, *Court Leet Records of Manchester*, II, pp. 169, 177; VI, p. 88; VII, p. 122.

73 Jeaffreson, *Middlesex County Records*, IV, p. 82.

74 Manchée, *Westminster City Fathers*, pp. 74–5.

75 *OBSP*, 11–14 Oct. 1721, p. 8.

76 Edward Ward, 'The Dancing Devils' (1729), p. 4 [pagination restarts with each piece in this volume].

77 Earwaker, *Court Leet Records of Manchester*, VII, pp. 163, 248.

78 Ibid., VI, p. 157.

79 Ibid., VI, pp. 166–7, 203–4.

80 BRO, Council Minute Book 1, pp. 79 (31 Mar. 1634), 168 (25 June 1638); Redford, *History of Local Government in Manchester*, I, p. 109.

81 Salter, *Oxford City Properties*, pp. 317–18; *Oxford Council Acts 1626–1665*, p. 119.

82 *Oxford Council Acts 1626–1665*, pp. 112, 375.

83 *VCH Oxon*, IV, p. 82.

84 *VCH Oxon*, IV, pp. 351–3; *Oxford Council Acts 1626–1665*, pp. 119, 426–7.

85 *Oxford Council Acts 1626–1665*, pp. 399–400.

86 Anthony à Wood, *The Life of Anthony à Wood from the year 1632 to 1672 written by himself, and published by Mr Thomas Hearne* (Oxford, 1772), pp. 345–6.

87 Massie, *Essay*, p. 12.

88 See *A new and compleat history of London*, pp. 259, 261.

89 McLaughlin, *Coprophilia*, pp. 97–8; *A new and compleat history of London*, p. 261.

90 Stow [updated by Strype], *A Survey of London*, I, book III, p. 278 (this severs White-friars from Salisbury Court).

91 McLaughlin, *Coprophilia*, p. 98; J. G. Waller, 'The Fleet River', *The Gentleman's Magazine and Historical Review*, Jan. 1855, pp. 24–32 at pp. 28–9. 'You recollect the cinder heap, Vot stood in Gray's Inn Lane, sirs': William Thomas Moncrieff's *The Literary Dustman*, in Brian Maidment, *Reading Popular Prints 1790 to 1870* (Manchester, 1996), p. 99.

92 Hanway, *A Letter to Mr. Spranger*, p. 17.

93 Robert Lovell, *Panzoologicomineralogia; or a compleat history of animals and minerals* (Oxford, 1661), p. 271; Mandeville, *Fable of the Bees* (1714), preface, sig. A6v.

94 Evelyn, *Fumifugium*, p. 14.

95 *A new and compleat history of London*, p. 259.

96 Hanway, *A Letter to Mr. Spranger*, pp. 17–18. Hanway also moaned that ramming and were levelling insufficient, reducing the durability of the streets and causing them to break up easily under pressure.

97 See E. L. Jones and M. E. Falkus, 'Urban improvement and the English economy in the seventeenth and eighteenth centuries', in P. J. Uselding (ed.), *Research in Economic History*, 4 (1979), pp. 193–233.

98 *Court Leet Records* (Southampton), p. 572.

99 Mandeville, *Fable of the Bees* (1714), preface, sig. A6v.

100 Hanway, *A Letter to Mr. Spranger*, p. 26.

101 Jeaffreson, *Middlesex County Records*, III p. 227; Manchée, *Westminster City Fathers*, pp. 133–4.

102 BLC, MS B914–238, p. 122; *A Description of England and Wales* 10 vols, London, 1769–70), VIII, p. 127; Power, *Liverpool Town Books*, pp. 153, 181.

103 LMA, MJ/SBB/133, fol. 39.

104 GL, MS 68, fols 3v, 6, 24v, 26v, 29v, 32, 35, 39v, 42v, 45; see also LMA MJ/SR/1336, recognizance no. 22.

105 Chandler, *Liverpool*, pp. 337, 347, 368; Power, *Liverpool Town Books*, pp. 63, 66, 68, 77, 81.

106 Power, *Liverpool Town Books*, pp. 92, 116; in 1665 the bellman was given the additional duty of supervising swine control, p. 177; pigs also created major and continuing problems in Southampton in the seventeenth century. In 1603 the Southampton jurors labelled the 'disorderly keeping of hoggs and piggs' a 'disgrace to the governm[ent]'. Despite draconian threats, it was noted that porcine abuses 'dayle more & more encreaseth': *Court Leet Records* (Southampton), pp. 385, 402.

107 Earwaker, *Court Leet Records of Manchester*, II, pp. 185, 195, 199, 203, 222–3, 265–6, 287, 307; III, pp. 21, 103, 115–16, 211, 215; VI, pp. 6, 15, 28, 32, 42, 48, 68, 104, 110–11, 119, 122, 134, 145, 149, 165, 180, 190, 194, 207, 220, 228, 236, 249 .

108 Ibid., VII, pp. 77, 238; see also Earwaker, *Constables' Accounts*, II, p. 86.

109 Earwaker, *Court Leet Records of Manchester*, VII, p. 96.
110 Ibid., VII, pp. 17, 44, 77, 96, 117, 131, 137, 185, 239; VIII, pp. 9, 40, 49, 117, 125.
111 GL, MS 3018/1, fol. 137v.
112 Shesgreen, *Criers and Hawkers of London*, p. 78. A bow-string maker from London's St Sepulchre's parish kept pigs in 1695: Hardy, *Middlesex County Records 1689–1709*, p. 138. In 1715 two Johns – Serjant and Perrin – kept swine 'to the great Annusance of their Neighbours' in Portsoken Ward: GL, MS 2649/1 (unfoliated), presentments for 1715.
113 *VCH Oxon*, IV, p. 86.
114 City of Cambridge, *Whereas divers disordered people . . .*
115 *Court Leet Records* (Southampton), pp. 385, 424, 446.
116 For eighteenth-century examples see Earwaker, *Court Leet Records of Manchester*, VIII, pp. 38, 77, 117, 121.
117 Ibid., VII, p. 122; see also pp. 68, 128; VIII, p. 27.
118 Jones, *Butchers of London*, pp. 84–5; see also p. 95.
119 Stow [updated by Strype], *Survey of London*, I, book III, p. 283; see also Jones, *Butchers of London*, p. 95.
120 See, for example, Gwynn, *London and Westminster Improved*, pp. 18–20; Robey, '"All asmear with filth"', pp. 1–2.
121 'Gentleman of the Temple', *Public nusance considered*, pp. 21–3.
122 Court of Common Council (London), *Act of Common Councel 1655*, pp. 8–9; Earwaker, *Court Leet Records of Manchester*, VII, p. 188.
123 Earwaker, *Court Leet Records of Manchester*, VII, p. 215.
124 Betty Masters, *Public Markets of the City of London, surveyed by William Leybourn in 1677*, London Topographical Society, 117 (London, 1974), p. 15.
125 Wilson, *Surgery, Skin and Syphilis*, p. 35.
126 Bond, *Compleat Guide*, p. 239.
127 GL, MS 4069/2, fol. 373v (1688 onwards).
128 Ayres, *Building the Georgian City*, p. 57; Bond, *Compleat Guide*, p. 239.
129 *A new and compleat history of London*, p. 261.
130 Ayres, *Building the Georgian City*, p. 42.
131 Earwaker, *Court Leet Records of Manchester*, VI, pp. 12, 15.
132 London, Mercers' Company Archive, Gresham Repertory 1669–1676, p. 155. Their response was to let the stones already there be sawn, but the masons were to import no more thereafter. My thanks to Natasha Glaisyer for this reference. See also the case of a stonemason presented to the wardmote of the Vintry Ward in 1716 and 1718: GL, MS 68, fols 79v, 84v.
133 *OBSP*, 6–11 Sept. 1732, pp. 183–5.
134 Fuller, *Gnomologia*, p. 55.
135 Reddaway, *Rebuilding of London*, p. 79.
136 30 George II, ch. 65 (1757). See, for example BRO, Council Minute Book 7, pp. 66–7 (25 June 1753), p. 195 (24 Jan. 1757).
137 For example see the Bristol Act, 22 George II, ch. 20 (1749), in *The Statutes at Large, From the Seventh Year of King George the Second, To the Twenty third Year of King George the Second, inclusive* (6 vols, London, 1758), V, p. 650.
138 Hanway, *A Letter to Mr. Spranger*, p. 33.
139 Earwaker, *Court Leet Records of Manchester*, VII, pp. 236, 239.
140 Fox, *Coventry Constables' Presentments*, p. 40.
141 *Court Leet Records* (Southampton), pp. 510, 537.
142 Bond, *Compleat Guide*, p. 257.
143 *A new and compleat history of London*, p. 261.
144 Earwaker, *Court Leet Records of Manchester*, VI, p. 238.
145 GL, MS 3018/1, fol. 98v.
146 See Corporation of London, *Lawes of the Market*, sig. B1r for late sixteenth-century rules.

147 GL, MS 3018/1, fol. 126.
148 Earwaker, *Court Leet Records of Manchester*, II, p. 205.
149 Ibid., VIII, p. 118.
150 Ibid., III, pp. 181, 322–4; Redford, *History of Local Government in Manchester*, I, p. 109.
151 BRO, Council Minute Book 2, insert attached to p. 343 (1663).
152 In Cambridge a fine was set at three shillings and fourpence for citizens found to have swept dust, dirt or filth into a kennel: City of Cambridge, *Whereas divers disordered people . . .* ; Hardy, *Middlesex County Records 1689–1709*, p. 223.
153 BRO, Council Minute Book 1, p. 53 (21 Jan. 1633).
154 Earwaker, *Court Leet Records of Manchester*, VI, p. 15; see also pp. 209, 237.
155 Ibid., VI, p. 115; see also VII, p. 8.
156 *OBSP*, 11–14 July 1694, pp. 2–3.
157 GL, MS 4069/2 (part 1), fol. 58v.
158 Ibid., fol. 77r; see also 88v, 94r.
159 Fuller, *Gnomologia*, p. 39.
160 Swift, 'Description of a city shower', in *Miscellanies*, p. 410.
161 *Oxford Council Acts 1626–1665*, pp. 45, 54, 66, 189, 265; see also pp. 319–20; Salter, *Oxford City Properties*, p. 354. Oxford's waters were still troubled in 1665 when the council brought in some ancient city fishermen for a brainstorming session: *Oxford Council Acts 1626–1665*, pp. 337, 350.
162 *VCH Oxon*, IV, p. 86.
163 Anthony à Wood, *The ancient and present state of the City of Oxford* (London, 1773), p. 253; Clark, *Life and Times of Anthony à Wood*, II, p. 16.
164 *Court Leet Records* (Southampton), pp. 376, 444, 448, 458, 459, 477, 501, 523, 542, 551, 597.
165 BRO, Council Minutes Book 7, p. 21 (30 Mar. 1752), p. 245 (1 Apr. 1758); BRO, Quarter Sessions Book, 1743–1776, presentments for 25 Apr. 1751.
166 Commissioners of Sewers of the City of London, *At a Court of Sewers held at the Guild Hall, London; on Saterday the fifth of Feb. in the year of our Lord 1652* (London, 1653); Reddaway, *Rebuilding of London*, pp. 208–10; McLaughlin, *Coprophilia*, p. 60.
167 Weinstein, 'New urban demands', pp. 39–40.
168 Stow [updated by Strype], *Survey of London*, I, p. 12.
169 'Citizen of London', *A new and compleat survey of London*, 1, p. 631.
170 Daniel Defoe [?], *Due preparations for the plague, as well for soul as body* (London, 1722), pp. 35–6; see also George, *London Life*, p. 85.
171 Alexander Pope, *The Dunciad. An heroic Poem. In three books* (Dublin, 1728), p. 28.
172 *Statutes at Large*, 6th edn (8 vols, London, 1768–70), VI, p. 124; 'Citizen of London', *A new and compleat survey of London*, 1, p. 631.
173 *London Penny Post*, 22 Dec. 1749, cited in McLaughlin, *Coprophilia*, p. 99.
174 Campbell, *London Tradesman*, p. 216; Schneider, 'Fantastical colours', in Orlin, *Material London*, p. 113; Earwaker, *Court Leet Records of Manchester*, VI, pp. 205, 223, 257.
175 Stanford, *Ordinances of Bristol*, p. 40.
176 Campbell, *London Tradesman*, p. 263.
177 Stanford, *Ordinances of Bristol*, pp. 36, 55.
178 *Manchester Mercury and Harrop's General Advertiser* (no. 836), 2 June 1767, p. 1.
179 Earwaker, *Court Leet Records of Manchester*, VI, pp. 8, 12, 118, 158, 166, 183, 196; VII, p. 38.
180 GL, MS 2649/1 (unfoliated), presentments for 1692.
181 *OBSP*, 28 Feb.–5 Mar. 1728, p. 5.
182 Jones, *Butchers of London*, p. 135.
183 BRO, Council Minute Book 4, p. 173 (7 July 1718), p. 184 (29 Dec. 1718), p. 279 (1 Jan. 1722), p. 451 (1 Jan. 1728); Book 5, p. 23 (24 Jan. 1729), p. 213 (1 Apr. 1734);

Book 6, p. 239 (8 Dec. 1747); Book 7, pp. 50–60 (various dates); Book 8, p. 16 (29 June 1761), p. 201 (1 July 1765).

184   For the situation in London see Mark S. R. Jenner, 'From conduit community to commercial network? Water in London, 1500–1725', in Griffiths and Jenner, *Londinopolis*.

185   King, 'How high is too high?', p. 449.

186   Bond, *Compleat Guide*, p. 239.

187   Earwaker, *Court Leet Records of Manchester*, II, p. 268; III, pp. 31, 121–2, 160, 176.

188   *Court Leet Records* (Southampton), p. 378; see also pp. 399–400, 416, 421.

189   Court of Common Council (London), *Act of Common Councel 1655*, p. 9; *Court Leet Records* (Southampton), p. 383.

190   J. A. Hassan, 'The impact and development of the water supply in Manchester, 1568–1882', *Transactions of the Historic Society of Lancashire and Cheshire*, 133 (1983, published 1984), pp. 25–45 at pp. 27–8.

191   Earwaker, *Court Leet Records of Manchester*, VII, p. 45.

192   Fox, *Coventry Constable's Presentments*, p. 83.

193   Smollett, *Humphry Clinker*, II, p. 6.

194   Ware, *Complete Body of Architecture*, p. 121.

195   Huddesford, *An address*, pp. 3, 10.

196   H. D. Rack, 'The Manchester Corporation project of 1763: legend or history?', *Transactions of the Lancashire and Cheshire Antiquarian Society*, 84 (1987), pp. 118–42 at pp. 135–6.

197   Wood, *Essay*, I, pp. 216–17.

198   Fawcett, *Bath Administer'd*, p. 90.

199   Joseph Draper, 'Brief Description of Bath in a Letter to a Friend' (London?, 1747), pp. 13–14, cited in Fawcett, *Voices of Bath*, p. 6.

200   Mitchell and Penrose, *Letters from Bath*, p. 52.

201   Kielmansegg, *Diary of a Journey*, p. 130.

202   30 George II, ch. 65 (1757).

203   6 George III, ch. 70 (1766).

204   Fawcett, *Bath Administer'd*, pp. 26, 109; BRO, Council Minute Book 8, p. 222 (20 Dec. 1765).

205   30 George II, ch. 65 (1757); Fawcett, *Voices of Bath*, p. 7.

206   Hardy, *Middlesex County Records 1689–1709*, pp. 40, 144, 209, 305.

207   Commissioners of Sewers, Corporation of London, *At a Session of the Commissioners of Sewers, Pavements, &c. London, held at Guildhall, on Friday, the [blank] Day of [blank] 174[blank]* (London, *c.*1740). Purbeck stone was superior to the Kentish ragstone commonly used before.

208   Corporation of London, *To the Commissioners of the Sewers*, p. 9.

209   Hanway, *A Letter to Mr. Spranger*, p. 38.

210   Corporation of London, *To the Commissioners of the Sewers*, p. 8.

211   Hanway, *A Letter to Mr. Spranger*, p. 20.

212   Noorthouck, *A new history of London*, pp. 414–15.

213   Hanway, *A Letter to Mr. Spranger*, pp. 15–16, 26; Manchée, *Westminster City Fathers*, pp. 133–4.

214   Corporation of London, *To the Commissioners of the Sewers*, p. 8; Hanway, *A Letter to Mr. Spranger*, p. 23.

215   Hanway, *A Letter to Mr. Spranger*, p. 11.

9. Gloomy

1   Thomas Cogan, *The Haven of Health* (London, 1584), pp. 7, 262.

2   Neve, *The City and Countrey Purchaser*, p. 58.

3   *Diseases of Bath*, p. 13.

4   Evelyn, *Diary*, III, p. 140; see also Magalotti, *Travels of Cosmo*, p. 205.

5   Exwood and Lehmann, *William Schellinks' Travels*, p. 150; see also Edward Leigh, *England Described: or, the several counties & shires thereof briefly handled* (London, 1659), pp. 40–1.

6   Wood, *Essay*, I, sig. A3v.

7   *The Bath and Bristol Guide*, p. 14.

8   *Diseases of Bath*, p. 13.

9   Deering, *Nottinghamia*, pp. 6, 77–8, 85.

10 Robert G. Frank Jr, 'Medicine', in Nicholas Tyacke (ed.), *The History of the University of Oxford, Volume Four: Seventeenth-century Oxford* (Oxford, 1997), pp. 505–58 at p. 505.

11 Salmon, *The Present State of the Universities*, pp. 31–2.

12 Brimblecombe, *The Big Smoke*, pp. 34–5.

13 Ryder, *Diary*, p. 309.

14 Evelyn, *Fumifugium*, p. 16; Peter Brimblecombe, a modern environmental historian, has cast doubt on Evelyn's assertion that domestic fires were not key polluters and argues that the very visible nature of the plumes of smoke arising from the major industries drew attention to their discharge, but the multiplicity of domestic fires would have contributed much to the general blanket of smoke. See Peter Brimblecombe, 'Interest in air pollution among early Fellows of the Royal Society', *Notes and Records of the Royal Society of London*, 32:2 (1978), pp. 123–9.

15 See Deering's account of Nottingham's blacksmiths and tanners, *Nottinghamia*, p. 16.

16 LMA MJ/SBR/1, fol. 420; CLRO, rep. 78, fol. 306v.

17 Ayres, *Building the Georgian City*, p. 60.

18 BRO, Council Minutes Book 3, p. 251 (28 Mar. 1698).

19 Louis Simond, *Journal of a Tour* (1810), cited in John Woodforde, *Georgian Houses for All* (London, 1978), p. 59.

20 Evelyn, *Fumifugium*, p. 8.

21 Gwynn, *London and Westminster Improved*, p. 11.

22 C. H. Collins Baker and M. I. Baker (eds), *The Life and Circumstances of James Brydges, First Duke of Chandos, Patron of the Liberal Arts* (Oxford, 1949), p. 288.

23 James Howell, *Epistolae Ho-Elianae. Familiar Letters Domestic and Forren*, 2nd edn (London, 1650), p. 105.

24 Cited in Bowler and Brimblecombe, 'Control of air pollution in Manchester', p. 74.

25 Deering, *Nottinghamia*, p. 88.

26 Sir William Petty, *A treatise of taxes and contributions shewing the nature and measures of crown-lands, assessments, customs, poll-moneys, lotteries, benevolence, penalties, monopolies, offices, tythes, raising of coins, harth-money, excise &c* (London, 1662), p. 23.

27 Hardy, *Middlesex County Records 1689–1709*, p. 94.

28 Wood, *Essay*, II, p. 343; see also Wood's comments about George Street, p. 335.

29 Clavering, *An Essay on Chimneys*, p. 76.

30 Evelyn, *Diary*, III, p. 122.

31 Geoffrey Vaughan Blackstone, *A History of the British Fire Service* (London, 1957), p. 31; Lucas, *Kalm's Account*, pp. 88–9; Gay, *Trivia*, p. 77.

32 *The Spectator*, no. 131, 31 July 1711 [Addison].

33 Hooke, *Diary*, p. 251.

34 Bachrach and Collmer, *The English Journal: Huygens*, p. 134. Conrad von Uffenbach ensured that he climbed the tower of St Paul's Cathedral in the early morning, in order to enjoy the city prospect before the coal smoke obscured it: Quarrell and Mare, *London in 1710*, p. 32.

35 Mare and Quarrell, *Lichtenberg's Visits*, pp. 62, 111.

36 Evelyn, *Fumifugium*, Dedicatory and 'To the reader', sigs A2, A5v.

37 John Norden, *The Surveiors Dialogue* (London, 1610), p. 87.

38 John Graunt, *Natural and Political Observations. Mentioned in a following index, and made up on the Bills of Mortality* (London, 1676), esp. pp. 92–5.

39 Tryon, *Tryon's Letters*, p. 79.
40 Evelyn, *Fumifugium*, pp. 5, 10.
41 *OBSP*, 14–19 Jan. 1732, p. 56.
42 Evelyn, *Fumifugium*, esp. sig A2v–A3, pp. 15–16, 23–6, passim.
43 Hardy, *Middlesex County Records 1689–1709*, pp. 12, 62.
44 Wood, *Essay*, I, p. 224; II, pp. 362, 364.
45 Cited in Fawcett, *Voices of Bath*, p. 19.
46 Fuller, *Gnomologia*, p. 240.
47 Guillery, *Small House*, p. 118.
48 Campbell, *London Tradesman*, p. 106.
49 Baker and Milsom, *Sources of English Legal History*, p. 603.
50 Ramazzini, *De Morbis Artificum*, p. 33; Campbell, *London Tradesman*, p. 320.
51 Schneider in Orlin, *Material London*, p. 112; Baker, *Plants and Civilization*, pp. 160–4.
52 *Leet Court Records* (Southampton), p. 504.
53 Ibid., pp. 523, 540, 557, 599.
54 Weinstein, 'New urban demands', pp. 38–9; King, *Beer has a History*, p. 72; Power, 'The East London working community', p. 112; N. G. Brett-James, *The Growth of Stuart London* (London, 1935), p. 300. See also Cook, 'Policing the health of London', p. 18.
55 Campbell, *London Tradesman*, p. 277.
56 Ramazzini, *De Morbis Artificum*, p. 137.
57 *Oxford Council Acts 1583–1626*, p. 331.
58 GL, MS 2649/1 (unfoliated), presentments 1723.
59 *OBSP*, 28 June–3 July 1769, pp. 329–32.
60 *Oxford Council Acts 1583–1626*, p. 267.
61 Earwaker, *Court Leet Records of Manchester*, VII, pp. 64, 69, 77.
62 *Rex v. Pappineau* (1726), in Strange, *Reports*, pp. 686–9. On appeal the defence challenged the issue of appropriate location, arguing that the pits were near a highway, not on one. They also argued that a fine was inappropriate for a public nuisance, as it did not abate it. The defence also raised differences between permanent and temporary nuisances, and asked whether the pits themselves were a nuisance, or were merely the location of a nuisance.
63 Slack, *Impact of the Plague*, pp. 30, 45.
64 Deering, *Nottinghamia*, p. 83.
65 Tryon, *Tryon's Letters*, pp. 4, 79, 117–18, 120.
66 Cogan, *Haven of Health*, p. 318; Mead, *Pestilential Contagion*, p. 42.
67 Michael Foster, *A Report of some proceedings on the commission of oyer and terminer and gaol delivery for the trial of the rebels in the year 1746* (Oxford, 1762), pp. 74–5; see also J. M. Beattie, *Crime and the Courts in England 1660–1800* (Oxford, 1986), pp. 301–4.
68 Thomas, 'Cleanliness and godliness', p. 72; Slack, *Impact of the Plague*, p. 45.
69 *Oxford Council Acts 1583–1626*, pp. 192, 196.
70 *Oxford Council Acts 1626–65*, p. 341.
71 Mead, *Pestilential Contagion*, pp. 2–3.
72 Gerard William Groote, *Fumigating Ingredients to remove offensive smells, foul, putrid and stagnated air, from halls, chambers, courts of justice, distemper'd gaols* (London, c.1780).
73 *Aldred's Case* (1610), in Baker and Milsom, *Sources of English Legal History*, pp. 599–600.
74 *Leet Court Records* (Southampton), p. 599.
75 Jeaffreson, *Middlesex County Records*, IV, p. 74; K. Tweedale Meaby, *Nottinghamshire. Extracts from County Records of the Eighteenth Century* (Nottingham, c.1940), p. 210; see also Earwaker, *Court Leet Records of Manchester*, VII, p. 45; GL, MS 3018/1, fol. 106.

76 Harris, *The Life of Lord Chancellor Hardwicke*, I, pp. 266–70; see also the case of *Rex v. Burrell* (1757): Oldham, *The Mansfield Manuscripts*, II, pp. 897–9.
77 Jeaffreson, *Middlesex County Records*, I, p. 57.
78 Hawkins, *Pleas of the Crown*, I, p. 199.
79 Blackstone, *Commentaries*, III, p. 217; see also Burn, *Justice of the Peace*, II, p. 156.
80 Evelyn, *Fumifugium*, p. 21.
81 Jones, *Butchers of London*, p. 96.
82 BRO, Quarter Sessions Book 1743–1776 (unfoliated), 19 June 1755; see also 1 July 1756; Fawcett, *Bath Commercialis'd*, p. 18. There was a gradual increase in concern about slaughterhouses in the late eighteenth century. See Buchan, *Domestic Medicine*, p. 125. Christopher Otter has suggested that the key period for slaughterhouse reforms was 1840–1900: 'Cleansing and clarifying', esp. pp. 44–53.
83 Fuller, *Gnomologia*, p. 123.
84 Macray, *Register*, III, p. 40. I am indebted to Robin Darwall-Smith for his Latin translation.
85 BRO, Council Minutes Book 5, p. 98 (28 Dec. 1730).
86 Quarrell and Mare, *London in 1710*, p. 15.
87 Charles Jenner, extract from 'Eclogue IV. The Poet' (1772), in Roger Lonsdale (ed.), *The New Oxford Book of Eighteenth Century Verse* (Oxford, 1984), pp. 577–9.
88 Redford, *History of Local Government in Manchester*, I, p. 75.
89 Cook, 'Policing the health of London', p. 24.
90 Ward, *Field Spy* (1714), p. 24.
91 Gomme and Norman, *Lincoln's Inn Fields*, pp. 7–11.
92 8 George II, ch. 26 (1735).
93 Ibid. For evidence of 'disorders' see Jeaffreson, *Middlesex County Records*, IV, p. 183.
94 *Hell upon Earth*, p. 43.
95 Gomme and Norman, *Lincoln's Inn Fields*, pp. 9–11, 19–20.
96 Wood, *Essay*, II, pp. 331–2.
97 Massie, *Essay*, pp. 30–1.
98 Christoph Heyl, 'We are not at home: protecting domestic privacy in post-fire middle-class London', *London Journal*, 27:2 (2002), pp. 12–33 at p. 12.
99 See, for example, the various small, mean and nasty courts in Portsoken Ward, as described by John Strype in his update of Stow, *The Survey of London*, I (book II), pp. 27–8.
100 *VCH Oxon*, IV, p. 94.
101 Pantin, 'Domestic architecture in Oxford', pp. 136–9.
102 Thomas Short, *New Observations, natural, moral, civil, political and medical on city, town and country Bills of Mortality* (London, 1750), p. 65.
103 Peter Guillery, 'Waste and place: late eighteenth century development on Kingsland Road', *Hackney History*, 6 (2000), pp. 19–38 at p. 22.
104 Earwaker, *Court Leet Records of Manchester*, III, p. 86; VI, p. 183; GL, MS 2649/1 (unfoliated), presentments 1728.
105 For example see BRO, Council Minutes Book 1, p. 55 (1 Apr. 1633); Book 3, p. 537 (26 Dec. 1709); *Court Leet Records* (Southampton), pp. 580, 593.
106 Reddaway, *Rebuilding of London*, p. 38.
107 *Oxford Council Acts 1626–1665*, pp. 162, 253.
108 *Oxford Council Acts 1583–1626*, pp. 337, 426; *VCH Oxon*, IV, p. 86.
109 *Oxford Council Acts 1583–1626*, p. 326.
110 Crossley, 'City and university', p. 132; Salter, *Oxford City Properties*, p. xiii.
111 Clark, *Wood's City of Oxford, I: City and Suburbs*, p. 63.
112 Crossley, 'City and university', p. 132; *Oxford Council Acts 1626–1665*, p. 332.
113 *Oxford Council Acts 1626–1665*, p. 253.
114 *Oxford Council Acts 1626–1665*, pp. 253, 317; see also *Oxford Council Acts 1665–1701*, pp. 17, 32, 48, 49, 68, 180.

115 *VCH Oxon*, IV, p. 99.
116 Defoe, *A tour thro' Great Britain*, II, p. 254.
117 BRO, Council Minutes Book 5, pp. 331, 333, 336 (16 Jan. and 27 Mar. 1738).
118 Earwaker, *Court Leet Records of Manchester*, VII, p. 164.
119 Ibid., VII, pp. 164, 185, 228.
120 Earwaker, *Constables' Accounts*, III, p. 192.
121 Massie, *Essay*, p. 18.
122 Ibid., pp. 13–14, 18.
123 GL, MS 3018/1, fols 184v, 199v.
124 Corporation of London, *To the Commissioners of the Sewers*, p. 9; Hibbert Ware, *The Life and Correspondence*, p. 47; 22 George II ch. 20 (1749), in *The Statutes at Large, From the Seventh Year of King George the Second, To the Twenty third Year of King George the Second, inclusive* (6 vols, London, 1758), V, p. 650: lighting the streets was 'greatly hindered and obstructed by Signs'.
125 Massie, *Essay*, p. 32; see also Hanway, *A Letter to Mr. Spranger*, p. 21.
126 Sweet, 'Topographies of politeness', pp. 361–3.
127 Corfield, 'Walking the city streets', p. 149.
128 Fawcett, *Bath Administer'd*, p. 129; see also the state of the North Gate in Oxford, *Oxford Council Acts 1626–1665*, p. 84; *Oxford Council Acts 1665–1701*, p. 49.
129 BRO, Council Minutes Book 7, p. 62 (26 Apr. 1753), p. 69 (25 June 1753), p. 223 (3 Oct. 1757); Book 8, p. 37 (27 Jan. 1762), p. 56 (28 June 1762), p. 221 (20 Dec. 1765), p. 254 (30 June 1766).
130 Deering, *Nottinghamia*, pp. 4, 16. See also Ellis, *The Georgian Town*, esp. pp. 87–8.
131 BCL, MS B914–238, p. 80.
132 Salmon, *The Present State of the Universities*, pp. 28–9.
133 Hardy, *Middlesex County Records 1689–1709*, p. 172.
134 Wood, *Essay*, II, p. 340; see also p. 326.
135 Charles Robertson, *Bath: An Architectural Guide* (London, 1975), pp. 129–30.
136 BRO, Council Minutes Book 7, p. 168 (12 Apr. 1756).
137 Harland, 'The old market place in 1772', p. 211.
138 Bradshaw, *Origins of Street Names in Manchester*, p. 21.
139 Borsay, *English Urban Renaissance*, p. 63.
140 Fuller, *Gnomologia*, p. 93.
141 See Ekirch, *At Day's Close*.
142 *Oxford Council Acts 1583–1626*, pp. 240–1.
143 City of Cambridge, *Whereas divers disordered people . . .*
144 *Oxford Council Acts 1583–1626*, pp. 246, 412.
145 *Oxford Council Acts 1665–1701*, pp. 195–6; see also p. 251. In 1691 the constables and headboroughs of London parishes were to notify householders whose houses adjoined the street to hang candles or lanthorns from dusk until midnight: Hardy, *Middlesex County Records 1689–1709*, p. 27.
146 E[dmund] H[eming], *By virtue of a patent . . .* (n.p., 1691).
147 *The Case of Edmund Heming*, pp. 4–5.
148 Woodcroft, *Index of Patentees*, p. 586: 'Lighting streets and passages by lamps and lanterns' (1683), patent number 227.
149 *The Case of Edmund Heming*, p. 4; O'Dea, 'Artificial lighting', p. 320.
150 Malcolm Falkus, 'Lighting in the dark ages of English economic history: town streets before the Industrial Revolution', in D. C. Coleman and A. H. John (eds), *Trade, Government and Economy in Pre-industrial England* (London, 1976), pp. 248–73 at pp. 255–6.
151 Hardy, *Middlesex County Records 1689–1709*, p. 111.
152 9 George II, ch. 20 (1736).
153 Borsay, *English Urban Renaissance*, pp. 72–4.

154 BRO, Bath Council Minutes Book 3, p. 337 (22 Aug. 1702); Wood, *Essay*, II, pp. 375–6.
155 *Manchester Mercury and Harrop's General Advertiser*, no. 844, 28 July 1767, p. 2.
156 *The Case of Edmund Heming*, pp. 4–5.
157 A Parishioner, *An Address to the Ministers, Church-Wardens, and Parishioners of Newcastle upon Tyne* (Newcastle, 1755), p. 15; O'Dea, 'Artificial lighting', p. 322.
158 Ellis, *The Georgian Town*, p. 101.
159 *OBSP*, 7–9 Dec. 1757, p. 7.
160 Gill, 'Nottingham in the eighteenth century', pp. 42–3.
161 Mitchell and Penrose, *Letters from Bath*, p. 54.
162 *OBSP*, 20–27 Feb. 1771, p. 122; *OBSP*, 28–30 Aug. 1723, p. 7.
163 Hardy, *Middlesex County Records 1689–1709*, p. 281.
164 GL, MS 3018/1, fol. 254v.
165 Hardy, *Middlesex County Records 1689–1709*, p. 50.
166 Massie, *Essay*, pp. 22–3.
167 *OBSP*, 27–28 Feb. 1718, p. 2; see also *OBSP*, 7 June 1739, p. 90 (William Pattison stole three glass globe lamps).
168 *OBSP*, 16–19 Jan. 1747, pp. 53–4.
169 A Citizen, *A Candid Remonstrance*, p. 9.
170 30 George II, ch. 65 (1757).
171 Earwaker, *Constables' Accounts*, III, p. 53.
172 Ekirch, *At Day's Close*, p. 125: linkboys were known as mooncursers on account of the lack of customers on moonlit nights. Dillon, *Artificial Sunshine*, p. 14; *OBSP*, 23–27 May 1751, p. 169.
173 Pepys, *Diary*, I, pp. 41, 203, 208, 297.
174 Gill, 'Nottingham in the eighteenth century', p. 44.
175 Defoe, *Every-Body's Business is No-Body's Business*, p. 32.
176 See Gay, *Trivia*, p. 53; Earwaker, *Court Leet Records of Manchester*, II, pp. 169, 175; III, pp. 87, 125, 137; VII, pp. 39, 76; Power, *Liverpool Town Books*, p. 66.
177 Pepys, *Diary*, I, p. 246.
178 Fuller, *Gnomologia*, p. 93.
179 Earwaker, *Court Leet Records of Manchester*, II, p. 223; see also p. 306; VI, p. 35.
180 Clayton, *Friendly Advice to the Poor*, p. 39.
181 Chesterfield, *Letters to his son*, I, p. 163.
182 *OBSP*, 16–18 Jan. 1745, pp. 78–9.
183 *OBSP*, 12–15 Oct. 1726, p. 2.
184 Earwaker, *Court Leet Records of Manchester*, VII, p. 138; see also VI, p. 249; VII, pp. 110, 163.
185 Earwaker, *Court Leet Records of Manchester*, VII, p. 174; see also VIII, pp. 28, 41, 61.
186 Oldham, *The Mansfield Manuscripts*, II, p. 901.
187 Earwaker, *Court Leet Records of Manchester*, VIII, p. 51. The need to place 'a good and sufficient Light' on heaps of building rubble or rubbish or broken pavements to make them visible at night was enshrined in a York Act of Parliament of 1763: *The History and Antiquities of York* (3 vols, York, 1785), III, p. 177.
188 Huddesford, *An address*, pp. 3, 6, 11.
189 'A Citizen', *A Candid Remonstrance*, pp. 14–16.
190 Lettsom, *Medical memoirs*, pp. 33–4.
191 'A Citizen', *A Candid Remonstrance*, p. 15.

10. 'Such things as these . . . disturb human life'

1 Fuller, *Gnomologia*, p. 172.
2 Earwaker, *Court Leet Records of Manchester*, II, p. 195.

3   Campbell, *London Tradesman*, p. 245.
4   Ramazzini, *De Morbis Artificum*, p. 93.
5   Ibid., p. 69; Hooke, *Diary*, p. xv.
6   See chapter 6 above, 'Grotty'.
7   Ellis, *The Georgian Town*, p. 105.
8   See chapter 7 above, 'Busy'.
9   Swift, *Directions to Servants*, pp. 75, 86.
10   *Wits Cabinet*, p. 154.
11   Smollett, *Humphry Clinker*, II, p. 10.
12   *Diseases of Bath*, pp. 13–14.
13   Mead, *Pestilential Contagion*, p. 43.
14   Buchan, *Domestic Medicine*, p. 125.
15   Clayton, *Friendly Advice to the Poor*, p. 34.
16   Massie, *Essay*, p. 16.
17   *The Spectator*, no. 430, 14 July 1712 [Steele].
18   Amhurst, *Terrae Filius*, I, p. 112.
19   Mandeville, *Fable of the Bees* (1714), p. 98.
20   Clark, *Life and Times of Anthony à Wood*, II, p. 86.
21   See chapter 5 above, 'Noisy'.
22   Byrom [?], *A serious diswassive*, p. 9; Fuller, *Gnomologia*, p. 279.
23   GL, MS 2649/1 (unfoliated), presentments 1737.
24   Hardy, *Middlesex Country Records 1689–1709*, p. 211; see also Chetham's Library, Halliwell-Phillips Collection, [Mun. A.5.1] HP 2390: 'The case of the manufacturers and shop-keepers in Great-Britain; humbly recommended to the present Parliament'.
25   GL, MS 2649/1 (unfoliated), presentments 1737.
26   Fuller, *Gnomologia*, p. 91.
27   Haywood, *Present for a Servant-Maid*, pp. 21–2.
28   Deering, *Nottinghamia*, p. 72.
29   Clayton, *Friendly Advice to the Poor*, pp. 20–1.
30   Cavendish, *The Worlds Olio*, pp. 35–9.
31   'Gentleman', *The Gentleman's Library, Containing Rules for Conduct in all Parts of Life* (London, 1715), p. 68.
32   Ray, *Compleat Proverbs*, p. 210.
33   Michael Drayton, 'Poly-Olbion. The nineteenth Booke', in *A Chorographicall Description of all the Tracts, Rivers, Mountains, Forests and other Part of this Renowned Isle of Great Britain* (London, 1622), p. 2 [page numbering restarts with each song]. The immoral could also be compared to waste matter that rose to the surface. One upright moraliser moaned about 'the very *scum* and *refuse* of mankind': Byrom [?], *A serious disswasive*, p. 9.
34   Thomas Brown, 'The Gods on a day when their Worships were idle', in *The Works of Mr Tho. Brown* (4 vols, London, 1715–20), II, p. 226.
35   Hall, *The Loathsomnesse of Long haire*, p. 104.
36   John Spencer, *A discourse concerning vulgar prophesies wherein the vanity of receiving them . . .* (London, 1665), p. 49.
37   Trenchfield, *A Cap of Gray Hairs*, pp. 112–13, 189.
38   John Rouse Bloxam, *Magdalen College and King James II, 1686–1688*, Oxford Historical Society, 6 (Oxford, 1886), p. 215.
39   John Eliot, *Poems or Epigrams, Satyrs, Elegies, Songs and Sonnets, Upon several Persons and Occasions* (London, 1658), p. 60.
40   John Taylor, *A Bawd* (London, 1635), C1r.
41   Oldys, *The London Jilt*, p. 5.
42   Pepys, *Diary*, IX, p. 247; *OBSP*, 27 Feb.–1 Mar. 1734, p. 92.
43   Ray, *Compleat Proverbs*, p. 15; Thomas Newcomb, *The Manners of the Age: in Thirteen Moral Satirs* (London, 1733), p. 121.

44 *Twelve Ingenious Characters*, pp. 30–1.

45 Ward, *Nuptial Dialogues and Debates* (1710), I, p. 41.

46 Fuller, *Gnomologia*, p. 233.

47 Earwaker, *Manchester Court Leet Records*, various entries through various editions; Jenner, 'Circulation and disorder', p. 43; GL, MS 3018/1. Presentments for nuisances other than defective pavements and obstacles become less common after the 1690s.

48 Corporation of London, *To the Commissioners of Sewers*, pp. 10–11.

49 C[harles] W[alcot], *Considerations for the More speedy effectual Execution of the Act, for Paving, Cleansing and Lighting, the City and Liberty Of Westminster, and for Removing Annoyances therein* (London, 1763), p. 7.

50 Massie, *Essay*, p. 10.

51 Chandler, *Liverpool*, p. 410.

52 Corporation of London, *To the Commissioners of Sewers*, p. 15.

53 For a more detailed discussion of the ways in which services were gradually brought under public (or semi-public) management see Paul Slack, *From Reformation to Improvement: Public Welfare in Early Modern England: The Ford Lectures* (Oxford, 1999), p. 131.

54 Cooper, *Annals*, IV, p. 353.

55 *To the Occupiers of Houses in the Town of Cambridge* (Cambridge, 1769).

56 Henry Gunning, *Reminiscences of the University, Town, and County of Cambridge from the year 1780* (2 vols, London, 1854), I, pp. 319–22.

57 John Beckett and Catherine Smith, 'Urban renaissance and consumer revolution in Nottingham, 1688–1759', *Urban History*, 27:1 (2000), pp. 31–50 at p. 31.

58 Langford, *Public Life*, p. 448; see also Porter, 'Cleaning up the Great Wen', p. 67.

59 Lloyd, 'The Cit's Country Box'. A 'cit' was a slightly contemptuous term for a citizen.

60 *Country Gentleman's Vade Mecum*, pp. 6, 22–3.

61 Carl B. Estabrook, *Urbane and Rustic England: Cultural Ties and Social Spheres in the Provinces, 1660–1780* (Manchester, 1998), p. 256. See also Keith Thomas, *Man and the Natural World: Changing Attitudes in England, 1500–1800* (London, 1983), pp. 245–8.

62 Lloyd, 'The Cit's Country Box'.

63 Hanway, *Journal of Eight Days Journey*, p. 18. See also *The Spectator*, no. 118, 16 July 1711 [Steele].

64 Hanway, *Journal of Eight Days Journey*, p. 101.

65 Uglow, *Hogarth*, pp. 481–5.

66 Shuttleton, 'Mary Chandler's *Description of Bath* (1733)', p. 181.

67 Porter, 'Urban and rustic', p. 184.

68 Margaret Pelling, 'Skirting the city? Disease, social change and divided households in the seventeenth century', in Griffiths and Jenner, *Londinopolis*, pp. 154–75, esp. pp. 154–5. A contrary view is posed by Linda Levy Peck (who considers the early seventeenth century) in 'Building, buying and collecting in London', in Orlin, *Material London*, pp. 268–89 at pp. 273–7.

69 Cited in Port, 'West End palaces', p. 40.

70 Massie, *Essay*, p. 30.

71 See Ellis, *The Georgian Town*, p. 92.

72 Beresford, *East End, West End*, p. 125.

73 Wood, *Essay*, II, p. 347.

74 Borsay, *English Urban Renaissance*, pp. 74–9.

75 Porter, 'Urban and rustic', pp. 185–6.

76 Deering, *Nottinghamia*, pp. 6, 17, 77–8, 93–4.

77 Fuller, *Gnomologia*, p. 282.

78 Tryon, *Cleanliness in Meats*, p. 12.

79 Cogan, *Haven of Health*, p. 201.

80 Blount, *Blount's Essays*, p. 110.

81   Ibid., pp. 110–11.
82   Ramazzini, *De Morbis Artificum*, p. 137.
83   Tryon, *Tryon's Letters*, p. 121; Tryon, *Cleanliness in Meats*, p. 12.
84   Tryon, *Tryon's Letters*, pp. 4–5, 118.
85   Chris Galley, 'A model of early modern urban demography', *Economic History Review*, n.s., 48:3 (1995), pp. 448–69 at pp. 449–51; Paul Slack, 'Great and good towns 1540–1700', in Peter Clark (ed.), *The Cambridge Urban History of Britain, Volume II: 1540–1840* (Cambridge, 2000), pp. 347–76, and also John Langton, 'Urban growth and economic change: from the late seventeenth century to 1840', ibid., pp. 453–90; Sweet, *The English Town*, pp. 164–79.
86   Ray, *Compleat Proverbs*, p. 138; Fuller, *Gnomologia*, p. 282.
87   Mandeville, *Fable of the Bees* (1724), p. 91.
88   Mandeville, *Fable of the Bees* (1714), 'Preface', sig. A7r.
89   Campbell, *The London Tradesman*, p. 265–7.
90   Clavering, *An Essay on Chimneys*, p. 74.
91   Tryon, *Memoirs*, p. 47.
92   Mare and Quarrell, *Lichtenberg's Visits*, p. 111.
93   Brewer, *Pleasures of the Imagination*; Borsay, *English Urban Renaissance*.
94   Smollett, *Humphry Clinker*, II, p. 12.
95   Cited in Port, 'West End palaces', p. 35.
96   See, for example, Oldham, *The Mansfield Manuscripts*, II, pp. 882, 892.
97   Horner, 'Proper persons to deal with', p. 66.
98   Monson, *A Briefe Declaration*, p. 9.
99   Ibid., p. 21.
100 The urban historian Joyce Ellis has perceptively noted that a 'factor dulling contemporary reaction to the degradation of the environment was their imperfect understanding of the health dangers posed by the twin evils of uncontrolled industrial development and overcrowding. Noise, dirt and smoke were certainly thought of as unpleasant, but that was a venial sin when weighed against the wealth and activity of which they were an apparently inescapable symptom': Ellis, *The Georgian Town*, pp. 93–4.
101 Ibid., p. 97.
102 6 George III, ch. 70 (1766); Fawcett, *Bath Administer'd*, p. 26.
103 Mitchell and Penrose, *Letters from Bath*, p. 170.
104 Hibbert Ware, *Life and Correspondence*, p. 47; 'An Act for amending certain of the Mile-ways leading to *Oxford*', 11 George III, ch. 19: for details see Great Britain, *Statutes at Large* (1774), XI, pp. 78–109.
105 Sweet, 'Topographies of politeness', p. 361.
106 Hamlin, 'Public sphere to public health', pp. 190–1; Keith-Lucas, 'Some influences affecting sanitary legislation', p. 293.
107 Keith-Lucas, 'Some influences affecting sanitary legislation', p. 291.
108 Wright, *Clean and Decent*, p. 107.
109 Ellis, *The Georgian Town*, p. 94.
110 Alec Skempton (ed.), *Biographical Dictionary of Civil Engineers, Volume I: 1500 to 1830* (London, 2002), p. 336.
111 Tryon, *Memoirs*, p. 62.
112 Earwaker, *Court Leet Records of Manchester*, VII, p. 172; VIII, p. 112.
113 Lettsom, *Medical memoirs*, pp. 33–4; Thomas Short, *A Comparative History of the Increase and Decrease of Mankind in England* (London, 1767), p. 20; see also Porter, 'Cleaning up the Great Wen', p. 68.
114 *A Brief Description of the Cities of London and Westminster . . . by Sir John Fielding* [Fielding denied authorship of this text] (London, 1776), p. xxiii.
115 George, *London Life*, p. 10.
116 6 George III, ch. 26, in Great Britain, *Statutes at Large, from the Fifth year of King*

George the Third to the Tenth year of King George the Third (8 vols, London, 1771), VIII, pp. 231–49.

117 Noorthouck, *A new history of London*, p. 436.
118 Davis and Bonsall, *Bath*, p. 44.
119 Fawcett, *Bath Administer'd*, pp. 98, 108.
120 Borsay, *English Urban Renaissance*, pp. 67–8; Fawcett, *Bath Administer'd*, p. 54; BRO, Council Minutes Book 7, p. 332 (19 May 1760); Book 8, p. 298 (5 Jan. 1767).
121 Magdalen Bridge was in urgent need of repairs in the 1660s. By 1665 a part had fallen into the river and the rest was decaying fast. The bridge was propped up in 1666: *Oxford Council Acts 1626–1665*, pp. 223, 274, 294, 335, 405.
122 Hargreaves-Mawdsley, *Woodforde at Oxford*, p. 188; Octavius Ogle, 'The Oxford market', in Montagu Burrows (ed.), *Collectanea Second Series*, Oxford Historical Society, 16 (Oxford, 1890), pp. 1–136 at p. 43.
123 Noorthouck, *A new history of London*, p. 436.
124 Davis and Bonsall, *Bath*, p. 39.
125 Wood, *Essay*, II, p. 336.
126 Smollett, *Humphry Clinker*, I, p. 104.
127 Mitchell and Penrose, *Letters from Bath*, p. 103.
128 Cited in Fawcett, *Voices of Bath*, p. 168.
129 Cited in Guillery, *Small House*, pp. 39, 279.
130 Defoe, *Tour thro' Great Britain*, II, pp. 89–90.
131 *Proposals For Establishing a Charitable Fund in the City of London* (London, 1706), p. 19.
132 Cited in George, *London Life*, p. 98.
133 Oldham, *The Mansfield Manuscripts*, II, pp. 897–9.
134 Redford, *History of Local Government in Manchester*, I, p. 157.
135 Aikin, *A Description of Manchester*, p. 192. Aikin explains that funds intended for lamp oil were used for other purposes: 'Manchester was, as before the act, in total darkness.'
136 Sweet, *The English Town*, pp. 175–7.
137 Bowler and Brimblecombe, 'Control of air pollution in Manchester', p. 95.
138 Percival, *Philosophical, medical and experimental essays*, pp. 8–9; Aikin, *A Description of Manchester*, p. 192: Aikin remarked that 'In a house in Bootle Street, most of the inhabitants are paralytic, in consequence of their situation in a blind alley which excludes them from light and air.'
139 Hannah Barker, '"Smoke cities": northern industrial towns in late Georgian England', *Urban History*, 31:2 (2004), pp. 175–90 at p. 178.
140 Aikin, *A Description of Manchester*, p. 192.
141 Percival, *Philosophical, medical and experimental essays*, pp. 9–10.
142 J. P. Mayer (ed.), *Journeys to England and Ireland* (London, 1958), pp. 107–8.
143 Phillips, *Generosi Ludentes* (appended to his *Mysteries of Love and Eloquence*), pp. 31–3 (sigs X8–X8v).

Select Bibliography

The select bibliography lists sources mentioned more than once.

Manuscript Sources

Bath Central Library
MS B914–238 'MS account of a tour in several English Counties in 1725, including a description of Bath and Beau Nash'.

Bath Record Office
Council Minutes, transcription of volume I by Rev. Shickle.
Council Minutes Books 1–9.
Quarter Sessions Book 1743–1776.

Chetham's Library, Manchester
Mun A.2.137 'Edmund Harrold: His Book of R[e]m[ar]ks 1712 & ob[servation]s'.
Mun A.2.140 'Diary of Henry Newcome of Manchester Sept 30, 1661 to Sept 29, 1663'.

Corporation of London Record Office
COL/SJ/27/465 Viewers' Presentments, 1623–1636.
Misc. MSS 58/35, 'Committee investigating nuisances committed by Bridewell Boys in early 18th century'; 'Information ab[out] Bridewell boys taken 11 Nove 1715'.
Repertories of the Court of Aldermen – Reps 78–9, 121, 126 (1671–1722).

Guildhall Library, London
MS 68 Vintry Ward Wardmote Inquest Minutes, 1687–1774.
MS 2649/1 Portsoken Ward Wardmote Inquest Minute Book, 1684–1798.
MS 3018/1 St Dunstans-in-the-West Wardmote Inquest, 1558–1823.
MS 4069/1 Cornhill Wardmote Inquest Minute Book, 1571–1651.
MS 4069/2 Cornhill Wardmote Inquest Minute Book, 1652–1733.
MS 4069/3 Cornhill Wardmote Inquest Minute Book, 1734–1800.
MS 4829 Queenhithe Wardmote Inquest Book, 1667–1746.
MS 7090/4 Court Minutes of the Pewterers' Company, 1611–1646.
MS 12,071/5 The Armourers' and Braziers' Company Court Minutes, 1719–1733.
MS 12,071/6 The Armourers' and Braziers' Company Court Minutes, 1733–1746.
MS 22,207 'The humble petition of the Coppersmiths being freemen of London and many of them of this Company' (c.1600).

London Metropolitan Archives
MJ/OC/II, V   Orders of the Court of Middlesex 1730, 1744.
MJ/SBB/133   Middlesex Sessions of the Peace Book, 1654 (Microfilm X71/60).
MJ/SBB/424   Middlesex Sessions of the Peace Book, 1684–1685.
MJ/SBR/1   Middlesex Sessions Register, 1608–1613.
MJ/SR/541, 1252, 1336, 1663, 2363, 2376   Middlesex Sessions of the Peace Rolls
  (1615–1721).

Newspapers, Periodicals and Printed Ephemera

The Gentleman's Magazine, 1731.
Harrop's Manchester Mercury and General Advertiser, 1756.
The Manchester Mercury and Harrop's General Advertiser, 1757–1767.
The Spectator, nos 118–631.
The Tatler, nos 1–68.

Chetham's Library, Halliwell-Phillips Collection
HP 1239   'William Trunkett, at the Young Civet Cat, without Temple Bar, London,
  perfumer . . .' (London, c.1732).
HP 2106   'A just and exact account taken out of the books of several brickmakers, lime-
  burners, tilemakers, slaters, masons, and paviers: of the goods made, or brought by
  them . . . Humbly offer'd to the consideration of the Honourable House' (London,
  1712?).
HP 2122   'Some of the abuses complained of at Billingsgate, Bear-Key, and other publick
  markets within the City of London: humbly offer'd to the consideration of the
  Honourable House of Commons for redress'.
HP 2182   'Some Considerations humbly offer'd to the Honourable House of Commons
  by the tallow-chandlers in and about the cities of London and Westminster' (n.d., early
  eighteenth century).
HP 2390   'The case of the manufacturers and shop-keepers in Great-Britain; humbly
  recommended to the present Parliament' (London, 1730).

Published Contemporary Works

Aikin, John, *A Description of the Country from thirty to forty Miles round Manchester* (London,
  1795).
Amhurst, N[icholas], *Terrae Filius: or, the Secret History of the University of Oxford; in Several
  Essays* (2 vols, London, 1726).
*The art of governing a wife: with rules for batchelors. To which is added, an essay against unequal
  marriages* (Anon.) (London, 1747).
Bacon, Francis, *The Essayes or Counsels, civill and morall* (London, 1625).
Bailey, Nathaniel, *An Universal Etymological English Dictionary* (London, 1721).
——— *Dictionarium Britannicum: or a more compleat universal etymological English dictionary
  than any extant* (London, 1736).
——— *A Universal Etymological English Dictionary* (Anon.) (London, 1742).
The Bath and Bristol Guide: or, trademan's, and traveller's pocket-companion (Anon.) (Bath,
  1753).
Blackstone, William, *Commentaries on the Laws of England*, 4th edn (4 vols, Oxford, 1770).
Blount, Thomas, *Glossographia: or a dictionary, interpreting all such hard words, whether
  Hebrew, Greek, Latin, Italian, Spanish, French, Teutonick, Belgick, British or Saxon*
  (London, 1656).
Blount, Thomas Pope, *Sir Thomas Pope Blount's Essays on Several Subjects* (London, 1697).

Bond, J., *A Compleat Guide for Justices of the Peace. In two parts* (London, 1707).

Brathwaite, Richard, *Essaies upon the Five Senses, with a pithie one upon detraction* (London, 1620).

—— *Whimzies: or, a new cast of characters* (London, 1631).

Breton, Nicholas, *Fantasticks: serving for a Perpetuall Prognostication* (London, 1626).

Brown, Tom, *Amusements Serious and Comical. Calculated for the Meridian of London* (London, 1700).

Buchan, William, *Domestic Medicine: or, a treatise on the prevention and cure of diseases by regimen and simple medicines*, 2nd edn (London, 1772).

Burn, Richard, *The Justice of the Peace, and Parish Officer* (2 vols, London, 1755).

Burnaby, William, *The Reform'd Wife. A Comedy: As it is Acted, At the Theatre-Royal in Drury-Lane* (London, 1700).

Bury, Edward, *England's Bane, or, The Deadly Danger of Drunkenness Described* (London, 1677).

Byrom, Edward [?], *A Serious Disswasive from an intended subscription, for continuing the races upon Kersal Moore. Address'd to the inhabitants of Manchester*, 3rd edn (Manchester, 1733).

Cambridge, City of, *Whereas divers disordered people inhabiting amongst us, not regarding the good of this University and Town of Cambridge . . .* (Cambridge, 1635).

Campbell, R., *The London Tradesman; being a compendious view of all the trades, professions, arts, both liberal and mechanic now practised in the cities of London and Westminster* (London, 1747).

The Case of Edmund Heming (Anon.) (London, 1689).

Cavendish, Margaret [The Duchess of Newcastle], *The Worlds Olio* (London, 1655).

Chandler, Mary, *The Description of Bath. A Poem*, 7th edn (London, 1755).

Chesterfield, Earl of, *Letters written by the Late Right Honourable Philip Dormer Stanhope, Earl of Chesterfield, to his son* (2 vols, London, 1774).

'A Citizen', *A Candid Remonstrance to the Vice-Chancellor . . . City of Oxford* (London, 1764).

Clavering, Robert, *An Essay on the Construction and Building of Chimneys* (London, 1779).

Clayton, John, *Friendly Advice to the Poor; Written and Publish'd at the Request of the late and present officers of the Town of Manchester* (Manchester, 1755).

Cleland, John, *Memoirs of a woman of pleasure* (2 vols, London, 1749).

Cogan, Thomas, *The Haven of Health. Chiefly gathered for the comfort of students, and consequently of all those that have a care of their health*, 2nd edn (London, 1636).

Collins, Emanuel, *Lying Detected; or, some of the most frightful untruths that ever alarmed the British Metropolis, fairly exposed* (Bristol, 1758).

Coma Berenices; or, The Hairy Comet (Anon.) (London, 1674).

Cook, Ann, *Professed Cookery: containing boiling, roasting, pastry, preserving, pickling, potting, made-wines, gellies, and part of confectionaries*, 3rd edn (London, *c.*1760).

Cotgrave, Randle, *A Dictionarie of the French and English Tongues* (London, 1611).

The Country Gentleman's Vade Mecum for his Comparison for the Town (Anon.) (London, 1699).

Dalton, Michael, *The Countrey Justice. Conteyning the practise of the Justices of the peace out of their sessions* (London, 1618).

—— *The Country Justice: containing The Practice, Duty and Power of The Justices of the Peace, As well in as out of the their sessions* [eighteenth-century revised edition of the original, from 1618] (London, 1742).

Deering, Charles, *Nottinghamia Vetus at Nova or an Historical Account of the Ancient and Present State of the town of Nottingham* (Nottingham, 1751), reprinted as *The History of Nottingham by Charles Deering* (Wakefield, 1970).

Defoe, Daniel [pseud. Andrew Moreton], *Every-Body's Business is No-Body's Business; Or, Private Abuses, Publick Grievances* (London, 1725).

Defoe, Daniel, *A Tour Thro' the Whole Island of Great Britain*, 3rd edn (4 vols, London, 1742).

The Diseases of Bath. A Satire, unadorn'd with a frontispiece (Anon.) (London, 1737).

Dunton, John, *A Voyage around the World or, A pocket-library divided into several volumes* (London, 1691).

Earle, John, *Micro-cosmographie. Or, a Peece of the World Discovered; in Essays and Characters* (London, 1628).

Ellis, William, *The Country Housewife's Family Companion: or, profitable directions for whatever relates to the management . . . of the domestic concerns of a country life* (London, 1750).

England and Wales, *The Statutes at Large, Beginning with the Seventh and Eighth Year of the Reign of King William III* (3 vols, London, 1706).

Essays and Letters on Various Subjects (Anon.) (London, 1739).

Evelyn, John, *Fumifugium: or the inconvenience of the aer and smoak of London dissipated* (London, 1661).

Fielding, Henry, *The Temple Beau. A Comedy. As it is Acted at the Theatre in Goodman's-Fields* (London, 1730).

—— *The Intriguing Chambermaid. A comedy of two acts* (London, 1734).

—— *The Works of Henry Fielding Esq. with the life of the author* (4 vols, London, 1762).

Fuller, Thomas, *Gnomologia: Adagies and Proverbs; Wise Sentences and Witty Sayings, Ancient and Modern, Foreign and British* (London, 1732).

Gay, John, *Trivia: or, the art of walking the streets of London* (London, 1716).

'Gentleman of the Temple', *Public nusance considered under the several heads of bad pavements, butchers infesting the streets . . .* (London, 1754).

Gerard, Alexander, *An Essay on Taste. To which is added part fourth, of the standard of taste; with observations concerning the imitative nature of poetry*, 3rd edn (Edinburgh, 1780).

Glasse, Hannah, *The Art of Cookery, made Plain and Easy; Which far exceeds any Thing of the Kind ever yet Published* (London, 1747).

Graunt, John, *London's Dreadful Visitation* (London, 1665).

Great Britain, *The Statutes at Large, From the Thirtieth Year of the Reign of King George the Second To the End of the Second Year of the Reign of King George the Third* (8 vols, London 1768–70).

—— *The Statutes at Large from the Tenth year of King George the Third to the Thirteenth year of King George III* (11 vols, London, 1774).

Great Britain, Court of King's Bench, *Reports of Cases Adjudged in the Court of King's Bench* (3 vols, London, 1731–2).

Grose, Francis, *The Olio: Being a Collection of Essays etc.* (London, 1792).

Gwynn, John, *London and Westminster Improved, illustrated by plans* (London, 1766).

Hall, Thomas, *Comarum akosmia, the Loathsomnesse of Long haire* (London, 1654).

Hanway, Jonas, *A Letter to Mr. John Spranger, On his excellent Proposal for Paving, cleansing, and lighting the Streets of Westminster, and the Parishes in Middlesex* (London, 1754).

—— *A Journal of Eight Days Journey from Portsmouth to Kingston upon Thames* (London, 1756).

Hawkins, William, *A Treatise of the Pleas of the Crown: or, a System of the Principal Matters relating to that Subject, digested under their Proper Heads*, 4th edn (2 vols, London, 1762).

Haywood, Eliza, *A Present for a Servant-Maid: or, the sure means of gaining love and esteem* (London, 1743).

Hell upon Earth: or the Town in an Uproar (Anon.) (London, 1729).

Herbert, George, *Outlandish Proverbs, Selected by Mr G.H.* (London, 1640).

—— *Jacula Prudentum – Or Outlandish proverbs, sentences &c* (London, 1651).

Heywood, Thomas, *Philocothomista; or, the Drunkard, Opened, Dissected, and Anatomized* (London, 1635).

Hibbert Ware, Mrs, *The Life and Correspondence of the late Samuel Hibbert Ware* (Manchester, 1882).

Holme, Randle, *The Academy of Armory, or, A storehouse of armory and blazon* (Chester, 1688).

Hooke, Robert, *The Posthumous Works of Robert Hooke* (London, 1705).

Huddesford, William, *An address to the Freemen and other inhabitants of the City of Oxford* (Oxford, 1764).

Jacob, Giles, *Every man his own lawyer: or, a summary of the laws of England in a new and instructive method*, 2nd edn (London, 1737).

Johnson, Samuel, *A Dictionary of the English Language* (London, 1755).

Jones, Erasmus, *The Man of Manners: or, Plebeian Polish'd*, 2nd edn (London, 1737).

Jonson, Ben, *Epicoene, or The Silent Woman. A Comedie* (London, 1620).

Kames, Lord (Henry Home), *Elements of Criticism* (3 vols, Edinburgh, 1762).

Lettsom, John Coakley, *Medical memoirs of the General Dispensary in London, for part of the years 1773 and 1774* (London, 1774).

Lloyd, Robert, 'The Cit's Country Box' (1757), in *Poems by Robert Lloyd, A. M.* (London, 1762).

London, 'Citizen and native of', *A new and compleat survey of London in ten parts* (2 vols, London, 1742).

London, Corporation of, *The Lawes of the Market* (London, 1595).

London, Corporation of, *To the Honourable Commissioners of the Sewers of the City of London* (London, 1765).

London, Court of Common Council, *An Act of the Common Councel made the eleventh day of September, in the yeare of our Lord 1655. For the better avoiding and prevention of annoyances within the city of London, and liberties of the same* (London, 1655).

Mace, Thomas, *Profit, Conveniency, and Pleasure, to the whole nation being a short rational discourse, lately presented to his Majesty, concerning the high-ways of England* (London, 1675).

Magalotti, Lorenzo, *Travels of Cosmo the Third, Grand Duke of Tuscany, through England, during the Reign of King Charles the Second*, ed. Joseph Mawman (London, 1821).

Mandeville, Bernard, *The Fable of the Bees: or, private vices publick benefits* (London, 1714).

—— *The Fable of the Bees: or, private vices, publick benefits*, 3rd edn (London, 1724).

Massie, J[oseph], *An Essay on the many Advantages accruing to the Community, from the superior neatness, Conveniencies, Decorations and Embellishments of Great and Capital Cities* (London, 1754).

Mead, Richard, *A Short Discourse Concerning Pestilential Contagion, and the Methods To be used to Prevent it* (London, 1720).

'Miso-spilus', *A Wonder of Wonders: or, A metamorphosis of Fair Faces voluntarily transformed into foul Visages, or, an Invective against Black-spotted Faces* (London, 1662).

Monson, Robert, *A Briefe Declaration for What manner of Speciall Nusance concerning private dwelling Houses, a man may have his remedy by Assize, or other Actions as the Case requires*, 2nd edn (London, 1639).

Neve, Richard, *The City and Countrey Purchaser, and builder's dictionary; or, the compleat builder's guide* (London, 1703).

A new and compleat history and survey of the cities of London and Westminster (Anon.) (London, 1769).

Noorthouck, John, *A new history of London, including Westminster and Southwark* (London, 1773).

Oldys, Alexander, *The London Jilt, or, the Politick whore* (London, 1683).

Overbury, Thomas, *Sir Thomas Overburie His Wife, with new elegies upon his (now knowne) untimely death: whereunto are annexed, new newes and characters*, 7th edn (London, n.d., c.1614).

Percival, Thomas, *Philosophical, medical and experimental essays* (London, 1776).

Phillips, Edward, *The Mysteries of Love and Eloquence, or, the arts of wooing and complementing* (London, 1658).

Playford, Henry, *Wit and mirth: or pills to purge melancholy: being a collection of the best merry ballads and songs, old and new*, 2nd edn (London, 1705).

Pope, Alexander, *The Works of Alexander Pope* (3 vols, London, 1736).

Ray, John, *A Compleat Collection of English Proverbs; also the most celebrated proverbs of the*

Scotch, Italian, French, Spanish and other languages, 3rd edn (London, 1737).

Richardson, Samuel, *The History of Sir Charles Grandison in a series of letters*, 3rd edn (7 vols, London, 1754).

Salmon, [Thomas], *The Present State of the Universities and of the five adjacent counties* (London, *c*.1744).

Saltonstall, Wye, *Picturae Loquentes. Or Pictures Drawen forth in Characters. With a Poeme of a Maid* (London, 1631).

Satan's Harvest Home (Anon.) (London, 1749).

A satyr upon old maids (Anon.) (London, 1713).

Seaton, Thomas, *The Conduct of Servants in Great Families* (London, 1720).

Sheppard, William, *The Offices of Constables, Church-Wardens, Overseers of the Poor, Supravisors of the High-Wayes, Treasurers of the County-Stock; and some other lesser Country officers plainly and lively set forth* (London, 1650).

—— *A sure guide for his Majesties Justices of Peace* (London, 1669).

Smith, E[liza], *The Complete Housewife: or, accomplished gentlewoman's companion*, 17th edn (London, 1766).

Smollett, Tobias, *The expedition of Humphry Clinker* (3 vols, London, 1771).

Southall, John, *Treatise of Buggs* (London, 1730).

Stow, John, *A Survay of London* (London, 1598).

Stow John, [updated by John Strype], *A Survay of the Cities of London and Westminster: Containing The Original, Antiquity, Increase, Modern Estate and Government of those Cities* (2 vols, London, 1720).

Strange, John, *Reports of Adjudged Cases in the Courts of Chancery, King's Bench, Common Pleas and Exchequer, from Trinity term in the second year of King George I to Trinity term in the twenty-first year of King George II* (2 vols, London, 1755).

Stubbes, Phillip, *The Anatomie of Abuses: Contayning a Discoverie or Briefe Summarie of such Notable Vices and Imperfections as now raigne in many Christian Countreyes of the Worlde . . .* (London, 1583).

Swift, Jonathan, *Journal to Stella* (covers 1710–13), ed. H. Williams (2 vols, Oxford, 1974).

—— *Miscellanies in Prose and Verse* (London, 1711).

—— *Directions to Servants in General* (London, 1745).

Trenchfield, Caleb, *A Cap of Gray Hairs for a Green Head* (London, 1671).

Tryon, Thomas, *A Treatise of Cleanliness in Meats and Drinks* (London, 1682).

—— *Wisdom Dictates: or, aphorisms & rules* (London, 1691).

—— *A Pocket-companion containing things necessary to be known by all that values their health and happiness being a plain way of nature's own prescribing, to cure most diseases in men, women and children, by kitchen-physick only* (London, 1694).

—— *Thomas Tryon's Letters upon Several Occasions* (London, 1700).

—— *Some Memoirs of the Life of Mr Thomas Tryon, Late of London, Merchant: written by himself* (London, 1705).

Twelve Ingenious Characters: or, Pleasant Descriptions of the properties of Sundry Persons and Things (Anon.) (London, 1686).

Ward, Edward [Ned], *The Insinuating Bawd: and the Repenting Harlot* (London, 1700),.

—— 'A Step to Bath', in *The Reformer. Exposing the Vices of the Age in several Characters*, 4th edn (London, *c*.1701).

—— *The London-Spy, Compleat, in eighteen parts*, 4th edn (2 vols, London, 1709).

—— *Nuptial Dialogues and Debates, or an useful prospect of the felicities and discomforts of a marry'd life* (2 vols, London, 1710).

—— *Field Spy: or, the Walking Observator. A poem* (London, 1714).

—— *Hudibras Redivivus: or a burlesque poem on the times*, 3rd edn (2 vols, London, 1715).

—— *Hudibras Redivivus: or, a Burlesque poem on the Times. In Twenty four Parts*, 4th edn (London, 1722).

—— *Nuptial Dialogues and Debates: Or, An Useful Prospect of the Felicities and Discomforts of a Marry'd Life*, 3rd edn (2 vols, London, 1723).

——— 'The Merry Travellers: or, A trip upon Ten-Toes, from Moorfields to Bromley. Part 1', in *The Wandring Spy: or, the Merry Observator* (London, 1729).

——— 'The Dancing Devils', in *The Wandring Spy: or, the Merry Observator* (London, 1729).

Ware, Isaac, *A Complete Body of Architecture adorned with plans and elevations, from original designs* (London, 1768).

Wecker, [Johann Jacob], *Cosmeticks: or, The Beautifying Part of Physick* (London, 1660).

Wits Cabinet: or, a companion for Young Men and Ladies, 8th edn (London, 1698).

Wood, John, *An Essay towards a Description of Bath*, 2nd edn (2 vols, London, 1749).

Edited Primary Sources

Bachrach, A. G. H. and Collmer, R. G. (eds), *The English Journal 1651–1652: Lodewijck Huygens* (Leiden, 1982).

Baker, J. H. and Milsom, S. F. C., *Sources of English Legal History: Private Law to 1750* (London, 1986).

Beer, E. S. de (ed.), *The Diary of John Evelyn* (6 vols, Oxford, 1955).

Bold, J., 'The design of a house for a merchant, 1724', *Architectural History: Journal of the Society of Architectural Historians of Great Britain*, 33 (1990), pp. 75–82 .

Chandler, George (ed.), *Liverpool under Charles I* (Liverpool, 1965).

Chinnery, G. A. (ed.), *Records of the Borough of Leicester, Volume VII: Judicial and Allied Records 1689–1835* (Leicester, 1974).

Clark, Andrew (ed.), *Wood's City of Oxford, Volume I: City and Suburbs*, Oxford Historical Society, 15 (Oxford, 1889).

——— *The Life and Times of Anthony à Wood, Antiquary, of Oxford, 1632–1695, described by himself* (5 vols), Oxford Historical Society, 19, 21, 26, 30, 40 (Oxford, 1891–1900).

Colvin, Howard and Newman, John (eds), *Of Building: Roger North's Writings on Architecture* (Oxford, 1981).

Cooper, Charles Henry, *Annals of Cambridge by Charles Henry Cooper (Coroner of the Town)* (5 vols, Cambridge, 1842–53).

Davies, Godfrey (ed.), *The Autobiography of Thomas Raymond and memoirs of the family of Guise of Elmore, Gloucestershire*, Camden Society, 3rd Ser., 28 (London, 1917).

Earwaker, J. P. (ed.), *The Court Leet Records of the Manor of Manchester* (12 vols, Manchester, 1884–90).

——— *The Constables' Accounts of the Manor of Manchester from the Year 1612 to the Year 1647 and from the Year 1743 to the Year 1776* (3 vols, Manchester, 1891–2).

Exwood, Maurice and Lehmann, H. L. (eds and trans), *The Journal of William Schellinks' Travels in England 1661–1663*, Camden 5th ser., 1 (London, 1993).

Fox, Levi (ed.), *Coventry Constables' Presentments, 1629–1742*, Publications of the Dugdale Society, 34 (Stratford-upon-Avon, 1986).

Furnivall, Frederick J., *Phillip Stubbes's Anatomy of the Abuses in England in Shakspere's Youth, A.D. 1593*, The New Shakspere Society, 4 (London, 1877–9).

Galloway, David (ed.), *Norwich, 1540–1642*, Records of Early English Drama (Toronto, 1984).

Hardy, W. J. (ed.), *Middlesex County Records. Calendar of the Sessions Books 1689–1709* (London, 1905).

Hardy, William Le, *Calendar to the Sessions Records. New Series (Middlesex Quarter Sessions 1612–18)* (4 vols, London, 1935–41).

Hargreaves-Mawdsley, W. N. (ed.), *Woodforde at Oxford 1759–1776*, Oxford Historical Society, n.s., 21 (Oxford, 1969).

Harland, John (ed.) 'Diary of a Manchester wig-maker 1712–15', in *Collectanea relating to Manchester and its Neighbourhood at Various Periods*, Chetham Society, o.s., 68 (Manchester, 1866).

——— 'The old market place and neighbouring streets in 1772', in *Collectanea relating to Manchester and its Neighbourhood at Various Periods, Volume II*, Chetham Society, o.s., 72 (Manchester, 1867).

Hearnshaw, F. J. C. and Hearnshaw, D. M. (eds), *Court Leet Records, Volume I, Part III A.D. 1603–1624*, Publications of the Southampton Record Society, 4 (Southampton, 1907).

Hobson, M. G. (ed.), *Oxford Council Acts 1665–1701*, Oxford Historical Society, n.s., 2 (Oxford, 1939).

Hobson, M. G. and Salter, H. E. (eds), *Oxford Council Acts 1626–1665*, Oxford Historical Society, 95 (Oxford, 1933).

Jeaffreson, John Cordy (ed.), *Middlesex County Records*, Middlesex County Record Society (4 vols, London, 1886–92).

Kielmansegg, Countess (trans.), *Diary of a Journey to England in the years 1761–1762* (London, 1902).

Lucas, Joseph (trans.), *Kalm's Account of his Visit to England on his way to America in 1748* (London, 1892).

Manchée, W. H., *The Westminster City Fathers (the Burgess Court of Westminster) 1585–1901: being some account of their powers and domestic rule of the City prior to its incorporation in 1901* (London, 1924).

Mare, Margaret L. and Quarrell, W. H. (eds and trans.), *Lichtenberg's Visits to England as described in his Letters and Diaries* (Oxford, 1938).

Matthews, W. (ed.), *The Diary of Dudley Ryder, 1715–1716* (London, 1939).

Matthews, William and Latham, Robert (eds), *The Diary of Samuel Pepys* (11 vols, London, 1970–83).

Mitchell, Brigitte and Penrose, Hubert (eds), *Letters from Bath 1766–1767 by the Rev. John Penrose* (Gloucester, 1983).

Muyden, Madame Van (ed. and trans.), *A Foreign view of England in the reigns of George I and George II. The Letters of Monsieur César de Saussure to his family* (London, 1902).

Parkinson, Richard (ed.), *The Private Journal and Literary Remains of John Byrom, Volume I, Part I (1707–1728)*, Chetham Society, o.s., 32 (Manchester, 1854).

——— *The Private Journal and Literary Remains of John Byrom, Volume I, part II (1729–1735)*, Chetham Society, o.s., 34 (Manchester, 1855).

Pottle, Frederick A. (ed.), *Boswell's London Journal, 1762–1763* (London, 1985).

Power, Michael (ed.), *Liverpool Town Books 1649–1671*, Record Society of Lancashire and Cheshire, 136 (1999).

Quarrell, W. H. and Mare, Margaret (eds), *London in 1710, from the travels of von Uffenbach* (London, 1934).

Ramazzini, Bernardino, *De Morbis Artificum [diseases of workers]. The Latin Text of 1713*, Revised with translation and notes, ed. and trans. Wilmer Cave Wright (Chicago, 1940).

Robinson, Henry W. and Adams, Walter (eds), *The Diary of Robert Hooke F.R.S., 1672–1680* (London, 1935).

Sachse, William L. (ed.), *Minutes of the Norwich Court of Mayoralty 1630–1631*, The Norfolk Record Society, 15 (London, 1942).

Salter, H. E. (ed.), *A Cartulary of the Hospital of St John the Baptist, Volume I*, Oxford Historical Society, 66 (Oxford, 1914).

——— *A Cartulary of the Hospital of St John the Baptist, Volume III*, Oxford Historical Society, 69 (Oxford, 1917).

——— *Surveys and Tokens*, Oxford Historical Society, 75 (Oxford, 1923).

——— *Oxford City Properties*, Oxford Historical Society, 83 (Oxford, 1926).

——— *Oxford Council Acts 1583–1626*, Oxford Historical Society, 87 (Oxford, 1928).

Schofield, John (ed.), *The London Surveys of Ralph Treswell* (London, 1987).

Stanford, Maureen (ed.), *The Ordinances of Bristol 1506–1598*, Bristol Record Society Publications, 41 (1990).

Williams, Clare (ed.), *Thomas Platter's Travels in England 1599* (London, 1937).

Willis, Arthur J. and Hoad, Margaret J. (eds), *Portsmouth Borough Sessions Papers,*

1653–1688. A Calendar, Portsmouth Record Series, I (London and Chichester, 1971).

Willis Bund, J. W. (ed.), *Worcester County Records: the Quarter Sessions Rolls. Part 1. Kalendar to the Sessions Rolls 1591–1621*, Publications of the Worcestershire Historical Society, 11 (1899).

Woodcroft, Bennet, *Alphabetical Index of Patentees of Inventions*, revised edn (London, 1969).

Secondary Sources

Atherton, Herbert M., 'The "mob" in eighteenth-century English caricature', *Eighteenth Century Studies*, 12:1 (1978), pp. 47–58.

Ayres, James, *Building the Georgian City* (London, 1998).

Bailey, Peter, 'Breaking the sound barrier: a historian listens to noise', *Body and Society*, 2 (1996), pp. 49–66.

Baker, Herbert G., *Plants and Civilization*, 2nd edn (London, 1970).

Beresford, Maurice, *East End, West End: The Face of Leeds during Urbanisation, 1684–1842*, The Publications of the Thoresby Society, 60 (1988).

Blackwell, Mark, '"Extraneous bodies": the contagion of live-tooth transplantation in late-eighteenth-century England', *Eighteenth-Century Life*, 28:1 (2004), pp. 21–68.

Borsay, Peter, *The English Urban Renaissance: Culture and Society in the Provincial Town 1660–1770* (Oxford, 1989).

Bowler C. and Brimblecombe, P., 'Control of air pollution in Manchester prior to the Public Health Act, 1875', *Environment and History*, 6:1 (2000), pp. 71–98.

Bradshaw, L. D., *Origins of Street Names in the City Centre of Manchester* (Manchester, 1985).

Brenner, Joel Franklin, 'Nuisance law and the industrial revolution', *Journal of Legal Studies*, 3:2 (1974), pp. 403–33.

Brewer, John, *The Pleasures of the Imagination: The Emergence of English Culture in the Eighteenth Century* (London, 1997).

Brimblecombe, Peter, *The Big Smoke: A History of Air Pollution in London since Medieval Times* (London, 1987).

Chalklin, Christopher, *The Provincial Towns of Georgian England: A Study of the Building Process, 1740–1820* (London, 1974).

—— *The Rise of the English Town, 1650–1850* (Cambridge, 2001).

Cockayne, Emily, 'A cultural history of sound in England 1560–1760', Ph.D. thesis, Cambridge University, 2000.

—— 'Cacophony, or vile scrapers on vile instruments: bad music in early modern English towns', *Urban History*, 29:1 (2002), pp. 35–47.

—— 'Experiences of the deaf in early modern England', *Historical Journal*, 46:3 (2003), pp. 493–510.

Cole, Catherine, 'Carfax conduit', *Oxoniensia*, 29–30 (1964–5, published in 1966), pp. 142–166.

Cook, Harold, 'Policing the health of London: the College of Physicians and the early Stuart monarchy', *Social History of Medicine*, 2:1 (1989), pp. 1–33.

Corfield, Penelope, 'Walking the city streets. the urban odyssey in eighteenth-century England', *Journal of Urban History*, 16 (1990), pp. 132–74.

Cox, Margaret, *Life and Death in Spitalfields 1700 to 1850* (York, 1996).

Crossley, Alan, 'City and university', in Nicholas Tyacke (ed.), *The History of the University of Oxford, Volume 4: Seventeenth-Century Oxford* (Oxford, 1997), pp. 105–34.

Cruickshank, Dan, *Georgian Town Houses and their Details* (London, 1990).

Cunnington, C. Willett and Cunnington, Phillis, *Handbook of English Costume in the Eighteenth Century* (London, 1964).

Cunnington, Phillis and Lucas, Catherine, *Occupational Costume in England from the*

Eleventh Century to 1914 (London, 1967).

Davis, Graham and Bonsall, Penny, *Bath: A New History* (Keele, 1996).

Dillon, Maureen, *Artificial Sunshine: A Social History of Domestic Lighting* (London, 2002).

Doughty, Oswald, 'A Bath poetess of the eighteenth-century', *Review of English Studies*, 1:4 (1925), pp. 404–20.

Downes, Kerry, *Hawksmoor* (London, 1959).

Drummond, Jack Cecil and Wilbraham, Anne, *The Englishman's Food: A History of Five Centuries of English Diet. Revised and with a new chapter by Dorothy Hollingsworth* (London, 1957).

Ekirch, A. Roger, *At Day's Close: A History of Nighttime* (London, 2005).

Ellis, Joyce, *The Georgian Town, 1680–1840* (Basingstoke, 2001).

Eveleigh, David J., *Bogs, Baths and Basins: The Story of Domestic Sanitation* (Stroud, 2002).

Fawcett, Trevor, 'Chair transport in Bath: the Sedan era', *Bath History*, 2 (1988), pp. 113–37.

—— *Voices of Eighteenth-Century Bath: An Anthology of Contemporary Texts Illustrating Events, Daily Life and Attitudes at Britain's Leading Georgian Spa* (Bath, 1995).

—— *Bath Administer'd: Corporation Affairs at the Eighteenth-Century Spa* (Bath, 2001).

—— *Bath Commercialis'd: Shops, Trades and Markets at the Eighteenth-Century Spa* (Bath, 2002).

Filby, F. A., *A History of Food Adulteration and Analysis* (London, 1934).

Fussell, G. E., The *English Dairy Farmer, 1500–1900* (London, 1966).

George, M. D., *London Life in the Eighteenth Century*, 2nd edn (London, 1930).

Gill, Harry, 'Nottingham in the eighteenth century especially with reference to domestic architecture', *Transactions of the Thoroton Society of Nottinghamshire*, 16 (1912), pp. 41–90.

Gilman, Sander L., *Making the Body Beautiful: A Cultural History of Aesthetic Surgery* (Princeton, NJ, 1999).

Gomme, L. and Norman, P. (London County Council), *The Survey of London III. The Parish of St Giles-in-the-Fields, Part I: Lincoln's Inn Fields* (London, 1912).

Gowing, Laura, *Domestic Dangers: Women, Words and Sex in Early Modern London* (Oxford, 1996).

—— *Common Bodies: Women, Touch, and Power in Seventeenth-Century England* (London, 2003).

Griffiths, Paul and Jenner, Mark S. R. (eds), *Londinopolis: Essays in the Cultural and Social History of Early Modern London* (Manchester, 2000).

Guillery, Peter, *The Small House in Eighteenth-Century London: A Social and Architectural History* (New Haven, CT, and London, 2004).

Guillery Peter and Herman, Bernard, 'Deptford houses 1650–1800', *Vernacular Architecture*, 30 (1999), pp. 58–84.

Gunther, R. T. (ed.), *The Architecture of Sir Roger Pratt* (Oxford, 1928).

Hamlin, Christopher, 'Public sphere to public health: the transformation of nuisance', in Simon Sturdy (ed.), *Medicine, Health and the Public Sphere in Britain, 1600–2000* (London, 2002), pp. 189–204.

Harris, George, *The Life of Lord Chancellor Hardwicke* (3 vols, London, 1847).

Hatcher, John and Cardwell Barker, Theodore (eds), *A History of British Pewter* (London, 1974).

Horner, Craig Andrew, '"Proper persons to deal with": identification and attitudes of middling society in Manchester, *c*.1730–*c*.1760', Ph.D. thesis, Manchester Metropolitan University, 2001.

Jenner, Mark S. R., 'The great dog massacre', in W. Naphy and P. Roberts (eds), *Fear in Early Modern Society* (Manchester, 1997), pp. 44–61.

—— 'Circulation and disorder: London streets and Hackney coaches, *c*.1640–*c*.1740', in Tim Hitchcock and Heather Shore (eds), *The Streets of London: From the Great Fire to the Great Stink* (London, 2003), pp. 40–58.

Jones, P. E. (ed.), *The Worshipful Company of Poulterers of the City of London: A Short History*, 2nd edn (London, 1965).

—— *The Butchers of London: A History of the Worshipful Company of Butchers of the City of London* (London, 1976).

Keith-Lucas, B., 'Some influences affecting the development of sanitary legislation in England', *Economic History Review*, 2nd ser., 6:3 (1954), pp. 290–6.

King, Frank A., *Beer has a History* (London, *c*.1947).

King, Walter, 'How high is too high? Disposing of dung in seventeenth-century Prescot', *Sixteenth-Century Journal*, 23 (1992), pp. 443–57.

Lane, Maggie, *Jane Austen and Food* (London, 1995).

Langford, Paul, *A Polite and Commercial People: England, 1727–1783* (Oxford, 1989).

—— *Public Life and the Propertied Englishman, 1689–1798: The Ford Lectures* (Oxford, 1991).

Laugero, Greg, 'Infrastructures of enlightenment: road-making, the public sphere, and the emergence of literature', *Eighteenth Century Studies*, 29:1 (1995), pp. 45–67.

Lemire, Beverly, 'The theft of clothes and popular consumerism in early modern England', *Journal of Social History*, 24 (1990), pp. 255–76.

Lewis, Jeremy, *Tobias Smollett* (London, 2003).

Lowe, Donald M., *The History of Bourgeois Perception* (Chicago, 1982).

Lowe, N. F., 'Hogarth, beauty spots, and sexually transmitted diseases', *British Journal for Eighteenth-Century Studies*, 15:1 (1992), pp. 71–9.

—— 'The meaning of venereal disease in Hogarth's graphic art', in Linda E. Merians, *The Secret Malady: Venereal Disease in Eighteenth-Century Britain and France* (Lexington, KY, 1996), pp. 168–82.

McIntyre, Sylvia, 'Bath: the rise of a resort town 1600–1800', in Peter Clark (ed.), *Country Towns in Pre-industrial England* (Leicester, 1981), pp. 198–249.

McLaughlin, Terrence, *Coprophilia; or, A Peck of dirt* (London, 1971).

Macray, W. D., *A Register of the Presidents, Fellows, Demies, Instructors in Grammar and in Music, Chaplains, Clerks, Choristers, and other members of Saint Mary Magdalen College in the University of Oxford, from the foundation of the College to the present time*, new series (7 vols, Oxford 1894–1915).

Meldrum, Tim, 'Domestic service, privacy and the eighteenth-century household', *Urban History*, 26:1 (1999), pp. 27–39.

Melville, Jennifer Dawn, 'The use and organisation of domestic space in late seventeenth-century London', Ph.D. thesis, Cambridge University, 1999.

Miller, William Ian, *The Anatomy of Disgust* (Cambridge, MA, and London, 1997).

Neale, R. S., *Bath 1680–1850: A Social History, or, A Valley of Pleasure, Yet a Sink of Iniquity* (London, 1981).

O'Dea, W. T., 'Artificial lighting prior to 1800 and its social effects', *Folklore*, 62:2 (1951), pp. 312–24.

Ogborn, Miles, *Spaces of Modernity. London's Geographies, 1680–1780* (London and New York, 1998).

Oldham, James, *The Mansfield Manuscripts and the Growth of English Law in the Eighteenth Century* (2 vols, Chapel Hill, NC, and London, 1992).

Orlin, Lena Cowen, *Material London, ca 1600* (Philadelphia, 2000).

Otter, Christopher, 'Cleansing and clarifying: technological perception in nineteenth century London', *Journal of British Studies*, 43 (2004), pp. 40–64.

Pantin, W. A., 'The development of domestic architecture in Oxford', *Antiquaries Journal*, 27 (1947), pp. 120–50.

—— 'Houses of the Oxford region (i) Fisher Row', *Oxoniensia*, 25 (1960, published in 1961), pp. 121–5.

Paston Williams, Sara, *The Art of Dining* (London, 1993).

Paulson, Ronald, *Hogarth* (3 vols, Cambridge, 1992–4).

Pelling, Margaret, 'Appearance and reality: barber-surgeons, the body and disease', in A. L.

Beier and A. P. Finlay (eds), *London 1500–1700: The Making of the Metropolis* (London, 1986), pp. 82–112.

Piper, David, *The English Face*, ed. Malcolm Rogers (London, 1992).

Platt, Colin, *The Great Rebuildings of Tudor and Stuart England* (London, 1994).

Pointon, Marcia, *Hanging the Head: Portraiture and Social Formation in Eighteenth-Century England* (London, 1993).

Port, M. H., 'West End palaces: the aristocratic town house in London, 1730–1830' *London Journal*, 20:1 (1995), pp. 17–46.

Porter, Roy, 'Cleaning up the Great Wen: public health in eighteenth-century London', in W. F. Bynum and Roy Porter (eds), *Living and Dying in London*, Medical History Supplement, 11 (London, 1991), pp. 61–75.

—— *London: A Social History* (London, 1994).

—— 'The urban and rustic in Enlightenment London', in Mikulàs Teich, Roy Porter and Bo Gustafsson, *Nature and Society in Historical Context* (Cambridge, 1997).

Porter, Stephen, 'The Oxford fire of 1644', *Oxoniensia*, 49 (1984), pp. 289–300.

—— 'The Oxford fire regulations of 1671', *Bulletin of the Institute of Historical Research*, 58 (1985), pp. 251–5.

—— *The Great Fire of London* (Stroud, 1996).

Power, Michael, 'The East London working community in the seventeenth century', in P. J. Corfield and D. Keene, *Work in Towns, 850–1850* (Leicester, 1990), pp. 103–20.

Prescott, Sarah and Shuttleton, David E., 'Mary Chandler, Elizabeth Rowe, and "Ralph's Miscellany": coincidental biographical and bibliographical findings', *Notes & Queries* (Mar. 2001), pp. 31–4.

Reddaway, T. F., *The Rebuilding of London after the Great Fire* (London, 1940).

Redford, Arthur, *The History of Local Government in Manchester* (3 vols, London, 1939–40).

Rindisbacher, Hans J., *The Smell of Books: A Cultural-Historical Study of Olfactory Perception in Literature* (Michigan, 1992).

Robey, Ann, '"All asmear with filth and fat and blood and foam": the social and architectural reformation of Smithfield Market during the nineteenth century', *Transactions of the Ancient Monuments Society*, 42 (1998), pp. 1–12.

Schofield, John, 'The topography and buildings of London ca. 1600', in Lena Cowen Orlin (ed.), *Material Culture, ca. 1600* (Philadelphia, PA, 2000), pp. 296–321.

Sheppard, F. H. W., 'London before the L.C.C.: the work of the vestries', *History Today*, 3:3 (1953), pp. 174–80.

Shesgreen, Sean, *The Criers and Hawkers of London: Engravings and Drawings by Marcellus Laroon* (Aldershot, 1990).

—— *Images of the Outcast: The Urban Poor in the Cries of London* (Manchester, 2002).

Shuttleton, David E., 'Mary Chandler's *Description of Bath* (1733): a tradeswoman poet of the Georgian urban renaissance', in Rosemary Sweet and Penelope Lane (eds), *Women and Urban Life in Eighteenth-Century England* (Aldershot, 2003), pp. 173–94.

Skelton, Joseph, *Oxonia Antiqua Restaurata*, 2nd edn (London, 1843).

Slack, Paul, *The Impact of the Plague in Tudor and Stuart England* (Oxford, 1985).

Spufford, Margaret, 'Fabric for seventeenth-century children's and adolescents' clothes', *Textile History*, 34:1 (2003), pp. 47–63.

Stead, Jennifer, 'Necessities and luxuries: food preservation from the Elizabethan to the Georgian era', in C. Anne Wilson, *Waste Not Want Not: Food Preservation from Early Times to the Present Day*, Papers from the Fourth Leeds Symposium on Food History and Traditions, April 1989 (Edinburgh, 1991), pp. 66–103.

Stout, Adam, 'Three centuries of London cowkeeping', *Farmers Weekly*, 18 August 1978, pp. i–x.

Sweet, Rosemary, *The English Town 1680–1840: Government, Society and Culture* (Harlow, 1999).

—— 'Topographies of politeness', *Transactions of the Royal Historical Society*, 6th ser., 12 (2002), pp. 355–74.

Thane, Pat, *Old Age in English History: Past Experiences, Present Issues* (Oxford, 2002).

Thomas, Keith, 'Cleanliness and godliness in early modern England', in Anthony John Fletcher and Peter Roberts, *Religion, Culture and Society in Early Modern Britain* (Cambridge, 1994), pp. 56–83.

Todd, Dennis, *Imagining Monsters: Miscreations of the Self in Eighteenth-Century England* (Chicago and London, 1995).

Uglow, Jenny, *Hogarth: A Life and a World* (London, 1997).

Wall, Cynthia, *The Literary and Cultural Spaces of Restoration London* (Cambridge, 1998).

Weinstein, Rosemary, 'New urban demands in early modern London', in W. F. Bynum and Roy Porter (eds), *Living and Dying in London*, Medical History Supplement, 11 (London, 1991), pp. 29–40.

Westerfield, Ray Bert, *Middlemen in English Business, particularly between 1660 and 1760* (New Haven, Conn., 1915).

Whitaker, Katie, *Mad Madge: The Flamboyant Civil War Duchess of Newcastle* (London, 2003).

Wilson, Philip K., *Surgery, Skin and Syphilis: Daniel Turner's London (1667–1741)* (Amsterdam, 1999).

Woodward, Donald, '"Swords into ploughshares": recycling in pre-industrial England', *Economic History Review*, 2nd ser, 38:2 (1985), pp. 175–91.

Wright, Lawrence, *Clean and Decent: The Fascinating History of the Bathroom and the Water Closet* (London, 1960).

Wrightson, Keith, *English Society 1580–1680* (London, 1982).

Index